THE END OF NORTH'S MINISTRY
1780–1782

ENGLAND IN THE AGE OF THE AMERICAN REVOLUTION

(*General Editor:* SIR LEWIS NAMIER)

THE END OF NORTH'S MINISTRY 1780–1782

BY

IAN R. CHRISTIE

LECTURER IN MODERN HISTORY
UNIVERSITY COLLEGE, LONDON

LONDON
MACMILLAN & CO LTD
NEW YORK · ST MARTIN'S PRESS
1958

TO

MY MOTHER

PREFACE

I HAVE to acknowledge the gracious permission of Her Majesty the Queen to make use of the papers of King George III in the Royal Archives, Windsor Castle.

I also wish to thank the following who have kindly allowed me to quote from manuscripts in their possession: the Marquess of Abergavenny, O.B.E.; the Earl of Cardigan; the Earl Fitzwilliam and the Trustees of the Wentworth Woodhouse Estates, and the City Librarian of Sheffield; the Viscount Hinchingbrooke, M.P.; Mr. David Holland; the Baron Hotham; the Marquess of Lansdowne; the Duke of Portland, K.G., and the Trustees of the University of Nottingham. I would also like to express my appreciation for the help given — by the staffs of the British Museum, the Public Record Office, and of county record offices and local libraries and newspaper offices — which has contributed to the making of this book.

To Sir Lewis Namier I owe many thanks: first, when I had only met him in his books, for prompting in me a strong desire to know whether his picture of politics and party structure at the accession of George III was still valid for the period some twenty years later, when the political system was under strain as a result of defeat in the American War of Independence; and, since this study began, for his guidance and encouragement. He and Professor M. A. Thomson and Mr. R. R. Sedgwick have kindly read through this book in manuscript, and I am very grateful for their helpful suggestions and advice.

IAN R. CHRISTIE

1 *March* 1957

CONTENTS

INTRODUCTION

How secure in the support of parliament was the North ministry during the last two chequered years of its existence ? By what process was its position undermined after Great Britain's final defeat in the American War of Independence ? These are the two chief questions to which answers have been sought in this study. Domestic politics between 1780 and 1782 were dominated by the war situation. The Rockingham party and the other groups in opposition, convinced that the government's American policy was disastrous and that its members were in any case incompetent to carry it out, sought by any means to compass its overthrow. During the autumn of 1779 fortune had appeared to favour them, for the ministry seemed on the verge of dissolution. In the ensuing winter and spring, although there was insufficient support for a direct assault upon its war policy, indirect attack by the campaign for economical reform apparently came very near at one stage to destroying its parliamentary majority. Then came a check. The pendulum swung once more in favour of administration. The domestic history of the North ministry during the next two years is one of limited recovery followed by swift collapse.

Why was there a dissolution in 1780 ? What did the government hope to gain ? The initial impulse towards a general election arose from concern at the opposition's strength in the House of Commons during the campaign for economical reform ; but as spring passed into summer this motive was powerfully reinforced by other considerations. The impact of the Gordon Riots, splits in the ranks of opposition, a deceptive lull in the affairs of Ireland, better news from America — all these events, which the ministers interpreted far too optimistically, added to the attraction of the proposal ; indeed, made it appear criminal negligence to let slip so favourable an opportunity. Careful Treasury calculations seemed to confirm that a general election would greatly strengthen the government's position in the House. During August, preparations were pushed forward with the greatest secrecy, the opposition leaders were deliberately misled, and the elections were sprung upon the country on 1 September.

In Chapter II the efforts of the Treasury to improve the ministerial majority are examined in detail. Administration had only limited opportunities in the counties and larger boroughs: here it relied upon the support of friendly local interests backed by an expected favourable swing of popular opinion. Most of its arrangements concerned the 'close' constituencies controlled by government departments and by private patrons. Funds were made available by the King from his privy purse, but the actual amounts spent during the elections were not so great as has sometimes been supposed nor very large compared with expenses incurred by private interests. Much of this money was spent to no purpose: in particular, large sums were squandered in vain attempts to increase the government's prestige by winning seats in the metropolitan constituencies. The results of the elections were a blow to the ministers' hopes. Instead of the increased majority which they had expected, they were, so far as can be seen, weaker by five or six votes in the new House of Commons. They lost heavily in the counties and still retained the support of only a minority of the representatives of the larger boroughs, where the elections, on balance, made little change.

Compared with elections since at least 1747, politics played an appreciable part in the general election. Public controversy over American policy and economical reform was fairly widespread. This was probably the reason for the relatively large number of elections which were contested, despite various circumstances, such as a shortage of money, which might have been expected to reduce contests to a minimum. But even in the most 'popular' constituencies an election fight was not always a straight political battle, or even political at all, whilst in some instances political changes in the representation occurred without a contest. Opposition to the friends of administration was piecemeal, a series of individual actions fought by local groups and interests: for, despite the extent to which a great opposition party had come into being, grouped round Rockingham and his friends, no central organization for elections existed on the opposition side comparable to that provided for administration by the Treasury.

The new parliament opened with a tussle over the election of the Speaker. Administration regarded the former Speaker as hostile. When the one candidate acceptable to both sides of the House declined to be nominated, they determined to place a man of their own in the Chair, and they carried the day by a handsome majority. Not for several months, however, did North come to feel reasonably confident of the support of the House. The House, and the balance of political forces within it, are considered in Part II, Chapter I. Judged by the general characteristics of its membership, it differed but little from its predecessors since the beginning of the reign. The same types of members reappeared, in much the same proportions, though there were now rather fewer serving officers and rather more merchants. Parties still displayed the familiar characteristics of personal or family connection. But the American War had hardened party divisions and had increased the number of members of rather independent type who voted with parties upon principle and conviction, so that now about a third of the members had some party connection. Conspicuous among the parties was the great confederation of family, personal, and regional groups in opposition which acknowledged Rockingham's leadership.

The parliamentary events of January and February 1781 showed that administration could still depend on the support of the House. The victories of the previous summer in the southern colonies had re-established its credit both in the House and in the country: Anglo-Saxon dislike of looking realities in the face made men gloss over the fact that the Carolinas as yet were far from pacified. The outbreak of war with the United Provinces in December 1780 did not affect the government's position. The opposition thought it useless to assail either this new venture or the ministers' fixed policy with regard to America: its attack was launched on what seemed the most popular ground — economical reform. The reintroduction of Burke's Establishment Bill gave North some bad moments. He expected to be run very hard in the Commons and feared another long, wearing campaign like that of 1780. On at least one occasion he declined to divide the House for fear of losing the division or of winning only by so narrow a margin that the opposition would be encouraged to press their attack. But when, after careful preparation, he at last put the government's parliamentary strength to the test, his position was assured by a decisive majority; and for the rest of this session he had nothing to fear from the House, overcoming all opposition moves with ample majorities.

Yorktown transformed the situation. Disillusionment spread rapidly within the cabinet, in the House, and throughout the country. Politics soon centred upon two crucial questions — the ending of the war and the fate of the ministry. Most members of the cabinet felt that the war must be ended. But, irresolute and divided among themselves, they found it impossible to overcome the objections of George III until it was too late to save their political credit. A strong and determined group of ministers might have coerced the King with the threat of resignation, for there was no alternative war-ministry to which he might turn. Such action might have saved the government from destruction; at least it would have been better for the reputation of the ministers. As it was, North's protests were brushed aside by the King, who only gave up the American War at the end of February 1782, after the House of Commons had vetoed any further attempt to reconquer the colonies. Meanwhile rifts were opened in the ranks of administration, as its members suddenly, after years of power, found themselves faced with a struggle for political survival. Junior ministers began to press for changes in the cabinet which would purge it of its most unpopular members and so perhaps enable it to survive; and at the beginning of February Germain was obliged to resign. But this change was too little and too late. There was no longer in the Commons a sufficient measure of confidence in the government. Yorktown brought into the open a considerable mass of potential opposition to North's ministry, which had remained quiescent so long as the war appeared to be going, if not well, at least without disaster. This development would not alone have been enough to bring down the government. The opposition's success was the result of a comparatively small swing of opinion among members who had hitherto attended regularly in support of administration, but who now either abstained or voted against it. An important margin of its following had come from M.P.s who had little confidence in the capacity of the ministers, but who opposed the American demand for independence and could see no other possible administration which would resist it. Once the Commons had vetoed the reconquest of America they no longer had a motive for supporting it. The growth of this dissident trend among government supporters can be clearly traced through the weeks from mid-December 1781 up to the two critical divisions of March 1782, when the government only survived motions tending towards its removal by a margin of ten and then of nine votes. At that point it became clear to North, and to the independents who supported him in the Commons, that the House had virtually withdrawn its confidence from the ministers and that actual defeat on a motion of censure was imminent. The strongest representations were made to the King; at long last he accepted the situation; and on 20 March North announced the resignation of a government which had lasted for twelve years and had brought unparalleled disaster upon the British Empire. In its first years it had allowed an already critical situation to drift into civil war. Later it had conducted the war without energy or inspiration. At last it paid the price of failure, and the tasks of securing peace and recovery were left to its successors.

Military and naval events lie outside the scope of this study, save in so far as they had some bearing upon the attitudes of the politicians and upon parliamentary events. Similarly the diplomatic situation is sketched in only lightly and as from the viewpoint of Whitehall. I have not considered the motives behind Dutch or Russian policy and the skill or lack of it with which the British government assessed them: I have tried to show only how the ministers conceived of the situation and how this affected their outlook and in particular their handling of the Dutch crisis in parliament.

PART I

TOWARDS A NEW PARLIAMENT

(i)

THE GOVERNMENT AND ITS PROBLEMS

In August 1780 Lord North's ministry finally took the decision to seek the support of a new parliament. This course of action, adopted after much hesitation and anxious calculation, was, if not unprecedented, at least unusual. In the eighteenth century two circumstances rendered automatic a dissolution of parliament : one was a demise of the Crown ; the other, arising from the Septennial Act of 1716, was the lapse of seven years since the last general election. Usually it was one or other of these occurrences which gave rise to a dissolution. The power to dissolve at discretion still remained a part of the royal prerogative, but occasions for its employment had been rare since the beginning of the Hanoverian age. The legal time-limit was anticipated by a few weeks for the sake of convenience, but, except for this, parliaments tended to last the full legal term — those ending in 1754 and 1768 had provided recent examples. In 1774 North had deviated from custom to some extent by having parliament dissolved some seven months before the law required. But the dissolution of 1780 marked a much more startling departure from recent practice. The existing parliament had still over a year to run. Since the commencement of Hanoverian rule there had been only one instance (in 1747) of a parliament prematurely dissolved so long before its legal termination. However, in 1780 political motives overrode constitutional precedents. The explanation of the government's decision to dissolve is to be found in the political situation, and especially the situation in parliament, which faced it in the spring and summer of 1780.

During that spring the government appeared to be stronger within itself, and to have surmounted the danger of internal collapse which had seemed imminent the previous autumn.[1] Lord North himself had recovered from the nervous prostration which had then rendered him for many critical weeks totally inactive, and threw himself with some energy into the dispatch of pressing Irish commercial legislation and other business of his department. His strength lay in his agreeable personality and his considerable gifts as a House of Commons man. Cultured and affable, he won men by his personal friendliness and the gaiety and charm of his conversation: 'Never . . . was a First Minister less entrenched within the forms of his official situation'. Long familiarity had made him a master of the forms and procedures of the House, and a clear mind and a ready tongue secured him the respectful and affectionate attention of its members. Though he had not the Younger Pitt's genius for presenting financial information, his budgets were accounted 'peculiarly lucid, clear, and able'. Witty and good-humoured, he was imperturbable in debate, parrying with skilful repartee the most pressing attacks and winning respect by his capacity to take hard knocks with equanimity; rarely, even under the greatest provocation, did he lose his temper. His reputation for sincerity and integrity was never seriously challenged, although he had in full measure that essential gift of every politician, of being able when necessary to say nothing with persuasive eloquence. Attempts by opponents to force him into inconvenient disclosures were avoided with consummate skill; and Charles Fox admitted with rueful admiration that there existed not 'within these walls nor in the kingdom, a more complete master of language'.[2] Yet with all these considerable assets as a parliamentarian, North had grave shortcomings as the King's chief minister. He lacked energy and initiative; worse, he was devoid of any gift for leadership. Lord Buckinghamshire, the Lord-Lieuten-

[1] On the internal weaknesses of the government in the latter part of 1779, see H. Butterfield, *George III, Lord North, and the People, 1779-1780* (1949), 117-37.
[2] *The Historical and the Posthumous Memoirs of Sir Nathaniel William Wraxall, 1772-1784*, edited by H. B. Wheatley (5 vols., 1884) (cited below as Wraxall), i, 361-72.

ant of Ireland, even thought his abilities equal to the task of 'dictatorial minister', but North himself was foremost to admit that he lacked the force of personality for such a role.[1] Premier only in name, he was diffident and sensitive to snubs — 'Lord Sandwich', he once wrote to John Robinson, in a letter concerning some naval intelligence, 'has conceived such a mean opinion of all my intelligence, and all my suggestions (perhaps deservedly) that I do not think it would be of any service for me to write to him'.[2] In cabinet, far from trying to assert himself as a leader, he disclaimed responsibility for any but Treasury business. William Knox, under-secretary in the American department (whose information was largely gathered direct from his chief, Lord George Germain), described him as able and versatile in the House of Commons, of excellent judgment 'when he could be roused to an exertion of his faculties', but 'in his chamber and at the cabinet, inattentive, indifferent, and considering every proposition of a public nature as wholly irrelative to him . . . so far from leading the opinions of the other ministers that he seldom gave his own and generally slept the greatest part of the time he was with them'.[3] His colleague, Lord Thurlow, the Lord Chancellor, though allowing that his abilities were the best of all the cabinet, railed in exasperation at his inactivity — 'Damn him, nothing can goad him forward, he is the very clog that loads everything'.[4] Even Lord Hillsborough, a man of considerably less capacity, complained of his 'flimsy way of doing business'.[5] Unstable in temperament, the least reverse cast him back into the depths of depression, and the parliamentary set-backs of the spring wrung from him once more pleas to be allowed to retire.[6]

[1] Lord Buckinghamshire to Sir Charles Hotham Thompson, 30 May 1778, Hotham MSS.; North to George III, 16 Nov. 1778, *The Correspondence of King George III*, edited by Sir John Fortescue (Macmillan, 6 vols., 1927–8) (cited below as Fortescue), iv, no. 2452.
[2] 25 May 1779, Abergavenny MS. 217.
[3] William Knox, 'Anecdotes and Characters of the late Administration, 1782' (a narrative drawn up for George III), Windsor MSS.
[4] John Robinson to Charles Jenkinson, 26, 27 Jan. 1780, Add. MSS. 38213, ff. 77–80.
[5] To John Robinson, 18 Mar. 1780, H.M.C., *Abergavenny MSS.*, 28, no. 247.
[6] To George III, 7 Apr., 18 May 1780, Fortescue, v, nos. 2986, 3026.

Of the three Secretaries of State, Lord Hillsborough, the southern secretary, was little more than a cipher, a courtier rather than a statesman, a person of mediocre abilities, of whom the King himself had written that 'he did not know a man of less judgment', another weak man drawn in the wake of his friend, Lord North.[1] Recruited to the ministry in the autumn of 1779, to fill the gap left by the resignation of Lord Weymouth, Hillsborough had at least the merit of an intense interest in the affairs of Ireland, which had reached a most critical stage. He possessed large estates in Ireland, commanded five followers in the Dublin House of Commons, and believed strongly in the necessity for a union between the two countries on the lines of the Anglo-Scottish union of 1707.[2] But he was impulsive, indiscreet, cynical, and inactive. Within a few months of coming into office he had given offence both to the Lord-Lieutenant of Ireland and to the Russian Empress,[3] and neither the paucity of his letters in the Royal Archives nor the complaints of neglect in the private correspondence of the Lord-Lieutenant speak well for his industry.[4]

Lord Stormont in the northern department presented a contrasting picture of incessant activity.[5] A career diplomat, his abilities and his professional knowledge were considerable, and in debate he could speak 'with great precision of language and force of argument'. But these qualities were offset by

[1] Wraxall, i, 381-2; George III to John Robinson, 15 Oct. 1776, H.M.C., *Abergavenny MSS.*, 15, no. 118.
[2] W. H. Lecky, *A History of England in the Eighteenth Century* (6 vols., 1883), iv, 504-5; Robinson to Jenkinson, 13 Nov. 1779, Add. MSS. 38567, ff. 15-16.
[3] Lord Buckinghamshire to Sir Charles Hotham Thompson, 3 June, 10 Dec. 1780, Hotham MSS.; Sir James Harris to Lord Grantham, 27 Aug. 1782, *Diaries and Correspondence of James Harris, 1st Earl of Malmesbury*, edited by the 3rd Earl (4 vols., 1844), i, 531-2, 537. For an example of Hillsborough's cynicism, see his letter to Robinson, 27 Jan. 1782, H.M.C., *Abergavenny MSS.*, 47-8, no. 413.
[4] Lord Buckinghamshire to Sir Charles Hotham Thompson, 27 Apr., 6 Aug., 8 Nov., 1780, Hotham MSS.
[5] Between Jan. 1780 and Mar. 1782 Stormont was, after North, the King's most voluminous correspondent, and there remain over a hundred and fifty of his letters, plus more than fifty cabinet minutes and other enclosures : for the same period there are only fourteen letters from Hillsborough, and of these only three or four touch on matters of major political importance.

defects of personality. Dour and inflexible, he was lacking in the suppleness of conduct and subtlety of mind essential for success in the delicate diplomatic problems which beset him. His 'austere diligence' gave frequent offence, and, according to Knox, 'he was without skill in negotiation, for he knew not how to obtain an influence over the minds of others . . . swelled with his own importance he disdained to sooth or comply in order to gain, and not infrequently revolted the heart by the arrogance of his manner while he subdued the understanding by the force of his reasoning'.[1]

Lord George Germain, the third Secretary of State, had taken over the American department in 1775 from Lord Dartmouth, when events demanded its transfer to a man of action. Intimate contemporaries, Wraxall, Richard Cumberland, and William Knox, lauded his intelligence and gifts of exposition in conventional terms, but Knox adverted to incidents which modify his praise considerably. Germain's celebrated swiftness in doing business became a fault, since 'he was apt to be too hasty in forming his opinions', and his slavery to the clock caused him sometimes to leave matters unfinished. Knox, who was closely associated with Germain for several years in the American department, suspected him of diffidence in pushing his views in the cabinet, and his account of Germain also hints at a certain hesitation to assume responsibilities. But when sure of his ground, Germain was dogged to the point of recklessness. Blunt and forthright, he came with a soldier's obstinacy to the arena of politics and maintained his views inflexibly to the last. Opposition politicians in the House of Commons found it possible to exploit his lack of subtlety to elicit information which a careful minister would have kept unrevealed. On the American question he was every whit as stubborn as the King himself. As American Secretary he was responsible for all military operations in the colonies, but, although urged by Knox, he had never been able to secure control of auxiliary naval matters, which

[1] Charles Sackville to Sir Charles Hotham Thompson, 20 Oct. 1779, Hotham MSS. ; Wraxall, i, 381 ; Knox, 'Anecdotes and Characters . . .', Windsor MSS.

remained in the hands of the First Lord of the Admiralty, Lord Sandwich.[1]

Sandwich, who, in point of unbroken tenure of office, stood next in seniority to North in the cabinet, was little if at all inferior to any of his colleagues in ability, although that sober young Scotsman, John Sinclair, was unfavourably impressed, as doubtless were others, by his air of gaiety and dissipation. But even Horace Walpole, who had very little good to say about any minister after the retirement of his beloved cousin, General Conway, gave high praise to Sandwich for his diligence and capacity for business.[2] Sandwich's selection of subordinates at the Admiralty Board did him credit, for one of them at least, Constantine Phipps, Lord Mulgrave, was a man of first-class talent in his profession.[3] To some extent Sandwich's reputation during this period of his career suffered from misfortunes which it was out of his power to rectify. He succeeded to control of a navy which had suffered severely from the economy campaigns of the seventeen-sixties and which was pitted, during the American War, against allied fleets of considerably greater total strength. His situation was made more difficult, as controversy over colonial policy gave political edge to personal feuds among the naval officers for which he himself was certainly not wholly responsible. As a result some of the ablest naval commanders of the day refused to serve, and he was forced to rely upon elderly and unenterprising admirals of second-rate ability.

The other leading personality in the government was Lord Thurlow, the Lord Chancellor, an irascible lawyer, scornful of failure and bitter of tongue, a King's man, in whom the King placed high confidence, but a jarring and disrupting influence in the cabinet. Considerably younger than his colleagues, impatient of what he regarded as inefficiency, and suffering fools not at all, he was inclined, during the winter of 1779-80, to

[1] Wraxall, i, 386-9 ; Richard Cumberland, *Character of the late Lord Sackville* (1785) ; Knox, 'Anecdotes and Characters . . .', Windsor MSS.
[2] Wraxall, i, 398-403 ; *The Correspondence of the Right Hon. Sir John Sinclair, bart. . . . edited by himself* (2 vols., 1831), i, 77 ; Horace Walpole, *Memoirs of the reign of King George III*, ed. G. F. R. Barker (4 vols., 1894), iv, 170-1.   [3] Wraxall, ii, 172-3.

consider the continuance of North in office as 'destruction to the country',[1] but he refused (probably through loyalty to the King) to join in any intrigue to overthrow him.[2] John Robinson, who took pride and delight in Thurlow's friendship but fought tooth and nail against his hostility towards North, described him in candid terms: 'He has humours, he is overbearing perhaps in his opinions, sentiments and dictates, his superior abilities may lead to this, but he has a manly firmness and decisiveness about him that gives him great consequence, and would be of infinite support to take him along with them, and his judgment is sound, but he complains that business is never so formed when brought before them, as to enable people to judge properly'.[3] Thurlow was never able to conceal his contempt for North and Sandwich, and this circumstance continued to create strains and animosities within the government until its final collapse in 1782.

The remaining members of the cabinet played little part in the determination of events. Lord Amherst, the commander-in-chief, was a professional soldier, unconcerned with the intricacies of political intrigue. Lord Bathurst, the Lord President, the predecessor of Thurlow on the woolsack and considered 'the least efficient Lord Chancellor of the eighteenth century',[4] — another lawyer and a seeker of places — had formal responsibilities in connection with his office but was otherwise inactive. Lord Dartmouth, stepbrother to North, the Lord Privy Seal, was a mild and ineffective figure, liberal and sympathetic by temperament, but too soft and amiable to grapple effectively with problems of government. Knox summed him up as unsuited by character for political life.[5]

During the spring of 1780 this ill-assorted band of ministers faced a situation of increasing difficulty. Only American events seemed to offer them some hope. On one side they were harassed by Ireland, on the other by the development of the

---

[1] Robinson to Jenkinson, 26 Jan. 1780, Add. MSS. 38213, ff. 77-8.
[2] Richard Rigby to Georgiana, Countess Spencer, 26 Mar. 1780, Spencer MSS.
[3] To Jenkinson, 27 Jan. 1780, Add. MSS. 38213, ff. 79-80.
[4] *Dictionary of National Biography* (1908-9), i, 1328.
[5] Knox, 'Anecdotes and Characters . . .', Windsor MSS.

Armed Neutrality, whilst under their noses, by exploiting the popular movement for Economical Reform, the opposition very nearly succeeded in destroying the government's parliamentary majority and so rendering its position untenable.

In 1780 the American War was in its fifth year, and the insurgent colonists had been joined in their fight by France and Spain. Britain's naval power was strained to its limit. Nevertheless hopes were still nursed by the ministers, that a decisive blow might be struck against the colonists. For over a year past, following the reappraisals of the situation made necessary by Burgoyne's defeat at Saratoga, the main British offensive effort had been gradually turned against the southern colonies. There, it was believed, the loyalists were both numerous and ready to act in support of royal authority. In 1779 this policy paid impressive dividends with the capture of Georgia and its successful defence against three American attempts to recover it.[1] The government now hoped for still further successes in this quarter. In the autumn of 1779 the withdrawal of the French fleet from the American coast enabled Sir Henry Clinton, the commander-in-chief in America, to launch at last a major expedition to the southward. News of the embarkation of his troops at New York reached London during February 1780, by early April the arrival of the expedition near Charleston was known, and early in May a premature rumour was already circulating, that the town had surrendered on 19 April.[2] About the same time private letters reaching William Eden from New York gave ground for a belief that the rebels' finances were strained to breaking point.[3]

But while British fortunes in the colonies seemed more favourable, Ireland appeared ready to repeat the cycle of revolutionary America. American example, and also the economic depression caused by the war, had created a widespread public demand for release from the commercial and constitu-

---

[1] J. R. Alden, *The American Revolution* (1954), 227-30.
[2] Sir Stanier Porten to Knox, 3 Feb. 1780, and encl., C.O. 5/143; Stormont to Sir James Harris, 11 Apr. 1780, S.P. 91/104; George III to North, 6 May 1780, Fortescue, v, no. 3019.
[3] Eden to Germain, 30 Apr. 1780, H.M.C., *Stopford Sackville MSS.*, ii, 160.

tional restraints imposed by Great Britain.[1] The Volunteer Movement — the spontaneous creation, under the leadership of the Irish gentry, of para-military formations to defend the country now denuded of regular forces — excited the liveliest disquiet at Westminster, for though its members appeared to be absolutely loyal to the British Crown, their attitude in the event of a refusal of concessions could not be foreseen. Bowing to pressure, the British government gave way over one part of the Irish grievances in a series of commercial enactments passed during the winter of 1779–80.[2] Statutes prohibiting the export of Irish woollens and glass were repealed, and Ireland was placed on the same footing as Great Britain in regard to trade with the British colonies. Restrictions on the importation of bullion were removed and the right to participate in the trade of the Levant was conceded. But the constitutional problem remained. In January 1780 North judged from the parliamentary states sent over from Dublin by the Lord-Lieutenant that 'it did not appear . . . that it was in the power of any Lord Lieutenant to prevent the constitutional questions and save the country'.[3] A few weeks later the government received reports that every member of the Irish parliament would be given instructions at the assizes from his constituents and from the Volunteer associations, to support the repeal of Poynings' Law and other constitutional questions to be agitated. Grattan, so Lieutenant-General Cuninghame informed the ministers, had 'spoke out loudly, that this is the time to attack Great Britain in her weakness and obtain freedom to their constitution'.[4] However, Lord Buckinghamshire was at first successful in carrying out his instructions to prevent any constitutional proposals from being carried in the Irish parliament. During April Grattan's motion affirming the legislative independence of Ireland and Yelverton's proposals to amend Poynings' Law

---

[1] On the development of the Irish discontents, see Butterfield, 71-116, 138-61. For some further information on the public agitation in Ireland, see R. B. McDowell, *Irish Public Opinion, 1750–1800* (1944), chapters iii and iv.   [2] 20 Geo. III, ch. 6, 10, 18.

[3] Robinson to Jenkinson, 31 Jan. 1780, Add. MSS. 38213, ff. 99-104.

[4] Buckinghamshire to Hillsborough, 17 Feb. 1780, Henry Grattan, *Memoirs of . . . Henry Grattan* (5 vols., 1839-46), ii, 20-1 ; Robinson to Jenkinson, 25 Feb. 1780, Add. MSS. 38567, ff. 28-9.

were both defeated by small majorities.[1] But an indirect attack upon the right of the British parliament to legislate for Ireland was not so easily repulsed. Popular bodies began declaring the British Mutiny Act not valid in Ireland, and Irish magistrates refused to apply it. An Irish Mutiny Act thus became as much an immediate military necessity as a political manœuvre, and despite his instructions, the Lord-Lieutenant and his advisers at Dublin considered it impossible to oppose the Army Regulation Bill sponsored by Gervase Bushe.[2] In an attempt to forestall annual reaffirmations of the incompetence of the British parliament to legislate for Ireland, the Irish Secretary, Sir Richard Heron, sought to add a clause to Bushe's Bill to make the measure perpetual. But in face of violent opposition this proposal failed. On receipt of the Lord-Lieutenant's despatches of 3 July, the British ministers faced the delicate question, whether to approve Bushe's Bill in its original form, or to risk the possibly dire consequences of amending it.[3]

Abroad, the course of Dutch and Russian policy during the spring of 1780 increased the government's anxieties.

In March 1780 the cabinet considered it necessary to send a stiff memorial to the States General of the United Provinces. One complaint was the Dutch neglect to furnish naval and military assistance due by treaty, which had been frequently requested during the eight months since Spain had entered the war on the side of the colonists. But the main grievance put forward by the British government was the Dutch insistence upon their right under treaty to trade with France freely in practically all goods, including many war supplies, whilst declining their obligations under subsequent treaties to help Great Britain. The primary British concern was the maintenance of the blockade against France, and especially the denial to the French of supplies of naval stores imported in neutral bottoms. An Anglo-Dutch treaty of December 1674 left the

---

[1] Hillsborough to Buckinghamshire, 28 Mar. 1780, Buckinghamshire to Hillsborough, 21, 29 Apr. 1780, Grattan, ii, 31, 52-3, 78-80.

[2] Sir Richard Heron to Sir Stanier Porten, 8 Apr. 1780, Buckinghamshire to Hillsborough, 22 Apr., 8, 21 May 1780, Grattan, ii, 71-5, 85-91.

[3] Buckinghamshire to Hillsborough, private, 3 July 1780, S.P. 63/470, ff. 48-9.

Dutch free to carry naval stores and other goods, except a few enumerated war supplies, to the ports of powers at war with England. However, later Anglo-Dutch treaties of alliance, of 1678 and 1716, pledged the United Provinces to give military and naval assistance if Britain were attacked by any other power. Had the Dutch accepted this treaty obligation and declared war on the Bourbons, France would have been deprived of this most important source of naval stores; but their refusal to do this or even to limit their trade with France, and their insistence on their rights under the treaty of 1674, threatened to render useless the British weapon of blockade. In face of the British determination to intercept Franco-Dutch traffic if an end could not be put to it by diplomatic agreement, the Dutch, at the end of 1779, resorted to convoys. An armed incident became inevitable, and in the last days of December 1779 shots were exchanged when a British force under Captain Fielding attempted a search of Dutch vessels bound for French ports under the escort of Count Byland. Yet a further ground of complaint was the grant of facilities lately made by the Dutch to the American privateer, Paul Jones. Accordingly, on 14 March, the British government gave warning, that if the Dutch persisted in their conduct, all commercial privileges granted to Dutch subjects by treaty would be suspended.[1] On 17 April, as the States General had given no satisfactory answer, this threat was put into effect, and Dutch shipping was declared subject to search in the same manner as the vessels of other nations not privileged by treaty.[2] There, for the time being, the matter rested. 'We shall', Stormont told Sir Joseph Yorke, the minister to The Hague, on 16 May, 'certainly pursue our point with equal steadiness and moderation, act up to the King's order in council and not go beyond it unless the conduct of the Republic should force a rupture.'[3] But he was apprehensive what developments in the Dutch situation might result from the turn of events at Petersburg.

[1] *Annual Register*, 1780, 204*-5*, 344-5; Stormont to George III, 13 Mar. 1780, Fortescue, v, no. 2967; Stormont to Sir Joseph Yorke, 14 Mar. 1780., and encl., S.P. 84/569, ff. 215-20.
[2] *Annual Register*, 1780, 345-6; Stormont to Sir Joseph Yorke, 18 Apr. 1780, and encl., S.P. 84/570, ff. 254-8.   [3] *Ibid*. f. 40.

At Petersburg the British envoy, Sir James Harris, had been angling for two years, with complete lack of success, for an alliance which would secure Russian armed mediation on Britain's behalf.[1] Early in 1780 the seizure of two Russian ships by Spanish naval patrols aroused the passionate resentment of the Empress Catherine, and gave rise to some hopes that a Russian fleet might be sent to demonstrate against the Spaniards and so relieve the naval pressure upon Great Britain. Harris also anticipated a Russian *rapprochement* with Austria which might weaken French and Prussian influence at Petersburg. But he gave his government insistent warnings that the Empress shrank from any idea of participation in the war.[2] He did not foresee, however, the astonishing and unfavourable sequel to the Spanish incident. The British ministers first learnt of it on 1 April, while still in the midst of their controversy with the Dutch, when Simolin, the Russian ambassador, presented to Stormont a declaration of rules relating to navigation and contraband which, if accepted, would have virtually destroyed the British weapon of blockade. Neutral vessels, Russia declared, were free to pass from port to port along the coasts of countries at war. Hostile goods were to be protected at sea by a neutral flag, unless they had been defined as contraband by treaty between the neutral and the blockading power — in this case by the Anglo-Russian commercial treaty of 1766. Blockade of a harbour existed only when a naval force was in the immediate vicinity to enforce it.[3] For the British ministry to sacrifice the weapon of blockade by subscribing to these doctrines was unthinkable. 'The second article, if adhered to,' Stormont commented in a letter to the King, 'would totally destroy all that has been so properly resolved with regard to the Dutch.' But he had no wish to run the risk of alienating

[1] Earl of Suffolk to Harris, 9 Jan. 1778 ; Harris to Stormont, 15/26 Feb. 1780, *Diaries and Correspondence of James Harris, 1st Earl of Malmesbury*, edited by the 3rd Earl (4 vols., 1844) (cited below as *Malmesbury Corr.*), i, 157-60, 270-80.
[2] Harris to Stormont, no. 4, 17/28 Jan. 1780, nos. 11, 12, 15, 15/26 Feb. 1780, no. 16, 21 Feb./3 Mar., no. 17, 25 Feb./7 Mar. 1780, S.P. 91/104 (partly printed from Harris's copies, *Malmesbury Corr.*, i, 270-80, 283-4) ; Stormont to George III, 21, 28 Mar. 1780, Fortescue, v, nos. 2977, 2980.
[3] *Annual Register*, 1780, 347-8.

the Empress by a downright rejection of the declaration, and he advised that the best course would be 'to answer it in very civil general terms, and to instruct Sir James Harris to take a fit opportunity of explaining the mistake upon which the second article proceeds, and the consequences to which it would lead highly pernicious to this country and therefore contrary to Her Majesty's friendly intentions'.[1] By the commonly accepted rule relating to contraband, to which Great Britain adhered, all enemy goods found on neutral ships were liable to confiscation, unless the rule had been modified by treaty. But the official British reply to the Russian declaration avoided any controversy on this question, and Harris was instructed that, before handing it formally to the Russian minister, he should convey the British point of view as tactfully as possible to the Empress, by any unofficial channel which might be open to him.[2]

Harris executed these orders to the best of his ability, but his influence at Petersburg was now at its nadir. The Empress, although her navies had ruthlessly exercised similar rights of search in the Mediterranean during the recent Russo-Turkish war, was sensitive to the last degree about any interference with the tiny ocean-going Russian merchant marine and now declined to concede such rights to any other power. Furthermore, the effect of the soft answer returned by Stormont was spoilt by the indiscretions of Hillsborough, whose threatening and derogatory language about the Russian navy was reported to Petersburg and disgusted the Empress. Apart from these difficulties, Catherine had committed herself at the courts of other neutral powers to a neutral league for the defence of free navigation on the lines of her declaration, before hearing the case against it and without foreseeing the difficulties it would cause. Harris feared she could not quickly reverse her policy for fear of the blow to her dignity and pride. He feared also that his efforts to explain the British case to the Empress were frustrated by her Prussophil minister, Count Panin, who

[1] 1 Apr. 1780, Fortescue, v, no. 2983.
[2] *Annual Register*, 1780, 349; Stormont to Harris, no. 17, 11 Apr. 1780, S.P. 91/104.

appeared to want a breach with Britain and a French alliance. Accordingly, he was obliged to report himself powerless to check the development of the project for an Armed Neutrality, to which both Denmark and Sweden adhered during the summer.[1] He remained keenly on the watch for signs that the Empress might be having second thoughts about the question, and in June he was able to convey the slightly reassuring news that the Russian fleets despatched from Cronstadt to protect Russian shipping in West European waters had, contrary to the projected convention of the Armed Neutrality, no orders to succour vessels of other neutral powers.[2]

But the main burthen of Harris's despatches was anything but reassuring. Viewed from London, Russian policy gave the impression of veiled hostility and aroused the keenest suspicion — all the more, since, from March onwards, the British government knew that the Russian ambassador at The Hague was working in collusion with the anti-British faction in the province of Holland to draw the United Provinces into the proposed Armed Neutrality.[3] Why, wrote Stormont on 14 July, had the Empress not sought the addition of an article to the Anglo-Russian treaty of 1766, to exempt her shipping from search, instead of taking steps so detrimental to Great Britain? 'I own', he concluded, 'a strong suspicion that some secret plan highly prejudicial to this country has been adopted, not only by Count Panin, but by the Empress herself; and that nothing is wanting but an opportunity of disclosing this plan and of carrying it into execution.' And in a private letter of the same date to Harris he added: 'I cannot but suspect a deep and very hostile design, as it seems to be impossible that one of her penetration and ability should not see the consequences of the measures she pursues'.[4]

[1] To Stormont, nos. 49, 50, 51, 52, 15/26 May, no. 59, 19/30 May, no. 64, 2/13 June, no. 69, 9/20 June 1780, S.P. 91/105 (nos. 50, 52, 59, 69, partly printed, from Harris's copies, *Malmesbury Corr.*, i, 301-6, 307-10, 311-12, 315-7); to Grantham, 16/27 Aug. 1782, *Malmesbury Corr.*, i, 531-2, 537.
[2] To Stormont, no. 71, 12/23 June 1780, S.P. 91/105.
[3] Harris to Stormont, no. 11, 25 Feb./7 Mar. 1780, S.P. 91/104.
[4] To Harris, no. 39, 14 July 1780, and private letter of same date, S.P. 91/105.

At home the opposition's exploitation of the popular movement for Economical Reform during the early months of 1780 constituted a threat to the very existence of the government. Already foreshadowed in the speeches of opposition leaders before the Christmas recess, this attack began in earnest on 8 February, when Lord Shelburne introduced in the House of Lords his scheme for a Commission of Public Accounts, and Sir George Savile, member for Yorkshire, presented in the Commons a petition for economy from the freeholders of his county. A key passage in this Yorkshire petition summed up the central purpose of the attack as conceived by the opposition politicians. It declared that, 'notwithstanding the calamities and impoverished condition of the nation, much public money has been improvidently squandered, and that many individuals enjoy sinecure places, efficient places with exorbitant emoluments, and pensions unmerited by public service, to a large and still increasing amount; whence the Crown has acquired a great and unconstitutional influence, which, if not checked, may soon prove fatal to the liberties of this country'.[1] In the view of the opposition, passage of the Bills which it brought forward for the satisfaction of the petitioners of Yorkshire, and of twenty-five other English counties and eight large towns which submitted similar petitions, would amount to a successful vote of censure against the government on two counts — of governing with unnecessary extravagance, and of conducting relations with parliament in a manner which was morally wrong and which obscured the real will of the 'political nation'. Its object was to destroy the ministry, perhaps by discrediting it, but certainly by rooting out the supposed corrupt system, upon which alone, so thought people like Burke, its survival depended: eliminate a number of placemen, so ran Burke's reasoning, and then the ministry would fall and the virtuous politicians of the opposition would come into their own; on 11 February, summing up the advantages to be gained from his Establishment Bill, he pointed out that it would extinguish 'secret corruption almost to the possibility of its existence', and destroy 'direct and visible influence to the offices of at

[1] John Almon, *The Parliamentary Register*, xvii (1780), 72-5.

least fifty members of parliament'.[1] Burke's premises were quite mistaken. The North government did not stand by virtue of 'corruption'. But his object might nevertheless have been gained. From North's point of view, an adverse vote on this sort of measure was a repudiation by the Commons of his leadership. It signified a withdrawal of confidence. It also shook his nerve and touched his sensitive nature on the raw. When Dunning's resolution was passed, he drew the immediate conclusion that the House would no longer place confidence in him and that he must go; a week or two later he talked indiscreetly to Fox about his wish to retire.[2] One other, indirect, object can also be traced in the opposition's legislative programme — an implicit condemnation of the government's American policy, by an assault upon its symbol, Germain, and upon the machinery for controlling American administration. After one early indiscretion, this issue was carefully avoided throughout the debates on Economical Reform. But on 8 February Fox, perhaps inadvertently, cast a momentary light on the secret thoughts of his friends. 'Suppose the people should be of opinion', he declared while speaking in support of the Yorkshire petition, 'that there is no longer any need of a very expensive Board of Trade and Plantations, when that trade and those plantations . . . no longer exist, would it not become the noble Lord's duty, to sacrifice his particular opinion.'[3] It was, then, not on grounds of redundancy in general — as was afterwards argued — but of redundancy as a result of the war situation, that the first offices listed for the axe in Burke's Establishment Bill were the Third Secretaryship of State and the Board of Trade and Plantations. In the name of economy parliament was invited to accept the opposition's contention, that the American colonies were lost and beyond recovery — a view which, until after Yorktown, it consistently rejected whenever directly submitted to it.

[1] 'Speech on presenting . . . a plan for the better security of the independence of parliament and the economical reformation of the civil and other establishments', *The Works of . . . Edmund Burke* (12 vols., 1808-13), iii, 342.

[2] North to George III, George III to North, 7 Apr., Jenkinson to George III, 14 Apr. 1780, Fortescue, v, nos. 2986, 2987, 2993.

[3] Almon, xvii, 78.

As the government avoided the tactical folly of dividing against the Establishment Bill at its first introduction in the House of Commons on 11 February, the first trial of strength in the House took place on the 21st, when Sir George Savile moved for an Address to request the King to lay before parliament an account of all subsisting pensions granted by the Crown during pleasure or otherwise. North moved to limit the motion to such pensions as were payable at the Exchequer, and so to exclude from its scope those charged on the Civil List through the Secret and Special Service accounts. This amendment was carried by only two votes. A majority hardly more reassuring was secured on 9 March, on the division in committee on the first clause of Burke's Bill, when the ministry saved the third Secretary of State by seven votes only. On the 13th the Board of Trade was lost, opposition carrying the motion for its abolition by 207 to 199, and the same day Clerke's Bill for excluding government contractors from the Commons passed through committee without a division. On 20 March the government did not challenge a division on the third reading of Clerke's Bill. But the next business of the day was a crucial debate and division on Burke's Bill. Continuing the reading of the Bill in committee, Burke proposed the abolition of the separate treasuries within the royal household, with the object of ensuring the responsibility of the First Lord of the Treasury over the whole of the Civil List. This issue raised in acute form the question of parliament's right to intervene in matters which could be regarded as the King's private concern and within the scope of the royal prerogative, and the disquiet thus occasioned among the independent country gentlemen and the constitutional lawyers saved the ministers.[1] At 2 A.M. on the 21st the government carried its amendment against Burke's motion to abolish the Treasurer of the Chamber by 211 to 158, and the remaining sections of this part of the Bill were then negatived without a division. Regarding the pith and core of his Bill as destroyed, Burke confessed himself indifferent to its fate.

During these divisions the government's normal majority

---

[1] Butterfield, 304-8. Cf. the similar development concerning the divisions of 6 and 24 Apr. 1780, pp. 22-3 below.

had undergone first a distressing lapse and then a strong recovery. In actual votes its numbers had remained fairly constant. The substantial majority against Burke's Bill on the night of 20-21 March was due to the abstention of about fifty members who had previously voted in favour of its earlier clauses. But ministers had been made acutely aware of the insecurity of their position in the House of Commons, and this situation provoked the first discussions of the advisability of a dissolution.

(ii)

THE DECISION TO DISSOLVE

At the beginning of March, North had disclaimed 'any intention' of dissolving parliament before the usual time.[1] But on the 29th North's subordinate, John Robinson, confided to his friend, Charles Jenkinson, his own belief, that the project of a new parliament deserved the most serious attention. 'I humbly think', he wrote, '[it] calls for the most deliberate consideration of the K—— even more than the thoughts of his ministers. It strikes me as the most weighty business of His Majesty's reign . . . I shall be happy in an opportunity of talking this over with you.'[2] This was an expert opinion. Robinson had now served for ten years as parliamentary manager, and his knowledge of the subject was unsurpassed. Furthermore, it was an opinion addressed to the highest quarter. A mere Secretary to the Treasury could hardly correspond direct with his royal master on such a matter of high policy behind the back of his departmental chief; but Robinson had other ways of getting his views known, for through Jenkinson lay a recognized, confidential channel of communication with George III.[3]

In just over a week events themselves seemed to confirm Robinson's opinion and convinced the King, at least, that he was right. On 6 April the government again appeared to have

---

[1] Almon, xvii, 199.   [2] Add. MSS. 38567, ff. 78-9.
[3] Robinson to George III, George III to Robinson, 13 Mar. 1779, Abergavenny MSS. 208, 209.

lost hold of its majority in the House of Commons. Dunning proposed that the House should reverse its verdict on Burke's Bill, by giving its approval to two resolutions, the first 'that the influence of the Crown has increased, is increasing, and ought to be diminished', the second, 'that it is competent for this House to reform the civil list or any part of the public expenditure'. These were to be followed up by 'real, substantive, practical measures'.[1] Dunning's first — and famous — motion was carried after a hot debate by 233 to 215. His second motion was then passed without a division, and the House thus repudiated the ground on which a majority had quashed the Establishment Bill less than three weeks before. After that the House seemed to run quite wild. For good measure Thomas Pitt secured the passage, again without a division, of the motion, 'that it is the duty of this House to provide, as far as may be, an immediate and effectual redress of the abuses complained of in the petitions'.[2] Fox then carried a motion, that these resolutions be reported; this was done; and also a further resolution was passed, that the report be received. The opposition, in their anxiety to strike while the ministerial ranks were in confusion and while the independent members could be led to swallow the logical consequences of their votes on the first motion, before they had proper time to consider where it led, rode rough-shod over the normal conventions of parliamentary procedure.[3] To George III this scene of ministerial impotence was decisive: 'It would be madness', he wrote two or three days later to Robinson, 'not to call a new parliament as soon as we have hobbled through the present session.'[4]

To North the blow was none the less severe for being anticipated, and his immediate reaction was that he had lost his ascendancy in the Commons. 'It has happen'd as I expected', he wrote to the King. 'I humbly submit once more to your Majesty that it is absolutely necessary that I should be permitted to retire at the end of the Session, and some other arrangement take place.' But once again the King

---

[1] Almon, xvii, 447-54.   [2] *Ibid.* 474.   [3] *Ibid.*
[4] 10 Apr. 1780, H.M.C., *Abergavenny MSS.*, 29, no. 252.

rallied the spirits of his minister.[1] The opposition's majority of nearly twenty could not be sustained. On 10 April Dunning obtained a majority of two only for a declaration that the offices of the subordinate treasurers of the household and their staffs should be rendered incompatible with a seat in the Commons. Three days later Crewe's Bill for disfranchising revenue officers was defeated by 224 to 195. Several more ministerial supporters were whipped up during the recess which the illness of the Speaker made necessary in the following days : 'no one that I have weight with shall be neglected', Sandwich told Robinson.[2] When the House resumed on 24 April, Dunning moved for an Address to the King requesting there should be no dissolution or prorogation, 'until proper measures have been taken to diminish the influence, and correct the other abuses, complained of by the petitions of the people'. Like Burke's attack upon the treasurers of the household, this motion implied an invasion of the sphere of the royal pre-rogative, and it was rejected on a division by 254 to 203.[3] Government supporters were present in unprecedented force, but once again it was the independent members who tipped the scale. A comparison of the names of members voting with the opposition on 6 and on 24 April shows that nearly forty who supported Dunning on the first occasion deserted him on the second. Sixteen of these voted with the government on the 24th, of whom five were representatives for counties and twelve had previously been consistent supporters of reform, among them men of the most independent character, the Morgans of South Wales, Drake of Amersham, Lethieullier, and William Pulteney : the rest abstained, these including Sir William Wake, Samuel Whitbread, the younger Drake, Forester, Lister, Sir Fletcher Norton, and Sir John Palmer, all of whom had three or four votes against government to their credit during the previous weeks.[4] Had all, or nearly all, of

[1] North to George III, 7 Apr., George III to North, 7, 11 Apr. 1780, Fortescue, v, nos. 2986, 2987, 2991.
[2] 20 Apr. 1780, Abergavenny MS. 254.
[3] Almon, xvii, 488-90, 512-13, 525, 532-6, 557.
[4] *A correct list of the Members of the last House of Commons distinguished according to their votes in certain late public questions in which the rights and*

these members adhered to the opposition at the end of April, the government would have been again defeated and its existence would indeed have been in jeopardy.

Rumours of a dissolution were rife in the weeks after the passage of Dunning's resolutions,[1] and, indeed, provoked his tactical mistake on 24 April. But, for the moment, the blow which the resolutions struck at North's unreliable spirits made such an event less likely. North drew little comfort from the triumph of the 24th, or from the fact that thereafter the government's voting strength remained steady, successive stages of Burke's Bill and of Dunning's motions on the petitions being safely disposed of by sound majorities in committee, and General Conway's motion for a conciliation bill to facilitate a treaty with America being roundly rejected on 5 May by 123 to 18, only a small minority opposing the contention of Lord George Germain, that 'the moment of conciliation was near . . . that the majority of the people there were ready and desirous to return to their allegiance, but . . . were prevented by the tyranny of those who had got the power of government into their hands'.[2] For several weeks the King fought a disheartening battle to stiffen the resolution of his minister and to keep alive the project of a dissolution and a new parliament.[3] At last his tenacity seemed rewarded and the groundwork of Robinson's 'weighty business' soundly laid, for the end of the spring brought triumphs to the government and disintegration to the ranks of the opposition.

At the beginning of June the Gordon Riots gave an initial impetus to a reaction in favour of the government. On 2 June a mass demonstration round the Houses of Parliament, organized in support of the Protestant Association's petition for the repeal of the Catholic Relief Act of 1778, soon degenerated into riotous attacks upon Catholic chapels attached

liberties of the people were essentially concerned (1780). Add. MSS. 27837, following f. 7.
[1] Charles Jenkinson to Sir Robert Chambers, 19 Apr. 1780, Add MSS. 38307, f. 166.   [2] Almon, xvii, 661.
[3] North to George III, 7 Apr., 18 May 1780, George III to North, 7, 11, 25 Apr., 19 May 1780, Jenkinson to George III, 19 May 1780, Fortescue, v, nos. 2986, 2987, 2991, 3006, 3026, 3027, 3028 ; George III to Jenkinson, 19 May 1780, Add. MSS. 38564, f. 16.

to foreign embassies. For most of the next day there was a lull in the disorder, but during the evening there was renewed rioting, with destruction of Catholic chapels and private property. The disturbances continued spasmodically for nearly a week. On the 6th, Newgate prison was destroyed, Lord Chief Justice Mansfield's house was attacked and gutted, and the residences of various leading politicians were threatened with destruction. Next day — 'Black Wednesday' in Horace Walpole's record — a climax of destruction took place in scattered parts of London and Westminster, many rioters perishing in the fire and the drunken orgy that accompanied the wrecking of Thomas Langdale's distilleries. Only on the 8th, when large military reinforcements were hurried into the capital, were the riots at length brought under control.

Critics made much of the ministers' tardiness in enforcing law and order. Yet in the end they rather gained credit than lost it. For a moment the governing class found itself faced with the nightmare of mob rule, and even between bitter political opponents there was a reknitting of the ranks in defence of the established order. The riots were a warning, that there were limits beyond which public campaigns for discrediting the government could not be carried without serious risk. The most immediate dividend in the eyes of the ministers was a renewed breach in the ranks of the opposition. The riots and their aftermath completed the destruction for the time being of the uneasy combination of the parties led by the Marquis of Rockingham and the Earl of Shelburne. This alliance, never strong, was already, by late May, on the point of foundering over the issue of parliamentary reform. Burke and some other members of the Rockingham party condemned outright all proposals for altering the existing parliamentary system. Rockingham himself was not averse in principle to discussing the idea, but he countered it as far as he could, in order to try and preserve unity among the opposition factions. Shelburne insisted that some reform measures were necessary, gave encouragement to radical leaders of the county associations, and was indignant when he found Rockingham's connections working against him. At the beginning of June his patience gave way : in a series of speeches in the House of Lords on 3 June he spared neither ministry nor opposition and concluded with the threat, which he forthwith put into effect, of retiring from parliament and leaving the Rockinghams to their own devices. In the next week or two the Gordon Riots drove the two opposition leaders still further asunder, for Shelburne, as an anti-Catholic, stood directly opposed to such leading supporters of toleration among Rockingham's followers as Sir George Savile and Edmund Burke. Nor did he react as the Rockinghams did to the threat to law and order represented by the riots. On 3 June he laid the blame on the ministry for their pro-Catholic legislation, demanding the repeal of the Quebec Act of 1774, and in the following days he viewed with ill favour the Rockingham party's momentary co-operation with the government in the task of subduing the riots and restoring order.[1]

Ministers — Stormont at least — anticipated as early as 4 June the adoption of this course of action by the Rockingham party and greatly over-estimated its significance.[2] Their expectations that the Rockinghams were inclined to give up opposition seemed borne out by the zeal shown by Portland and Rockingham for the restoration of law and order, by the attendance of both at the privy council meeting summoned on 7 June to consider the use of the military against the rioters, and by Rockingham's offer to set out post-haste for Yorkshire to supervise counter-measures in case of outbreaks in the West Riding, of which he was Lord-Lieutenant.[3] In some ministerial circles at least (where wishes were rather too apt to father thoughts), these moves were interpreted as deliberate signals, as signs of a definite wish on the part of the Rockinghams to treat with North for a coalition.[4]

[1] See my paper, 'The Marquis of Rockingham and Lord North's offer of a Coalition, June-July 1780', *English Historical Review*, lxix (1954), 390-1.

[2] Stormont to George III, 4 June 1780, Fortescue, v, no. 3043.

[3] *The Last Journals of Horace Walpole*, edited by A. Francis Steuart (2 vols., 1910), ii, 311 ; Stormont to George III, 13 June 1780, Fortescue, v, no. 3072 (Rockingham's name is here incorrectly transcribed as 'Buckingham').

[4] Charles Jenkinson to George III, 17 June 1780, Fortescue, v, no. 3080.

Within a week of the quelling of the Gordon Riots news from America greatly increased the public credit of the ministry. All through April and the first days of May, Sir Henry Clinton had been pressing the siege of Charleston. On 12 May the town capitulated with over five thousand men and three hundred cannon. Despatches reporting this success reached London on 15 June and were immediately made public in an extraordinary issue of the *London Gazette*. The strategy of the southern campaign appeared amply vindicated, and further developments were presaged in Clinton's letters, which announced immediate plans for clearing South Carolina of the rebel forces and hopes of establishing at least a small detachment in the south of Virginia to support these operations.[1] It is very probable that the arrival of this news encouraged the ministers in the belief that the Rockinghams, disillusioned by the failure of their parliamentary campaign, would welcome the idea of giving up opposition and of joining the government.

Fortified in spirit by these favourable developments at home and in America, North, at the end of June, committed himself to two important decisions. On the 28th he approached Rockingham with proposals for a coalition ministry, employing as intermediary their common friend, Frederick Montagu, the member for Rockingham's borough of Higham Ferrers.[2] A day or two later he bowed to the wishes of the King and, on 1 July, submitted the question of a general election to the cabinet.[3]

The first of these moves, had it succeeded, would have altered considerably the character of the ensuing general election. Elections in the course of which the largest independent political group in the country acted as collaborators instead of opponents might well be conducted with the minimum of contests and of expense, and could be expected to produce a favourable House of Commons. It was true that the con-

[1] Clinton to Germain, 13 May, 14 May, secret, C.O. 5/99.
[2] On the commencement and progress of these feelers for a coalition, see my paper, 'The Marquis of Rockingham and Lord North's offer of a coalition, June-July 1780', *English Historical Review*, lxix (1954), 394-401.
[3] George III to Robinson, 29 June 1780, Add. MSS. 37835, f. 129; North to Thurlow, 3 July 1780, Egerton MSS, 2232, f. 36.

version of the Rockinghams to friends would ensure a government majority in any case, but this would be no reason for postponing a dissolution. One would have to take place within twelve months, and if North waited, he might lose the opportunity through a breakdown of the hoped-for coalition. On his part, then, the proposal for a coalition was ancillary to the project for an early general election and not an alternative. The one scheme, he hoped, would smooth the way to the other. But a few days proved how visionary were his expectations. On 28 June he sent via Montagu a request to Rockingham to outline the terms on which he and his friends might be willing to join the existing government. The answer he received next day from Rockingham was entirely uncompromising. On the three crucial questions of American policy, Economical Reform, and the distribution of offices within the proposed coalition, Rockingham laid down conditions which would destroy the existing ministry and all its works. The coalition, he declared, must have the King's leave to recognize American independence if it were found that the colonists declined to treat on any other terms. The main substance of Economical Reform must be conceded. Sandwich and Germain were to be eliminated from the cabinet. The posts of Secretaries of State were to be given to Fox and the Duke of Richmond, thus ejecting Hillsborough and Stormont from the two chief executive posts in the government.

These proposals were entirely unacceptable to George III; nor, indeed, were they of a kind to be given consideration by a ministry exulting in the news received from Charleston and anticipating further triumphs in the next despatches from America. The letters of Germain to Clinton and of Stormont to British envoys abroad reveal that already, in the first week of July, ministers were in a state of high elation and in no mind to give up their positions or listen to defeatist counsel. Stormont thought the fall of Charleston the 'most important' event to have occurred since the commencement of the American war.[1] 'I am sanguine enough to expect the recovery of the whole of the southern provinces in the course of the

[1] To Sir James Harris, circular no. 37, 16 June 1780, S.P. 91/105.

27

campaign', Germain wrote in reply to Clinton on 4 July.[1] The despatches reaching his office from America the following day still further raised the spirits of the ministers. Cornwallis's detachments, Clinton wrote, had 'completed the destruction of everything in arms against us in the province'. The inhabitants had hurried in to declare their allegiance, often after placing rebel leaders and officials under arrest. Loyalists in the back country were arming. 'I may venture to assert', Clinton concluded, 'that there are few men in South Carolina, who are not either our prisoners or in arms with us.'[2] And in a private letter written about the same time to William Eden he declared that if French or Spanish fleets did not intervene, 'I think a few works if properly reinforced, will give us all between this and Hudson's River'.[3] In view of this heady encouragement, the exaltation of ministers was understandable. It had been the persistent thesis of Lord George Germain that the bulk of the colonials were loyal and that they only needed the stimulus of some regular troops to rise and throw off rebel domination. For the moment this supposition seemed correct, and upon it expansive expectations were based. Clinton's successes, wrote Stormont, were of such a nature, 'as in all probability will have a great and immediate effect upon the minds of all his Majesty's rebellious subjects in America, and bring the colonies back to their connection with the Mother Country; ' and a few days later: 'the happy turn things have taken in America gives the greatest reason to hope that the other provinces will follow the example of South Carolina'.[4] At once published in an extraordinary issue of the London Gazette, the news raised public expectations as high as those of the ministers.[5] A trickle of congratulatory addresses began to come in from grand juries of counties and

---

[1] C.O. 5/99.

[2] 4 June 1780, *ibid.*, partly printed from a copy in Germain's papers, H.M.C., *Stopford Sackville MSS.*, ii, 167-8, and in print in the *London Gazette* (extraordinary), 5 July 1780.

[3] 30 May 1780, Sir Henry Clinton papers, William L. Clements Library, University of Michigan.

[4] To Harris, circular no. 38, 5 July, and despatch, 14 July, 1780, S.P. 91/105.

[5] Horace Walpole to Sir Horace Mann, 24 July 1780.

the corporations of cities and boroughs. These were doubtless a welcome change to the ministers from the economical reform petitions of earlier months, though it was to be observed that the addresses from the counties, in sharp contradistinction to those from the corporations, were confined to congratulating the King on the restoration of order in London and made no mention of events in America.[1]

On 7 July North referred back to Rockingham a series of questions which were intended, it would seem, to ascertain whether Rockingham would modify any of his conditions in view of the news received from America two days before.[2] Even a fortnight later, ministers seem to have expected a reply to this memorandum.[3] But Rockingham treated it as an outright rejection of his terms and as putting an end to the proposal for a coalition, and no reply was ever delivered to North. In view of the war situation and the development of a favourable public opinion, this was less to be deplored by the ministers than it otherwise would have been, and within a fortnight North himself was agreeing with the King that Rockingham's demands were unreasonable and not to be complied with.[4] However, North's anxieties about the dissolution were increased. He had hoped by some understanding with the opposition to pave the way for a quiet general election, but now it was clear that the elections could not be amicably arranged between the parties. Instead they would be forced into the semblance of a party contest, and no effort could be spared on the ministers' part to secure a majority in the new House of Commons.

In the first week of July, at the same time as the conversations with Montagu were proceeding, the preparations for the dissolution began to be pressed forward. The evidence shows that the ensuing general election was not simply a manœuvre for which George III himself was mainly responsible. Certainly the King believed a dissolution necessary. But the departmental

[1] *London Gazette*, 4-8, 11-15, 25-29 July, 1-5 Aug. 1780.
[2] North's memorandum for his conversation with Montagu, 7 July 1780, Fortescue, v, no. 3101 ; the date and purpose of the document is established by the reference to it in Robinson's letter to Jenkinson of 7 July, Abergavenny MS. 266.
[3] Jenkinson to Robinson, 22 July 1780, Abergavenny MS. 277.
[4] *Ibid.*

responsibility was North's; and North, to strengthen his hand, made sure that his colleagues endorsed his proposal and found them to be at least as eager for it as himself. The dissolution was a stroke deliberately and enthusiastically resolved upon, not merely by the King but by the cabinet.

Encouraged by the initial reception given to his proposal at the cabinet meeting on 1 July, North, by the 3rd, 'was full of his arrangements and the next parliament', and further discussions of the subject took place in the cabinet on the 4th and on following days.[1] The more the proposal was aired the more it was liked. On 13 July Robinson wrote to Jenkinson of 'an impatience in the cabinet, particularly Lord Bathurst to diss[olve]'.[2] The keenest enthusiasm was shown by Lord Sandwich, who felt it essential to exploit the credit gained by the government from the recent turn of events at home and abroad. On the 14th he wrote letters to Admiral Rodney warning him to make preparations if he wished to come into parliament, and to Lord Orford to make final arrangements about the return of two of his friends at Callington.[3] By the end of the month, when no final decision had yet been reached, he had grown out of all patience with the plodding caution of North and Robinson, and in a letter to Robinson urged the need for immediate action:[4]

> I think all your reasons for delay are weak when compared to the innumerable advantages of a speedy dissolution; it is unnecessary to run them over here, but I must join with Rigby in deprecating all further delay, which will be deciding against the thing without meaning to do so.
>
> It is not the dissolution alone but the *speedy* dissolution that appears to me to be the measure upon which the fate of this administration and government depends; this is the favourable moment for executing it, our opponents are depressed, the nation is set against riots and rioters of all kinds, events have been favourable beyond conception; will

[1] North to Thurlow, 3 July 1780, Egerton MSS. 2232, f. 36; Robinson to Jenkinson, same date, Add. MSS. 38214, ff. 66-7.

[2] Add. MSS. 38567, f. 55.

[3] Sandwich MSS., letter book, 'private letters 1776–1781', pp. 227 and 229-31.

[4] 1 Aug. 1780, Abergavenny MSS. 279.

you wait to give our enemies time to rally and re-unite, and for some blow in our military operations to turn the tide of popularity against us ? We may be worse, we cannot be better, therefore this is the time to bring things to an issue, if it is neglected I must think it an unpardonable oversight.

Sandwich's friends among the junior ministers, Richard Rigby and William Eden, joined in the campaign and bombarded Robinson with letters, which were duly passed on for North's perusal.[1] In a letter explaining the situation at the end of July, William Eden wrote to his friend, Lord Loughborough : [2]

> I had a visit from Lord Sandwich this morning, and the conversation would be interesting to you if I could throw it upon paper. It was occasioned by something which passed yesterday between us with Mr. Rigby on the ex-pediency of dissolving without an hours delay : in this we all fully agree, upon the grounds which you and I saw six weeks ago, of its being a moment when Government both personally and politically stands very high ; and that this popular favour will gradually evaporate and if bad events take place transfer itself to our adversaries, in which case we must either send writs through an ill-tempered country or try another session with the present wretched parliament. Lord Sandwich in talking over this matter stated with apparent and I believe real frankness all that has passed in different places on the subject — everybody except the Chancellor has long allowed it to be expedient ; and Lord Sandwich well observes that the delay risques all the bad effects of a decided negative — The Chancellor did not dis-agree but would only give sullen answers, such as 'Lord North ought to settle it. Why do you ask me ? I don't love this countenancing the damned nonsense of shortening the duration of parliaments, but if it is right in the present instance you must do what is right, etc.' . . . we are trying through several channels to accelerate the measure, which has been delayed only by some neglect about settling matters with Lord Edgecumbe, Mr. Eliot, and the Duke of Northum-berland, before they left Town.

[1] W. Eden to Lord Loughborough, 5 Aug. [1780], Add. MSS. 34417, f. 120.   [2] 31 July [1780], *ibid.*, f. 102.

A fuller explanation of the delay complained of by Sandwich and Eden is revealed in the papers and correspondence of North's Secretary to the Treasury. Certainly it did not spring from lack of industry. John Robinson, holder of a post of crucial importance at times of parliamentary elections, was well qualified to grapple with the labours which the decision to dissolve imposed upon him. Ability had carried him from small beginnings to a central position in parliamentary politics. Member of an 'obscure' Westmorland family, which had achieved a solid but not brilliant record in trade and the professions, and apprenticed to a country solicitor, his talents had earned him the esteem of his employer and patron, Sir James Lowther, through whose recommendation in 1770 he was taken into the Treasury by North. He had an unaffected and conciliatory manner, did not hesitate to be forthright when he felt it necessary, and possessed both good judgment and power of decision.[1] His reputation as a hard-working and efficient civil servant was well attested by his friends and colleagues. '[Lord North] makes you in fact do the whole of his business', Charles Jenkinson wrote to him on 2 September 1780, '. . . [and] finds you always ready as well as able, to do what he desires . . . the idea of your quitting the King's service can never take place; no-one, I am sure, will suffer it. The government could not go on without you.'[2] 'I am fatigued to death having been with my pen in my hand from eight in the morning till this hour, except one hour at dinner', Lord Sandwich once wrote to him on a later occasion, 'but I know you will laugh at my being fatigued with thirteen hours' work, as you make nothing of working double tides.'[3]

During his career at the Treasury, Robinson held the key place of parliamentary manager during the general elections of 1774 and 1780, and in 1784, as an unofficial but extremely active adviser, he played a considerable part in organizing a

---

[1] Wraxall, i, 428-30 ; Charles Best (Norcliffe), *Some Account of the Family of Robinson of the White House, Appleby, Westmorland* (Westminster, 1874), 20-53 ; Robinson to Jenkinson, 4 Feb. 1770, Add. MSS. 38206, ff. 207-8 ; Wedderburn to W. Eden, 3 July 1779, Add. MSS. 46490-1, 4th pkt.
[2] Abergavenny MS. 297. [3] 15 Feb. 1782, Abergavenny MS. 428.

third. It is with regard to the general election of 1780 that his papers are most informative and are most fully supplemented by his letters and memoranda in other collections.[1] From these sources it is possible to obtain some picture of the methods adopted in running the general election for the government, the extent of the operations undertaken, the nature of the objects which North and Robinson sought to attain, and the degree to which their efforts and their forecasts were successful.

These records also make clear the heavy burden assumed by Robinson in the organization and running of the elections. Once the decision to dissolve parliament had been taken in principle, the pressure upon him became extreme. He had now, with the utmost despatch, to interview several scores of people — members of parliament, prospective candidates looking for seats, peers and gentlemen with seats at their disposal, election agents — glean from them and digest into a summary information about their constituencies and their expectations; put pressure on Lord North to interview leading politicians and offer him advice about the distribution of favours; make responses to requests for assistance at elections, despatch candidates to constituencies, help in securing the attendance of voters, pull wires in all directions — and this all on top of the routine business at the Treasury Board. True, an occasional incident might produce some light relief amongst all these labours. In an undated letter of early September Lord Edward Bentinck wrote to his brother, the Duke of Portland: 'Port Eliot has dismissed Gibbon. Everybody rejoices. He is to be found from 8 in the morning to twelve at night in Robinson's

---

[1] The main sources of information regarding Robinson's part in the general election of 1780 are: (1) his correspondence and notes in the possession of the Marquis of Abergavenny (the selections from these papers printed in the *Historical MSS. Commission, 10th report, appendix part VI* and in *The Parliamentary Papers of John Robinson, 1774–1784*, edited by W. T Laprade (Camden Soc., 3rd ser., xxxiii, 1922) omit important letters and parts of letters); (2) his letters to Charles Jenkinson among the Liverpool Papers in the British Museum (Add. MSS. 38214 and 38567); (3) his correspondence with George III — mainly his own drafts and copies (Add. MSS. 37835); (4) his very informative analysis of the House of Commons and the constituencies as at the end of July 1780 preserved among the papers of George III in the Royal Archives at Windsor Castle.

ante-chamber and once being put into an inward room Robinson went out the back way and the maid not knowing anybody was left locked him in all night. This is the story as told.'[1] Robinson's own letters, though making no reference to this episode, certainly confirm the picture of a man driven by weariness to the point of evading suitors in sheer self-defence. 'I have very much to say to you on the transactions of this day', he wrote to Jenkinson shortly before midnight on 2 September, the day after the dissolution, '. . . but I am quite tired and worn out and can scarce hold my pen, and time will not allow it tonight', ending his letter, 'I am this minute broke in upon by electioneers, therefore must conclude'. Or again, at the height of the Westminster election three weeks later : 'Today I have been so tossed about that I have not got twenty words with Lord North uninterruptedly'.[2]

Early in July, probably immediately after the beginning of the parliamentary recess on the 8th, Robinson began to piece together an analysis of the parliament and the constituencies. By the 19th he was deeply immersed in this task to the exclusion of all other business — Hillsborough, who wished to talk with him on East India business, gave up hope of doing so until his 'parliamentary computations' were over.[3] By the 23rd he was able to inform George III that a fair copy of it was in preparation.[4] But finality in this work was impossible. As he explained to the King a week later : 'this is a business subject to fluctuation varying almost every day, the necessary additions and alterations have made the copy now sent to Your Majesty in several parts erased'.[5] Fresh, sometimes contrary, information was pouring in day by day, and the King's copy bore last minute additions dated 31 July.

The completed 'State' filled forty-nine pages of a foolscap size notebook. The roll of the House of Commons was set forth by constituencies in the manner of the contemporary *Royal Kalendars*, that is, the English and Welsh constituencies in alphabetical order, followed by those of Scotland. In

[1] Portland MSS.   [2] Add. MSS. 38567, ff. 71, 77.
[3] Hillsborough to Robinson, 19 July 1780, Abergavenny MS. 273.
[4] Add. MSS. 37835, f. 134.   [5] *Ibid.* f. 137.

column on the left of each page were entered the names of the constituencies. Against each of these Robinson entered the following information, passing to the right across the page : the names of the members sitting in July 1780; their political classification, indicated by a stroke, or figure one, in the appropriate one of four columns headed 'pro', 'hopeful', 'doubtful', 'con'; remarks about the constituency and the members, varying from the brief 'the same' noted, for instance, against Lord North at Banbury, to ten or fifteen lines of memoranda; and lastly, in a second set of four columns, the known or anticipated classification of the members certain or likely to be returned in the next parliament. With this information gathered and digested Robinson was able to explain, in his covering letter of 1 August forwarding the fair copy to George III : 'Except a few things necessarily to be done by Lord North and two or three things by Mr. Robinson which he shall attend to and he hopes to despatch while in town . . . he thinks he sees the measure now so forward as that he shall be able to put it in motion and execute it on any given ten days notice, which time the detail of it whenever fixed to take place, will be requisite for doing it properly previously to the day for the Council to dissolve'.[1]

The men at the Treasury, expert in the conduct of elections, viewed the question of the dissolution from an angle very different from that of Sandwich and Eden. North and Robinson attached much less importance to the state of public opinion. Public opinion was something intangible and incalculable; in any case, in more than half of the constituencies it had no importance whatsoever. They were concerned with the hard facts of the electoral system, much of them readily ascertainable and reducible to methodical analysis. What was the state of opinion among the hundred or so patrons of parliamentary boroughs? How many were friendly, how many definitely adverse? Reckoning up in advance what changes they were likely to make in their disposition of the seats which they controlled, how would the balance of parties be affected? Where, in the open constituencies, was there a

[1] Add. MSS. 37835, ff. 137-8.

likelihood of finding wealthy candidates prepared to stand a contest, with or without assistance from the government? It was in the light of such considerations as these that North and Robinson weighed the expediency of an early general election, and in their view no irretrievable step towards a dissolution should be taken until their knowledge in these matters had been checked and brought up to date. Edgecumbe, Eliot, and Northumberland, to whom William Eden alluded in his letter of 31 July,[1] together controlled fourteen parliamentary seats in Cornwall and four in Devon. While the arrangements in these boroughs were not yet complete, North and Robinson remained reluctant to commit themselves. It was the impatient Sandwich who forced the issue and secured what was practically a firm decision when the cabinet meeting of 3 August was about to disperse. In the absence of Thurlow, the only minister who viewed the proposal with disfavour, North found himself faced with an unanimous demand for an early dissolution: 'All', Sandwich told Eden, 'were for the measure without an hour's delay. Lord North concluded by promising it should be done in the course of the month', provided no 'bad event' took place in the interval.[2]

So far as North was concerned, the basis for this decision was the 'State' forwarded to the King by Robinson two days previously. There are, however, some curious deductions to be drawn from this document. Robinson found the state of numbers in the existing parliament to be:

'pro', 290 'hopeful', 19 'doubtful', 16 'con', 233.

Summing up the known or anticipated classifications of the members likely to be returned in the next parliament, he ended with the following totals:

'pro', 252 'hopeful', 47 'doubtful', 70, 'con', 189.

Adding the 'hopefuls' to the 'pros' and the 'doubtfuls' to the 'cons' in each of these sets of figures, it would appear that Robinson's initial calculations forecast a probable *reduction*, not an increase, of the government's theoretical maximum

---

[1] P. 31 above.
[2] W. Eden to Loughborough, 5 Aug. [1780], Add. MSS. 34417, f. 120.

majority in the House of Commons. In the existing parliament the totals were 309 and 249. In the next they might be 299 and 259, a transfer of ten votes from the government side of the House to the opposition. But after analysing the large number of uncertain cases in his forecast, Robinson then added to his 252 'pros' the 47 'hopefuls' and 44 out of the 70 classed as 'doubtful', and so reached the optimistic conclusion: 'the supposed numbers will therefore be 343 and 215'.

At a first sight the champions of an immediate general election could hardly have been given greater encouragement. And yet Robinson's final calculation proved highly misleading. In compiling the main body of the 'State' he had inevitably made wrong guesses about some constituencies, but the mistakes largely cancelled each other, and his original forecast turned out to be very nearly correct. But his redistribution of the 'doubtful' cases introduced errors of guesswork which were not countered by similar mistakes on the other side of his table: in some cases his assumption that friends would be returned was wrong, in others he correctly forecast the return of particular individuals but placed more reliance than was justified upon the extent of their loyalty to the government. Furthermore, the final calculation was based on inadequate data, some of which had already been superseded by 31 July. When Robinson added his notes dated 30 and 31 July to various entries in the fair copy of the 'State' sent to the King, he omitted to adjust the final calculation accordingly — omitted to note, for instance, that since the borough of Haslemere was now known to have been bought by Sir James Lowther, it could no longer be expected to return two friends. Or again, at that date, he assumed that friends would be returned for most of the seats controlled by Edward Eliot. This assumption was not entirely unreasonable, since Eliot, although himself in opposition, had agreed to re-elect placemen in 1778 and 1779; but it proved incorrect — a clear example of the flimsy premises upon which some of Robinson's calculations were based. Why Robinson ventured upon such dubious reassessments of seats which he had at first dismissed as 'doubtful' is not explained in his papers, but one or two probable explanations may be put forward. His original forecast, since it predicted a reduction of twenty in the government's theoretical maximum majority, provided no justification at all for a general election. But if Sandwich and other ministers were right about the wave of popular feeling in support of the ministry, it seemed likely that more friends might be returned in open boroughs than he had originally thought possible — hence the reclassification of seats at Bridport, Canterbury, Colchester, Evesham, London, Poole, and Yorkshire (all instances in which his first opinion was right and his second wrong). Perhaps, too, he was subconsciously influenced by his anxiety to justify a measure, which he himself had for months assumed to be necessary and upon which, as he knew, the King and most of the members of the cabinet had set their hopes. But whatever the considerations upon which Robinson acted, as a consequence North, coming to the cabinet as the ministerial expert on parliamentary affairs, was furnished with a brief which cast a far too rosy light on the electoral situation. It can hardly be imagined that he and Robinson had not made some downward revision of the predicted majority of 128 before the decisive cabinet meeting of 3 August, in the light of the extra information which had been gathered during the last two or three days of July; but, even so, the picture would still have been misleading and the hopes of success unrealistically high. It is evident to what an extent they were dealing in uncertainties, despite the careful analyses undertaken by Robinson. Yet after 3 August North was morally bound by his promise to carry through the measure within the month, unless new adverse circumstances — such as military or naval defeat — arose meanwhile and made it advisable to rescind the decision.

In this week of decision the ministers also plucked up courage to deal firmly with one other pressing question — the fate of the Irish Mutiny Bill. This matter had been left unsettled throughout July, and warnings had been received from Dublin that difficulties in the Irish House of Commons were anticipated if amendments making the Bill perpetual were added by the British privy council.[1] At the beginning of August the government was ready to face this risk, the alteration was made, and the Bill was returned to complete its legislative stages at Dublin. At the same time changes unpalatable to the Irish sugar trading interests were inserted in the heads of an Irish sugar duty bill. Resistance to these two revised bills proved unexpectedly feeble, and the complaisance of the Irish parliament seemed to justify the firmness shown by the government. The modified Mutiny Bill passed all its stages with gratifying ease and on 19 August received the royal assent from the Lord-Lieutenant.[2]

In due course Hillsborough wrote complacently congratulating the Lord-Lieutenant on the successful conclusion of the parliamentary session, and anticipating the extinction of factious opposition.[3] But the British ministers both over-rated this triumph and badly misjudged the Irish situation. Throughout the year they had been labouring under a basic misconception regarding Irish politics, for the origin of which they themselves were largely to blame. Buckinghamshire, from the start of his lord-lieutenancy, had felt it essential to recruit support for Irish government among men of consequence in Irish public life, even though some of them might have personal connections with the opposition in England.[4] The pro-English faction at Dublin Castle could not, in his view, give his administration sufficient weight in the Irish parliament. This policy was resented and condemned by some pro-English politicians, especially John Scott, the Irish Attorney-General, and John Robinson's particular friend, John Beresford. The British ministers' fault was to give too much credence to the complaints of Scott and Beresford and too little confidence to their Lord-Lieutenant — here, as with America, they listened only to what they wished to hear. Buckinghamshire, resentful of the

---

[1] Sir Richard Heron to Sir Stanier Porten, 11 July, 9 Aug. 1780, Grattan, ii, 484-5, 125-6 ; Sir John Irwin to Germain, 11 July 1780, H.M.C., *Stopford Sackville MSS.*, ii, 270-1.

[2] Buckinghamshire to Hillsborough, 17 Aug. 1780, Grattan, ii, 126-7, 19 Aug. 1780, and encl., S.P. 63/470, ff. 296, 300.

[3] Hillsborough to Buckinghamshire, 14 Sept. 1780, Grattan, ii, 139.

[4] Buckinghamshire to Sir Charles Hotham Thompson, 11 Mar. 1777, Hotham MSS.

mistrust which he encountered, primed his brother-in-law, Sir Charles Hotham Thompson, in a series of private letters, with a defence of his political tactics, hoping perhaps that Thompson, while carrying out his duties as a Groom of the Bedchamber, might have some chance of representing his views to the King.[1] Neither Scott nor Beresford, he explained, had political connections of adequate weight to provide a basis of support for the government. Those two excepted, 'almost every individual' in public life in Ireland was 'in some degree a patriot'. But this did not mean that support for government had not been forthcoming, even from men whose private connections were with members of the English opposition. 'Those gentlemen', he wrote, 'are greatly mistaken who conceive that the English opposition influence either Mr. Conolly or the Duke of Leinster. Conolly supported government upon principle. The Duke of Leinster stands personally pledged to me.' It was a satisfaction to him in August 1780 that these two men were induced to take the lead in the two Houses of Parliament in condemning public agitation against the revised Sugar Duty and Mutiny Acts.[2] In December he reiterated his conviction that the support of such men had been essential: 'The distresses and the discontents of Ireland has been such, the danger of American contagion so much to be apprehended, and the conduct of those who formerly never presumed to form an opinion so fluctuating, that unless men who, in some degree, possessed the confidence of the nation had given their assistance anarchy must have been the consequence. As to those who are *emphatically* styled the friends of English Government, they have neither numbers nor parliamentary abilities.'[3]

Beresford and Scott, and a number of politicians of the same kidney at Dublin, had other views. They condemned Buckinghamshire's temporizing policy as weakness, and, estimating the strength of their political connections more highly than Buckinghamshire, they impressed their own valuation of it upon British ministerial circles. The Lord-Lieutenant,

[1] 11 Feb., 3, 30 June, 10 Dec. 1780, *ibid.*
[2] Buckinghamshire to Hillsborough, 21 Aug. 1780, Grattan, ii, 132-4 ; to Sir Charles Hotham Thompson, 25 Aug. 1780, Hotham MSS.
[3] To the same, 10 Dec. 1780, *ibid.*

who seems to have been ready to give them their due, regarded their judgment rather than their integrity as at fault: they were, he wrote, 'ever ready to stand forth as the champions of English Government; but . . . they seem very often what the Italians would style *innamorati del' impossibile* and sacrifice the *bon* to vain attempts of obtaining the *mieux*'.[1] Their opinions seriously misled the British ministers. North, Hillsborough, and Robinson were confirmed in the belief that Irish politics were a mere matter of factions and that Buckinghamshire was completely mismanaging the game.[2] Following the myopic guidance of the men whose judgment they trusted more than that of Buckinghamshire, they continued to ignore the realities of Irish discontent, which made the more knowledgeable Lord-Lieutenant liken his charge to a fireship which a touch of a match would reduce to ruin.[3] In August, as Hillsborough's congratulatory letter indicated, they regarded the parliamentary victory in Ireland as the end of their difficulties with that country. It was an over-confident body of ministers that looked forward during August to the approaching dissolution — over-confident about America, over-confident about Ireland, over-confident about the outcome of the elections.

In mid-August the last arrangements fixing the date of the dissolution were decided on the advice of Robinson — whose main concern, in proposing the first day of September, was to ensure that he had adequate opportunity for last-minute election arrangements and that the new parliament would meet in time to despatch essential financial business before the Christmas recess. At the same time plans were laid for keeping the decision to dissolve a secret until the last possible moment. On the 14th Robinson wrote in reply to a letter from North:[4]

I would recommend that you should not formally adjourn the Treasury, but have it considered as adjourned from Thursday or Friday next, and let only the rotation of clerks

[1] To the same, 3 June 1780, *ibid.*
[2] *E.g.*, Robinson to Jenkinson, 30, 31 Jan., 2, 15 Feb. 1780, Add. MSS. 38213, ff. 89-97, 99-104, 110-12, 38567, f. 26.
[3] Buckinghamshire to Sir Charles Hotham Thompson, 11 May 1780, Mrs. A. M. W. Stirling, *The Hothams* (2 vols., 1918), ii, 190-1.
[4] Abergavenny MS. 286.

be in attendance, that your Lordship should if you and your family think it right and propose to go into Kent, they perhaps sooner, your Lordship on Saturday morning early, set forward thither; and have it publickly given out that you were gone thither for three weeks or a month. This would cover the business more than anything whatever otherwise can do it; and especially if during this time parliament should be prorogued from the 24th of August to which it now stands prorogued, until Tuesday the 31st day of October or Thursday the 2nd of November, which is the very last day the meeting can be postponed to, so as to get the money by the 23rd of that month for as there is always several days lost in the usual forms at the beginning of a new parliament, it will be near a week before we can get to real and essential business, I therefore doubt whether the earlier day, the 31st of October is not the best day. In this case the Council should be held on Thursday the 31st of August or Friday the 1st of September, the proclamation issued and the writs bear teste the 1st or 2nd of September. . . . Your Lordship might stay in Kent until Monday the 28th of August, and return to Bushy on that day unknown and unexpectedly, for while you and the ministers are still in and about town and particularly so about the time of next prorogation, a momentary dissolution is expected.

A few more days elapsed before the day of the dissolution was finally fixed. On the 21st the King understood it to be Wednesday, 30 August, but that same day North informed him: 'Mr. Robinson seems inclined to the first of September, as it will give him two more days for notices round the kingdom'.[1] This arrangement received final approval at a meeting of the cabinet on 24 August, when it was agreed: 'That it be humbly recommended to His Majesty to dissolve the present parliament on the 1st of September next and to call a new parliament to meet for the dispatch of business on Tuesday the 31st of October'.[2]

[1] George III to Robinson, 21 Aug. 1780, H.M.C., *Abergavenny MSS.*, 34, no. 290; North to George III, same date, Fortescue, v, no. 3121.
[2] Minute of cabinet meeting held at Lord Stormont's, 24 Aug. 1780, Sandwich MSS.

North's open departure from London and secret return was not the only deception arranged for the benefit of the politicians in opposition. Other ministers similarly departed into the country.[1] Charles Jenkinson, the Secretary-at-War, retired to his country retreat at Addiscombe. The Secretaries to the Treasury deserted their offices, Cooper for Worlingham near Newmarket, Robinson for his house at Sion Hill in Isleworth, where he remained sufficiently close in touch with men and affairs : there, on the 29th, he was joined by North.[2] The Lord Chancellor took himself and his humours off to Bath, whence he was by no means pleased to be dragged back at the end of the month in order to complete the formalities for the dissolution.[3]

These manœuvres were fairly successful in their object. Rockingham and his friends were highly suspicious of the government's intentions, but Rockingham himself did not believe that a dissolution was imminent, and, like his colleagues, he was loath to incur expenditure before it was necessary. On 21 August he and Lord John Cavendish paid a visit to York to discuss election matters with their supporters, and that evening he wrote to his wife :[4]

> The principal objection to calling a meeting of the Club is that it might raise a wish among *all the freemen* to have a *festival too*, and that it would lead on to opening houses and treating etc. etc. — all of which in the present time is thought unnecessary. I have had no further account from the Duke of Portland relative to a speedy dissolution of parliament. I believe that the ministers will delay it some time.

Portland seems to have remained near London in order to provide members of the Rockingham connection with early

[1] C. Jenkinson to Lord Hardwicke, 2 Sept. 1780, Add. MSS. 35617, f. 9.
[2] North to George III, 29 Aug. 1780, Fortescue, v, no. 3124, dated from Sion Hill.
[3] Robinson to George III, 22 Aug. 1780, *The Parliamentary Papers of John Robinson, 1774–1784*, edited by W. T. Laprade (Camden Soc., 3rd ser., xxxiii, 1922), 34 ; Thurlow to Robinson, 16, 19, 27, 28 Aug. 1780, Abergavenny MSS., 287, 288, 294, 295.
[4] Rockingham MSS. R. 158.

advice in case of a dissolution. His correspondence shows that he and his friends there were on tenterhooks about the middle of August: as Robinson told North, they were expecting the announcement to be made about the time the next prorogation was due (on 24 August). On the 17th Portland was stampeded into sending out a sheaf of warning letters. 'My Dear Lord,' he wrote to Rockingham, 'I think it may be material for you to know that *Mr. Charles Townshend* stopped Lord Richard Cavendish and my brother as they were coming here to dinner, to inform them that parliament would actually be dissolved immediately after the prorogation . . . He told them that he knew Rigby had given this intelligence to General Philipson, but that he himself knew it from still better authority which he was not at liberty to name.' [1] On the 21st — North having meanwhile departed into Kent — he was reassured in a letter from Charles Townshend, that it was understood that the ministry had now given up the idea of having a dissolution that week, but that 'the middle of next month or the latter end of it would be the time'.[2] Only on 30 August did Portland receive authentic reports that parliament would be dissolved in two days' time and send out immediate warnings to his friends.[3] Rockingham's confusion at being thus caught unprepared is sufficiently evident from the terms of his reply : [4]

I am exceedingly vexed at the sudden dissolution of parliament. I think it a *wicked* measure in the *advisers*.

In such a state as the affairs of this country now are — I should have thought that a sudden *call for parliament to meet* — was a much more becoming measure. The only idea on which the measure of the dissolution can be adopted — must be — that his Majesty's advisers think, that delay might risk the *influence of the Crown* getting out of their hands, and that *his Majesty* and they wish to secure as many tools to be elected — as possible — in order to have a large body of Banditti — to controul, thwart, and betray — *any*

---

[1] Rockingham MSS. R. 139-4 ; Lister and Lord Thanet to Portland, 20 Aug. 1780, acknowledging his warnings, Portland MSS.   [2] *Ibid.*
[3] Charles Townshend and Lord Duncannon to Portland, 30 Aug. 1780. Portland MSS. ; Lord John Cavendish to Rockingham [1 Sept. 1780], Rockingham MSS., R. 139-59.   [4] 1 Sept. 1780, Portland MSS.

men who venture to undertake administration — when the present ministers perhaps flye their country.

The secrecy so carefully preserved till the last moment by the government, although it had its drawbacks in preventing Robinson from making open preparations, probably reduced the bustle of the elections when they took place, and, by giving the opposition leaders little time to plan, lessened the number of contests and so helped to limit the demands which were subsequently made upon the slender financial resources at North's disposal. Every effort was made to maintain it till the last possible moment and to increase the confusion which reigned in the minds of the ministers' adversaries. Rumour was countered by rumour, and misleading reports were conveyed to the public press: the *General Evening Post*, for instance, printed on 26 August the statement: 'The Cabinet have resolved to postpone the dissolution of Parliament until after Christmas. The present Parliament will therefore meet early in November, to pass the land and salt duties etc. There will be very little private business, and the dissolution will certainly take place early in the Spring. This is the present settlement.' But that same day Robinson's messenger was posting down to Bath with a letter summoning Thurlow to the Council for the dissolution.[1] The bustle that overtook Westminster on 30 August made further concealment impossible. 'There were so many expresses sent off last night to every part of England', the London correspondent of the *Nottingham Journal* reported next morning, 'that horses could not be procured by the post office — the utmost secrecy was enjoined by the ministers to the different messengers, but it very soon transpired, and the friends of their country were advertised of the intended dissolution, as well as the friends of the Minister.'[2]

[1] Acknowledged by Thurlow on the 27th, Abergavenny MS. 294.
[2] Creswell and Burbages' *Nottingham Journal*, Saturday, 2 Sept. 1780.

THE GENERAL ELECTION

(i)
THE CONSTITUENCIES

A COMPREHENSIVE analysis has been made by Sir Lewis Namier of the character of the English electoral structure at the accession of George III, and there is no need to re-elaborate, from the documents relating to a period only twenty years later in the reign, the general picture he has presented.[1] Except for changes of detail the system remained as in 1761. But a brief recapitulation is not out of place. The counties and boroughs, and the various interests which affected them, were to the organizer of parliamentary elections as are the hills and dales, and the transport facilities giving access to them, to the staff officer directing a military operation. They were his terrain; and, like the staff officer, the political manager of the eighteenth century required his maps — only these were not cartographical but tabular in form, statements of information sorted and analysed. Just as the lie of the land conditions military manœuvres, so the complexities and variations within the old, unreformed electoral system determined the lines of action of the political manager — he had to conduct his operations within the limits set by its 'natural features'. It is necessary to consider some, at any rate, of the main features of the electoral map as it presented itself in 1780 to John Robinson, if the nature of his activities as organizer of elections for the government is to be appreciated.

At the same time a further question may be posed and answered. Had there been any recent increase in the extent to which the government could intervene with decisive effect

[1] *The Structure of Politics at the Accession of George III* (1957), 62-157.

in the constituencies ? For over a decade leaders of the parliamentary opposition had been loud in their denunciations of government influence, and the bill brought in year after year, first by Dowdeswell and later by Crewe, for the disfranchisement of revenue officers was intended to reduce ministerial manipulation of the electorate. Crewe's Bill was taken up as an essential plank of policy by the Rockingham party and eventually enacted in 1782. Did the facts justify the insistence with which it was pressed ?

The most 'independent' constituencies in England were the forty counties, each returning two members on the votes of the forty-shilling freeholders. The 'interest' and the point of view which the knights of the shire reflected were predominantly those of the landed class. But too much must not be made of the division between land and commerce. A short perusal of the record of the labours of the shire representatives in the *Commons Journals* shows that they were by no means narrow-minded in their interests. With very few exceptions they came of landed families. But if they sat for counties where an active commerce and industry were established, these subjects took up no small part of their time in the House of Commons. In Warwickshire, for instance, a large and important section of the electorate felt it necessary that their representatives should have some knowledge of local business activities. When the freeholders of the Birmingham district learned in 1780 that both the old members were retiring from parliament, they called upon Sir Robert Lawley to be one of their knights of the shire, as it was of great importance that 'gentlemen may, if possible, be chosen for the county who are connected with the people and not entirely uninformed of the particulars in which their interest consists'.[1] There were usually at least a few men among the county members with direct commercial experience. In 1780 one, Thomas Harley, was a leading banker in London; another, Henry Fletcher, was active in the East India Company; three more — Sir George Cornewall, Sir Joseph Mawbey, and Thomas Halsey,

[1] Thomas Gem to the Earl of Dartmouth, 14 Sept. 1780, H.M.C., *Dartmouth MSS.*, iii, 252-3.

representing the counties of Hereford, Surrey, and Hertford — came of business families and had themselves had commercial experience; others, like the members for Cornwall, Edward Eliot and Sir William Lemon, or like John Hanbury of Pontypool, M.P. for Monmouthshire, had diverse banking or mining interests.

Though the county franchise was exceedingly wide, and embraced persons of fairly humble standing, the effective voice in the selection of the representatives lay with the smaller circle of men of substance, the landowning peers and country gentlemen. As lords-lieutenants, magistrates, militia officers, squires, incumbents of parishes, the peers and gentry dominated a local society still shot with patriarchal, semi-feudal traits in its personal relationships; a society in which the lesser men were bound to the greater by a variety of all-pervading ties — leases, employments, trade, charity, and minor patronage of every description. Ignorant of political affairs, and drawn by loyalty or coerced by interest, the humbler freeholders followed at election time the instructions of their social superiors. Probably not one voter in twenty could freely exercise his statutory right.[1] A minority of local landed proprietors, which varied considerably within itself from county to county in range of wealth and point of numbers, played the main part in determining the course of elections. In some counties the members of this *élite* were fairly equal in economic status, numerous and independent — as they were in Yorkshire, or in some of the midland and south-western counties, or in Kent, where 'a kind of happy equality [prevailed] in the fortunes of all the country gentlemen, all of whom, of any note, possess about, and few or none exceed, £3,000 or £4,000 per annum'.[2] Elsewhere the accretion of great fortunes gave rise to narrower oligarchies of wealthy magnates, with whom the chief influence in their county lay. Such was the situation, for example, in Nottinghamshire, about which Sir George Savile of Rufford wrote in 1769: 'The idea I gave Lord Rockingham of this county was, four Dukes, two Lords, and three rabbit warrens,

---

[1] Namier, *Structure of Politics*, 73.
[2] *British Public Characters*, vol. x (1809-10), 534.

which I believe, in fact, take in half the county in point of space'.[1] No county, even Westmorland, could be described as under the absolute dominance of a single patron: but in about ten of them one or two leading families were conceded an undoubted primacy. The Cavendishes held one seat in Derbyshire, but on a tacit understanding that they would leave the choice of the other member entirely to the gentlemen of the county.[2] By some similar arrangement the Percy family at Alnwick carried one seat in Northumberland, as did the Gowers in Staffordshire, and the Manners family and the Yorkes in Cambridgeshire. In one or two instances aristocratic preponderance of this kind came near to making nonsense of the traditional eighteenth-century claim, that county constituencies were uniquely 'popular' and 'independent' in character. Oxfordshire, with its fiercely fought contest of 1754, provided an electoral *cause célèbre* in the middle of the century. But the expense had been fearful — the 'Old Interest' alone spent just over £20,000, of which over £11,000 came out of the pockets of the two 'Tory' candidates—and such an undertaking was not lightly to be repeated. By 1780 it seemed almost unthinkable that anything should shake the electoral compromise achieved between the groups headed respectively by the Duke of Marlborough and the Earl of Abingdon.[3] In the summer of 1782 Marlborough's brother, Lord Charles Spencer, offered a sinecure post which would necessitate his re-election, reassured Shelburne: 'I am not in the least hurry about it. I will only mention that there is no objection to my seat in parliament being left open, for there is no more danger of an opposition to me in Oxfordshire than in a burgage tenure.'[4] Sir James Lowther came near to enjoying a controlling influence in Westmorland, and he and the Duke of Portland had the leading interests in Cumberland. In one or two of the counties

---

[1] Albemarle, *Memoirs of the Marquis of Rockingham and his Contemporaries* (2 vols., 1852), ii, 138. Cf. T. H. B. Oldfield's account in 1816, *The Representative History of Great Britain and Ireland* (6 vols., 1816), iv, 317.
[2] Rockingham to Edmund Burke, 8 Jan. 1775, Rockingham MSS., R. 1-856.
[3] R. J. Robson, *The Oxfordshire Election of 1754* (1949), 158-9, 167; Oldfield, *Representative History*, iv, 350.
[4] 2 Aug. 1782, Lansdowne MSS.

the country gentlemen had little power to take an independent line if the big men were agreed between themselves. In Huntingdonshire, for instance, the rival houses of Montagu each conceded the other's claim to influence the choice of one member. On 16 February 1780 — well in anticipation of the event — Lord Sandwich wrote to the Duke of Manchester : [1]

> As prudence requires that those who are concerned in county elections shou'd begin to look to what may happen at the next general election, I hope there is no impropriety in my asking your Grace whither you will allow me to wait upon you in order to concert measures for preserving the peace and quiet of the county in which we live, and which I am well assured may be easily effected, if our sentiments coincide upon that subject.

Twelve years later, Oldfield described the county as being 'as much under the influence of two individuals as any rotten borough in the Kingdom'.[2] Similarly the electoral 'truce' established in Cumberland between the Duke of Portland and Sir James Lowther secured the peace and quiet of that county also : the attempts of the independent gentlemen to put up members of the Pennington family as candidates failed both in 1774 and in 1780, and in 1780 John Pennington publicly declared that he had withdrawn his candidature because Lowther threatened complete ruin to a large proportion of the inhabitants of Whitehaven, among whom Pennington had at first found much support during his canvass.[3]

Some very limited direct influence was possessed by the government in Kent and Hampshire, through naval bases and military installations, the revenue and postal services, the Cinque Ports and the Crown tenants in the New Forest, and in Cornwall through the numerous revenue officers. But in 1780 the seats in all three counties went to men in opposition, and it was found impossible even to find candidates to contest them.

In 1780 there were twenty boroughs with over 1000 voters,

[1] Sandwich MSS., letter book, 'private letters 1776–1781', 242.
[2] *An entire and complete history, . . . of the boroughs of Great Britain* (3 vols., 1792), ii, 138.   [3] *The General Evening Post*, 3-5 Oct. 1780.

ranking next below the counties in the grades of 'independent' constituencies, and ranging from Westminster with an electorate of 11,000, to Lincoln, Hull, and Leicester, each of which had about 1100 voters.[1] Twenty-six more had electorates varying from about 500 to 1000,[2] and another eleven had about 500 voters each.[3] After these came the great number of 'narrow' constituencies — small towns and villages with insignificant populations, and larger centres like Bath, Plymouth, Portsmouth, or Salisbury, where the franchise was restricted to a close corporation: there were 146 boroughs in this category, returning 290 members to the House of Commons.

Not one of the boroughs with over 1000 voters was subject to 'influence', although they were by no means immune from the formation of 'interests' by the government and by influential individuals. Revenue officials and other government employees provided the nucleus of a corps of voters in the ministerial interest, but the opposition tended to exaggerate the size and importance of these groups — Oldfield later wrote in his account of Hull that among the 1180 burgesses shown in the poll book for 1780 there were only forty-two customs men and three officials of the excise who were shortly to be disfranchised on the passage of Crewe's Act.[4] Traditional loyalties of a semi-feudal kind existed at Newcastle in favour of the Ridley family, and at Durham towards the

[1] The figures for the electorates given below are taken from the supplement to the *Royal Kalendar* of 1782.
The twenty parliamentary boroughs with the largest electorates were Westminster (11,000), London (7000), Bristol (5000), Norwich (3000), Newcastle-on-Tyne (2500), Gloucester, Nottingham, and Worcester (about 2000), Colchester, Coventry, Exeter, New Shoreham, Southwark, York (about 1500), Durham, Hereford, Liverpool (1200), Lincoln, Hull, and Leicester (1100). New Shoreham ranked as a borough, although, having, as a result of a particularly corrupt disputed election, been merged with the Rape of Bramber for election purposes by Act of Parliament in 1771, it was in character more a division of a county than a town.

[2] St. Albans, Bedford, Beverley, Canterbury, Chester, Lancaster (1000), Monmouth, Newark, Northampton, Rochester, Sudbury (800), Bridgnorth, Cirencester, Derby, Dover, Hertford, Maidstone, Sandwich, Great Yarmouth (700), Evesham, Ipswich, Lichfield, Oxford, Preston, Reading, and Maldon (over 500).

[3] Aylesbury, Berwick, Carlisle, Chichester, Newcastle under Lyme, Shrewsbury, Stamford, Taunton, Tewkesbury, Wareham, Warwick.

[4] *Representative History*, v, 275.

Lambtons and the Tempests. At York one seat was usually conceded to friends of the Marquis of Rockingham, whose connection there depended mainly upon the friendships he cultivated in the city and upon the respect felt for him and his opinions by its leading figures, backed by profuse hospitality at election times to the less politically minded voters in the drinking society known as the 'Rockingham Club'.[1] At Coventry the Seymour-Conways had a certain interest; Robinson thought in 1784 that this influence joined to that of the ministry might carry one seat; when Lord Hertford, contrary to expectation, went into opposition, it proved too weak to do so alone.[2] Westminster, the 'giant' among the borough constituencies, was not immune from the establishment of 'blocks' of voters. A considerable number of electors were employed in one way or another in the government service, or were connected with it by way of trade. The Dukes of Bedford and Northumberland also carried weight in the city: correspondence about the election of 1780 indicates that both sides had hopes of the support of the Bedford interest and were anxious about the way in which it would be employed.[3]

The degree of independence enjoyed by the towns with electorates of medium size — 500 and upwards to 1000 — varied from place to place, but only 21 of the 73 seats in these boroughs were subject to the control of a patron. The influence of the Cavendishes in Derby was a conditional one, relations with the borough being conducted on the same lines as with the county, one seat being conceded to them provided the other were left to the leading gentlemen of the borough and its neighbourhood. Portland learnt in September 1780 from his brother, Lord Edward Bentinck: 'they have given out in Derbyshire, that if Mr. Coke is opposed in the town, a gentleman will be set up for the county'.[4] Carlisle, in a

[1] See the account of Rockingham and the York city election, pp. 111-114 below.   [2] Laprade, 107.
[3] G. Stanhope and G. P. Gooch, *The Life of Charles, third Earl Stanhope* (1914), 24 ; C. Jenkinson to Robinson, 24 Aug. 1780, H.M.C., *Abergavenny MSS.*, 34, no. 292 ; Lord Carlisle to W. Eden, 6 Sept. 1780, Add. MSS. 34417, f. 178 ; Lord Ed. Bentinck to Portland, same date, Portland MSS.
[4] 4 Sept. 1780, Portland MSS.

different category, was 'open' only in the sense that it was the bone of contention between powerful neighbouring magnates, who compromised, or fought over, its representation — in 1774, the Earl of Carlisle and Sir James Lowther came to an agreement, and a supporter of each was returned; but in 1780 Lowther did not renew this arrangement and ousted Carlisle's candidate with the aid of the Duke of Portland and Lord Surrey, Surrey winning the second seat.[1] At one extreme in this group of towns was Sudbury, 'as open as the day and night too, and it is hard to say who may come in' :[2] at the other were places like Stamford or Newcastle under Lyme, completely controlled by the Earl of Exeter and by Earl Gower respectively.

By contrast, only thirty of the 'narrow' constituencies could be described as 'open', and some of these nursed quasi-feudal loyalties. Thus King's Lynn, long after the death of the great Walpole, continued to return members of his family, without expense to them.[3] In 104 of these boroughs the seats were wholly at the disposal of patrons (including in a few cases the Treasury and other government departments). The remaining twelve small boroughs, as also eight of those of medium size, were of a 'mixed' type — that is, one seat was controlled by patronage, whilst the other was, at least to some extent, 'open' to competition.

Of the 405 borough seats about 240 were controlled by patronage.

Excluding 24 seats under the influence of the Treasury and other government departments, there were 221 seats at the disposal of private patrons. A list of these is given below, which is compiled primarily from the information gathered by Robinson in the parliamentary 'States' which he drew up in preparation for the general elections of 1780 and 1784. In order to facilitate comparison with the situation which existed at the beginning of the reign, the list is presented in similar form to that compiled by Sir Lewis Namier for 1761,[4] and an

[1] 'State, 1780', 9, Windsor MSS.; Portland to Lord Egremont, 30 Aug. 1780, Portland MSS.   [2] Laprade, 77.
[3] Horace Walpole to Sir Horace Mann, 13 Feb. 1757; to William Langley, 13 Mar. 1767.   [4] *Structure of Politics*, 144-8.

attempt has been made to apply the same criteria of 'influence'. One new feature is introduced — one which indeed would not have applied in 1761 : the names of those patrons who were in opposition to the government, and the names of their boroughs, are printed in italics. In the then existing state of politics this was information of essential concern to the manager of parliamentary elections, and it is possible to see at a brief glance what Robinson himself could gather from his 'State', the extent to which the close boroughs presented hopes of support in a new parliament.

Names of Patrons	Nomination	Influence
BOROUGH PATRONAGE OF PEERS		
Earl of Abingdon (2)	*Westbury* (2)	
Earl of Ailesbury (4)	Great Bedwin (2)	
	Marlborough (2)	
Duke of Ancaster (1)	Boston (1)	
Earl Bathurst (1)		Cirencester (1)
Duke of Beaufort (1)		Monmouth (1)
Duke of Bedford (3) *	Tavistock (2)	Okehampton (1)
Viscount Bolingbroke (2) †		Wootton Bassett (2)
Duke of Bolton (1)		*Totnes* (1)
Duke of Bridgwater (2)	Brackley (2)	
Earl of Bristol (1)		*Bury St. Edmunds* (1)
Lord Brownlow (1)		Grantham (1)
Earl of Carlisle (2)	Morpeth (2)	
Duke of Chandos (1)		Winchester (1)
Earl Cornwallis (2)	Eye (2)	
Duke of Devonshire (3)	*Knaresborough* (2)	*Derby* (1)
Lord Mount Edgecumbe (6)		Fowey (1)
		Bossiney (1)
		Lostwithiel (2)
		Plympton (2)
Earl of Exeter (2)		Stamford (2)
Viscount Falmouth (5)		St. Mawes (1)
		Tregony (2)
		Mitchell (2)
Earl Fitzwilliam (1)		*Peterborough* (1)

* In 1780 the fifth Duke was a minor, and control of his borough interests was divided between his grandmother, who favoured the Rockingham party, and associates of his late grandfather, who supported the government.

† Lord Bolingbroke's hold on the second seat at Wootton Bassett was not very certain.

Names of Patrons	Nomination	Influence
Lord Foley (2)		*Droitwich* (2)
Earl Gower (3)	Lichfield (1)	Newcastle under Lyme (2)
Duke of Grafton (3)		*Thetford* (2)
		Bury St. Edmunds (1)
Earl of Guilford (1)		Banbury (1)
Earl of Hardwicke (1)	Reigate (1)	
Lord Harrowby (1)		*Tiverton* (1)
Earl of Hertford (2)		Orford (2)
Duke of Marlborough (4)	Woodstock (2)	Oxford (1)
	Heytesbury (1)	
Viscount Montague (2)	Midhurst (2)	
Duke of Newcastle (6)	Aldborough (2)	Newark (1)
	Boroughbridge (2)	E. Retford (1)
Duke of Northumberland(6)	Beeralston (2)	Launceston (2)
		Newport (2)
Earl of Orford (4)	Castle Rising (1)	Ashburton (1)
	Callington (2)	
Earl of Onslow (1)		Guildford (1)
Earl of Pembroke (2)		*Wilton* (2)
Lord Pelham (1)		Lewes (1)
Duke of Portland (2)		*Wigan* (2)
Earl of Portsmouth (1)		*Andover* (1)
Earl of Powis (2)		Ludlow (2)
Earl of Radnor (1)		*Salisbury* (1)
Duke of Richmond (2)		*Chichester* (2)
Marquis of Rockingham (3)	*Malton* (2)	
	Higham Ferrers (1)	
Duke of Rutland (3)	*Bramber* (1)	*Newark* (1)
		Grantham (1)
Earl of Sandwich (2)		Huntingdon (2)
Earl Spencer (1) *		*Okehampton* (1)
Earl Temple (2)		*Buckingham* (2)
Earl of Thanet (1)		*Appleby* (1)
Viscount Townshend (1)		Tamworth (1)
Earl of Warwick (1)		Warwick (1)
Earl of Westmorland (2)		Lyme Regis (2)
Viscount Weymouth (3)		Tamworth (1)
		Weobley (2)
Lord Wycombe (*Earl of Shelburne*) (3)		*Calne* (2)
		Chipping Wycombe (1)
Scottish Peers :		
Earl of Bute (1)		Bossiney (1)
Viscountess Irwin (2)	Horsham (2)	

* In addition, Earl Spencer had influence amounting almost to control of one seat at St. Albans.

Names of Patrons	Nomination	Influence
BOROUGH PATRONAGE OF COMMONERS		
W. A'Court Ashe (1)	*Heytesbury* (1)	
W. Aislabie (2)	Ripon (2)	
G. Anson (1)	*Lichfield* (1)	
H. Bankes (1)	Corfe Castle (1)	
M. Barne (1)		Dunwich (1)
J. Bond (1)	Corfe Castle (1)	
Sir H. Bridgeman (1)		*Wenlock* (1)
J. Buller of Morval (2)	West Looe (2)	
J. Buller, senior (2)		East Looe (2)
Sir H. Burrard (2)		Lymington (2)
J. Calcraft, jun. (2)		Wareham (2)
Sir R. Clayton (1)	*Bletchingley* (1)	
W. Clayton (1)		Great Marlow (1)
Lord Clive (2)		Bishop's Castle (2)
Sir C. Cocks (1)	Reigate (1)	
Sir E. Dering (2)		New Romney (2)
W. Drake (2)	*Amersham* (2)	
Sir L. Dundas (2)	*Richmond, Yorks.* (2)	
Edward Eliot (6)	*Liskeard* (2)	*Grampound* (2)
	St. Germans (2)	
M. Fonnereau (2)		Aldeburgh (2)
G. Forester (1)		*Wenlock* (1)
Sir T. Frankland (2)	*Thirsk* (2)	
Lord Galway (2)	Pontefract (2)	
Lord George Germain (2)	East Grinstead (2)	
Sir H. Gough (1)	Bramber (1)	
W. C. Grove (1)		Weymouth and Melcombe Regis (1)
A. Holdsworth (2)		Dartmouth (2)
Sir J. Honywood (2)		*Steyning* (2)
Edward Hooper (2)		Christchurch (2)
Miss Howard (1)	Castle Rising (1)	
George Hunt (1)		*Bodmin* (1)
J. C. Jervoise (1)		*Yarmouth, Hants* (1)
W. Jolliffe (2)		Petersfield (2)
J. Kenrick (1)	Bletchingley (1)	
Ed. Lascelles (1)	Northallerton (1)	
Peter Legh (2)	Newton, Lancs. (2)	
Thos. Lister (2)	*Clitheroe* (2)	
Thos. Lockyer (2)		Ilchester (2)
Sir Jas. Lowther (5)	*Cockermouth* (2)	
	Appleby (1)	
	Haslemere (2)	
J. F. Luttrell (2)		Minehead (2)
T. H. Medlycott (2)		Milborne Port (2)

Names of Patrons	Nomination	Influence
J. Nesbitt (1)		Winchelsea (1)
Lord Newhaven (2)	Gatton (2)	
Sir F. Norton (1)		*Guildford* (1)
Earl Nugent (1)		St. Mawes (1)
Robert Palk (1)		*Ashburton* (1)
Henry Peirse (1)	*Northallerton* (1)	
Henry Penton (1)		Winchester (1)
Jon. Philips (2)		Camelford (2)
Thos. Pitt (2)	*Old Sarum* (2)	
H. M. Praed (1)		St. Ives (1)
P. Rashleigh (1)		*Fowey* (1)
Sir J. Rushout (1)		*Evesham* (1)
G. A. Selwyn (2)	Ludgershall (2)	
Rob. Shaftoe (2) *	Downton (2)	
Gab. Steward (3)		Weymouth and Melcombe Regis (3)
Thos. Townshend (2)	*Whitchurch* (2)	
C. Tudway (1)		*Wells* (1)
Sir G. W. Vanneck (1)		*Dunwich* (1)
Earl Verney (2)		*Wendover* (2)
Edm. Waller (1)		Chipping Wycombe (1)
Lord Westcote (1)		Bewdley (1)
Thos. Whitmore (1) †		*Bridgnorth* (1)
Edm. Wilkins (2)	Malmesbury (2)	
Rev. L. T. Holmes (1)		Yarmouth, Hants (1)
Rev. L. T. Holmes		
Sir F. Barrington } (2) ‡	Newton, Hants (2)	
Sir R. Worsley		

* Shaftoe's control of Downton was contested by Lord Radnor : their wives were co-heirs of the Duncombe estate which commanded the borough.

† In 1784 Whitmore carefully avoided any pretensions to control both seats (*Berrow's Worcester Journal*, 1 Apr. 1784 : cf. Laprade, 116).

‡ 'Newtown consists of a farm-house and two fishing huts ; and is the divided property by a contract tripartite of the Rev. Mr. Holmes, Sir Richard Worsley, and Sir Fitzwilliam Barrington, who . . . nominate the members in succession. The right of election is in burgage tenures which consist of seven little fields.' *Parliamentary Characters, 1779–1781*, 62 (Scrap-book in the possession of Sir Lewis Namier).

Fifty-two peers enjoyed absolute control or decisive influence over the elections for 113 seats, and 67 commoners a similar power over another 108. In all 119 patrons disposed of 221 seats. The number of peers controlling seats had declined by three since 1761, whilst there had been an increase of eleven in the number of commoners — though the distinction between these two categories had little significance, and within a few years the tempo of grants of peerages to commoners who were patrons of boroughs was to quicken appreciably. The total number of seats at the command of peers and commoners had increased by sixteen since 1761, but this did not represent such an extension of the patronage system in parliamentary boroughs as appears at first sight, for nearly half the increase was due to the 'capture' by individuals of seats formerly controlled by the Treasury. In 1761 three peers and one commoner had each been able to control five or six seats. In 1780 the number of such larger-scale borough-mongers had slightly increased — four peers were now in this position and two commoners — the period 1774 to 1780 saw the deliberate creation by purchase of two such electoral 'empires' by Sir James Lowther and the Duke of Northumberland; but no political patron had built up a block of seats beyond the number of six. It is clear from these figures that there had been comparatively little extension of the system of nomination and influence over elections and no significant engrossment of parliamentary patronage in the hands of great subjects since the beginning of the reign.

Changes since 1761 in the list of boroughs controlled by patrons arose from a variety of circumstances. In one or two instances a patron had been able to extend his control from one seat in a borough to two, as the Duke of Richmond had managed to do at Chichester — though his hold on the second seat was somewhat precarious. A few boroughs had, for the time being at least, shaken off external control, and a slightly greater number had been added to the number of places under influence. At Truro the corporation, backed by a neighbouring magnate, Sir Francis Basset, revolted in 1780 against the decision of Lord Falmouth to return two members of his own family, insisted upon keeping a junior minister, Bamber Gascoyne, a Lord of the Admiralty, as one of the representatives, and selected one of their own number, Henry Rosewarne, a leading merchant of the town, to be the other. This momentary emancipation was the result of a local rivalry between Falmouth and Basset, the latter seeking to extend his electoral influence at Falmouth's expense.[1] At Helston a situation had developed which can only be described as bizarre. The rivalry of two borough families had produced a feud within the corporation which threatened it with extinction. No mayor could be elected, and no new corporators co-opted. One faction, with the support of the Godolphin family which had for long patronized the borough, sought in 1774 to circumvent their opponents by obtaining a fresh charter, setting up a new corporation from which their rivals were excluded. But the surviving members of the old corporation maintained their claim to be the sole rightful parliamentary electors in Helston, and in 1775 and again in 1781 their cause was upheld by committees of the House of Commons at the trials of disputed elections. As a consequence of this ludicrous situation, the electorate of Helston had been reduced by 1780 to three persons; and in that year, and for one or two later occasions, the Godolphin faction was unable to control the representation of the borough.[2]

At Wigan the Clayton family had a strong interest. But in 1768 the Duke of Portland had succeeded, by dint of great expense, in obtaining a controlling influence, which rested mainly upon the creation of friendly outvoters — this 'invasion' of Wigan was reputed to have cost him up to £20,000.[3] Robinson wrote of Wigan in his minutes of July 1780:[4]

> This borough is canvassed against because the Duke of Portland is supposed to have weight there and may with proper attention probably succeed in bringing in some friends, altho' it has been thrown out that it is open and Sir R. Clayton, the heir of Chief Justice of Ireland Clayton, who has the most natural interest there has been mentioned as having intentions to stand. If he succeeds he is a friend.

When the elections came on in September:

> Sir Richard Clayton considering the outvoters illegal would not poll any. The great majority in favour of Mr.

[1] P. Jennings, 'Notes on the Parliamentary History of Truro', *Journal of the Royal Institution of Cornwall*, xix (1913), 231-3.
[2] H. Spencer Toy, *The History of Helston* (Oxford, 1936), 200-75.
[3] Oldfield, *Representative History*, iv, 118.
[4] 'State, 1780', 39, Windsor MSS.

Bridgeman arose from his having the whole of Sir Richard's interest; and it is expected that Sir Richard will prefer a petition to parliament complaining of the undue election of Mr. Walpole.[1]

Henry Bridgeman was in politics a friend of Portland, as was also Horatio Walpole, who was related to him through the Cavendishes. Portland's hold on Wigan was not challenged by a petition. Robinson still thought the borough 'open' in 1784;[2] but the Duke continued to control its representation until the end of the century. Another example, Minehead, about 1761 was an 'open' borough, though some influence was ascribed to Lord Egremont.[3] But by 1774 Henry Fownes Luttrell had won complete control, reviving an old family interest derived from his Dunster estate. This was achieved by co-operation with the Treasury: in consequence of the representations which Luttrell made to Grafton in 1768, the government 'gave him the immediate patronage of all offices at Minehead'. This policy was continued by North when he succeeded to the Treasury in 1770; but Luttrell was quick to react against any hint that this arrangement gave the government any claim to nominate members, and in 1774 North was obliged to write an explicit disclaimer of any such pretensions:[4]

> From the time that you explained to me that the borough was intirely in your hands, I have always disposed of the offices there at your recommendation. That Sir Charles Whitworth should not be tempted to give you any trouble, I fixed him above half a year ago as a candidate for Dover. As soon as I heard from you that he was making some stir at Minehead, I wrote to him to desist. It was from your own suggestion that I thought of recommending a candidate at Minehead, and it was upon your objecting to Mr. Legge and appearing, as I thought, willing to accept of my recommendation of another gentleman, that I took the liberty of mentioning Governor Pownall to you.

[1] *Adam's Weekly Courant*, Tuesday, 19 Sept. 1780.
[2] Laprade, 116.
[3] Miss N. Jucker, *The Jenkinson Papers, 1761–1766* (Manchester, 1950), 27 n.
[4] Sir H. C. Maxwell Lyte, *A History of Dunster* (1909), i, 248-9, 255-6.

This, I solemnly declare, is all that I have done with respect to Minehead, and I cannot conceive how you can form, from any part of this conduct, an idea that I look upon it as a Government borough.

In 1780 North seems to have been disappointed in an attempt to persuade Luttrell to bring in another friend.[1] The patron was taking no risks. 'This borough belongs to the family of Lutterell of Minehead', Robinson minuted in December 1783.[2]

Conspicuous among these shiftings of borough patronage was the acquisition of six seats by the Duke of Northumberland, who, in 1761, had no substantial borough interest at his disposal. In 1775 Humphrey Morice, owner of the estate of Werrington on the borders of Devon and Cornwall and patron in virtue thereof of the twin boroughs of Launceston and Newport, found age, gout, climate, and the trouble of dealing with shifty, venal, and disloyal voters too much for him. Northumberland seized his opportunity, and was willing to pay a purchase price of £41,000 for this estate of only £1200 a year for the sake of securing the parliamentary interest, the nursing of which had cost Morice all the £1200 each year and another £3000 annually besides.[3] Before the general election of 1780 Northumberland also purchased from Sir Francis Henry Drake of Buckland the estates giving a controlling influence over both seats at Beeralston.[4] He thus moved forward at a bound into the position of one of the leading borough-mongers of England.

The politics of the borough patron often indicated the

[1] North to Robinson, 7 Sept. 1780, Abergavenny MS. 301.
[2] Laprade, 88.
[3] North to George III, 27 Apr. [1775], Fortescue, v, no. 3013 (misdated by Fortescue as 1780), and Morice's accompanying memorandum; memorandum of conveyance of Werrington Barton and lands in Werrington Parish, Manor of Lanson Lands, Borough of Newport and parishes of St. Mary Magdalen, Launceston, St. Thomas and St. Stephen in General, '21 to 22 Apr. 1775', Alnwick MSS. (information kindly supplied by my colleague, Dr. F. M. L. Thompson). The purchase price was well under half that set by rumour — £100,000 (W. P. Courtney, *The Parliamentary Representation of Cornwall* (1889), 371).
[4] 'State, 1780', 4, Windsor MSS. In 1761 the borough had been divided between Drake and Lord Buckinghamshire, but before the sale Drake's influence seems to have been predominant: in June 1780 he wrote to Buckinghamshire telling him of the sale and referring to his colleague as brought in by him on Buckinghamshire's recommendation, H.M.C., *Blickling MSS.*, 366.

politics of the man he had brought, or would bring, into parliament. Detailed information concerning the general election of 1780 and the members who sat before and after it in the House of Commons, bears out the conclusion drawn by Porritt from evidence ranging over many decades, that the patron usually dictated his nominees' political line, though there were frequent exceptions to this practice : there were always some men in the House who were returned with the assistance of friends by whom few or no restrictions were set upon their parliamentary behaviour or who stipulated for, and obtained, complete freedom of action when bargaining for their seats.[1] Generally speaking, it was the aristocratic patrons seeking to cut a great figure in politics who placed most conditions upon the disposal of their borough seats : thus, when a vacancy was imminent at Huntingdon in 1775, Sandwich sought to secure the political services of Captain Constantine Phipps, R.N., one of the most promising younger officers in the profession, but made it clear that Phipps must accept his conditions, 'the thinking and acting as I do in all American points and supporting the present administration in their whole system'.[2] It was in virtue of his knowledge of the politics of the patrons that John Robinson, compiling his preliminary data for the general election, was able to make many accurate forecasts of the line likely to be taken by new members, and to foretell correctly the rejection of men who had voted with the government in the late parliament; for instance, by Lord Temple at Buckingham, by the Earl of Pembroke at Wilton, by the Earl of Abingdon at Westbury.[3] Against the borough of Cockermouth he noted : 'If these two gentlemen don't come in again, yet Sir James Lowther will bring in two gentlemen against'; of Knaresborough : 'It will clearly be two friends of the Duke of Devonshire — 2 con'; of Thirsk : 'Sir Thomas Frankland being disappointed over Greenwich Hospital will not let a friend of government come in for that place as he once talked of'.[4]

[1] E. and A. G. Porritt, The Unreformed House of Commons (2 vols., Cambridge, 1903, 1909), i, chapter xvi.

[2] Sandwich to Robinson, 6 Sept. 1775, H.M.C., Abergavenny MSS., 11, no. 70.

[3] 'State, 1780', 6, 38, 40, Windsor MSS.   [4] Ibid. 11, 21, 36.

Concerning Lord Shelburne's unpolitical brother, Thomas Fitzmaurice, he wrote in his notes against Chipping Wycombe: 'As Mr. Fitzmaurice does not attend it does not answer Lord Shelburne's wishes and therefore it may be doubtful whether he will bring Mr. Fitzmaurice in again' — in the new parliament, Fitzmaurice was replaced by the eager young radical politician, Lord Mahon.[1]

But sometimes, Robinson found, such information failed him. The election arrangements made by those borough patrons who did not habitually engage in party politics were sometimes quite unpredictable, the patron being more concerned to serve a relation or friend than to give support to either the government or the opposition. At Pontefract, Lord Galway, who voted with the administration, brought in his relative, William Nedham, a nephew of the great Lord Chatham, who constantly opposed it. Edward Eliot of Cornwall, who went with the opposition in 1780, had accepted Treasury nominees for his boroughs in 1774 and was to do so again in 1784: but, alike on all three of these occasions one of his seats was made available — for the usual premium — to his friend, Samuel Salt, a barrister of the Inner Temple, who had attached himself to the Rockinghams in the 'sixties and adhered to them till the end of his career. One more example in 1780 is furnished by the Earl of Ailesbury, one of the Brudenells, a family prominent at Court but without much interest in politics.[2] When news of the dissolution reached Ailesbury, his most pressing concern was to arrange for one of his borough seats to be available in future when his son should come of age. His first hope was that his friend, Sir James Long, would agree to continue as representative for Marlborough for the interim period — on 1 September he wrote to Long:[3]

You must recollect your declaration to me at the last general election with regard to your seat in Parliament if my son had been of age. As that event will happen, please God, March two years, I should be glad to know whether

[1] *Ibid.* 41.
[2] Sir Lewis Namier, *Personalities and Powers* (1955), 22-3.
[3] Savernake MS. 1708.

it will be agreeable to you to continue one of the representatives for Marlborough until that time. I know there were instances at the last election particularly in the present Duke of Rutland and Lord Middleton of minors being chosen a year or two before they were of age, but I should prefer the more usual method of vacating a seat if you have no objection to being elected on that footing.

This plan fell through on Long's deciding to accept nomination at Devizes, and Ailesbury took further counsel with his friends and agents: 'Mr Peck came . . . and after showing a letter from Sir James Long I proposed my son to succeed him but he thought it more regular to have somebody for his *locum tenens* which I observed was an awkward thing to propose to anybody and fortunately my friend Mr. Woodley . . . proposed it', he noted afterwards.[1] Only a close friend could be asked to act thus as a stop-gap; but while Woodley's kindness was gratifying, his politics presented a difficulty; writing to him a day or two later about another vacancy, at Great Bedwin, Ailesbury observed: 'I will own to you disposition to support Government (let who will be the minister) is a *sine qua non*, and your delicacy on that point I well remember'.[2] Under these circumstances, Woodley's helpful offer could only be accepted with conditions, which Ailesbury outlined in a letter of 8 September:[3]

I know no man better qualifyed to act as a friend and *stop gap* (as you call it) than yourself, and I thankfully accept your kind offer of keeping a seat *warm* till I shall want it, or whoever succeeds me, and I have no doubt of your assurance likewise of not opposing, tho' it may be sometimes contrary to your inclination to support Government in that situation. Upon the faith of your compliance with these conditions which I understand you most kindly offer in your last very obliging favor, I am going to propose that upon the idea of being a *locum tenens* (as one of my most intimate friends) for my son who will be of age, please God, March two years.

[1] A memorandum by Lord Ailesbury narrating his borough arrangements in 1780, Savernake MS. 1709.
[2] Draft, 3 Sept. 1780, Savernake MS. 1713.
[3] Savernake MS. 1710.

The other candidate for Marlbro' will be your old acquaint-
ance Ld. Courtown.

Woodley accepted the bargain, and adhered faithfully to it, so
that his name appears in no division list for this parliament
until after the fall of North's ministry. But that could be
only small consolation to Robinson, who had counted both
seats at Marlborough as 'pro' before the general election.[1]

Occupying a very central place in Robinson's planning for
the general election was the little block of 'government
boroughs'. In 1761 government had about thirty seats under
its more or less immediate patronage — 'not all of them very
safe'.[2] The incessant complaints of opposition politicians
during the first twenty years of George III's reign give the
impression that this core of government influence had been
substantially increased by 1780. In fact the very reverse
process had occurred. In 1780 only twenty-four seats in
fifteen boroughs could be classed as under government control.
Of the nineteen dominated by the Treasury in 1761, the
government had abandoned Orford outright to the Earl of
Hertford;[3] its tenuous hold upon Totnes had been replaced
by a dependence on the private interest of Chief Justice Francis
Buller; control at Dartmouth had been usurped by the local
manager, Arthur Holdsworth; and three seats at Newton and
Yarmouth in the Isle of Wight had fallen under the domination
of the local families of Worsley, Holmes, and Clark Jervoise.
Against these losses could be set only the acquisition of a
temporary bargaining power over one seat at Winchelsea and
of a rather uncertain influence over one seat at Hythe. Apart
from these two gains the Treasury retained control only of one
seat at Dover and both seats at Harwich, Newport, Isle of
Wight, Hastings, Seaford, and Rye. Between 1761 and 1780
the Admiralty interest suffered less damage. The Admiralty
still controlled one seat at Queenborough, one at Sandwich,
and both seats at Plymouth, Saltash, and Portsmouth; but in
all three of the last-named boroughs opposition was started in

---

[1] 'State, 1780', 24, Windsor MSS.
[2] Namier, *Structure of Politics*, 142.
[3] *Ibid.* 389-401, where this episode is narrated in detail.

1780, and Sandwich and Robinson soon foresaw that ministerial control over Portsmouth at least could not be maintained much longer. At Rochester the Admiralty had lost one seat, but soon afterwards it temporarily secured control of one at Scarborough, and so still had ten seats at its disposal in 1780. As in 1761, one seat at Queenborough was under the control of the Board of Ordnance. It was thus a reduced, not an increased, 'electoral domain' which stood at the government's disposal in 1780 — this is one instance (and not the only one) where detailed investigation exposes the flimsiness of that constitutional bogy, the increasing influence of the Crown, puffed up and constantly paraded by the opposition in the years from 1770 to 1782.[1]

Constituencies in the Principality of Wales returned twenty-four members to the House of Commons, twelve from counties and twelve from boroughs or groups of boroughs. For the most part the borough franchise was wide — the outstanding exceptions were Beaumaris in Anglesey, and Montgomery, controlled respectively by Viscount Bulkeley and by the Earl of Powis. But in the choice of representatives the voters usually paid a semi-feudal deference to local magnates — this was an influence not due to corrupt inducements, but 'to popularity and hospitality of men of considerable property, whose residences are contiguous . . . and who are ready to serve them with that assistance and advice, which the exigencies of their situation may require'.[2] In the counties, also, the social and financial primacy of a few families gave them political leadership in their districts — for instance, the Morgans in Brecon (and also in the English border county of Monmouth), the Vaughans in Merioneth, the Wynns in Denbigh, the Mostyns in Flint, the Owens in Pembroke. Contests were few, and the political scene presented a picture of greater stability than either England or Scotland: Robinson's notes against the Welsh constituencies in 1780 (and again in 1784) were confined time and again to a brief 'the same'.[3]

In Scotland, the representative system favoured without

[1] My paper, 'Economical Reform and the Influence of the Crown', *The Cambridge Historical Journal*, vol. xii (1956), 144-54.
[2] Oldfield, *Representative History*, vi, 1.
[3] 'State, 1780', 6, 8, 12, 15, 16, 25, 26, Windsor MSS.; Laprade, 94-8.

exception the limitation of effective influence over parliamentary elections to a narrow circle of landed proprietors — this although two-thirds of the constituencies in Scotland were counties. But even the county franchise was greatly restricted and could be manipulated by corrupt practices. The right to vote in county elections was associated with forty-shilling freeholds of 'old extent', that is, lands which had been so rated in medieval times, or else it could only be claimed by those enfeoffed in or seized of estates worth at least £400 Scots *per annum*. Furthermore, only direct tenure from the Crown of such estates or freeholds conferred the franchise. The tenant holding directly from the Crown had the 'superiority' of the land, and he did not, by parting with his property, necessarily transfer or alienate the right of voting. Such was the state of the law, that effective property in an estate and the 'superiority' over it might be entirely divorced and pass into different hands. During the eighteenth century, the great landowners of Scotland exploited this legal situation on an extensive scale in order to create parliamentary votes in their own favour : they transferred their 'superiorities' to relations, friends and dependents whom they could trust to follow their political line, but kept their hold on their estates. The mode of procedure was succinctly described in the petition presented to the House of Commons in favour of parliamentary reform by the Society of the Friends of the People in 1793 : [1]

> The process by which this operation is performed is simple. He who wishes to increase the number of his dependent votes, surrenders his charter to the Crown, and parcelling out his estate into as many lots of four hundred pounds *per annum* as may be convenient, conveys them to such as he can confide in. To these, new charters are upon application granted by the Crown, so as to erect each of them into a superiority, which privilege once obtained, the land itself is reconveyed to the original grantor, and thus the representatives of the landed interest in Scotland may be chosen by those who have no real or beneficial interest in the land.

[1] *The Annual Register*, 1793 (Chronicle), 87.

The number of county electors remained limited, and this facilitated the predominance of aristocratic interests. A few years later, in 1788, the number of voters varied from twelve in Bute to rather over two hundred in the county of Ayr, and there were only ten counties in which the county roll held more than a hundred names : in all the counties together there were only some 2500 electors.[1]

The Scottish burghs similarly were subjected to aristocratic interference. Except for Edinburgh, where the corporation, numbering about thirty persons, returned one member, the burghs were grouped four or five together for the purpose of representation, and the member of parliament was elected by a convention consisting of one delegate from each municipal council within the group. The right to choose delegates was everywhere confined to the councils, and these narrow, often self-perpetuating bodies were easily controlled by neighbouring patrons, who packed them with their own supporters and victimized recalcitrant voters.[2] The system of indirect election gave additional opportunities for outside interference with parliamentary elections, and the considerable extent to which the burgh seats were at the disposal of a few individuals is clearly to be seen, for instance, in a memorandum relating to December 1773 preserved in Robinson's papers.[3]

The Scottish constituencies thus apparently presented a ready field for the traditional forms of election management practised by the Treasury ; but in fact, while it had to pay due attention to the pretensions of various magnates, its interest in Scottish elections was small. Most of the leading figures in Scottish political life were accustomed to support the King's government in parliament, whoever the ministers might be, and contested elections (which were proportionately much more frequent than in England) normally reflected not political differences but local family rivalries, in which the ministry tried to

[1] On this, see *View of the Political State of Scotland in the Last Century*, ed. Sir Charles Elphinstone Adam (Edinburgh, 1887).
[2] E. and A. G. Porritt, *The Unreformed House of Commons* (2 vols., Cambridge, 1903, 1909), ii, 120-8.
[3] Laprade, 5-9.

avoid entanglement.[1] Such elections were not matters of political urgency to the government. In 1780 Robinson might have annotated most Scottish constituencies as he did Kirkcudbright or Roxburgh — 'the same to government whoever succeeds'; 'whichever way a friend'.[2]

(ii)

THE ELECTIONS: THE GOVERNMENT 'CAMPAIGN'

In the eighteenth century elections were in practice a part of the business of government, a part for which the First Lord of the Treasury was responsible. Under his direction the Secretary to the Treasury in charge of patronage managed elections wherever ministerial interest might reach. It was their joint task to survey the constituencies, to allot candidates to a number of them, and to support these and also other friendly candidates by such diverse methods as were available. Thus a hard core of support in the House of Commons was obtained for the government. This practice harmonized with the contemporary theory of the sovereign's place in the British constitution. The King was still regarded as the active head of the executive branch of government: to him properly belonged the function of choosing ministers to run his departments of state, and so, to some small extent, of directing broad lines of policy. There was no competing centre of power in the country which could set up an effective counter-claim against the King's right to choose a government — certain aristocratic factions which virtually made such a challenge could not be regarded as 'centres of power' in any real sense. A general election was thus not an occasion for the people to choose a ministry. It was not primarily a struggle for mastery in the country between two opposing parties (although the general elections of 1780 and 1784 were contests of this kind to a limited extent): although the politicians habitually coalesced for the easier

[1] *Intimate Society Letters of the Eighteenth Century*, ed. the Duke of Argyle (2 vols., *c.* 1910), i, 168-9.
[2] 'State, 1780', 45, 46, Windsor MSS.

pursuit of their ambitions into loosely connected factions, to
which the term 'party' was often applied, the generally accepted
theory and practice of politics gave no recognition to the idea
that government should be in the hands of a party. On this
subject Edmund Burke spoke as a voice in the wilderness:
significantly, the men with whom he was associated from 1765
to 1790, the Rockingham, later the Portland, 'Whigs', held
office during that period for an aggregate of barely two years;
and some of them finally secured an enduring lease of power
only when the French Revolution drove them to abandon the
attempt to apply his theory. Far more in accordance with the
constitutional concepts of the age were the denunciations of
party uttered by Chatham and George III.

The true dichotomy in the national politics of the eighteenth
century consisted of Court and Country, of Government and
People — the term 'People' in this context being used to denote
the 'political nation', the small section of the community which
was politically articulate and qualified by wealth and education
to play a part in public affairs. These two factors were the
permanent features of the political landscape. More transitory,
the parties, such as those led by Rockingham, Bedford, Grenville, North, Fox, and Pitt, sprang up and burgeoned, grouped
and regrouped, withered and renewed themselves, like the
flowers in their seasons. A general election was not primarily
a campaign fought out between the parties, but an occasion
for an adjustment of the balance in the House of Commons
between the Court and the Country. Country and Court
were not necessarily opponents: they were opposites, upon
the co-operation of which the harmonious conduct of governmental affairs depended. Superimposed upon this process of
adjustment between them, like eddies on the placid surface of
a river, were the rivalries of the various party groups —
those of them called into office by the King being intent to
exploit the facilities of administration to forward both their
own and the Court's political interests — interests which they
often did not distinguish, nor wish to distinguish, one from
the other.

On the one hand, to the 'Country', the 'People', that is,

par excellence, the independent country gentlemen ambitious only for primacy in local affairs, general elections were periodic opportunities for ensuring that parliament reflected their opinions when discharging its constitutional function of checking and scrutinizing the activities of the government. To attach the term 'country party' to this section of the political community or to its representatives is inappropriate, for the word 'party' implies a degree of coherence and organization entirely absent from either. 'Country interest' is more admissible as a description of it. Its members thought locally rather than nationally, save when great matters of state like the American War touched their consciences or their interests. They did not face a general election or any other major political event as a group at all. Whilst they were independent and at times aloof from the government of the day, they were not necessarily by virtue of their classification opposed to it, and indeed no eighteenth-century government could last unless it enjoyed the regular support of many of their number. It follows then, that one cannot expect to find, on the side of the country interest, any trace of an election organization of any kind in opposition to that which existed in the Treasury.

On the other hand, to the Court, to the Government — that is, to the King and the politicians whom he had chosen to direct the departments of state — a general election was an occasion which imposed the necessity of conciliating, or defeating, factious combinations of politicians who, for one reason or another, were out of office, and wanted to get in, and who hoped to get in by increasing their bargaining power in the Commons. This view was but a shade removed from the more positive one, that a general election was an opportunity for strengthening the government majority in parliament; and at times of political strain, as in 1780, this more positive view gained ground. It seemed no anomaly to George III and his ministers, that an increase in this majority was to be achieved in part by negotiation with a limited number of peers and gentlemen and only in part by an appeal to an electorate, still less that the government itself should descend *qua* government into the arena and organize elections, and that the actual apparatus of national administration should be used for the purpose. This appears less strange, however, when it is remembered that, in the working of the eighteenth-century parliamentary system, the electorate was not expected to make a choice of an alternative government, and that no government majority was in any sense of the word a 'party majority', being compounded of courtiers, administrators, independents, and the members of the political factions to which the King committed the direction of the country's affairs.

The parliamentary 'State' which John Robinson prepared — as has already been described [1] — in the latter part of July served a triple purpose : it was a guide to the constituencies, a plan of action, and a progress chart. Robinson and North, scanning these notes, could see readily where the government might be able to take further action, to provide candidates, to support friends, to encourage attacks upon members of the opposition. Even at this early date, four weeks before the dissolution, the 'State' was beginning to take shape as a day-by-day record of the dispositions already made during July by the Treasury and by various individual borough patrons. Notes as to possible future action were also entered. It is probable that had Robinson's rough copy survived among his papers, it would have been found to bear further notes under dates in August, which would have provided additional information about the arrangements made by the government and by its leading supporters — in a number of instances, the further action which was indicated by, or at least foreshadowed in, the entries made during July, is traceable in the correspondence of Robinson during August and September. Combining the information in the 'State' and that contained in this correspondence, it is possible to present a fairly detailed picture of the extent of what may well be described as the 'government campaign' ; but owing to the disappearance of much of North's election and patronage correspondence, this picture certainly is not complete.

[1] Pp. 34-8 above.

THE GENERAL ELECTION

(A) The Counties

Of the 245 English constituencies (40 counties, 203 boroughs,[1] and the 2 universities) the greater number lay beyond the reach of government intervention. Government 'interest' of some kind extended, it is true, to all but the remotest parts of the country, but it was often of only minor electoral importance, and there were many boroughs under the control of individual patrons with which the government did not meddle at elections. Least of all was it possible for it to exert any appreciable influence in the counties.

Just because of this last circumstance, the forty English counties were regarded at election times as the most crucial constituencies. When political divisions in the country were sharp, as they were in 1780, then success or failure in the counties was of the utmost significance. When the new parliament met, Richard Fitzpatrick, seconding the opposition amendment to the Address, was able to strike telling blows in debate owing to the government's failure to receive support in the county constituencies. Philip Yorke informed his uncle, Lord Hardwicke, that Fitzpatrick 'ridiculed' the government's claim that the King was 'acquainted with the sense of his people from the late elections. He observed that in most of the counties the elections had been carried against the ministry; it was a sufficient cause for the people to reject a candidate if he was supported by the administration . . . as the right of voting is more extensive in the counties, the county elections were the fairest criterion of the people's sense'.[2]

Even before the dissolution the government enjoyed only meagre support from the English county representatives. Of these eighty members fifty-two were wholly opposed to it and two more were in the category of 'doubtful'. Only twenty were whole-hearted supporters, and another six were rated by Robinson as 'hopeful'.[3] But here, where an addition of

[1] Weymouth and Melcombe Regis is counted as one borough in this total.
[2] 7 Nov. 1780, Add. MSS. 35379, f. 246. (Yorke's letter supplements the account of this speech printed in Almon and Debrett's *Parliamentary Register*, i, 30-31).
[3] These figures are abstracted from the 'State' of July 1780 (Windsor MSS).

strength would be of most value, the government was least able
to strive after it. At most it might hope to extend aid in one
or two counties to friendly groups of magnates and country
gentlemen, and the references to county election matters in
Robinson's papers are accordingly few.

In a number of counties, for instance Gloucester, Huntingdon, Oxford, the ministry simply relied upon the interests of
well-disposed magnates — the Duke of Beaufort, the Earl of
Sandwich (himself a minister), the Duke of Marlborough —
to keep one seat in friendly hands. In Yorkshire, rather
similarly, Edwin Lascelles was expected to hold his seat, on
the strength of his own interest in the county together with
such help as could be given by other friendly peers and gentlemen — this hope proved abortive. Looking again to the great
men, Robinson, in his memoranda of July, speculated whether
the influence of the Duke of Newcastle in Nottinghamshire and
of the Duke of Northumberland in Northumberland might not
secure, in the former a first, and in the latter a second member
friendly to government; [1] but there is no further mention in
his papers of either project. In Cambridgeshire, the ministry
now cultivated the friendship of the Yorkes, although a few
years before Lord Hardwicke and his brothers had been
associated with the Rockingham group. It was Robinson's
hope that Hardwicke's nephew, Philip Yorke, would be returned
together with a very cordial ministerial supporter, Sir Sampson
Gideon, and that the attempt by the Duke of Rutland, now in
opposition, to capture one seat for his brother would be thus
defeated.[2] But Yorke and his uncle, who gave him continual
advice in this his first electoral adventure, were too doubtful
of Gideon's success to think of joining with him; and Gideon
was left to test what the power of money would do, while the
ministers gave every possible encouragement to the Hardwicke
interest. In July the King himself expressed to Hardwicke his
good wishes for Yorke's success, and gave orders for the
disposal of offices in Cambridgeshire in the way best calculated
to bring him support; while Sandwich, a member of the
cabinet, gave full promises of his personal assistance and, in

[1] 'State, 1780', 28, Windsor MSS.   [2] *Ibid.* 7, Windsor MSS.

September, did his utmost to see that Cambridgeshire free-holders resident in Huntingdonshire came over to Cambridge to vote for Yorke.[1]   It proved impossible to obtain the election of Gideon as well as that of Yorke ; and it was the county interests, not any 'court engine' (to use Oldfield's phrase) which determined the outcome of the election.[2]

In Kent, where Robinson was concerned to preserve one seat from the clutches of the opposition groups, he encountered one of the difficulties which frequently checked the attempts of the government to improve their voting strength among the county members — that of finding a suitable candidate. About mid-August, he tried every means he could to secure the services of Lord Lewisham, the son of the Lord Privy Seal, Lord Dartmouth, but met with repeated failure. At the end of the month he bemoaned the fact: 'Kent I find every day would do was there but a good man. But we have no ardour amongst our friends.' And in September the two opponents of government were returned without opposition.[3]

The same difficulty arose in Hampshire, where the government had a distinct but limited interest of its own, of a complex kind, deriving from the docks and harbours at Portsmouth and Gosport, crown tenants in the New Forest, and political dependants in the Isle of Wight. Many references to this county occurred in Robinson's election correspondence, but they only serve to show how limited was the government's power to intervene. A contested by-election the previous December had been a severe set-back, Sir Richard Worsley being defeated despite his solid backing of some five hundred freeholders in the Isle of Wight, the support of the Lord-Lieutenant, the Duke of Chandos, and the grant of £2000 from the King's election fund.[4] Of the members sitting at the

[1] Hardwicke to P. Yorke, 14 Apr., 15 July, P. Yorke to Hardwicke, 5 May, 11 June 1780, Add. MSS. 35379, ff. 45, 143, 87-8, 121 ; Hardwicke to Sandwich, 13, 16 Apr. Sandwich MSS. ; Jenkinson to Robinson, 15 July, Abergavenny MS. 268 ; Sandwich to Hardwicke, 13 Sept. 1780, Add. MSS. 35617, f. 40.   [2] Oldfield, *Representative History*, iii, 119.
[3] Robinson to Jenkinson, 21, 22, 28 Aug. 1780, Add MSS. 38567, ff. 59, 61, 65 ; *Canterbury Journal*, 19 Sept. 1780.
[4] T. Luttrell to J. Wilkes, 18 Dec. 1779, Add. MSS. 30872, f. 159 ; Sir Rich. Worsley, the Duke of Chandos to North, 12 Dec. 1779, Abergavenny MSS. 234, 235 ; Laprade, 57.

dissolution, Sir Henry Paulet St. John was fairly friendly, but as for the other seat, Robinson thought in July : 'After the late severe brush it is not likely that anyone will be found to fight this county'. Nevertheless, the ground was to be surveyed : 'The reconciliation of the Duke of Gloucester to the King is one material alteration : many other interests of the good friends of Govt. which were engaged stood neuter ; or which were not active last time might be secured and act with Govt. on a plan well formed and above all better management, for that was wretchedly bad the last time'.[1] In the following weeks there was desultory and evidently indecisive discussion about candidates : Robinson thought Henry Herbert of Highclere might do, Sandwich favoured the naval hero, Admiral Sir George Rodney, and the name of Sir Thomas Heathcote, one of the leading friends of the government in the county, was also canvassed.[2] Then at the end of August St. John decided to retire from parliament, and Robinson found it doubtful whether even one seat could be kept in friendly hands. Rodney could not be spared from Westminster, where his popularity with the crowd was an indispensable asset, and Heathcote resisted continued pressure to stand. 'I have sent for Penton to be here at breakfast tomorrow to consult about Hampshire', Robinson informed Jenkinson on 28 August. 'I have proposed to Lord North to write by a messenger again to Sir Thos. Heathcote to desire he would consider and consult the friends as to a proper person to stand for the county, and to offer to support such person whoever it should be, and then to get Mr. Penton to follow this letter and go down to negotiate, what think you of this.' Evidently these steps produced no result, for Jenkinson advised him on 3 September : 'If you can get no other candidate for Hants, Sir R. Worsley would now do very well.' A week later Jenkinson was in Winchester and reported that undoubtedly friends of government would carry one seat (provided a candidate were ready) : 'Any one may be chosen for this county that government pleases without either

[1] 'State, 1780', 17, Windsor MSS.
[2] *Ibid.* ; Robinson to Jenkinson, 21 Aug. 1780, Add. MSS. 38567, f. 59 ; Jenkinson to Robinson, 24 Aug. 1780, Abergavenny MS. 292.

trouble or expence. The opposition has had a meeting and say they will not put up a second candidate.' But Robinson and his Hampshire friends were unable to produce as a candidate any local gentleman who was really reliable in support of government. At the county meeting on 13 September, Heathcote and Thomas Dummer, *faute de mieux*, proposed, and carried without a contest, the election, vice St. John, of Robert Thistlethwayte, an independent gentleman acceptable to both sides; but he subsequently turned out to be a consistent voter against the North administration.[1]

In Surrey the problem of finding a candidate was at last solved. But other conditions were unpromising and the government fared no better than in Kent or Hampshire. Robinson's first reports gave little hope: 'The gentlemen are so divided and jealous of each other that it is very hazardous they will agree even to oppose persons against whom they all exclaim and consequently it is probable these gentlemen may come in again'; both the sitting members, James Scawen and Sir Joseph Mawbey, were in opposition. But on 31 July Robinson was able to add to his notes: 'Lord Onslow now says that he has hopes of this county for his son'.[2] Onslow held a court appointment and his family connections were zealous supporters of the government. Here were a candidate and an interest which merited the full backing of the ministry. Robinson and Jenkinson both exerted themselves personally on the Onslows' behalf, Sandwich added his quota of information and advice, and £2000 were contributed from the King's election fund. Up till within a week of the election Lord Onslow continued to be entirely confident of his son's success.[3] But the opponents of the government in Surrey included many of the most influential men in the county — Lords Spencer,

---

[1] Robinson to Jenkinson, 28 Aug. 1780, Add. MSS. 38567, f. 65; Jenkinson to Robinson, 3, 10 Sept., Robinson to George III, 13 Sept. 1780, Abergavenny MSS. 298, 304, 307; *Parliamentary Characters, 1779–1781* 58.   [2] 'State, 1780', 36, Windsor MSS.

[3] Lord Onslow to Sandwich, no date (mid-Sept. 1780) Sandwich MSS.; Robinson to Jenkinson, 17 Sept. 1780, Add. MSS. 38567, f. 75; Robinson to George III, 22 Sept. 1780, Fortescue, v, no. 3146; Lord Onslow to Jenkinson, 21 Sept. 1780, Add. MSS. 38458, ff. 133-4; Laprade, 58 — further payments totalling another £2,000 were made later.

Midleton, King, Radnor, and Suffolk, Sir Robert Clayton and Sir William Meredith — and they were supported by a strong group representing the radical interests of the metropolis: the committee which sponsored the candidature of Rockingham's friend, Admiral Keppel, in opposition to Onslow, included Thomas Scott and Thomas Wood, Nathaniel Polhill and Sir Richard Hotham, the first two leading freeholders in Middlesex who supported John Wilkes, the others merchants in Southwark, all of them connected with the radical movement.[1] The Onslows were reluctantly drawn into a contest — on 23 September they were on the point of withdrawing,[2] and it is probable that the payment of £2000 to them on that day was made to keep them in the field — and on the 28th Thomas Onslow abandoned the contest having fallen nearly six hundred votes behind Keppel.[3] Keppel and his colleague, Sir Joseph Mawbey, the victors in this election, were among the most violent opponents of the government.

Thus in four counties — Cambridgeshire, Kent, Hampshire, and Surrey — Robinson made appreciable efforts to stir up friends of the government without obtaining the slightest advantage. In 1780 Cambridge and Surrey were the only counties in which contests were carried to a poll by candidates and local groups friendly towards the ministry: in the first a member was lost, in the second an attempt to gain one failed. In the counties as a whole the elections were a decisive reverse. Prior to the dissolution twenty-six of the county members were favourable to the government ('pro' or 'hopeful') and fifty-four adverse. But when, in February 1781, Robinson drew up new lists of the House of Commons, the ministry was able to count only fifteen county members in its following. A friend had been displaced by an opponent in each of the following counties — Bedford, Cambridge, Kent, Leicester, Salop, Hants, Suffolk, and York — while three other members, Sir Thomas Clavering (Durham), John Morgan (Monmouth), and Lucy

---

[1] Keppel to Rockingham, 26 Sept. 1780, T. R. Keppel, *Life of Augustus, Viscount Keppel* (2 vols., 1842), ii, 286-8 ; *General Evening Post*, 19-21 Sept. 1780.

[2] George III to Robinson, 23 Sept. 1780, Add. MSS. 37835, f. 173.

[3] *The Canterbury Journal*, 3 Oct. 1780.

Knightley (Northants) were no longer rated as supporters.[1] Before the general election there were four counties of which both the representatives were friends of government — Cambridge, Leicester, Durham, and Stafford; after it, only one.

Furthermore, although the fifteen friendly county members sat for what were considered most representative and independent constituencies, not all of them were typical independents. Lord Lewisham was son of the Lord Privy Seal, Lord Hinchingbrooke of the First Lord of the Admiralty. Lord Charles Spencer enjoyed a court employment as Treasurer of the King's Chamber. Thomas Harley sat for the county of Hereford in virtue of his family's landed interest in the west of England, but as a London merchant and banker under contract to supply funds to the forces in America, he was closely connected with the government. Nor is it entirely accurate to classify as independents the following members: G. B. Brudenell, a minor placeman, member of a court family whose head, the Duke of Montagu, his cousin, was Master of the Horse; Nathaniel Curzon, whose father, Lord Scarsdale, drew an official salary as Chairman of the Committees in the House of Lords; or Sir John Eden, whose three younger brothers were all in government service — Robert, titular governor of Maryland, Morton in the diplomatic service, and the restless, ambitious William, about to become principal secretary to the Lord-Lieutenant in Ireland, who usually dictated the family's political line. This reduces to eight the number of genuinely 'independent' members sitting for English counties whom the government could reckon as supporters in the new parliament.

(B) THE OPEN BOROUGHS

In the open boroughs, as in the counties, the opportunities for the government to gain advantages from the elections

[1] Morgan and Clavering, however, voted fairly consistently for the government during the last critical months of its existence. Figures for the politics of the county members before and after the general election were:

	'pro'	'hopeful'	'doubtful'	'con'
July 1780	20	6 (=26)	2	52 (=54)
February 1781	13	2 (=15)	6	59 (=65)

depended largely upon local initiative. Possibilities of intervention depended upon the existence of pro-ministerial local groups and individuals, whom the ministry might be prepared to back with such interest as was at its disposal. In July, sixteen of the open and ' mixed ' boroughs — Andover, Arundel, Beverley, Bridport, Dover, Hedon, Honiton, Leominster, Liverpool, London, Great Marlow, East Retford, Salisbury, Scarborough, Westminster, Windsor — claimed the attention of Robinson as places where action was being taken on the government's behalf or where the chances of intervention should be explored.[1] In about half of these cases, as in the instance of Beverley cited below,[2] enquiries apparently proved that there was little hope of success for, so far as is known, no action seems to have followed. Later Robinson's attention was also turned to certain other boroughs.

The twenty boroughs with over a thousand voters were, like the counties, sufficiently large to provide arenas for conflicts between genuine political groups and interests. Also their electorates were too numerous for the government to exert much influence upon elections. Twelve of these constituencies were contested in 1780, and, in three more, contests were begun but not carried to a poll. But five only out of these fifteen figure in Robinson's correspondence as places where there was co-operation between the government and local groups to find and support candidates — Bristol, London, Westminster, Gloucester, and Worcester.

The metropolitan prestige attaching to London and Westminster caused both to be the regular objects of government intervention at general elections. The past record of North's attempts in the City was not a happy one.[3] Nevertheless the ministry hoped that their friends might bring in one member, and an initial £1500 were paid from the King's election fund in support of Alderman Richard Clark. But the efforts of his supporters were half-hearted: by 13 September Robinson knew he could not 'be supported to any great effect', and kept

---

[1] 'State, 1780', 2, 4, 6, 13, 18, 19, 21, 23, 24, 32, 33, 39, 40, Windsor MSS.   [2] Pp. 87-8 below.
[3] George III to Robinson, 31 Aug. 1780, North to Robinson, 1 Oct. 1781, H.M.C., *Abergavenny MSS.*, 43, no. 381, 45, no. 391.

in view only the more modest object — which was attained — of excluding the violent radical, John Sawbridge, by backing a moderate candidate, Alderman Newnham.[1]

Westminster with its 11,000 inhabitant voters — next to London the most populous urban constituency in the kingdom — presented a formidable prospect to political undertakers — so formidable, indeed, that ten years later Pitt and Fox agreed to compromise upon it.[2] But in 1780 the opponents of government were strongly organized in the Westminster Committee of Association and were as fully determined to bring in Fox as North and Robinson were to keep him out. The abilities, the personality, and the popularity of Fox made the struggle a crucial one. 'It is no trifle to keep out such a man as Fox, at the opening of such business as must of necessity come on', Edmund Burke wrote to Lady Rockingham, after the poll had been closed but while a scrutiny of votes was still proceeding. 'The spirit which appears at the beginning of the next session may have a very great influence upon all that is done in that, and perhaps in the succeeding sessions of the present parliament.'[3] One seat, left vacant by the withdrawal of Lord Malden, was virtually compromised, for both sides welcomed the candidature of Admiral Rodney, though the government gained more from it.[4] In opposition to Fox's attempt to capture the other, the ministers again supported Lord Lincoln, son of the Duke of Newcastle. This candidature was only arranged with difficulty. On 14 August Newcastle agreed that his son should stand. But in the following days he wavered, fearing that the hostility of the Bedford interest would make Lincoln's success impossible. On the 24th Jenkinson urged that the King should intervene himself, or through North, and that it should be clearly explained to Newcastle that Palmer, the agent for the Bedford estates, would throw that

---

[1] *Ibid.*; Laprade, 58; Robinson to George III, 13 Sept. 1780, Jenkinson to Robinson, 14 Sept. 1780, Abergavenny MSS. 307, 308; Robinson to Jenkinson, 14 Sept. 1780, Add. MSS. 38567, f. 74.
[2] Stanhope, *Life of Pitt* (4 vols., 1861–2), ii, 52-3.
[3] 27 Sept. 1780, Rockingham MSS., R. 140-4.
[4] Francis Place, Memoranda on Reform Politics in Westminster, Add. MSS. 27849, f. 56; Jenkinson to Lord Amherst, 1 Sept. 1780, Add. MSS. 38307, f. 208.

interest on the side of the Court instead of following the
Duchess of Bedford in supporting Fox: this alone, he thought,
would make Lincoln's candidature certain. It was made clear
also that government would bear all the expense.[1] North and
Robinson thus ensured that Lincoln would stand a poll, and
the government engines were put to work to whip up votes,[2]
but on 22 September he was obliged to admit defeat. Robinson
blamed the negligence of his agents and their mistaken tactics
half-way through the election, in trying to poll government
supporters for Lincoln only instead of for him and Rodney
jointly. It was still hoped for a few days that a scrutiny would
lead to the disqualification of a sufficient number of Fox's
votes to let in Lincoln,[3] but even this last resort failed, and on
10 October the High Bailiff reported that Fox had been duly
returned.

At Gloucester, Robinson's original aim was to hold on to
the one seat which was in friendly hands. For this purpose he
relied upon the candidature of George Selwyn of Matson, who
had represented the borough since 1754; but difficulty arose
early from the reluctance of Selwyn, now ageing and no longer
inclined to face a stiff contest for the town where his long-
established family interest was on the wane. Robinson thought
in July that his withdrawal would probably admit a member
opposed to the government — 'but whether to be let in without
an opposition must be considered and determined. It will be
a pity it should be given up quietly when it has so long returned
one friend.'[4] So, a day or two after the submission of the
'State', Selwyn was 'mightily pressed to go to Matson . . . to
engage in the bustle and disputes of that abominable town of
Gloucester'. North's request was not without justification,
for Selwyn admitted, in a letter to his friend, Lord Carlisle:
'There is a great party for me both in the corporation and in
the town, and among the gentlemen on the side of administra-

---

[1] Robinson to North, 14 Aug. 1780, Laprade, 32 ; Jenkinson to Robinson, 24 Aug. 1780, Abergavenny MS. 292.

[2] Jenkinson to Amherst, 1 Sept., to Robinson, 2, 14 Sept. 1780, Add.
MSS. 38307, f. 208, Abergavenny MSS. 297, 308.

[3] Robinson to George III, 15, 22 Sept. 1780, Add MSS. 37835, ff. 167,
171.   [4] 'State, 1780', 16, Windsor MSS.

tion dispersed in the several counties, my interest is not so inconsiderable. The clergy are as so many turnspits ready to be put into the wheel, and to turn it round as the Minister pleases. There may be something consistent in all this, and with these tools I can work very well if my health permits.'[1] Had the election managers remained satisfied with holding on to the one seat, all might have been well. But at an interview with North, arranged by Robinson a week later, Selwyn was persuaded to take a step he soon regretted and join with another government supporter to try to win both.[2] A visit to the town convinced him that there was no hope of this, but neither North nor Robinson would accept defeat: 'We have much to do', Robinson wrote on 28 August, 'to prevent Selwyn throwing up the game at Gloucester, which seems fair for both'.[3] Local customs officers were whipped up to support him, North busied himself to secure voters resident at his own borough of Banbury, and £1500 was contributed from the King's election fund. But in the end, Selwyn rated his chances too low to risk the expenses of a poll: on 13 September two opponents of government were returned unopposed.[4]

Worcester, Bristol, and Liverpool made only fleeting appearances in Robinson's election correspondence: here, again, local interests were the determining factors in elections. In July Robinson's notes on Worcester read: 'It is an uncertain place depending much on popularity. If the gentlemen of Worcester and the neighbourhood can agree among themselves they will bring in a person. If not Sir W. Lewes or some such man [i.e. a man in opposition] will get in perhaps.'[5] As the retirement of John Walsh left one seat disengaged, North and Robinson were concerned to secure a friendly successor, and it is possible, but not certain, that two aspirants, Edward

---

[1] 3 Aug. 1780, H.M.C., *Carlisle MSS.*, 441.
[2] Robinson to Selwyn, 8 Aug. 1780, Jesse, *George Selwyn and his Contemporaries* (4 vols., 1843-4), iv, 360 ; Selwyn to Carlisle, 11 Sept. 1780, H.M.C., *Carlisle MSS.*, 442-3.
[3] Selwyn to North, 22 Aug. 1780, Jesse, 362-3 ; Robinson to Jenkinson, 28 Aug. 1780, Add. MSS. 38567, f. 65.
[4] Dr. Warner to Selwyn, 7 Sept. [1780], Jesse, 386 ; Laprade, 35, 58 ; *General Evening Post*, 14-16 Sept. 1780.
[5] 'State, 1780', 40, Windsor MSS.

Bearcroft and Sir Charles Cocks,[1] who tested the ground during August but decided not to stand, did so at their instigation. In the first week of September, with the dissolution announced, there was still no ministerial candidate set up against Lewes. Tentative plans were made to put up Edmund Poulter, a young barrister belonging to a Worcestershire family and connected by marriage with the Bishop of Worcester, Brownlow North; and Lord North was ready to contribute £1000.[2] But nothing came of this arrangement, and the Treasury does not seem to have concerned itself further with the election: in the end, it was the local gentry who found a candidate from amongst their own number.[3] At Bristol, as soon as the decision to dissolve was taken, the government had a candidate ready in Richard Combe, newly appointed Treasurer of the Ordnance, and a contribution of £1000 was made from the King's election fund towards his expenses.[4] But there is no information about Bristol affairs during September 1780 in Robinson's surviving papers, and the ministerial faction seems to have been left to its own devices — apart, no doubt, from the usual attention paid to the voting of revenue officers. Liverpool was 'undertaken' by Bamber Gascoyne, another junior minister, whose son defeated a virulent opponent of government, Richard Pennant. It is reasonable to conclude that Gascoyne was strongly encouraged by North and Robinson, though he got no promise of financial assistance and his requests for some contribution to the expenses of his son's election were still being fobbed off by North eighteen months later.[5]

There is no indication in Robinson's correspondence that he or North took any substantial part in election arrangements in any of the other fourteen boroughs in this group. In the three with which they were chiefly concerned there was a loss

---

[1] Cocks, as a government official (Clerk of the Ordnance) and as owner of an estate at Eastnor some ten miles from Worcester, was just the sort of man from whom the Treasury would hope for assistance.

[2] Dr. North to his brother, Lord North, 5 Sept. 1780, Abergavenny MS. 299; North to Robinson, 7 Sept. 1780, Laprade, 35.

[3] On the course of this election, see pp. 147-51 below.

[4] Laprade, 57; Ed. Burke to Portland (for Rockingham), 3 Sept. 1780, Rockingham MSS., R. 140-11.

[5] North to George III, 16 Apr. 1782, Fortescue, v, no. 3663.

of two seats. At Bristol, Liverpool, and Worcester, where there was little or no governmental participation, five seats were gained.

In 1780 there were 52 open boroughs with electorates of 1000 or less, returning 102 members,[1] and another 20 which, for convenience, may be described as 'mixed', one seat being open, the other under the control of a patron. In these constituencies the activities and the successes of North and Robinson were on an even more modest scale.

Robinson's correspondence reveals attempts, sometimes unsuccessful, to provide friendly candidates at five places — Bath, Bridgwater, Hedon, Honiton, and Windsor. Both members for Bath in the previous parliament had been government supporters. One, Abel Moysey, a legal placeman, and son of a medical practitioner resident in the town, was sure of re-election. The retirement of his colleague, General Sebright, left Robinson with the problem of finding someone acceptable to the corporation to contest this seat against an opposition candidate, John Jeffreys Pratt, son of Lord Camden. Another soldier was thought most appropriate, and unsuccessful attempts were made to get the services first of Lieutenant-General Amherst and then of Lord Ligonier: in the end Moysey and Pratt were returned without a contest.[2] At Bridgwater, where Earl Poulett had some interest, his brother, Anne Poulett, one of its members since 1769, believed that 'with assistance' he might carry the other seat.[3] At the end of August, Robinson was advised by Lord Chancellor Thurlow, then at Bath, to send down a second candidate.[4] But in this instance he acted too late. Captain Thompson was despatched to Bridgwater, but before he arrived Poulett had taken as

[1] Abingdon and Monmouth were single-member constituencies.
[2] Jenkinson to Robinson, 24 Aug. 1780, Abergavenny MS. 292; Robinson to Jenkinson, 24 Aug. 1780, Add. MSS. 38567, f. 63; Jenkinson to Lord Amherst, 1 Sept. 1780, Add. MSS. 38307, f. 208; George III to North, 1 Sept. 1780, Add. MSS. 37835, f. 149; Lord Camden to Thomas Walpole, 20 Nov. 1780, Lullings MSS.
[3] 'State, 1780', 6, Windsor MSS.
[4] 27, 28 Aug. 1780, Abergavenny MSS. 294, 295. Though Poulett was not a reliable supporter, he was preferable to the other member, Benjamin Allen, who was entirely opposed to government and was making a bid to carry the second seat for Fox.

colleague John Acland, a cadet member of one of the leading families of Somerset, whose later conduct justified North's foreboding that Thompson would have been a better member.[1]

At Honiton the government gave backing to Captain Macleod, a retired East Indian, who won his election, but was too careless in the dispensation of favours to the electors to keep his seat when his opponent petitioned.[2] There was better fortune at Hedon, of which Robinson was already able to record in July: 'It is hoped this borough is so settled as to return two good members'.[3] At Hedon a fair proportion of the voters were employed in the revenue services: the borough was small and extremely venal,[4] and it proved susceptible to a combination of government pressure and private wealth. The successful candidates were Christopher Atkinson, a well-do-do corn-factor and government contractor, who had been cultivating an interest at least since 1775, and Robinson's wealthy relation by marriage, William Chaytor of Spennithorne. At Windsor the ministry won another success, as the result of a change of opinion on the part of the corporation. George III himself, encouraged by the new friendliness he found among its members, worried Robinson as early as April to fix on a candidate, busied himself with ensuring that the properties he owned in the town conferred as many votes as possible on members of his household, and, when North found a Berkshire gentleman, Penyston Portlock Powney, who would undertake the borough, made shift to get his tradesmen to support him.[5] Powney stipulated for £1000 to assist with his expenses, and received in September £1500.[6] The outcome was a triumph

---

[1] Robinson to Jenkinson, 5 Sept. 1780, Add. MSS. 38567, f. 73 ; North to Robinson, 7 Sept. 1780, Abergavenny MS. 301. The election was contested, and Benjamin Allen, through corrupt practices on the part of his friend, the mayor and returning officer, was able to secure the return of himself though not of Fox. But he was unseated on petition in favour of Acland in March 1781.

[2] Robinson to Jenkinson, 28 Aug. 1780, Add. MSS. 38567, f. 65.

[3] 'State, 1780', 18, Windsor MSS.

[4] Oldfield, *Representative History*, v, 312-13.

[5] George III to Robinson, 10 Apr., 3 May (2) 1780, H.M.C., *Abergavenny MSS.*, 29, no. 252, 30, nos. 258, 259.

[6] North to Robinson, 13 Apr. 1781, *ibid.*, 41, no. 359. Powney extracted further payments from North totalling £1,100 in January and May 1781 (Laprade, 58).

for the King and the government, Powney displacing Admiral Keppel, an outspoken opponent of their American policy.

At three other places financial assistance from the King's election fund was given to friendly candidates. £700 were issued on 1 September to aid Richard Whitworth at Stafford. Three payments totalling £1600 were made on account of Reading between May and September, and in July £1500 for Taunton. Whitworth failed; but a seat was gained at Taunton, where the Treasury backed a local army officer, Colonel John Roberts, and spurned an attempt at compromise by Alexander Popham, a follower of Shelburne.[1]

These exhaust the instances to be found in Robinson's letters and papers of specific aid or intervention by the government in the open boroughs. Their action, and the situation which faced them, in connection with other towns where Robinson in July had hoped intervention might be possible, is probably represented by the case of Beverley as it is revealed in two letters in the Hotham correspondence. In July Robinson had noted against Beverley: 'It is doubtful whether the same gentlemen will come in again; but it [is] equally doubtful whether a friend may be got in for this place. If Sir C. Thompson could be prevailed on to stand, he would it is hoped carry it. He should be talked to on it. Col. Masters of the East York Regt. would also make a good candidate.'[2] The sequel to this minute was an appeal for assistance sent by North on 22 August to Sir Charles Hotham Thompson:[3]

When I sent [to] you, I had received intelligence from Beverley that the electors there were not much pleased with their present members, and as I have no great reason to be more pleased with them than the electors, I wish'd to know whether it would be agreeable to you to declare yourself a candidate upon this opening, as I suppose that no man in Great Britain is so likely to succeed there as you are. I do not know that we can be of much service in a Beverley contest, but what service we can do will certainly be at your command, if you think proper to call for it. . . .

[1] Laprade, 57; Shelburne to Sir John Jervis, 11 Sept. 1780, Add. MSS. 29914, f. 147.
[2] 'State, 1780', 4, Windsor MSS.   [3] Hotham MSS.

Thompson, however, had washed his hands of Beverley. On the 27th he wrote declining the suggestion that he should stand, on the ground of his ill health and the ingratitude to his family shown by the electors at his previous attempt.[1] Doubtless North made similar abortive enquiries about Andover, Bridport, Dover, and other constituencies noted for possible future action in Robinson's State. Probably also he gave encouragement to independent friends or to placemen who sought to win or retain parliamentary seats: among placemen, John Kenrick at Bedford, William Masterman at Bodmin, Francis Eyre at Great Grimsby;[2] contractors, Anthony Bacon at Aylesbury, Cator at Wallingford, Fitzherbert at Arundel; independents, Robert Vyner at Lincoln, Sir John Delaval at Berwick-on-Tweed. But such men were for the most part concerned primarily with getting themselves into the House and only secondly, if at all, with fighting the government's battles, and their candidatures cannot be regarded as a part of the Treasury's planned election campaign.

(c) THE CLOSE BOROUGHS

Of a different character — and also somewhat greater in extent — were the operations of the government in connection with the close boroughs. With the majority of friendly patrons who controlled only one or two seats and returned themselves or their relations and dependents, North and Robinson had little concern: in Robinson's notes of July the brief entry, 'same again', appeared repeatedly against their boroughs. But negotiations with the owners of more extensive borough interests who were willing to place their seats at the disposal of ministry loomed large among their election preparations. Also of importance was the arrangement — in co-operation with the heads of various departments — of nominations of members to be returned for those constituencies where the government had a direct controlling interest.

[1] Draft, filed with North's letter, *ibid.*
[2] Kenrick was clerk of the deliveries in the Ordnance, Masterman clerk, register and secretary to the Duchy of Lancaster, and Eyre solicitor for plantation appeals.

Since nominations to the government boroughs could be settled in North's office, or by verbal arrangement with other ministers — Sandwich, for instance, met North on 22 August, 'to settle about Admiralty boroughs and men' [1] — scarcely any mention of them occurs in Robinson's papers. The main government outlay in such places being in salaries to placemen and wages to dockyard employees, only incidental expenses in connection with them appear in the election accounts and in the secret and special service accounts kept by the two Secretaries to the Treasury.[2] In this group of constituencies the ministry had a fairly secure block of twenty-four seats, which were distributed among its close supporters, about a third of them to active members of the administration — government servants among these nominees were : at Harwich, John Robinson and North's son, and private secretary, George Augustus North ; at Hastings, Lord Palmerston, a Lord of the Treasury, and John Ord, Chairman of Ways and Means; at Winchelsea, C. W. Cornwall, Speaker ;[3] at Queenborough, Sir Charles Frederick, Surveyor-General of the Ordnance; at Saltash, Sir Grey Cooper, Secretary to the Treasury, and Charles Jenkinson, Secretary-at-War ; at Sandwich, Philip Stephens, Secretary to the Board of Admiralty.

The leading ministers, the nine members of the cabinet, could muster only six seats between them — a fact confirming the conclusion already drawn for an earlier period in the reign, that borough interest counted for comparatively little in attaining ministerial office.[4] Five of the cabinet ministers, Lords Thurlow, Dartmouth, Stormont, Hillsborough, and Amherst, had no seats at their disposal. Lord Bathurst, and Lord North through his father Lord Guilford, controlled one each. Lord Sandwich and Lord George Germain each disposed of two seats in one borough. Their united interest was no greater than that possessed by the Duke of Newcastle or the Duke of Northumberland, by Edward Eliot or by Lord Mount

[1] Robinson to Jenkinson, 21 Aug. 1780, Add. MSS. 38567, f. 59.
[2] Secret and Special Service Accounts, 1779–82, Windsor MSS.
[3] I include the Speaker and the Chairman of Ways and Means, since both positions carried official perquisites and were not regarded as so detached from government as they are at the present day.
[4] Namier, *Structure of Politics*, 10. Of the nine patrons who controlled four or five seats in 1780, not one was in the first rank in politics.

Edgecumbe. The contribution thus available to strengthen the government in the Commons was small indeed, for as North and Germain both occupied seats for their family boroughs, only four were left for the return of friends (who, in all cases, were relations or particular clients of the ministers to whom they owed their elections).

Next, there were, in 1780, over forty seats controlled partly by aristocratic patrons, partly by hangers-on of administration, to which the government could lay claim with varying degrees of confidence for men of its choice. In Cornwall — despite the defection of Edward Eliot, who declined to accept any ministerial nominations and opened his boroughs to the opposition — about twenty-one seats were available (though two or three of these proved to be required by the patrons for themselves or their clients) — four of the Duke of Northumberland, five of Lord Falmouth, four of Lord Mount Edgecumbe, four controlled by the Buller family in the Looes, Lord Orford's two seats at Callington, and two managed by the Philips family at Camelford. The Duke of Northumberland and Edgecumbe each had also two seats for disposal in Devon. The Duke of Newcastle had four seats in Yorkshire and two in Nottinghamshire. There were also about twenty seats in the hands of lesser patrons, scattered about the south and south-western counties, where the government might expect to plant nominees — Gatton, Horsham, Ludgershall, Malmesbury, Midhurst, Milborne Port, Wareham, Weymouth and Melcombe Regis, Wootton Bassett, and Yarmouth.

North and Robinson attached the utmost importance to the continuance of support by the few great patrons who each controlled five or six seats. By the end of July they were assured of the friendship of the Dukes of Northumberland and Newcastle.[1] Northumberland kept two seats for his son and for a client, John Coghill, and accepted nominees of the Treasury for the remaining four.[2] Newcastle returned members of his

[1] Robinson to Jenkinson, 7, 28 July 1780, Abergavenny MS. 266, Add. MSS. 38567, f. 56 ; 'State, 1780', 1, 4, 5, 21, 26, Windsor MSS.
[2] Lord Cranborne, Treasurer of the Household, and Thomas Bowlby, Commissary General of the Musters at Launceston ; Lord Maitland at Newport ; Lord Macartney at Beeralston.

family at East Retford and Newark, where the name of Pelham-Clinton, but not a mere *fiat*, would carry one seat, but put in three dependents of the government at Aldborough and Boroughbridge, where he had absolute control.[1] No difficulty was experienced with Lord Falmouth, Robinson's notes of July correctly forecasting that friends would come in for his boroughs.[2] Lord Orford's two seats at Callington were secured by a direct negotiation undertaken by Lord Sandwich.[3]

It was less certain that arrangements could be made with the two western magnates, Lord Mount Edgecumbe and Edward Eliot. At the end of July this was the reason pleaded by the Treasury to excuse delay in fixing the date of the dissolution.[4] On 14 August Robinson wrote to North that he had little more business with which to trouble him if only he would make a clear plan of proposed appointments, and 'if it were possible to get decision in our favour with Lord Edgecumbe and Mr. Eliot which to be sure are great and material considerations in the business of Parliament, but which indeed seems almost alone the King's remaining to settle'.[5] A week later Edgecumbe had declared his friendship. His ambition was an earldom, but he made no embarrassing demands: 'He takes all our men', Robinson wrote to Jenkinson on the 21st. 'He is good natured and only wanted a little civility, he trusts everything to the King's goodness.'[6] £18,000 was paid to him in December 1780 for the return of friends for his six seats in Devon and Cornwall, but not all of this was government money, some of it being afterwards recovered by Robinson

---

[1] Sir Richard Sutton and Charles Mellish at Aldborough; Charles Ambler at Boroughbridge.

[2] 'State, 1780', 24, 37, Windsor MSS.

[3] Sandwich to Orford, 14 July 1780, letter book, private letters, 1776–81, pp. 229-31, Sandwich MSS.; Sandwich to Robinson, 15 July 1780, Abergavenny MS. 269; 'State, 1780', 7, Windsor MSS.

[4] W. Eden to Loughborough, 31 July [1780], Add. MSS. 34417, f. 102.

[5] Abergavenny MS. 286.

[6] Add. MSS. 38567, ff. 61, 55. Edgecumbe became a Viscount in March 1781, a promotion said to be in consideration of damage done to his estates by repairs to fortifications at Plymouth. Doubtless his complaisance over the election contributed to his advancement, for the King was ready to grant him this step in August 1780 (Jenkinson to Robinson, 19 Aug. 1780, H.M.C., *Abergavenny MSS.*, 34, no. 289).

in the form of contributions from the members concerned.[1] But Eliot with his six Cornish seats could not be won. For the last four years Eliot had shown growing disapproval of the government's American policy: on this account he had resigned in 1776 from the Board of Trade. In July 1780 he was 'violent against administration' and returned evasive answers to Robinson's enquiries. Though North thought it would do no good, as late as 22 August Robinson still made attempts to gain him. But long before that Eliot had determined his course, and his boroughs were put at the disposal of the leaders of opposition.[2]

Most of the remaining seats of this class could be settled by the government without much difficulty. A number were in the hands of men who stood little higher than borough managers and who were too dependent on government favours to neglect its wishes. Thus Philips of Camelford was brought up to London to settle his borough, which was eventually disposed of for cash to two East Indians, John Pardoe, an East India Company director (for his son), and James Macpherson, agent to the Nabob of Arcot and a government pamphleteer.[3] Wareham in Dorset was looked after during the minority of John Calcraft junior, by his brother-in-law, Anthony Lucas, a Commissioner of Excise.[4] Three seats at Weymouth and Melcombe Regis were under the control of Gabriel Steward, who held the office of Paymaster of Marines (£6000 p.a.) and whose brother was Receiver General for Dorset: he kept one seat for himself and accepted government nominees for the other two.[5] Malmesbury was under the patronage of Edmund Wilkins, Receiver General for Wilts and the recipient of an annual subsidy of £720 from the secret and special account

---

[1] Laprade, 58-9. On the source of this sum, see pp. 99-101 below.

[2] 'State, 1780', 15, Windsor MSS.; North to Robinson, 13 Aug., Robinson to North, 14 Aug. 1780, Abergavenny MSS. 285, 286; Robinson to Jenkinson, 21, 22 Aug. 1780, Add MSS. 38567, ff. 59, 61. On Eliot's conduct with regard to the election, see pp. 108-11 below.

[3] 'State, 1780', 8, Windsor MSS.; Laprade, 58-9.

[4] North to Lord March, 19 Jan. [1774], Cely Trevelyan Collection, in the possession of the Society of Antiquaries of London, for whose permission to use this information I make grateful acknowledgment; Laprade, 86.

[5] Oldfield, *Representative History*, iii, 381-4; Laprade, 86.

for the upkeep of his interest.[1] T. H. Medlycott accepted
large sums from the government to assist in preventing the
re-election of Temple Luttrell at Milborne Port and brought
in himself and a friend of ministry.[2] Lord Montague, Protestant member of a Roman Catholic family whose fortunes he had
dissipated, had a pension of £1000 as a retainer on his interest
at Midhurst.[3] Ludgershall was controlled by George Selwyn,
beneficiary from the sinecures of Registrar of Chancery in
Barbados and of Surveyor of the Meltings and Clerk of the
Irons in the Mint: in 1774 the annual pension paid to him for
his borough interest had been raised to £1500.[4] In 1780 he
kept one seat for himself and re-nominated for the other Lord
Melbourne, a courtier connected with North. Still, the
importance of the material ties with administration in all these
cases must not be pressed too far. Selwyn had his distinct
political loyalties, in relation to which his places and pensions
stood (in his view) in the nature of a proper reward for service,
not a bribe — he scorned the mere pursuit of place as an end
in itself.[5] Even Edmund Wilkins of Malmesbury, not at all a
high type to judge from the account of him given by Oldfield,
continued to support North at the general election of 1784
instead of following his natural lodestar, the Treasury.[6]

These election arrangements in the close constituencies
might be described as a holding operation by the government
rather than an electoral offensive. Such negotiations with
patrons offered only small prospects of increasing the ministerial
majority in the Commons, for the seats were normally disposed
of ministerially at any general election and had been filled with
friends by North himself in 1774. In the intervening six years
a few of these members had turned against the government and
the opportunity was now taken to oust them. Eight seats

---

[1] T. H. B. Oldfield, v, 180-2 ; Secret and Special Service Accounts,
1779–82, Windsor MSS.

[2] *The Last Journals of Horace Walpole*, edited by A. Francis Steuart
(2 vols., 1910), ii, 282 ; Laprade, 57.

[3] North to George III, 20 Apr. 1782, Fortescue, v, no. 3674. This
pension was virtually an equivalent of an outright purchase price, and after
North's friends, Henry Drummond and Sir Sampson Gideon, had paid
for their seats in 1780 it was discontinued.   [4] *Ibid.*

[5] Selwyn to Lord Carlisle, 16, 18, 27, [28], 30 Mar. 1782, H.M.C.,
Carlisle MSS., 596-613.   [6] Laprade, 118.

were won for friends in this way; [1] but these gains were largely offset by the transfer from the side of government to that of opposition of five of the seats in the gift of Edward Eliot (Eliot's sixth member, Samuel Salt, having been throughout in opposition).

As in the boroughs within reach of negotiation by the Treasury, so also in some of the other narrow constituencies a similar readjustment of representation took place, patrons excluding members whose opinions were not in agreement with their own. Among these borough owners Robinson could count on the government side a number of independent gentlemen or minor placemen who occupied their own borough seats — such, for instance, as John Bond and Henry Bankes at Corfe, Sir Henry Gough at Bramber, and Robert Shaftoe at Downton. Also friendly were Lords Gower and Weymouth, who had dissociated themselves from North's ministry in 1779 but avoided any action smacking of opposition to the Crown, and whose nominees in their parliamentary boroughs continued to vote on the side of the government. Despite the hostility of the redoubtable dowager Duchess of Bedford — whose influence in the counties of Bedford and Cambridge and in the city of Westminster was exerted against the ministry during the general election — her late husband's associates, who supported North, continued to sit for the Bedford boroughs.[2] Only in the relatively small number of twenty-one cases did changes of membership in these privately managed constituencies reflect a change of voting strength in the Commons. Here the government drew less advantage from the general election than the opposition, for only eight of the changes were in its favour, while thirteen went against it. The over-all picture of the elections in the close boroughs disposes of any idea that here was a field in which the government could make large additions to its strength in the House of Commons.

---

[1] Those occupied by John Amyand (Camelford), who died just before the general election: Lord George Gordon (Ludgershall); C. J. Fox (Malmesbury); Temple Luttrell (Milborne Port); Sir A. Leith (Tregony); W. G. Hamilton (Wareham); Robert Scott (Wootton Bassett); and William Baker (Aldborough).

[2] Richard Rigby (Tavistock), and Richard Vernon (Okehampton).

The voting behaviour of a few of the members returned in 1780 is difficult to assess for lack of clear evidence — Robinson was still not sure about a number of them even four months later [1] — but it would appear that the net effect of the elections in the close constituencies was a gain of one seat by the government.

(D) DOUBLE RETURNS

In the eighteenth century the term 'double return' was in common use to describe the practice of standing and securing election for two, or even three, constituencies.[2] This was a familiar method of reinsurance for owners of boroughs who were about to try their fortunes in counties or other open constituencies. The outcome of such a sortie could rarely be foretold with confidence, but the risk of being left out of parliament could thus be completely avoided. If the candidate was successful in his venture, he could dispose of his reserve seat in his own borough to a relative or political associate and so add to the weight of his interest in the House of Commons. In the event of defeat, the reserve seat enabled him nevertheless to enter the House.

This technique of reinsurance could also be used by the government, and was deliberately employed in 1780. When Jenkinson, after the elections, importuned Robinson to provide a seat for John Cator, a timber contractor, who had unavailingly fought the battle of administration at Wallingford, Robinson informed him : [3]

It is true that there were two or three double returns kept open to answer the purposes of government, but they were not easy, nor can they possibly be yet arranged, as Lord North has some gentlemen thrown on his hands, who

[1] List of the parliament, February 1781, Abergavenny MSS.
[2] It is in this sense that the term is used in the following passage. But it was also employed to describe the situation when a returning officer in a borough declined to judge the voting rights of two different descriptions of electors and returned the two candidates or pairs of candidates chosen on the different franchises, leaving it to the authority of the House of Commons to decide which election was valid.
[3] 3 Oct. 1780, Add. MSS. 38567, f. 83.

must be taken care of, as Sir George Osborne thrown out by a manœuvre of Mr. Holmes's, Sir Andrew Hammond who fought the battle of government at Gloucester most manfully and two or three more in the same situation. Until these things are done therefore it is impossible for Lord North to say with certainty what he can do for his other friends, but thus far I can venture to say, that I know he will give a preference to every man who has fought and been disappointed, and that he will be happy to provide for them all if possible.

Such a reserve of seats was quite essential to the government, for its credit, no less than that of any private patron, depended upon its willingness and ability to serve friends whose prospects had been blighted in the elections. Thus, on 4 September, Loughborough reassured the despondent Gibbon: 'It would be bad policy in administration to suffer either you or Langlois . . . to wait long for a seat, because it behoves a government to shew that no protection is so powerful as theirs'.[1] In the election arrangements made by North and Robinson the following hedging returns were included : Lord Cranborne (Launceston and Plympton); Lord Lewisham (Horsham and Malmesbury); John St. John (Midhurst, Lostwithiel and Newport); Thomas Onslow, the ministerial candidate for Surrey, at Rye; and Sir Richard Sutton, who intended to contest Sandwich, at Aldborough. As Lord Cranborne, on the death of his father the Earl of Salisbury, became a peer a few days after the elections, as Lewisham was also returned unopposed for Staffordshire, and as Sutton won at Sandwich, North found himself with three extra seats at his disposal in addition to the four close seats about which he could be certain. Yet another was made available by the unexpected return of Robinson for Seaford at the instigation of the East India shipper and government contractor, John Durand — an event which amusingly illustrates the embarrassments in which the Treasury might sometimes be involved by its friends. Durand found his seat at Plympton otherwise allotted at the general election. He proposed to contest Lyme Regis, but received a strong warning

[1] Add. MSS. 34486, f. 113.

not to do so, since Lord Westmorland, the patron of Lyme, was a friend of North and a staunch supporter of the government.[1] As a last resort he assumed the unauthorized character of a government candidate at Seaford. The rest of the tale is well told by the anonymous author of the sketch of Durand in *Parliamentary Characters, 1779–1781* : [2]

> The circumstances of his last election are a sufficient demonstration of his peculiar excellence in the *niceties* of *commercial* management . . . Lord North had actually exercised his privilege of indefeasible dominion . . . and had named General Gage and Mr. Mellish [*an error for Medley*] in private for the representation of Seaford. Mr. Durand soon obtained the knowledge of this secret, from his intimacy at the Treasury, and not perceiving any reason why he should not avail himself of the Minister's influence as well as another man, and so save the *trouble* of a contested election at his old borough, without leaving any intimation of his purpose behind him, proposed himself and Mr. Robinson as the candidates for that place. Mr. Mellish, with all the confidence of unsuspecting certainty, gave himself little trouble about the matter, and did not arrive till a few days previous to the election. . . . It was in vain to contest against the Secretary to the Treasury and his friend.

By way of these seats, once parliament had assembled and the writs could be moved, there re-entered the House Sir Sampson Gideon, who had lost his contest for Cambridgeshire; Sir George Osborn, a relation of North, rejected by Holmes at Yarmouth; George Johnstone, formerly M.P. for Appleby, aggrieved at being left out of Sir James Lowther's first arrangement of his boroughs, and thus, on the advice of Lord Loughborough, finally separated from his old patron; [3] Christopher D'Oyly, left out, owing to a misunderstanding, from North's first disposal of seats; [4] the Earl of Bute's son, James Stuart, for whom there were pressing personal reasons (probably debts) that he should be in the House of Commons

---

[1] North to Robinson, 7 Sept. 1780, Abergavenny MS. 301.
[2] Pp. 16-17.
[3] Loughborough to Robinson, 8 Sept. 1780, Abergavenny MS. 302.
[4] North to D'Oyly, 4 Sept. 1780, *Gentleman's Magazine*, 1829, i, 506-7.

before his return to England from the West Indies ;[1] and three other men, John Calvert, junior, Edward Onslow, and C. G. Perceval, to whose families Lord North owed political obligations. But these eight seats were quite inadequate to meet the government's requirements. Other friends still remained unsatisfied, including Benjamin Langlois, Edward Gibbon, a Lord of Trade, and the candidates at Wallingford and Gloucester, John Cator and Sir Andrew Hamond. Charles Jenkinson's brother was out, and he himself in doubts about the outcome of a petition to be made against his return at Saltash. With seats, as with places, the Treasury never had enough to go round, much to the disgust of its clients : 'Lord North has not yet finally fixed the vacant seats', Robinson wrote to Jenkinson on 17 November, 'but I am very sorry to say that he is so entangled by *absolute* promises, that I don't see hopes of any such arrangement for your brother as we talked of, only positive assurances that in case of accidents you shall be taken care of'.[2]

(E) THE KING'S ELECTION FUND

The account of the King's election fund was kept by Robinson entirely distinct from the secret and special service accounts.[3] In November 1777, in preparation for the next general election three to four years ahead, George III began to put aside £1000 each month out of his privy purse for election purposes. Periodically these sums were handed over to North or Robinson. When Robinson closed his accounts in March 1782, after the fall of the North administration, £40,000 had been contributed in this way, for every month up to February 1781, and another £13,000 was due for the period March 1781 to March 1782 inclusive. All these sums had by that time been spent, and more. In December 1780 North had been obliged to take up a loan of £30,000 from Messrs.

---

[1] Bute to Jenkinson, 28 Oct. 1780, Charles Stuart to Robinson, 7 Nov. 1780, Jenkinson to Robinson, 30 Oct., 17, 18 Nov., 1780, Jenkinson's memorandum, Nov. 1780, Abergavenny MSS. 320, 320A, 323, 326, 327, 329.   [2] Add. MSS. 38458, f. 139.
[3] Abergavenny MSS., printed, Laprade, 56-60.

Drummond, in order to meet outstanding election claims. He intended that this should be paid off from the future contributions out of the privy purse, but none of the debt had been repaid up to the time of his resignation.[1]

Robinson's papers contain the record of this election fund under the heading of 'His Majesty's Private Account', presenting first a statement of the sums received from the King and those repaid by private individuals, and the amount still due to North when the account was closed in April 1782, and secondly a running statement of payments made in respect of various constituencies from September 1779 to April 1782. There is also a supplementary statement showing sums received by Robinson from North and from some private contributors. Further information about the fund is contained in two important explanatory letters of 16 and 20 April 1782 from North to the King.[2]

One obstacle to an understanding of the use made of the King's election fund is that Robinson included in the election account disbursements of sums received into it as contributions from candidates, some of whom he omitted to name. The total received from individuals by April 1782 was £31,010 : 17s. Up to January 1782 five named individuals (or their fathers on their behalf) contributed sums totalling £13,300 — these were Lord Walsingham for Thomas de Grey (£1000), John Pardoe for his son (£4000), James Macpherson (£4000), John Townson (£3500), and Edward Gibbon (£800). In April 1782 £1000 was received from Bute for the election of his son, James Stuart, at Plympton. But in the meantime North had also received from other contributors, and banked, the sum of £16,710 : 17s., which on 18 January 1782 he withdrew and handed to Robinson.[3] The provenance of most of this sum cannot be traced with certainty from Robinson's papers.

[1] North to George III, 16 Apr. 1782, Fortescue, v, no. 3663 ; note at the end of the 'Most Private State', Laprade, 56.

[2] Fortescue, v, nos. 3668, 3663, and 3674 : no. 3663 is the final portion of the first of these letters.

[3] Laprade, 60. This sum entered in the account clearly was the balance of the private subscriptions, since when added to the contributions from Lords Bute and Walsingham, and from Pardoe, Macpherson, Townson, and Gibbon, it produces the correct total of £31,010 : 17.

A small part of it can be attributed to two subscribers. William Strahan was later stated to have paid for his election, and the sum disbursed for his return at Wootton Bassett was £2000 (in two instalments).[1] Gibbon would appear to have paid the balance of £2200 due for his seat at Lymington, since no sum for Lymington appears in North's list of government expenses at by-elections in his letter to George III of 20 April.[2] Individual contributions can thus be accounted for to the total of £18,500. A residuum remains of £12,510 : 17s., about which Robinson's accounts furnish no precise information regarding either the individuals who contributed it or the amounts related to particular constituencies. To the questions, who were the individuals and which the constituencies, a partial answer only can be deduced. Eliminating from the list of seats for which payments were made, those known to be paid for by the candidates, and those for which the Treasury was directly responsible, there remain eleven seats in seven boroughs, about which clear evidence is lacking :

Place	Members	Known to have been paid by the Fathers of the Members	Total Sums issued from the Election Fund
Mitchell	Hale		} £2,625
	Hanger		
Horsham	Wallace		} £5,325
	Ld. Lewisham, followed by Sir George Osborn		309 15 6 *
Malmesbury	J. Calvert, junior		£1,184 10
Plympton	Sir R. Payne		} £3,000
	Ld. Cranborne, followed by James Stuart	£1000	450 *
Lostwithiel	J. St. John, followed by George Johnstone		£3,000
			450 *
	T. De Grey	£1000	£3,000
Bossiney	H. L. Luttrell		£3,000
Fowey	Ld. Shuldham		£3,000
		£2000	£28,344 5 6

* These small sums for Horsham, Plympton, and Lostwithiel were paid for by-elections (Laprade, 59).

[1] Laprade, 58, 113.   [2] Fortescue, v, no. 3674.

Of the members named in this list, no contributions would be made by Lords Cranborne and Lewisham, or by John St. John, for their elections at Horsham, Plympton, and Lostwithiel merely created 'double returns' for the convenience of the government. Cranborne, in view of the illness and imminent death of his father, Lord Salisbury, refused to think of tackling an expensive seat and wanted only a temporary arrangement; [1] and Lewisham's father, Lord Dartmouth, was reluctant to 'spend a farthing' on his son's election.[2] But the remaining members all belonged to the type from whom governments in this period expected contributions,[3] and it is likely that all of them paid something towards their elections, though less than North — as he explained to the King — had hoped to receive. The table above indicates the extent of the government's total liabilities in this group of boroughs, though not the bills which it had to foot in each singly : its share of these election expenses was £13,833 : 8 : 6 — a figure obtained by deducting from the total of £28,344 : 5 : 6 the £2000 received in part payment for Plympton and Lostwithiel and the £12,510 : 17s. received by North from members whose individual subscriptions were not disclosed in Robinson's papers.

The total expenditure noted in the election account being £103,765 : 15 : 2, and £31,010 : 17s. being contributed by individuals, the amount spent by the government in the period for which it ran (to the nearest pound) was £72,755. Not all this sum was spent on the general election of 1780. Payments from the account ran in date from September 1779 to March 1782 and included a number of by-elections. North listed these in his letter to the King of 20 April as : Hampshire, Gloucestershire, and Coventry, £2000 each, Bristol £5000, and sundry re-elections £2000. But he was attempting to palliate the offence of overspending, and, while it was literally correct, it was hardly just to include the sundry re-elections, as they

[1] 'State, 1780', 4, 18, Windsor MSS.
[2] Robinson to Jenkinson, 22 Aug. 1780, Add. MSS. 38567, f. 61.
[3] In 1784 Robinson included Hale in a list of friends willing to purchase seats (Laprade, 124). Sir Ralph Payne's readiness at an earlier date to spend money for a seat in parliament is on record in the Grafton MSS. ('Memo from Mr. Woodley regarding Mr. Payne', not dated but probably of the winter of 1767–8) and also in Abergavenny MS. 103.

arose from the redistribution of seats kept in hand by double returns at Midhurst, Horsham, Plympton and Lostwithiel, and from the return of Gabriel Steward at Weymouth in place of his *locum tenens*, Warren Lisle.[1] The sums for the re-elections properly belong to the general election expenditure. The expenses arising from the general election were therefore rather under £62,000.

The following analysis includes all the payments of government money out of the election fund except the sums issued in connection with the four by-elections noted above :

1. Twelve open constituencies in England
    English counties : Surrey (£4000)
    English boroughs : Aylesbury (£1625), Barnstaple £1500), Bristol (£1000), Gloucester (£2600), London (£4209), Penryn (£650), Reading (£1600) Stafford (£1541), Taunton (£2924), Westminster (£8123), Windsor (£2600) £32,372
2. Scotland : Orkney and Edinburgh * 2,915
3. Three government boroughs, where opponents provoked contests (Plymouth, Hythe, Sandwich) . . 3,384
4. Writs and petty expenses at Haslemere and at various government boroughs (Harwich, Newport, Portsmouth, Rochester) 628
5. Close constituencies in England under private patrons :
    Lord Townshend, for Tamworth † . . . £4,000
    T. H. Medlycott, for Milborne Port, being the balance not covered by Townson's contribution . 3,931
    Lord Montague, for Midhurst, for the by-election of November 1780 ‡ 200
    Gabriel Steward, for his re-election at Weymouth . 500
    Seven boroughs, where the government paid part of the charge for seats § 13,833
    ———— 22,464

                                                  Total   £61,763

* Selkirk in Laprade (p. 58) is an error of transcription.
† North to George III, 16 Apr. 1782, Fortescue, v, no. 3668.
‡ A note that this payment was for the by-election occurs in an analysis made by Robinson of secret and special service payments (Add. MSS. 37836, f. 137).
§ See pp. 100–1 above.

[1] The premature general election caught Steward in the situation of mayor and returning officer, so that it was impossible for him to stand : his return at a by-election followed as soon as his term of office as mayor was over. On his expenses see Welbore Ellis to Robinson, 10 Feb. 1782, H.M.C., *Abergavenny MSS.*, 49, no. 421.

Expenditure was almost equally divided between open and close constituencies. It was certainly not North's intention to have spent over £30,000 on the open constituencies, and not all this sum was actually made available during the course of the elections. Up to the end of September only £18,500 was issued for Surrey and the eleven English boroughs. Probably North's promises spurred friends in some of these constituencies to rely on contributions from the election fund greater than those actually received up to the time of the elections, and so the extent of the government's financial interference must be assessed as rather higher than £18,500. But it is fairly certain that North's promises did not go nearly as far as £32,000. After September he was anxious to keep down further expense, and it is clear that some of the money later paid out for these elections was made available only with reluctance, partly from a feeling of duty towards friends of government who had spent beyond their intentions or their means, partly for fear of offending them. Thus, the ministerial party in Surrey received £2000 for the general election in September, but they made further demands eliciting three later payments totalling £2000 more, and still had other claims outstanding in April 1782. Powney, the victor over Admiral Keppel at Windsor, at first undertook the borough on condition he received an aid of £1000. This estimate he presumably found too low, for in September 1780, at the time of the election, he received £1500. But he later presented claims and received payments for expenses totalling a further £1100. North felt obliged to give way similarly to demands in connection with the by-elections at Bristol and Coventry: 'Really', he complained to Robinson, 'the demands on this occasion are exorbitant beyond the example of any former time.' [1]

Opposition politicians were wont to complain of the weight of government money thrown against them at elections. But it is necessary to put this ministerial expenditure in the open constituencies in proper perspective. £19,000, or even £32,000 was relatively moderate in scale, when compared with the sums which could be put forward by local groups of George III's

[1] 13 Apr. 1781, H.M.C., *Abergavenny MSS.*, 41, no. 359.

subjects. An amount larger than this was spent in 1780 on the contested Cambridgeshire election alone by the three rival parties. When the battle was over and the counting of the cost had begun, John Butcher, the Duke of Rutland's agent, confidently assured Rutland that his expenses would be under £12,000. Philip Yorke told his uncle, that he thought £15,000 would clear his side of the business. He added his belief that the three parties had probably spent £50,000 in all; and since the third participant, Sir Sampson Gideon, relied more on wealth and less on social status than his rivals, and had set the pace in spending money in the county, this estimate was quite possibly very near the mark.[1] Nor did this example stand alone. The recent Gloucestershire by-election of 1776 was believed by North to have cost one side only, the friends of government, from £20,000 to £30,000.[2] Again, £32,000 could soon be swallowed up in three or four contests in open boroughs, where each side might easily spend £8000 or more — this was the bill incurred by ministerial supporters at Bristol, and by the government itself at Westminster in 1780;[3] while Richard Rigby spent not far short of this sum the following year at Colchester, in the aid of a government man.[4]

The return for this £32,000 was extremely modest. Seats were won or retained in half of the twelve constituencies, but the government's candidates were beaten in all three constituencies where its greatest contributions were made. £8000 was paid for the lost cause of Lincoln against Fox at Westminster (it cannot be said that Rodney's election cost the government anything, for it was not really contested), £4000 was similarly lost in London, and £4000 in Surrey, and nearly £5000 more in Stafford, Gloucester, and Penryn — two-thirds of the funds used in open constituencies was spent in vain.

On close constituencies in England the government disbursed about £26,000. This was little enough — the con-

---

[1] Butcher to Rutland, 21 Sept. 1780, H.M.C., *Rutland MSS.*, iii, 37; Philip Yorke to Hardwicke, 5 May, 11 June, 2 Oct. 1780, Hardwicke to Yorke, 24 July 1783, Add. MSS. 35379, ff. 87-8, 121, 233, 35381, f. 124.
[2] North to George III, 20 Apr. 1782, Fortescue, v, no. 3674.
[3] *Ibid.*   [4] North to George III, 16 Apr. 1782, Fortescue, v, no. 3663.

ventional price of such seats varied in 1780 from £3000 to £4000, so that the sum spent on the King's behalf was equivalent to only six or seven seats. The effect, however, in terms of seats, in September 1780, was greater than this, since in some cases the government advanced or guaranteed payments to patrons, which it expected to recover afterwards from candidates. But the political effect of such payments was probably slight. Lords Mount Edgecumbe and Falmouth, for instance, were court politicians, who did not disagree with the North government's policy. It is hard to imagine their violating the code of respect for the King's administration and returning men who would be opposed to it, even if they had not received payment through the ministry. On the other hand, as the case of Eliot shows, such men, if they came to disapprove of the government's policy, threw their seats open to the opposition, whatever the price dangled before them by the Treasury: Edgecumbe himself had been in opposition during the 'sixties. The government, in its capacity of election broker, did not buy loyalty — the loyalty was already there. It bought convenience, the convenience of being able to place a small number of reliable supporters in the House of Commons without risk of their losing their elections. Had money not been so tight owing to the war, and had the government not fallen eighteen months after the general election, it is probable that private contributions would have considerably reduced the government expenditure on the close constituencies.

In April 1782 North reminded the King that the general election of 1774 had cost 'near £50,000'. If this figure was correct, then there was an increase in expenditure in 1780 of about twenty per cent. But the cost, North felt, had been fully justified by the circumstances, if not by the results. 'At the time of the election', he wrote to the King on 20 April, 'it was thought of the first importance to secure a number of friends in the House of Commons.' And in his previous letter of the 16th he thus summarized the causes of the increase: [1]

the strength of the Opposition to Government, which comprehending many powerful and rich families, and being very

[1] Fortescue, v, nos. 3663, 3668, 3674.

eager and zealous in their cause, were enabled to stir up
and maintain many, and those formidable, contests in several
of the counties and boroughs of England and Scotland:
add to this, that the difficulties of the times obliged several
of the friends of Government to apply for assistance from
Administration, who could have helped themselves better if
the times had been more favourable for obtaining pecuniary
assistance or credit from private persons.

The total sum expended was about twice the amount estimated
to have been spent on the general election of 1754, but still
small in comparison with other forms of pressure on elections :
this increase gives no reason for denying the truth for 1780 of
the conclusion reached by Sir Lewis Namier for 1761, that
such funds 'constituted only a small addition to official
patronage and to the vast sums spent openly year after year
on voters and members, through offices, sinecures, and contracts, which were employed for advancing the Parliamentary
"interest" '.[1]

The records of the 'secret and special service' accounts
kept by the secretaries to the Treasury [2] show that only an
inappreciable trickle of the money spent by the government
under that head went to supplement the election fund. Most
of this money was spent on naval and military intelligence and
on highly confidential diplomatic activities outside the 'normal
channels'. Disbursements also included a few pension payments to members of parliament,[3] genuine pensions to retired
courtiers and to such *literati* as Dr. Johnson and Thomas
Sheridan, and charitable payments to members of the aristocracy in straitened circumstances. Sir Grey Cooper made
small occasional payments to William Masterman, the Treasury
agent for Saltash — a borough with the management of which
he, as one of its members, was particularly concerned.[4] Robinson, in an analysis of his payments drawn up in April 1782,
noted under the heading of 'Payments for Parliamentary

---

[1] *Structure of Politics*, 213, 209.
[2] Add. MSS. 37836, ff. 58-140 ; Secret and Special Service Accounts,
Windsor MSS.   [3] Pp. 186-7 below.
[4] To Lady Day, 1779, £300 ; 1780, last quarter, £489 ; 1781, first
quarter, £60 ; Secret and Special Service Accounts, Windsor MSS.

Purposes' a number of routine disbursements to managers of the ministerial interest in nine constituencies : [1]

Camelford	Mr. Phillips	£100⎫	£150
	Mr. Carpenter	50⎭	
Rochester	Mr. Whitehead		50
Harwich	Yearly towards the expenses of the Corporation at Lady Day		100
Truro	Rose £100 and incidental expenses £100		200
Hythe	Towards the yearly expenses		160
Rye	Mr. Lamb yearly		150
Malmesbury	Yearly payment in May		720
Seaford	Mr. Chambers		100
Winchelsea	Mr. Vousden	10⎫	110
	Mr. Adcroft	100⎭	
	Mr. Gybbon dead £100 but applied for by Mr. Buller and Mr. Dawes		

Some of these payments would appear to have been merely agents' salaries. The annual total was less than £1800, and the only charge making possible 'corruption' of electors on a large scale was the £720 for Malmesbury. Rather bigger amounts were paid in the year of the general election — £300 for Hythe, £250 for Harwich — but the scale of this secret service expenditure was entirely trivial.

(iii)

THE ELECTIONS: THE OPPOSITION PARTIES

Despite the considerable size of the Rockingham party in 1780,[2] and its close links with other smaller groups, nothing comparable with the range of Treasury election organization and activity was to be found on the side of the opposition. The various leaders of minor factions — Abingdon, Rutland, Shelburne, Sir James Lowther — arranged their own borough elections independently and fought separate election battles in their various areas of interest and influence. So too did the magnates connected more closely with Rockingham — the

---

[1] Add. MSS. 37836, f. 138ᵛ.   [2] See pp. 210-21 below.

Duke of Richmond in Sussex and at Chichester, the Duke of Portland in Nottinghamshire, Cumberland, and at Wigan, Anderson Pelham in Lincolnshire and at Great Grimsby, Lord Upper Ossory, with the support of the Dowager Duchess of Bedford, in Bedfordshire, the Cavendishes in Derbyshire and at Lancaster.

Rockingham's activities extended to more constituencies than those of any one of his chief colleagues, but he occupied no position of director in elections comparable with that held on the government side by North and Robinson. His papers and his letters to Portland indicate that, apart from the arrangement of his own boroughs — Malton and Higham Ferrers — his electioneering was almost entirely confined to Yorkshire and to a negotiation with Edward Eliot of Cornwall.

Rumours of a dissolution, and the certainty that one must take place within the next twelve months, led Rockingham and Portland to give some thought to questions of seats and candidates soon after the break-down, early in July, of the *pourparlers* for a coalition government. Both had heard that Sir Thomas Frankland was inclined to dispose of his seats at Thirsk, but might prefer to 'barter them' for Greenwich Hospital; and Rockingham proposed that enquiries be made in the hope that, if Frankland 'was angry with the ministers and wished to sell to *Whigs* . . . perhaps some creditable *Yorkshire Gentleman* might be found and a little hint — that £3000 was a good fair price'.[1] The further stages of this affair are not recorded in their correspondence; but Frankland's hopes about Greenwich remained unsatisfied,[2] and two 'creditable Yorkshire gentlemen' were duly returned for Thirsk at the general election.[3]

During the summer Rockingham and Portland also carried on a desultory discussion with Edward Eliot of Cornwall,

---

[1] Rockingham to Portland, 28 July 1780, Portland MSS.
[2] 'State, 1780', 36, Windsor MSS.
[3] These were Beilby Thompson (1742-99), who had usually acted with Rockingham during the last twelve years, who now withdrew from Hedon in order to try and secure his brother's election on his interest there; and Sir Thomas Gascoigne (1745-1810), who recanted his Catholic faith in 1780 as a preliminary to entering parliament and who later attached himself politically to Earl Fitzwilliam.

about the provision of candidates for his borough seats, for which he was determined not to re-elect supporters of North's ministry. A last meeting was held early in August, before Rockingham retired to Yorkshire and Eliot, on the 12th, to Cornwall. Rockingham arranged two candidates with Eliot and provisionally mentioned a third, and, a few days later, told Portland that he had ascertained that all three were 'decisively fixed to accept' — these were Thomas Lucas, a city merchant with West Indian connections, a Governor of the South Sea Company, and President of Guy's Hospital, introduced to Rockingham by John Scudamore, M.P. for Hereford; Sir John Ramsden, Rockingham's brother-in-law; and Dudley Long, a friend of Lord Richard Cavendish.[1] A fourth seat was initially earmarked for Portland's friend, John Christian. But Christian declined, wishing to contest Carlisle; and Portland, though he had three or four other names in view, was unable to fix upon a single candidate. In mid-August he suggested the names of John Bullock, William Hale, and Sir Abraham Hume to Eliot, who replied that he had no objection to any of them, 'unless the Baronet is a North Briton'.[2] But in each of these cases there were monetary difficulties or political doubts. On Eliot's suggestion Portland tried to arrange that William Windham should accept nomination. But this proposal failed also. Eliot had to complete his arrangements with speed at the beginning of September without hearing further from Portland, and had, after all, no other seat available; and in any case Windham was not able to pay his price.[3]

These preparations were at first pursued with little sense of urgency, for Rockingham did not believe that a general election was really imminent, and, when overtaken by the event, was 'much vexed' that he had not written in good time to

[1] Rockingham to Portland, 17 Aug., 1 Sept. 1780, Eliot to Portland, 14 Sept. 1780, Portland MSS.; Eliot to Rockingham, same date, Rockingham MSS., R. 139-29.

[2] Portland to Rockingham, 14 Aug. 1780, Rockingham MSS., R. 2-142 — in this letter Portland referred merely to 'Mr. Hale', but as this was a person in touch with Portland's friend, William Plumer, it is fairly certain he was William Hale of King's Walden, Herts; Eliot to Portland, 20 Aug. 1780, Portland MSS.

[3] Eliot to Portland, 27 Aug. 1780, Windham to Lord Richard Cavendish, 7 Sept. 1780, Portland MSS.

Eliot to complete his arrangements.[1] The dissolution forced him into hasty attempts to repair this omission. On 1 September he wrote confirming his three original candidates, and adding the name of Charles Duncombe, the brother of one of his close friends in Yorkshire, Henry Duncombe of Copgrove, in case Eliot had still received no nomination for the fourth seat.[2] But meanwhile, Eliot found his own friend, Samuel Salt, who had formerly been expected to retire, desirous of being re-elected, had promised a seat to Wilbraham Tollemache, a friend of Shelburne, and needed his last one for his son, E. J. Eliot, and so only the first three men recommended by Rockingham were returned.[3] So far as is indicated by the correspondence on the subject, all three candidates paid the conventional contribution of £3000, and no financial liability was incurred by either Portland or Rockingham.[4] The course of the negotiations well illustrates the difficulties encountered by the opposition leaders, first in finding candidates, and then in finding seats at the last moment when caught unprepared. Of the friends whom Portland considered nominating, Christian insisted upon standing for Carlisle (though in the end he withdrew from Carlisle also); John Bullock, Portland feared, would not be '*prepared*' in due time (presumably with money); William Hale, so their common friend, William Plumer, informed him, 'would not find it convenient at present to part with the sum required'; and Hume's 'patriotic principles' were regarded with scepticism by Rockingham.[5] 'I think it right to say that I am afraid £3000 is more than I could advance without embarrassing myself too much', Windham wrote (for Portland's information) to Lord Richard Cavendish.[6] Rockingham, for his part, was left with a candidate

[1] Rockingham to Portland, 1 Sept. 1780, Portland MSS.   [2] *Ibid.*
[3] Eliot to Rockingham, 14 Sept. 1780, Rockingham MSS., R. 139-29; to Portland, same date, Portland MSS.
[4] Eliot to Rockingham, 17 Nov. 1780, Rockingham MSS., R. 1-1078; to Portland, same date, Portland MSS. Lucas's £3000 was paid into Portland's hands during September (Portland to Rockingham, 26 Sept. 1780, Rockingham MSS., R. 139-46). This conclusion is also indicated by the weeding out of Portland's friends who were not prepared to face the costs of election — see below.
[5] Portland to Rockingham, 14 Aug. 1780, Rockingham MSS., R. 2-142.
[6] 7 Sept. 1780, Portland MSS.

on his hands — Charles Duncombe — for whom he was unable to obtain a seat, although he wished most heartily to do so.[1]

In the city of York, where Rockingham's interest, through the 'Rockingham Club', was considerable, the Marquis had peculiar difficulties to face. He desired the re-election of his two friends, Lord John Cavendish and Charles Turner of Kirkleatham. There was no danger of a ministerial opposition against them, but serious embarrassment seemed to threaten from the proposal ardently pressed by Christopher Wyvill and other associators, that votes should be promised only to parliamentary candidates who undertook to work for the constitutional reforms demanded by the Committees of Association — shorter parliaments and an addition to the number of county members. Less conservative than his political mentor, Edmund Burke, Rockingham was not averse to the consideration of such propositions; but he was keenly aware of their danger as a source of discord in the ranks of the opposition.[2] The demand that representatives should give firm pledges to their constituents, objectionable in itself to the more aristocratic politicians, was doubly objectionable on this account. Thus political expediency made it impossible to support the plan of the associators, and Rockingham went to York himself soon after his return north from London, to see how best the danger might be averted. At first he anticipated little difficulty. To his wife, on 21 August, he reported:[3]

> The particular manœuvre of putting questions to Lord John and requiring his approbation of the objects of the Association — is said not to be at all likely to be played off against *us*. Our *friends* in general are thought to be sufficiently aware — that it would not be submitted to — and I trust if any such thing is proposed — many of our friends will immediately resist it, and declare their full confidence

[1] Rockingham to Portland, 22 Sept. 1780, Portland MSS.; to Eliot, 8 Oct. 1780, draft, Rockingham MSS., R. 140-92.

[2] Rockingham to Pemberton Milnes, 28 Feb., to Rev. Henry Zouch, 23 Mar. 1780, Rockingham MSS., R. 1-1049 and 1051, partly printed, Albemarle, ii, 395-400, 402-6, to Crofts, 23 Mar. 1780, R. 1-1052; to Sir George Saville, 17 Sept. 1780, H.M.C., *Savile-Foljambe MSS.*, 154-7.

[3] Rockingham MSS., R. 158.

in Lord John, and that they think their experience of *his conduct*, etc., is the best security.

Four days later he reassured her : [1]

> I have had conversations with several of *our friends here.* I think it will have done good. I am very much pleased with *many of them.* I have some hopes that men's minds begin to feel that there has been an intemperate imprudence in the manner of acting in regard to the measure of the association.

The next week, in a letter giving news of the dissolution, he sent a plain warning to Stephen Crofts, one of his leading supporters in the city : [2]

> I have stated my ideas very fully to you and to many of our friends with whom I had the pleasure to converse at York, and I must again repeat — that if the conduct of Lord John Cavendish in Parliament, and I may add my own conduct in politicks thro' life — are not or have not *been sufficient testimony's* of our love and adherence to the interests, welfare, happiness and liberty of our country, he and I may lament the prevalence of new and speculative dogmas — but cannot be the abettors of doubtful propositions.

On the same day as Rockingham penned this letter, Robert Sinclair, another of his supporters at York, sent him a reassuring account of the state of politics in the city : [3]

> With regard to the effect or operation of the Association even upon those who have given it their names I am still strongly of opinion that its influence is by no means coextensive with the apparent encouragement it has met with. I have had some conversation yesterday with several freemen who are firm friends to Lord John Cavendish, and who from novelty, imitation or particular persuasion have set their names to the Association, and I found from their atachment to his interest they were ready to adopt any finespun explanation in order to get disengaged from the

[1] 25 Aug. 1780, *ibid.*   [2] [3 Sept. 1780], *ibid.* R. 136-14.
[3] *Ibid.* R. 139-7.

obligation of their signatures — thus in the plan of association there is something of an optional alternative 'Unless
the candidate declares his atachment to the plans of reformation etc. by signing the association *or in such other form as
to each candidate shall seem most eligible.*' — of this clause
I saw they were not unwilling to avail themselves — so
that I am apt to think a few general verbal assurances from
Lord John of his atachment to the rights and privileges of
the people coupled with a reference to his past parliamentary
conduct, would be such a form of declaration as would
satisfy many of his associating constituents.

But this message was the prelude to an anxious week during
which Cavendish nearly abandoned his candidature and
Rockingham was obliged to intervene strongly, to stiffen his
morale and guide the campaign against the associators. Rockingham's task was all the more difficult, since Cavendish's
colleague, Charles Turner, had given a more or less open
promise to support the plan of the Association, a promise
which it now became necessary to oblige him to withdraw.[1]

When the dissolution was announced, Wyvill and a few of
his friends among the leading spirits of the Yorkshire Association were already at York, and they immediately seized the
chance to propound their views among the electors and to try
to force Cavendish to subscribe to the plan of the Association.
On 4 September, Cavendish informed Rockingham, the Rev.
William Mason came to him :

expressed Mr. Wyvill's wishes and hopes that I might be
induced to say something which would enable them to
support me consistently with their engagements : which I
peremptorily refused. He then gave me to understand that
they should think themselves obliged to support some candidate who would subscribe, for his own part he (Mason)
would go out of the town.[2]

Unwilling to face the 'vexation and tiresomeness' of an election
fight, Cavendish professed himself determined to withdraw if
this threat materialized.[3] At his urgent plea, Rockingham

[1] Lord John Cavendish to Rockingham, [4, 5, 6, Sept. 1780], *ibid*
R. 141-6, -8, -10, -11.   [2] *Ibid.* R. 141-7.   [3] *Ibid.*

hastened from Wentworth Woodhouse to near-by Tolston
Lodge to give help and advice. Rockingham's cure for the
situation was simple — to stir up the jealousies of the citizens
of York against the interference of outsiders in their election.
'I have particularly desired Lord John to state', he wrote to
his wife the night of his arrival at Tolston, 'that he looks to
the *approbation and support of the citizens* of York and that he
shall not submit to be *catechized* by *persons* who are not under
that description.' This scheme worked to perfection. By the
7th Rockingham was confident that the associators could not
'do any essential harm'; by the 9th he was able to return to
Wentworth from Tolston; [1] on the 11th Cavendish and Turner
were re-elected unopposed 'without the least expense', and,
in a heavy downpour, 'covered each with an umbrella', were
chaired through the city in the usual fashion. [2]

Rockingham's other main concern was with the county of
York. He welcomed heartily the decision of Henry Duncombe
of Copgrove to stand against Edwin Lascelles on the score of
opposition to the North ministry. On 8 September he replied
to Duncombe's request for his 'very important interest' on the
canvass: [3]

> I had the honour to receive your letter late last night.
> *The necessity that there appears to be in the present critical
> situation of affairs — of having two county members who may
> be depended upon as opposers to the present ruinous administra-
> tion* — which you state in your letter to me — I most heartily
> concur in.
>
> The knowledge and insight into your principles, and
> into your way of thinking on public affairs for several years
> past, which the intercourse of private friendship has afforded
> me the opportunity of forming, are and must be strong
> incitements in my mind to promote your wishes on this
> occasion.

'Duncombe has acted very well', Rockingham wrote that same
night to his wife, 'and you know has long been a favourite

[1] To Lady Rockingham, 5, 7, 8 Sept. 1780, *ibid.*, R. 158, R. 141-4, -3.
[2] William Siddall to Rockingham, 11 Sept. 1780, *ibid.* R. 139-13.
[3] *Ibid.* R. 1-1070.

with me.'[1] For the next few days he worked indefatigably, soliciting support for both Duncombe and Sir George Savile from all the people of influence he could approach, who might have any interest in Yorkshire.[2] Differences with the associators were hastily buried before the common desire to turn out a government supporter.[3] 'No time should be lost in regard to securing all votes and interests in favour of Sir George Savile and Mr. Duncombe', he concluded an urgent appeal for help to the Duke of Rutland. 'I have been so hurried and fatigued with writing letters, etc., on this subject, that I feel quite exhausted.'[4] 'Mr. Henry Duncombe offered himself', Lady Rockingham informed Burke on the 17th, 'My Lord . . . has scarcely ceased writing ever since, till he is quite worn down with fatigue.'[5]

Exhausted Rockingham might be, but he had not done a tithe of the election business undertaken by Robinson and North in the last week of August and the first week of September. Excluding his ancillary participation in contests, or preparations for contests which were not fought to a conclusion, in various constituencies where he had friends or other interests, and considering only those places where he took a leading part in election arrangements, or management, or campaigning, his activities extended to no more than a dozen seats in seven constituencies. Eight of these seats were in Yorkshire, one was his single-member borough of Higham Ferrers, three more were those of Eliot of Cornwall. Only the city and county of York presented large popular electorates responsive to some extent to the sway of political ideas and party slogans. And the county only involved a campaign against the government, for in York the threatened contest was internecine, a struggle between two factions which were alike hotly opposed to the ministry. Further than this Rockingham did not venture. Faced with an opportunity to attempt the capture of another

[1] *Ibid.* R. 141-3.
[2] Lord Bessborough to Rockingham, 18 Sept., Lord Carmarthen to Rockingham, 14, 16 Sept., Lord Ailesbury to Rockingham, 14 Sept., *et alia, ibid.*
[3] Rockingham to Zouch, 11 Sept. 1780, H.M.C., *Lonsdale MSS.*, 138.
[4] 12 Sept. 1780, Rutland MSS.
[5] Burke papers (Sheffield), 1-927.

seat, at Great Grimsby, he rejected it outright. At the end of August, Anderson Pelham wrote both to him and to his nephew, Earl Fitzwilliam, suggesting that they might propose and support a second candidate to stand there on his interest. Fitzwilliam wrote hastily to Rockingham, almost in terms of appeal, that if Rockingham would defray half the expenses of supporting his brother, George Fitzwilliam, he would pay the rest.[1] But Rockingham disapproved the suggestion entirely. Although thanking Pelham heartily for his offer, he explained : [2]

> I do not think it at present an eligible matter. The expense might not be large — but there undoubtedly is risk at *Grimsby*. I think your family were always sure of *one member* there, but as I recollect — there was always an opposite interest. You are the best judge, whether it is advisable for you to attempt to carry *both* members.

And, with a reference to his arrangements with Eliot :

> I have been trying to secure some *certain* seats in Parliament — by the desire of some friends — whether they will succeed or not — I cannot answer, but at least I have secured that they should run neither risk of money or trouble. I would by no means wish you to enter into such an agreement.

Rockingham's aim was safety, and a known, minimum expenditure. Costly electoral ventures were not to his taste.

(iv)

POLITICS IN THE ELECTIONS

The feature most distinguishing the general election of 1780 from those which had taken place during the middle of the century was the clear, abrupt division which sundered two groups of parties in parliament. In 1754, in 1761, and in 1768 there had been no great conflicts over national questions

---

[1] 1 Sept. 1780, Rockingham MSS., R. 158.
[2] 2 Sept. 1780, *ibid*. R. 140-83.

between the politicians, and, consequently, no widespread opposition to government. Neither of these conditions obtained in 1780. The ministerial cohorts in parliament were now faced by a numerous opposition, its core being the strong and coherent party led by Rockingham. Fifteen or more years of argument about colonial policy, and, in particular, five years of bitter controversy over the American War, had given to the two sides a certain stability and permanence, arming them with policies and declarations of principle, which made the distinction between them more clear-cut. Each had a cause to defend which exerted a wider, more general appeal to interests, loyalties, passions, and ideas than the mere call to support one faction against another. On one side the Court and the groups which made up North's ministry stood for the unity of the Empire and the maintenance in America of a protectionist economy. On the other the Rockinghams, and the various minor groups in opposition, such as the friends of Shelburne, and the Wilkite radicals of the metropolis, were at least united in a determination to end the war, though by no means agreed upon the form that a peace with America should take. In the months prior to the dissolution the opposition had gained popularity by taking up another plank of policy, the attack against the influence of the executive in parliament; though, on this question also, there was sharp disagreement among its various component parts about solutions. Practically all of the proposals for dealing with this largely mythical danger were met alike by the government with a decided negative. But here ministers were at a certain disadvantage — youthful zeal and the attraction of novelty were on the side of their opponents, and a purely negative programme does not so easily rouse enthusiasm. Two groups of parties thus faced each other in parliament, bound by opposing views and conflicting policies, separated — as the *pourparlers* of July had shown — by a gulf too wide for compromise. How did this affect the pattern of the general election?

In 1780 the number of contested elections in Great Britain was substantially higher than in 1761. The number of constituencies which went to the polls was 86 as against 49: for

England alone the respective figures were 68 and 42.[1] True, the total of elections contested in 1761 seems to have been abnormally low. In 1760 the advanced age of George II had acted as a brake on preliminary electioneering — men hesitated to undertake the trouble and expense of contests, which, since the King was not likely to live long, carried little promise of the usual fairly safe septennial tenure — and preparations were for the most part crowded into the last four months before the elections. This factor was not present in 1780: the King was hale, and the new parliament might be expected to last its full legal term. But a similar effect was produced by the government's concealment of its intention to dissolve:[2] in consequence, preparations and elections were largely confined to three hectic weeks, the first three weeks in September. Few preliminary dispositions had been made before September by the leaders of the opposition. Even on the ministerial side arrangements were restricted, and delayed, for fear of letting out the secret. George Selwyn, for instance, complained afterwards of the failure of the government to get the Duke of Beaufort and other influential men to support him at Gloucester.[3] Some candidates and many voters could only be released from military duties with their militia regiments at the last moment, and even within a week of the dissolution Jenkinson was nervous about the despatch of instructions concerning them. 'Lord Amherst's letter to the general officers commanding at camps will disclose the whole business of the dissolution: I submit, therefore, whether it should be sent so soon as Monday', he wrote to Robinson on 26 August.[4] The financial circumstances in 1780 presented some similarity to 1761: once again the national economy was disturbed by heavy war expenditure and the dislocation of trade; credit was short, and this also helped to check electioneering activities.[5] It might have been expected, therefore, that in 1780 the number

---

[1] The figures for 1761 are taken from Sir Lewis Namier's *Structure of Politics*, 159 and note [2], with the addition of one for a contest in Rutland, which is not included in those totals.   [2] Pp. 41-5 above.
[3] Selwyn to Carlisle, 11 Sept. 1780, H.M.C., *Carlisle MSS.*, 443.
[4] H.M.C., *Abergavenny MSS.*, 34, no. 293.
[5] Namier, *Structure of Politics*, 171; North to George III, 16, 20 Apr. 1782, Fortescue, v, nos. 3663, 3668, 3674.

of contested elections would again have been low. There is thus all the more significance in the much larger number of contests fought to a finish — the elections reflected the gathering tempo and the far greater extent and intensity of political controversy in the years of the American War.

Politics, however, had no place at all in the conduct of elections in many constituencies, except in so far as a patron like Edward Eliot or Sir James Lowther would alter the representation of boroughs under his control to accord with the change in his own political views. But clearly, politics did not enter into the calculations of the voters in the close boroughs, whose conduct was determined by financial sanctions and financial inducements. When Sir James Lowther bought in 1780 the burgage houses in Haslemere to which the right of voting was attached and faced the problem of conveying these holdings to reliable dependents in order to create votes,[1]

> not thinking it safe to trust any of the inhabitants with a conveyance of these freeholds, he actually sent forty of his labourers from his collieries in the north of England, to reside in this borough, erected cottages for their accommodation, and allowed them half a guinea a week each, besides what they might earn with their labour if they thought proper to work.

In return, and to avoid being made homeless and destitute, they were obliged to vote at his direction. This involved no hardship of conscience, for questions of national politics passed far above the heads of uneducated pit workers. Again, in the case of Malmesbury, it came out in evidence during the hearing of an election petition, shortly after the end of the century,[2]

> that a Mr. Edmund Wilkins, an apothecary of this borough, had obtained the control of the corporation in 1768, by allowing ten out of the thirteen capital burgesses an annuity of £30 *per annum* each, for the corrupt purpose of returning two members of parliament; that he continued to pay this annuity and nominate the members till the time of his death in 1804, and that he obtained for himself the lucrative place of receiver-general for the county of Wilts. . . . The

---

[1] Oldfield, *Representative History*, iv, 599.   [2] *Ibid.* v, 180, 187.

money . . . was a little clandestinely, and indeed whimsically paid; sometimes it was conveyed under a cabbage, and sometimes . . . it was left in a more indecorous manner in a chamber utensil that had been used by Mr. Wilkins after a feast which he gave to the burgesses.

The forms of pressure in such boroughs were not always so simple as this, and to a varying degree good-will and personal loyalty to the patron played a part in determining voting, especially where the electorate was more numerous than at either Haslemere or Malmesbury; but they were usually effective. In hardly any of the close boroughs did an election involve a competition between men of opposing political principles, between whom the electors had to make a choice determined by their own judgment or feelings regarding political events.[1] To find elections into which a genuine political element entered, we must turn to those few constituencies which had large electorates — though even in these elections were not always political in character.

(A) THE COUNTIES

Two counties only went to the polls in 1780, Cambridge and Surrey. The number is small, and, by comparison with other elections during the second half of the century, might at first sight seem abnormally low — in 1754, five were contested; in 1761, four; in 1784, and again in 1790, seven. But since the last general election in 1774 five counties had been contested at by-elections, two of them — Hampshire and Middlesex — as recently as the autumn of 1779. Apart from Surrey and Cambridge, considerable electioneering took place in several other counties in 1780, where a challenge was presented to the re-election of the former representatives, or where rival claimants aspired to a seat become vacant by the retirement of the old member. Changes in the county representation were

[1] There were one or two exceptions, as for instance Plymouth and Portsmouth where radical groups tried to break down the grip of the close corporation upon which governmental control of elections depended.

uniformly unfavourable to the government: friends of the ministers were displaced by opponents in Bedfordshire, Cambridgeshire, Kent, Leicestershire, Salop, Suffolk, and Yorkshire.

In Bedfordshire, Lord Ongley, a supporter of the government, was ousted by St. Andrew St. John, an enthusiastic young ally and close personal friend of Charles James Fox. Bedfordshire politics were dominated by a small ring of wealthy landowners, and the county was a stronghold of Fox's connections. The St. Johns of Bletsoe were one of its leading families, and were about to be connected by marriage with one of its richest men, the brewer Samuel Whitbread. Fox's brother-in-law, the Earl of Upper Ossory, with his seat at Ampthill, also carried weight in the county; but his strength lay in his connection with the Russells, whose interest usually secured the election of one member, and sometimes of two. During the minority of the fifth Duke of Bedford the influence of his House was organized and directed by the widow of the fourth Duke — Lord Ossory's aunt — the formidable Dowager-duchess Gertrude, whose considerable energies were employed in 1780 in support of Ossory and St. John.[1] As member for the county since 1761, Lord Ongley had enjoyed the support of the Russells, and in parliament he had belonged to the fourth Duke's political circle, the old Bedford party; but now, in consequence of his continuing to support the ministry, he was abruptly abandoned by all his old associates in the county. His supplanter, St. John, stood as a declared opponent of North's administration: Ossory, writing to solicit Rockingham's support, informed him that St. John had offered his services to the county ' *as a determined enemy to that wretched system of government that now prevailed, etc., etc.*' [2] The weight of interest and of opinion was so strongly with St. John that Ongley, although he had considerable support, declined a contest.

In Yorkshire the political issue was as plainly posed as in Bedfordshire. Before the dissolution the county had been represented by one opponent and one supporter of administration,

[1] P. Yorke to Hardwicke, 15 Sept. 1780, Hardwicke to P. Yorke, 16 Sept. 1780, Add. MSS. 35379, ff. 220, 223.
[2] 15 Sept. 1780, Rockingham MSS., R. 139-32.

and both members, Sir George Savile and Edwin Lascelles, were expected to stand again. But opposition to the ministry was widespread throughout the county, and an instrument for its service lay ready to hand in Wyvill's Committee of Association. The leaders of the Association, shelving for the moment the more radical parts of their programme, combined with those moderates and conservatives whose connections were with Savile and Rockingham to throw out Lascelles and bring in two opponents of government.[1]

Savile's election address, dated 5 September, set the tone for a predominantly political election.[2] The style of this address, a vigorous political polemic, was one not often found in the eighteenth century: it anticipated the electioneering of a later age. Savile described the country, under the control of the existing ministers, as 'maimed and weakened, its treasure lavished and mis-spent, its honours faded, and its conduct the laughing stock of Europe', its principal privileges 'impeached and mangled', and its constitution threatened by the discretionary power lately claimed for the military (as a result of the Gordon riots) to act against rioters without awaiting the authority of the civil magistrates. The supposed corrupt nature of the chief minister's power was next expounded:

> the modern improved art of corruption by contracts, subscriptions, and jobs, is attended with this perverse and vexatious consequence; that their benefit is not only unconnected with yours, but it grows upon your distress. They feed on the expence; they fatten on every extravagance that art and ill conduct can engraft in the natural disadvantages of a remote, rash, ill-fated, impolitic and unsuccessful war: the minister's direct interest (nay his safety) meanwhile requiring him to push the desperate game, and even in self defence to increase that very expence which is his crime: to entrench himself still deeper in corruption, and by headlong and unmeasured extravagance, to have the means of justifying to the faithful Commons his former mismanagement and misdeeds.

[1] A. Gooder, *The Parliamentary Representation of the County of York* (2 vols., Wakefield, 1935–8), ii, 149.
[2] *The Annual Register*, 1780, 399-404.

Lastly, Savile pledged his support for parliamentary reform, though this, he explained, was more because his constituents wanted it than because he was persuaded it would be of much use. An addition of county members might, he thought, be of some benefit, and although there were difficulties in the way of such a reform, these must be overcome, for the constitution was in danger: 'This is no time to talk of small rubs or difficulties. If something be not done, you may indeed retain the outward form of your constitution but not the power thereof.' This broadside was well calculated to appeal to those divergent elements in the Yorkshire electorate, including the Associators, who considered the continuance of the North ministry a national disaster. Fired with this conviction, the opposition leaders in the county welcomed the nomination as fellow candidate with Savile of Henry Duncombe of Copgrove, whose appeal for assistance was greeted with the greatest enthusiasm by Rockingham.[1] Duncombe offered himself as a candidate determined, if elected, to oppose the North ministry and to press for an end of the war against the colonies — on 11 September Rockingham explained to his friend, the Rev. Henry Zouch:[2]

> He says he is induced to offer himself as a necessity appears in the situation of the affairs of this country that two members of the county should be chosen who might be depended upon as opposers to the present ruinous administration.
>
> I have long known his way of thinking on the measures which have brought on all the calamities of this country. Particularly — the horrid, wicked, and abominable American War. His words include a positive declaration upon that subject, though not in a manner which might make some gentlemen who heretofore were abettors of it take offence.

The proposal to carry two candidates against the government proved highly popular in Yorkshire. In a few days £12,000 was subscribed to an election fund in support of Duncombe and

---

[1] Rockingham to Duncombe, 8 Sept. 1780, to Lady Rockingham, same date, Rockingham MSS., R. 1-1070, R. 141-3.
[2] H.M.C., *Lonsdale MSS.*, 138.

Savile;[1] and Edwin Lascelles, after holding a meeting of his friends to test public feeling, declined to face the bustle of a contest.[2]

This pattern of successful opposition to friends of the government on party and public grounds emerged also in the elections for Surrey and Kent, and, to a limited degree, in Hampshire.

Prior to the dissolution, both members for Surrey, Sir Joseph Mawbey and James Scawen, had voted regularly against the government. Mawbey stood for re-election in 1780; but the retirement of Scawen encouraged the Lord-Lieutenant, Lord Onslow, to put up his son for the county, and this course was warmly supported by the Treasury (which provided Thomas Onslow with an alternative seat for Rye in case of defeat), because it seemed to offer a chance of bringing one seat into friendly hands. The intervention of Admiral Keppel soon blighted this prospect. His candidature was a clear gesture of defiance against the ministers, following, as it did, immediately after they had employed all their available influence to oust him from Windsor. A friend of Richmond and Rockingham, Keppel was a leading figure in opposition and a thorn in the flesh of the ministers in the House of Commons. The famous court-martial arising from his quarrel with Palliser had created personal ill-feeling between him and Sandwich, and as the Rockinghams' First Lord of the Admiralty designate he was also Sandwich's rival for office. Both Keppel and Onslow could rally the support of active politicians among the country gentlemen of Surrey. Charles Jenkinson, Sir George Howard, and the Nortons of Wonersh gave assistance to Onslow, and among those who supported Keppel can be distinguished representatives of two distinct political groupings. There was a strong body of friends of Rockingham with estates in the county, the chief of them being Earl Spencer, Lord Bessborough, Lord Midleton, Sir Robert Clayton, Sir William

---

[1] W. Siddall to Rockingham, 5 Dec. 1780, Rockingham MSS., R. 1-1079.
[2] Rockingham to Rutland, 16 Sept. 1780, H.M.C., *Rutland MSS.*, 36; Loughborough to Carlisle, 18 Sept. 1780, H.M.C., *Carlisle MSS.*, 445; Loughborough to Eden, same date, Add MSS. 29475, f. 18; *The Leeds Intelligencer*, 19 Sept. 1780. Loughborough thought Lascelles's chances good, and considered his conduct pusillanimous.

Meredith.[1] Also there was a circle of business men, who had carried Sir Joseph Mawbey as member in 1775, despite much social prejudice against him, and whose affiliations were with the radicals of London and Westminster; at their head in 1780 were the members for Southwark, Nathaniel Polhill and Sir Richard Hotham.[2] Some men in this group wished Keppel to subscribe to the reform policies of the Associators, but he declined, basing his appeal for support simply on his past conduct as an opponent of government;[3] nevertheless the Associators gave him official support.[4] Together these parties marshalled far greater forces in the county than could be rallied to Onslow; and Onslow had fallen well behind his rivals at the poll when he at last decided to cut his losses and abandon the contest.

In Kent, as in Yorkshire, opposition to the government was connected with the associating movement and the agitation for reform; and Filmer Honywood, a close friend of Charles James Fox, was nominated, together with Charles Marsham, 'at a patriotic meeting',[5] many weeks before the dissolution. Both candidates had already established a reputation as opponents of the American War, and in September 1780 no one could be found willing to stand against them. The same insuperable difficulty, the lack of a candidate, was encountered by the government in Hampshire. In this county the battle had been fought out the year before, when the anti-ministerial forces had defeated the candidature of Sir Richard Worsley in the by-election of December 1779. Both the Rockinghams and the London radicals had their connections in the county as well as the ministry,[6] and although the 'opposition' decided

[1] T. R. Keppel, *Life of Augustus Viscount Keppel* (2 vols., 1842), ii, 286-8.   [2] *The General Evening Post*, 19-21 Sept. 1780.
[3] Rockingham to Keppel, 1 Oct. 1780, Rockingham MSS., R. 140-90.
[4] *The General Evening Post*, 21-23 Sept. 1780.
[5] 'State 1780', 20, Windsor MSS.
[6] There existed in the county a Hampshire Club, 'established for the support of public liberty in general and the freedom and independence of the county in particular', which looked to Rockingham's associate, the Duke of Portland, for patronage, William Faithful to Portland, 22 July 1777, Portland MSS. During the by-election of 1779, Temple Luttrell wrote to John Wilkes : 'A line or two from you to some of the staunch whigs at Newport and its environs might render very essential service to Mr. Jervoise' (Add. MSS. 30872, f. 159).

not 'to put up a second candidate', thus preserving 'the peace of the county', the least unsatisfactory candidate the supporters of the government could find was Robert Thistlethwayte, who soon showed himself an opponent rather than a friend.[1]

But if there were county elections in 1780 at which political issues were prominently canvassed, there were also others in which they were secondary or of little importance. In Leicestershire, the choice of a new member to replace Sir John Palmer on his retirement was arranged by agreement between the two factions into which the leading men of the county were divided;[2] and the candidates, J. P. Hungerford and William Pochin, although they were to take opposite sides in the House of Commons, solicited the support of the voters by a joint election address.[3] In Cambridgeshire, the contested election bears out the later dictum of Oldfield, that 'a contest . . . would only be a struggle for the pre-eminence of aristocracy'.[4] The illness of one of the old members, Sir John Hinde Cotton, foreshadowed a vacancy which Hardwicke was anxious to secure for his nephew and heir, Philip Yorke; and Hardwicke regarded a threatened incursion by the Manners family with jealousy and alarm. 'Lord Rockingham . . . called upon me', he informed his nephew towards the end of February 1780; 'and he told me from the Duke of Rutland that he should put up his brother for the county. . . . I desired he would ask of the Duke what his meaning was, and that I could not think his Grace had so good pretensions as my family had to represent the county.'[5] Rutland, however, was determined to carry the election of his brother, Lord Robert Manners, eventually running up expenses to the tune of some £12,000.[6] In the contest which took place, one friend of government, Sir Sampson Gideon, was displaced by Manners; but the theoretical gain to opposition of one member was simply an incidental con-

[1] Abergavenny MSS. 304, 307.
[2] Oldfield, *Representative History*, iv, 122; Rutland to Lord Robert Manners, 10 Mar. 1780, H.M.C., *Rutland MSS.*, iii, 25.
[3] *General Evening Post*, 16-19 Sept. 1780.
[4] *Representative History*, iii, 118.
[5] 25 Feb. 1780, Add. MSS. 35379, f. 13.
[6] John Butcher to Rutland, 21 Sept. 1780, H.M.C., *Rutland MSS.*, iii, 37.

sequence of the rivalry of the Yorke and Manners families. Had Rutland been really concerned to add an effective vote to the opposition and to his own following in the House of Commons, he might have found a candidate better able to attend parliament than his sailor brother, whose duties kept him constantly at sea (in fact Manners died of wounds while on active service without ever taking his seat). The lack of concern for party issues during the election is also clear from the way in which the Yorkes conducted their part in it. So far as the electors of the county were concerned, Hardwicke avoided connection with either the friends of government or their opponents. 'By joining *now* Lord Robert', he told his nephew in April, 'we should hurt those over whom the Court has influence in Cambridgeshire, or by joining Sir Sampson, the patriotic party, so we seem strongest on our own ground.'[1] Hardwicke continued to follow this course up to, and during, the election five months later. But, while not committing himself to either side, he sought any aid that served his family interest, whether it came from friends or foes of the ministry. Professing friendship for the government, he secured an interview with the King, gained his support, and enjoyed the effective assistance of at least one of the ministers, Lord Sandwich.[2] But at the same time he was in touch with the leaders of factions opposed to the administration. During the summer he and his nephew approached Rockingham in order to secure the interest of Earl Fitzwilliam with Cambridgeshire voters resident at Peterborough,[3] and an understanding existed between him and the oppositionist Duchess of Bedford regarding the friendly use of their interests in the counties of Bedford and Cambridge.[4]

Similarly, the contest which was threatened in Cumberland had nothing to do with national politics. Sir James Lowther and the Duke of Portland, the two men with the greatest

[1] 14 Apr. 1780, Add MSS. 35379, f. 45.
[2] C. Jenkinson to Robinson, 15 July 1780, Abergavenny MS. 268; Sandwich to Hardwicke, 13 Sept. 1780, Add. MSS. 35617, f. 40.
[3] P. Yorke to Rockingham, 10 July 1780, Rockingham MSS., R. 139-2.
[4] P. Yorke to Hardwicke, 15 Sept. 1780, Hardwicke to P. Yorke, 16 Sept. 1780, Add. MSS. 35379, ff. 220, 223.

influence in the county, had agreed since 1774 to share control of the representation, and both were in 1780 equally hostile to the North ministry. But the understanding between them did not prevent Cumberland from being agitated on behalf of the Penningtons of Muncaster, a family which sought to revive the honour it had formerly enjoyed of providing representatives. The Penningtons gathered behind them all the discontent in the county against the domination of the elections by two great magnates. Sir Joseph Pennington had forced a contest in 1774, and his son, John, offered himself as a candidate in 1780. A friend of the Duke of Grafton, in politics he was an independent: though he entered the House in 1781 as a friend of administration, he voted against North in February and March 1782. No challenge against Lowther could succeed, and Pennington seems to have tried to secure the Lowther interest. At the county meeting for the nomination of candidates his name was put forward by Sir Gilfrid Lawson, who had first proposed Lowther,[1] and he emphasized his intention of displacing the other old member, Portland's associate, Henry Fletcher. His attack upon Fletcher was pitched entirely in a personal key. Thomas Benson, Lord Egremont's agent in Cumberland, reported to Portland the proceedings of the county meeting:[2]

> Mr. Fletcher was then proposed by Lord Surrey, and immediately objected to by Mr. Pennington, who attacked him in a very severe, and I could almost say indelicate manner. He charged him with a total neglect of his duty . . . that lukewarmness which Mr. F. was so remarkable for was by no means equal to the important trust of a member of the House of Commons, that he never spoke upon any question whatsoever, that his fortune in Cumberland was very insufficient and consequently his interest small.

Pennington carried on his campaign and his canvass up to the eve of the poll; but he was then obliged to withdraw, finding that the many electors under the domination of Sir James Lowther had instructions to give their second votes to

---

[1] Thomas Benson to Portland, 11 Sept. 1780, Portland MSS. [2] *Ibid.*

Fletcher, in accordance with Lowther's election bargain with Portland.[1]

The counties were habitually praised by contemporaries — and rightly — as the most representative of the parliamentary constituencies. But it would be vain to generalize about awareness of political questions governing their elections, even in such times of grave national crisis. Of the two contested elections, that for Surrey, which was clearly political in tone, registered no change in the balance of parties in the House of Commons; while in Cambridgeshire, where a change did occur, the struggle was one of family interests. In the counties within easy reach of the capital, leading elements in the electorate were thinking and acting on political and party lines. Bedford, Kent, and Surrey are cases already cited. In Middlesex, the presence of John Wilkes as a representative was a standing challenge to the government, and no one could be found to oppose him. The man chosen as his colleague in 1780 was George Byng, a friend of Portland and the parliamentary whip of the Rockingham party. In Essex John Robinson, passing through Chelmsford on the day of the county meeting for the nomination of candidates, found political arguments being raised on the subject of the recent petitions. 'There seeming to be a desire to start an opposition', he informed the King afterwards; '. . . the idea went off in a little speaking by Sir Robert Smith, and Mr. Chiswell about the petitions and by Mr. Bramston denying such petitions to be the sense of the county'.[2] Nearly all the representatives for these counties were already hostile to the government; and the increased discontent of the electors, or at least of those who

---

[1] George Mounsey to Portland, 28 Sept. 1780, *ibid.*; *General Evening Post*, 3-5 Oct. 1780.

[2] In Essex, where the parties were evenly balanced, the opponents of the ministry, who returned one member, seem to have found their main strength in the western part of the county, lying nearest to London; for the strength of the friends of government lay in the east, including the outports — 'Mr. Bramston's friends attending in numerous bodies from different parts of the county, Mr. Rigby from his part, Harwich, and all the eastern part coming with about 600 freeholders, and their appearing to be near 1,000 ready to have supported Mr. Bramston. . . .' — so Robinson wrote elsewhere in this letter, dated 13 Sept. 1780. (Abergavenny MS. 307).

were politically aware and active, was made manifest at the elections by the transfer of seats in Bedford, Kent, and Suffolk to the opposition, and by the defeat of the ministerial attempt to recover one seat in Surrey. These counties, whether contested or not, gave a clear verdict against the government. But in the outlying counties, Yorkshire stood alone; the Cambridge election was not a political fight; and neither the ministers nor the leaders of the opposition appear to have had any connection with the election in Shropshire, the only other county constituency in which there occurred a change adverse to the government. Elsewhere — this can usually only be surmised — the electors were satisfied with their existing representatives, or else opposing groups of local politicians were too evenly balanced to dare the hazards of a contest. 'It is not quite certain', Robinson wrote of Dorset, 'that Mr. Sturt and Mr. Pitt will come in again both being threatened for their conduct by different parties, but as it is not easy to get gentlemen to stand forwards in a county contest against persons of large property and weight in possession of a county, probably it may remain as at present.'[1] Humphrey Sturt and George Pitt voted on opposite sides in the House of Commons: there was no contest for Dorset, and both men continued as its representatives. In Gloucestershire and Lancashire feelers were put out by candidates wishing to oppose men friendly to the ministry; but nothing came of them in either case.[2] There was talk during the summer of opposing Sir John Thorold in Lincolnshire; 'His conduct in all points opposing government has given offence to many persons of consequence and interest', was Robinson's note; but Thorold was returned again without a contest.[3] Huntingdonshire, according to Sandwich, was a hot-bed of political animosities, 'divided between two parties . . . Government and Opposition'.[4] It had been one of the petitioning counties in the previous February, and its electorate included a band of radicals under

[1] 'State 1780', 13, Windsor MSS.
[2] *Ibid.* 16, 21.
[3] *Ibid.* 17.
[4] Sandwich to Dartmouth, 24 Sept. 1780, H.M.C., *Dartmouth MSS.* iii, 253.

the leadership of Sir Robert Bernard.[1] But the determination
of both Sandwich and his rival, the Duke of Manchester, to
avoid trouble and expense, damped down any possibility of a
contested election. In nearly half the counties of England, a
balance existed similar to that in Dorset or Huntingdon and
remained undisturbed during the elections. In these outlying
counties, national politics were by no means ignored, but no
definite trend emerged either for or against the government.

(B) THE BOROUGHS

Since examples are found of county elections conducted
with little or no reference to questions of national politics, it is
not surprising that instances of this kind were still more
common among even the larger urban constituencies. A
survey of press columns and notices would indeed give the
impression that politics were rarely considered. At times of
general elections local newspapers and the London press were
filled with the advertisements of candidates notifying their
intention of offering their services, but it is rare to find in
them a trace of a political manifesto. With a few exceptions,
mainly to be found among the supporters of the movement
for shorter parliaments and electoral reform, candidates did
not brandish their political views and intentions before the
electors. Politics were considered above the heads of the
greater part of the urban voters. When Daniel Parker Coke,
in 1784, was addressing the electors of Nottingham — a
borough with an electorate of some 2000 — he declared he
would do anything he was able in the service of the town, but
'he declined then entering into the discussion of political
questions, as they very frequently caused confusion': if any
great constitutional question was introduced in parliament, he
would 'vote and act, as he was conscious he had heretofore done,
without any view of place or emolument, but from principle

---

[1] Sandwich to Robinson, 20 Apr. 1780, Abergavenny MS. 254; Lord
Carysfort to Rev. C. Wyvill, n.d. (? Dec. 1782), *Wyvill Papers*, ii, 128;
Sir Robert Bernard's obituary, *Gentleman's Magazine*, 1789, i. 98.

and a thorough conviction of the side he should take being right'.[1] In an urban constituency a prospective member had perforce to stress his independence, his disinterestedness, and his willingness to attend to local interests : but political questions, if they were discussed at all, were generally of concern to relatively small groups of leading citizens, who were the organizers and heads of local caucuses and party clubs.

Of the twenty boroughs with over 1000 voters, thirteen went to the polls,[2] but in only eight of these contests did declared partisans of the two sides, government and opposition, confront each other. In London, the right of election was in the members of the livery companies. This solid commercial vote was overwhelmingly hostile to the government, and of the six candidates who stood for election only one, alderman Richard Clark, was a known supporter of the ministers. Three of the members returned were Wilkites, and the fourth was an independent whose sympathies also proved to be with the opposition : Clark ended bottom of the poll. In Southwark, the position of Henry Thrale, a supporter of the government, was successfully challenged by Sir Richard Hotham, a local merchant connected with East India shipping circles, and a man who busied himself in party politics in Surrey, where he took a leading part in conducting the election for Admiral Keppel. At Westminster, both sides joined to support Admiral Rodney — so far as the electors were concerned, politics had no part in his candidature, and Rodney's great triumph at the polls was purely a testimony to his enormous popularity as a naval hero ;[3] but a stern political fight was waged for the second seat between Charles Fox and a ministerial candidate, Lord Lincoln. Government and opposition candidates were also ranged against each other at Bristol, at Liverpool, and at Norwich. At Colchester, there was a successful last-minute intervention by Sir Robert Smyth of Berechurch Hall, a

---

[1] Creswell and Burbage's *Nottingham Journal*, 3 Apr. 1784.
[2] Bristol, Colchester, Coventry, Hull, Lincoln, Liverpool, London, Newcastle upon Tyne, Norwich, Nottingham, Southwark, Westminster, Worcester.
[3] Add. MSS. 27849 (Place Papers), f. 56 ; Oldfield, *Representative History*, iv, 233-4.

leading figure in the associating movement in Essex,[1] whom
the voters in this usually venal borough welcomed and, according to one report, elected without soliciting or bribery.[2] At
Coventry two friends of government, John Baker Holroyd and
Edward Roe Yeo, were confronted by two candidates connected with the London radicals, Sir Thomas Hallifax and
Thomas Rogers — but this election was also a further round in
the struggle between the corporation (which favoured Hallifax
and Rogers) and the 'independent interest'.[3] The elections in
the five remaining boroughs within this group — Hull, Lincoln, Newcastle, Nottingham, Worcester — showed less conformity to any pattern of party politics. David Hartley at
Hull, Lord Lumley (a nephew of Sir George Savile) at Lincoln,
and Sir Watkin Lewes at Worcester were all party men opposed
to the government, Hartley and Lumley being connected with
the Rockingham faction, and Lewes with the London radicals.
But in none of these elections was there a straight party fight.
The contest at Hull was provoked by the personal ambition of
William Wilberforce, whose patrimony, derived from banking
in the city, gave him a great advantage in dealing with an
electorate whose venality was notorious.[4] Lord Lumley's
rivals at Lincoln, Robert Vyner and Sir Thomas Clarges, were
both independent country gentlemen, well disposed towards
administration. At Worcester local interests gave support to
Lewes's rivals regardless of their political alignments. At
Newcastle and at Nottingham local and personal interests
dominated the elections. As the following examples show,
the contests in the large boroughs ran through the whole scale
of variations, from those which were predominantly political
in character to those in which politics virtually played no part.

In the metropolitan area generally, and in Westminster

[1] *The Political Magazine*, 1780, 117. In the winter of 1779–80 Smyth
took a leading part in promoting the Essex petition for economical reform;
and as Chairman of the Essex Committee of Association he was in correspondence with Burke upon the subject (Burke papers (Sheffield)).

[2] T. H. B. Oldfield; *op cit.* iii, 459.

[3] T. W. Whitley, *The Parliamentary Representation of Coventry* (Coventry
1894), 165-83.

[4] Oldfield, *Representative History*, v, 275-7; Robert Isaac and Samuel
Wilberforce, *Life of William Wilberforce* (5 vols., 1838), i, 13-16.

particularly, political issues loomed large in the elections. Both in London and in Westminster the elections were contests between avowed supporters and opponents of the ministry, and this point was made clear to the electors. A broadsheet issued by the printers Almon and Debrett (who were closely connected with the London radicals) was designed to appeal to voters to support the opposition and the reformers in both constituencies. It reproduced lists of recent parliamentary divisions with notes and comments intended to convey that only placemen supported the ministers, and it appealed to the electors to choose 'honest independent representatives':

> Let not any lucrative motive tempt you to lift into the senate any prostitute gamester, any avaricious contractor, or Asiatic plunderer; they will be the first to offer you up as victims to the shrine of corruption, and will glory in advancing themselves upon your ruin. The reduced value of your lands and the decay of your commerce, the increase of your debt and taxes, and the division and depopulation of your country, call aloud for the exertion and concurrence of the wisest and best men in the nation.

The authors, however, were reformers, not merely opponents of the government. In support of the proposition that some reform of parliamentary representation was necessary, this manifesto presented a series of figures to demonstrate the disparity between constituencies and taxable wealth and the injustice to the metropolitan area from the existing arrangement. Middlesex, it was noted, paid rather over a seventh of the land tax raised throughout the whole of England and yet had only eight representatives, Cornwall paid only about a tenth of this amount and yet returned forty-four; whereas Middlesex should have nearly fifty representatives, Cornwall but five. All the opposition candidates in London and Westminster were known from their past utterances to favour electoral reform, and this appeal was clearly expected to rally support for them.[1]

Politics were well to the fore in Fox's election campaign in Westminster. Fox's activities in the Westminster Committee

[1] Add. MSS. 27837, between ff. 7-8.

of Association identified him with the cause of parliamentary reform, and he had publicly committed himself the previous April to work for annual parliaments and an addition of a hundred county members to the House of Commons.[1] Now, six months later, he was much more concerned to emphasize his opposition to North's ministry and its policies — his election address trumpeted forth the promise: 'You will always find me . . . a determined enemy to that wretched system of government which has reduced us to our present calamitous situation'.[2] On 7 September, in a speech nominating Fox, George Byng declared: 'The times required men of abilities to discern, and of his resolution to oppose the ruinous plans of weak and corrupt ministers'. And Fox, in his speech accepting nomination, declaimed against the 'knavery and folly of the authors of our calamities'.[3] Owing to the rejection by parliament of Economical Reform, 'the Minister', he declared, 'still retained the power of influencing a corrupt parliament'; and he stated the party nature of the contest in decisive terms: [4]

> I hope my past conduct will speak for me; it has been a uniform system of opposition to the uniform absurdities of the present administration, and will always be so till they change their measures, that is, till they withdraw from their situations. I have a respect . . . for the private character of [Lord Lincoln] . . . but he is from situation, from connection, and from avowed principle one of the strongest adherents to the present minister and his measures. The contest therefore, gentlemen, is not between Lord Lincoln and me, but between Lord North and the electors of Westminster. It is whether you will chuse a representative for yourselves, or whether an implicit dependent of Lord North shall be forced upon you.

The election literature relating to the contest in the City of London in 1780 is deceptively devoid of political content.[5]

[1] Speech at the meeting of the electors of Westminster, 6 Apr. 1780, *London Chronicle*, 6-8 Apr. 1780.   [2] *Public Advertiser*, 4 Sept. 1780.
[3] *Ibid.* 8 Sept. 1780.   [4] *Adam's Weekly Courant*, 12 Sept. 1780.
[5] British Museum, broadsheets, ref. 1850. c. 10, ff. 117 seq.; Guildhall Library, Noble Collection, C. 78 (filed under names of various candidates with other biographical material).

But three of the opposition candidates had little need to re-affirm their political line in their election appeals to the livery-men : alderman Frederick Bull, an associate of John Wilkes, George Hayley, Wilkes's brother-in-law, and John Sawbridge, had all been conspicuous in their opposition to the government during the previous parliament and in their support for measures of electoral reform, and in April 1778 all three had signed, on behalf of their respective wards, an association which had as its object the securing, by lawful means, a more equal system of representation.[1] In 1780 the one matter regarding which Sawbridge felt it necessary to clear his reputation with the electors was Roman Catholicism, about which passions had been stirred during the summer : on 12 September he issued a notice affirming that he was no friend of popery and had sup-ported the protestant petition. The politics of a fourth candidate, John Kirkman, were sufficiently indicated when these three hardened city politicians joined his candidature with theirs. The only broadsheet with a real political flavour relating to this contest to be found in the collections in the Guildhall Library or in the British Museum was issued when these four found it necessary to publish an answer to a public attack launched against their joint candidature by another candidate, alderman Nathaniel Newnham. It was hoped in government circles that Newnham might prove a more moderate opponent in parliament than Sawbridge, and ministerial influ-ence was exerted in his favour,[2] though it seems doubtful from his subsequent behaviour that this was done by agreement with him, still less at his desire. The suspicion that he was connected with the government — one circular openly solicited votes for Newnham and for alderman Clark, who was known to be a government supporter[3] — was too good a lever to be neglected by the Wilkite group, and Newnham's protest at the coalition against him[4] provoked an immediate reply in which their hostility to the government was directly avowed.

[1] *General Evening Post*, 9-12 Sept. 1780.
[2] John Robinson to George III, 13 Sept. 1780, Abergavenny MS. 307.
[3] Brit. Mus., broadsheets, 1850. c. 10, f. 125.
[4] *Ibid.* f. 127.

Under the heading 'Against Mr. Alderman Newnham', it declared : [1]

> Mr. Newnham will probably be taught, by the present poll, that the Livery are not to be misled by two or three vague high-sounding expressions. . . . there was no motion made, either at the previous meeting or at the Common Hall, for any junction of candidates ; nor would even the three old members, under those circumstances, have presumed to join before the commencement of a contest, had not their unparalelled unanimity in all public matters, throughout the whole of the last parliament, rendered their interests as public men, as inseparable as their public opinions — But when the contest began, it became the duty of the friends of liberty not only to promote the interest of four candidates, actuated by the same love of freedom with themselves, but to use every fair endeavour to exclude men either of avowed ministerial attachments or men whose language and conduct were *more than suspicious*. Mr. Alderman *Clark*, nay even Mr. Alderman *Newnham* himself, *must not* be angry with those liverymen who thought it no time to make a compliment of their votes to such characters.

So, despite the almost entire absence of public political argument during the election, the City contest was in large measure a straight political fight between four opponents and one supporter of the government, complicated by the intrusion of another independent (and anti-ministerial) candidate.

Even in London, however, local considerations entered to some extent into the elections : Sawbridge's defeat in 1780 was attributed by one observer to the hostility of the sugar refiners, the group to which his successful rival, Newnham, belonged.[2] Elsewhere, this interplay of national politics with local interests and group rivalries was often clearly apparent. At Liverpool, for instance, the ministerial cause was maintained by the corporation in alliance with Bamber Gascoyne senior, whose estate of Childwall lying near to the town helped him to establish a strong personal interest among the electors. The

[1] Guildhall Library, Noble Collection, C. 78 (Newnham).
[2] A. Storer to Lord Carlisle, 24 May 1781, H.M.C., *Carlisle MSS.*, 485.

two members returned in 1774, Sir William Meredith and
Richard Pennant, were both in opposition. Consequently
electors seeking favours from the government turned to
Gascoyne as their intermediary, incurring obligations which
proved of the greatest service to him in 1780. Moreover, in
support of his interest, Gascoyne was prepared to make heavy
contributions from his own fortune. The combination of
Gascoyne and the corporation proved so formidable that
Meredith, on the plea of ill-health, declined to stand. His colleague, Pennant, was defeated, and Gascoyne's son was returned
— at an alleged cost of £8000 — together with Henry Rawlinson, a leading Liverpool merchant. Local newspaper reports
give no indication that political arguments were publicly
canvassed by either side during the election.[1] Again, at
Norwich, a group of leading citizens friendly to the North
ministry put up two candidates, Edward Bacon, one of the late
members, and John Thurlow, a brother of the Lord Chancellor,
who had lately served as mayor in the city. Their object was
to oust the other late member, Sir Harbord Harbord, an
independent who was opposed to the American war and
associated in opposition with the Duke of Portland. In self-
defence, for the purpose of denying the second votes of his
supporters to his rivals, Harbord decided to adopt a colleague
for the election, choosing — in his absence abroad — William
Windham of Felbrigg, a young friend of Charles James Fox.
The lists were thus set for a party fight between supporters and
opponents of the government. But the contest was also a
further round in the struggle between the independents in
Norwich and a junto of wealthy merchants, linked together
by trade and family connections, who had long sought to
dominate the city, and who secured the support of the ministerial
interest by backing Bacon and Thurlow. Even so, this group
could only carry one of its candidates, and the two old members

[1] Oldfield, *Representative History*, iv, 106; 'Ignotus', *A letter to the
Earl of Sefton*, cited in Miss N. Jucker, *The Jenkinson Papers, 1761–1766*
(Manchester, 1950), 208, n. 2; Gascoyne to Sandwich, 30 Sept. 1780,
Sandwich MSS.; North to George III, 16 Apr. 1782, Fortescue, v, no.
3663; *Williamson's Liverpool Advertiser and Mercantile Chronicle*, 14, 21
Sept. 1780.

were returned. Cries of 'no family compact' accompanied the shouts of 'no placemen' against Bacon and Thurlow at the hustings.[1]

A third example of this interplay of local factions and national politics was furnished by Bristol.[2] The lives and fortunes of its people were intimately bound up with transatlantic trade, a good number of them had knowledge of, or contact with, America, and loyalists and rebels each commanded many sympathizers among them. Two local party machines existed in the city, the 'Union Club' and the 'Steadfast Society', through which were organized the politics of those who called themselves respectively by the old names of 'Whigs' and 'Tories'. These political groups, which at bottom represented local rivalries for power and influence, were, by 1780, also sharply divided over the American question. Up to 1774 the 'Union Club' had returned ministerial supporters, but in that year it terminated its connection with Lord Clare on account of his agreement with governmental policy towards America and gave its support to opponents of the ministry; while, on the other hand, the 'Steadfast Society' took up the role of ministerial party in Bristol, and, in the following years, raised nearly £9000 in subscriptions, the greater part for bounties given to recruits, the rest 'advanced for wounded soldiers in America'.[3] To the local parties, or at any rate to their leaders, rivalries in the city had become bound up with the great issues of national policy, and the elections of 1774 and of 1780 were party fights between friends and opponents of North's administration: Edmund Burke for instance did not hesitate, in his speech to the electors at the Guildhall on 6 September 1780, to reiterate his detestation of the American War.[4] In 1774 the 'Union Club' carried both seats, securing

[1] R. W. Ketton Cremer, *The Early Life and Diaries of William Windham* (London, 1930), 204-5.

[2] On this election, see my essay, 'Henry Cruger and the end of Edmund Burke's connection with Bristol', *Transactions of the Bristol and Gloucestershire Archaeological Society*, vol. 74 (1955), 153-70.

[3] G. E. Weare, *Burke's Connection with Bristol from 1774 to 1780* (Bristol, 1894), 27-8; Fortescue, v, 470.

[4] Speech of Edmund Burke at the Guildhall in Bristol, 6 Sept. 1780, *The Works of . . . Edmund Burke* (12 vols., 1808-13), iii, 371-2, 398-9.

the return of Burke and Henry Cruger. In 1780 the 'Steadfast Society' prepared to take its revenge and put up two local men as candidates. Matthew Brickdale, a prominent Bristolian, wealthy and popular, had previously sat in its interest in the parliament of 1768. Richard Combe had occupied borough seats elsewhere by ministerial arrangement, and as a sign of governmental favour and encouragement was appointed Treasurer of the Ordnance a day or two after the dissolution. It is some measure of the firmness and strength of the 'Steadfast Society' in 1780, that its efforts were hardly checked for a moment by Combe's death in the first week of September: another candidate, Sir Henry Lippincott, immediately offered himself, and the 'Tories' swept on triumphantly to win both seats.

This success was at least partly due to a breach in the ranks of the 'Whigs', and it was here that local and personal issues entered to affect the course of the election. In 1774 the union between the supporters of Burke and of Cruger had been extremely successful. Yet, from the first, these two men had differed in their conceptions of the proper relations between member and constituents : and while Cruger seemed to express himself 'in favour of the coercive authority' of instructions from the electors, Burke, in a famous passage, repudiated this view.[1] It shocked Burke subsequently to find 'how very little the local constituents attend to the general line of conduct observed by their members', and how they judged of him solely by his merits as their 'special agent'.[2] Nevertheless, he was not prepared to sacrifice his judgment to the electors of Bristol, and, for some time before the general election of 1780, he had displeased large sections of them by his support for the Catholic Relief Act of 1778, and for measures relaxing the law against debtors and lifting restraints upon Irish trade. For the 'Whigs', the election was to turn more upon these points, and upon the personal standing of Burke and Cruger, than upon the great public questions on which they

---

[1] Speech to the electors of Bristol, 3 Nov. 1774, *ibid.* 18-20.
[2] *The Correspondence of . . . Edmund Burke*, edited by Earl Fitzwilliam and Sir Richard Bourke (4 vols., 1844), ii, 166.

were agreed — Economical Reform, and the ending of the American War.

Cruger, far more concerned than Burke to curry popular favour and preserve his position in the city, had already resolved, several months before the dissolution, not to stand jointly with Burke again. Neither he nor Burke's friends thought that the forces of the 'Union Club' could a second time carry both seats : but Cruger was determined that Burke, not he, should quit. Intent upon securing his own re-election, he undermined the authority of the leaders of the 'Union Club' and established his own ascendancy among the smaller tradesmen who supported their party ; and he had no scruples about exploiting against Burke local irritation about the Irish trade and the anti-Catholic feeling stirred up by the Gordon Riots. To gain his end he would be 'both Whig and Tory, American and anti-American, a strong supporter or a violent opponent of government, according to the sentiments of the voters he is canvassing'.[1] The old heads of the Whig connection, 'the most opulent, the most sober, the most understanding part', remained loyal to Burke.[2] They were, in Champion's phrase, a 'good body of officers' : but unfortunately they were short of troops to lead, for more than half their rank-and-file had been stolen away. As Cruger withheld his assistance, they had no hope of carrying Burke's re-election ; even a tentative offer which they made to purchase a seat for Cruger elsewhere in return for his support for Burke proved fruitless : they had either to acquiesce in Cruger's triumph, or else to try to break him at the cost of a 'Tory' victory. This last was the course they chose. When the poll began, and Cruger to the last maintained his defiance of the wishes of the 'Club', and offered the courtesy of one or two split votes to Brickdale ; from that moment, so far as the 'Whigs' were concerned, the question of opposing the members put up by the friends of government had become entirely subordinated to the struggle between the old caucus and the new, the first headed by Champion, Noble, and other leaders of Bristol society, the other by the demagogue,

[1] Richard Champion to Portland, 1 Sept. 1780, Portland MSS.
[2] Burke to Portland, 3 Sept. 1780, Rockingham MSS., R. 140-11.

Cruger, and his father-in-law, Samuel Peach. Burke having retired from the contest, the old caucus now withheld the votes without which Cruger could have no hope of success; and Champion, in a letter written to Portland after the election was over, dilated with grim satisfaction upon Cruger's defeat : [1]

> Mr. Cruger has declined this morning. The neutrality of our friends must now convince him, how little he ought to have depended upon that vain security, which made him act so treacherous a part. He has since been as despicably mean in his apologies and offers to us to assist and support him. But they were at once rejected. He has dug a pit for Mr. Burke, into which he has fallen himself, and had the folly to think that we would help him out. Some of our friends, from hatred to the tories, could not be kept back, but with every assistance he has polled only 1271. Our friends have in general been steady, which has left a great number unpolled.

No wonder the 'Tories' had triumphed! But the success of Matthew Brickdale and Sir Henry Lippincott was far more an indication of the weakness of their divided opponents than of the existence of an anti-American majority among the electors of Bristol.

Newcastle, Nottingham, and Worcester provide examples of election contests fought in larger urban constituencies in 1780, with little or no reference to national politics.

Three candidates stood independently for Newcastle.[2] One of these, Sir Matthew White Ridley, was entirely secure — from 1747 onwards, there existed a 'quasi-feudal' tradition in favour of the Ridleys — and the contest resolved itself into a struggle for the second seat between Thomas Delaval, one of the Delavals of Seaton Delaval, and Andrew Robinson Bowes, the disreputable Irish adventurer who had married the Dowager Countess of Strathmore. Both Delaval and Bowes were connected with a 'radical' movement in the town : with the help

---

[1] 19 Sept. 1780, Portland MSS.
[2] A. R. Bowes, Wednesday Morning (? Aug. 1780), Jesse Foot, *The Lives of Andrew Robinson Bowes, Esq., and the Countess of Strathmore* (London, 1812?), 71.

of its leaders Delaval had unsuccessfully contested the borough in 1774, and Bowes in 1777 : [1] but this fact had little to do with their candidatures in 1780. Writing to the Duke of Portland to solicit his support, Delaval explained, in the hackneyed phrase of the time that, 'if I shall have the honour to be one of the representatives of that important place, I will exert my best endeavours to promote the welfare of the public and the prosperity of Newcastle'.[2] In September he pressed unsuccessfully for support from Ridley's friends, but Ridley stood firmly aloof from both Delaval and Bowes.[3] Bowes, at the beginning of 1780, was 'fully engrossed with our patriotic meetings and *their* appendages' : [4] but he was ready to take assistance wherever he could find it, and about the same time he was also courting ministerial circles, and hoping through the mediation of the Edens to gain the goodwill of Ridley [5] — although the Edens supported the government and Ridley opposed it.

A study of the voting at Newcastle confirms the impression that at best local and personal issues, at worst hard cash, were the main points on which the election turned and that no consistent party division swayed the electorate. There are in the British Museum two poll books relating to Bowes's two attempts at Newcastle — at the by-election of 1777 and at the general election of 1780 — each of them bearing additional manuscript notes.[6] A sample comparison of the lists indicates that about two-thirds of the electors who supported Bowes against Sir John Trevelyan in 1777 voted again for him in 1780, and that he received in 1780 about a third of those votes which had previously been cast against him in favour of Trevelyan, who had stood on the Blackett interest. In 1780 nearly two-thirds of Trevelyan's votes of 1777 were split between Ridley and Delaval, although Delaval had been

[1] Namier, *Structure of Politics*, 95-8.
[2] 3 July 1780, Portland MSS.
[3] Nicholas Ridley to Richard Ridley, 25 Sept. 1780, Blagdon MSS.
[4] Jesse Foot, 68.
[5] North to W. Eden, Add. MSS. 46519, f. 75, undated but assignable to the winter or spring of 1780.
[6] The press marks of these copies of the poll books are 809 e 25 and 26.

opposed to Sir Walter Blackett in 1774, when the quarrel over the grant of leases on the town moor had raised a genuine local issue at the election. But Blackett was now dead, and his nephew, Trevelyan, had withdrawn from Newcastle; and Bowes scraped home at the poll ahead of Delaval by means of a combination of votes from the two groups which had stood opposed to each other in 1777. He himself had no interest in party politics, and paid little attention to his parliamentary duties when he found that his personal ambitions were ignored. 'The fact was, that, as he has told us', wrote his biographer, 'he meant to make something of his parliamentary seat; that he aimed at an Irish peerage, and finding the administration recoiled at it, he grew sulky and abusive.' [1]

Delaval entered a petition against the return of Bowes, alleging bribery of the electors; but he withdrew it when the case came up for hearing. A memorandum concerning this petition scribbled in the back of one of these poll books indicates the general level of this contest:

This petition of Mr. Delaval's was presented merely to harrass Mr. Bowes and was supposed to be set on foot by Mr. Brandling, Mr. Bigg and others the friends of Sir Matthew Ridley and Mr. Delaval. There was another presented against Sir Matt. Ridley by the burgesses to intimidate Sir Matthew's friends for them to withdraw Mr. Delaval's petition but as this had not the desired effect, and as Sir Matt. had behaved with the greatest disinterested honour during the poll and acknowledged so by Mr. Bowes after the poll, Mr. Bowes wou'd not proceed against Sir Matt. but withdrew the burgesses' petition a few days before the 15th Feb. [1782, when Delaval's was to be heard] . . . .

Mr. Delaval was in this business made a mere tool of — certain gentlemen were determined to sacrifice both Mr. Delaval and Sir Matt. to their enmity against Mr. Bowes. No matter if all the three went out provided that Mr. Bowes was incapacitated to serve and it was even said that it was the wish of certain persons that the three should ruin one another by the evidence against each to avoid the election

[1] Jesse Foot, 80.

for two other gentlemen to serve in their places. Mr. Bowes procured copies of letters that passed between Mr. Delaval and his friends, by these letters it appeared Mr. Delaval expected to be supported with cash by his friends as was promised — the answer to him was Mr. Bowes must be first turned out and all expences shall be paid.

Contemporary references to the town of Nottingham indicate that its leading citizens concerned themselves with political affairs and were sharply divided on the issue of the American War. There was a considerable nonconformist community, well entrenched in the corporation, which sympathized strongly with the American cause. In December 1777 Lord Sandwich received this report from Thomas Rawson: [1]

This town is without any exception the most disloyal in the Kingdom, owing in a great measure to the whole corporation (the present mayor excepted) being dissenters, and of so bitter a sort that they have done and continue to do all in their power to hinder the service by preventing as much as possible the enlistment of soldiers.

An important section of opinion in the town felt just as strongly the other way. It was the misfortune of the brothers Howe, whose family interest with the corporation had long been considerable, that their attempts in the early stages of the American War to follow a course of compromise pleased neither side among their constituents. In 1780 General Howe was anxious to retain his seat for the borough, and in August Frederick Montagu reported to Portland that the two brothers, Lord Howe and the general, had arrived there, and were attempting to explain their conduct while in America, but without much success: 'Half the town abhor them for going to America, and the other half detest them for doing so little there', he wrote — and again, next month: 'The extreme awkwardness and ill-management of the Howes has totally demolished the

<hr>

[1] *The Sandwich Papers*, edited by G. R. Barnes and J. H. Owen (Navy Record Society, 4 vols., 1932–8), i, 340. Cf. Thomas Bailey, *Annals of Nottinghamshire* . . . (4 vols., 1852–5), iv, 48.

corporation interest'.[1]   *The Political Magazine* (a periodical with a ministerial bias) informed its readers : [2]

> The most respectable people in the town waited on the brothers, and acquainted them that the electors of Nottingham had formerly . . . revered the name and family of Howe: but that reverence had lately been obliterated by other sentiments : they saw the present distresses of their country : they imputed them to the conduct of the General and Noble Lord when in America : therefore the General could have no hopes of carrying his election.

Howe's former supporters adopted as their candidate, Daniel Parker Coke, of Derby, a barrister, and a man of very independent conduct in politics.[3] As member for Derby in the late parliament he had usually supported government but had voted with the opposition in all the divisions on economical reform during the past few months. Both parties in the town supported the candidature of Robert Smith, the eldest son of Abel Smith, a leading Nottingham banker : [4] and it is as unprofitable to try and correlate the parliamentary votes of Smith with the views of the electors who supported him, as it is in the case of Coke. Smith voted constantly with the opposition to North's ministry, but his father, M.P. for St. Ives, voted just as consistently for the government; and Robert's election for Nottingham reflected the dominant position of his family in the town rather than any political alignment among the voters. Abel Smith was now one of its leading citizens. In local affairs he was closely connected with the Duke of Newcastle,[5] who was an ally of the ministry, and he himself had connections with the Treasury through contracts and banking interests. But to Abel the re-election of his eldest son for Nottingham was more important than the return of a reliable friend of government; for it confirmed, amidst the ruin of Lord Howe's interest, the ascendancy of his own and his family's influence in the borough.

---

[1] 22 Aug., 10 Sept. 1780, Portland MSS.
[2] *The Political Magazine*, 1780, 577.
[3] *Parliamentary Characters, 1779–81*, 11.
[4] *Ibid.* 53.   [5] *The Sandwich Papers*, i, 340.

No government candidate appeared at Nottingham to challenge these two local interests. When Major John Cartwright, the reformer, decided to stand on a programme of parliamentary reform,[1] he found little support, and was beaten ignominiously, receiving only 149 votes to the 571 and 343 cast for Smith and D. P. Coke.

The general election at Worcester followed on this occasion its usual course, that of a conflict between the corporation and a strong corps of independent voters among the freemen. The circumstances of the contest were not a little entertaining; but, except for the interest shown in the result by Lord North, and by his brother who was bishop of the diocese, there was precious little politics to be found in it.

At this period the independents were sufficiently numerous to give trouble, but never strong enough to carry their candidate in a contest, though they regularly made the attempt. Between 1773 and 1780 they found a champion in Sir Watkin Lewes, an alderman of London (he was, however, a retired barrister, not a merchant), who flung away a fortune in this, one of the most corrupt of English boroughs. The general election of 1780 was the occasion of his fourth and last attempt to become its representative.

The corporation prided itself upon never losing an election. But the retirement of one of its protégés, John Walsh, placed it in a position of some difficulty. Walsh's colleague, Thomas Bates Rous, another East Indian, was standing for re-election; but it was not easy to find a colleague to run with him and to shoulder part of the expenses of a contested election on the corporation's behalf. During August three gentlemen with an interest in the borough were approached, but each in turn declined to face a contest.[2] The last of these, Sir Charles Cocks, of Eastnor Park in Herefordshire, was an official of the Board of Ordnance, and his canvass may have been attempted at the prompting of North and Robinson, who were concerned to keep out Sir Watkin Lewes in view of his connections

[1] Cresswell and Burbage's *Nottingham Journal*, 9 Sept. 1780.
[2] Henry Beaufoy, of Claverley, Shropshire, Edward Bearcroft, a London barrister, and Sir Charles Cocks of Eastnor Park.

with opposition circles in the City of London.[1]   However, it was not as a ministerialist, but simply as an interloper, that Cocks's intended candidature was opposed by the supporters of Lewes.   The day before his arrival a meeting of the independent freemen passed resolutions against the introduction of any 'third man' into the city :[2] and the sequel was related by Lewes in his speech to the electors at the opening of the poll :[3]

> [Sir Charles Cocks] declined also, a respectable deputation having waited on him with the resolution of the citizens not to break the peace of the city by supporting any third man.   This gentleman was pleased to say that 'he would not disturb your peace, that he was deceived and had been brought to believe that he was invited by the unanimous wishes of the city.'   And finding that he could not succeed unless honest men broke their word the gentleman declined.

At the end of August, with the general election upon them, the members of the corporation redoubled their efforts.   Both Rous (with their interest) and Sir Watkin Lewes were busy canvassing the voters ;   and in their endeavour to block Sir Watkin's prospects, the corporation were obliged to announce an anonymous candidate.   The following notice was inserted in Berrow's *Worcester Journal* on 31 August (and again on 7 September) :

> To the worthy Freemen of the City of Worcester
>
> Gentlemen,
>   You are earnestly requested not to engage your votes for the ensuing general election ;   as you may be assured that a spirited gentleman of abilities integrity and fortune will, in a few days personally solicit your suffrages.
>
> A CITIZEN

At this date not even the advertisers had the slightest idea who the 'spirited gentleman' might be.   The steps taken by the corporation to find one are revealed in a letter sent, on 5

---

[1] For Robinson's anxiety over Worcester, see Laprade, 53-6.
[2] Berrow's *Worcester Journal*, 31 Aug. 1780.
[3] *Ibid.* 14 Sept. 1780.

September, to Lord North, by his half-brother, Brownlow North, the bishop of Worcester: [1]

DEAR BROTHER,

I think it right to state to you the circumstances of the City of Worcester, and beg an answer by my messenger upon the subject, it is a mortification to me that the seat should fall to the lot of Sir Watkin L[ewe]s against the wishes of the prevailing interest. But Sir Charles Cocks and Bearcroft having declined, *before the dissolution*, there is now no competitor with Sir Watkin. The Corporation have sent two of their body privately to me wishing that a friend of mine should stand. Their account of the matter is that the Corporation have never yet been beaten, that they are stronger now than they ever have been, as the Quakers are with them, that they have the assistance of all the country gentlemen against the knight and that in short they are certain of success if I will procure them a candidate with £1,500.

Under these circumstances if truly stated . . . Mr. Poulter an active young man and now a little known in this country might really be made useful to rescue this seat out of disagreeable hands. . . .

Two of the members of the Corporation are now gone to Mr. Harley [2] to solicit Mr. Drummond [3] to stand, and this case is only thought of in case they return without a candidate. . . .

While these and other schemes were being tried, the corporation was obliged to bluff its adversaries still further, and a new notice over the signature of 'A Citizen' appeared in the *Worcester Journal* of 7 September:

Notwithstanding the many falsehoods issued forth by the partisans of Sir W. Lewes, intimating that no gentleman whatsoever dare oppose him at our next general election, nevertheless I hope my honest brethren will not despair of having a worthy man to represent, since there are now not

[1] Abergavenny MS. 299.
[2] Thomas Harley, 1730–1804, M.P. for Herefordshire, a banker in London, and a government contractor.
[3] Probably Harley's business partner, Henry Drummond, 1731–1795.

less than four men of most distinguished character . . .
ready to offer their services.

This notice was dated 6 September, and in the light of the
Bishop's letter of the previous day, it was clearly untrue.
There is no doubt either that the independent party were
aware of the corporation's embarrassment, and the same issue of
the paper carried a jeering rejoinder :

> Whereas the opposition to Sir W. Lewes have for a long
> time past *seriously* threatened this city with a *spirited* third
> man, who should *ruin* himself in a few days : and whereas
> it is admitted that the opposition were only joking when
> they set up Mr. Bearcroft and Sir Charles Cocks : for these
> and diverse other good causes, they are advised to be a little
> more expeditious than they have hitherto been, otherwise
> it will seriously be thought that no third man can be found
> to oppose Sir W. Lewes.

In another paragraph in the same issue of the paper, a facetious
correspondent put his finger on the root of the difficulty
encountered by the corporation ; a candidate must be found
willing and well able to spend money among the voters :

> Public notice is hereby given [he wrote] that two horses,
> viz. Liberty [1] and Nabob [2], are entered for our election
> plate, which is to be run for next Tuesday — Liberty is a
> strong active horse full of fire . . . the odds are, Liberty
> against the field.
>
> Nabob, it is thought, will run lighter by some pounds
> than he used to do, being lately observed to be very much
> sweated.
>
> A third is expected to enter at the post ; various are the
> conjectures and reports concerning this horse ; but it is agreed
> on all hands, that he will be obliged to pay double entrance.

Next week, however, the corporation had solved its problem
and the third man had been found. He was neither the
stranger from London, Henry Drummond, nor the young
kinsman whom the Bishop had suggested as a possible candidate ; but William Ward, whose elder half-brother, John,

[1] Sir Watkin Lewes.   [2] Thomas Bates Rous.

second Viscount Dudley and Ward, had formerly sat in two parliaments for the city. The Wards were a family of consequence in the West Midlands, deriving considerable wealth from the rich coal-bearing estates they owned in Staffordshire, and it may be surmised that William was well able to bear his share in a contested election. On Tuesday, 12 September, he was duly present on the hustings when the candidates addressed the freemen at the opening of the poll. Publicly he had not associated himself with Rous, but it was common knowledge that both men had the support of the corporation, and Sir Watkin Lewes waxed sarcastic at this hidden junction of interests.[1] Sarcasm, however, as Lewes was to find, was no substitute for votes. And, although, by the instigation of a riot near the hustings, he was able to keep away some of Ward's voters, and maintain a lead during the first day's poll, he lost it on the second, and finished well over a hundred votes below his rival.[2]

From first to last, during the whole course of this election, no trace of a reference to political affairs is to be found in the notices and addresses published in the *Worcester Journal*, nor in the reported speeches of the candidates before the commencement of the poll. Even Lord North's brother tended to present the issue as a local one, the preservation of the corporation's interest. The Ministry and the corporation, in wishing to keep Sir Watkin Lewes out of the borough, discovered a purpose in common; but the corporation was not inclined to oppose Rous because he usually voted with the opposition in parliament, and in 1780 it bestowed its favour impartially on Rous whose politics were known, and on Ward, who was untried but expected to be friendly towards the government.

A survey of the contested elections in the open boroughs with less than a thousand voters produces a similar mixed picture and one which shows that it is not possible to dismiss even quite small constituencies as unaffected by political considerations. Often contests took place between candidates of

---

[1] Berrow's *Worcester Journal*, 14 Sept. 1780.
[2] *Ibid.* 14, 21 Sept. 1780. The figures at the end of the poll were Rous 1106, Ward 847, Lewes 711.

opposite political persuasions. Less often, but still frequently, these borough electorates included independent or radical groups whose activities were directed by genuine political motives — groups which sought representatives ready to vote against the American War or to support parliamentary reform. Among the boroughs of from 500 to 1000 voters, there were contests of a political character at Bedford, Hertford, Maidstone, Reading, Rochester, and Sandwich, and politics probably also played some part at Canterbury. At Bedford the influence of Sir Robert Bernard, a leading radical of neighbouring Huntingdonshire, was exerted in favour of Sir William Wake against John Kenrick, a newly promoted member of the Board of Ordnance.[1] At Hertford Burke's admirer, William Baker, ousted a staunch ministerialist, John Calvert. Reading, despite its reputation for corruption, included amongst its electors a strong body of independents who captured one seat in 1774 and secured the re-election of their member, Francis Annesley, in 1780, and also in four later parliaments. In February 1780 this group contributed a petition in support of the campaign for Economical Reform : possibly it provided some of the support given at the general election to an unsuccessful Wilkite candidate, Temple Luttrell.[2] At Maidstone a large nonconformist element provided backing for an independent party which in 1780 triumphed over the influence of the ministerial Earl of Aylesford.[3] At Rochester the Middlesex election crisis of 1769 had brought into being a 'patriotic' party, which was able to carry one seat against the Admiralty interest from 1774 onwards ; probably some members of this group encouraged the candidature in 1780 of a second opposition man, Shelburne's friend, Nathaniel Smith, of East India House.[4] At

---

[1] Oldfield, *Representative History*, iii, 19 ; *Parliamentary Characters, 1779-81*, 60 ; North to George III, 5 Sept. 1780, Fortescue, v, no. 3128 ; Richard Fenton to Rockingham, 18 Sept. 1780, Rockingham MSS., R. 139-39.

[2] *Parliamentary Characters, 1779-81*, 2 ; Annesley's obituary, *Gentleman's Magazine*, 1812, i, 491 ; John Man, *History and Antiquities of Reading* (Reading, 1816), 74.   [3] Oldfield, *op. cit.* iv, 76.

[4] Obituary of John Calcraft, *The Canterbury Journal*, 8 Sept. 1772 ; W. Gordon to Sandwich, 16 Oct. 1771, Abergavenny MS. 19A ; George III to North, 24 Aug. 1772, Fortescue, ii, no. 1119. In 1774 Robert Gregory, a connection of Rockingham, was returned on the independent interest after

Sandwich Charles Brett, a connection of the Howes, and in opposition, was displaced after a stiff fight by a government candidate, Sir Richard Sutton.[1] But in other boroughs within this category political lines were blurred or non-existent. A 'patriotic' contest was started at Ipswich,[2] where radicals put up two supporters of parliamentary reform, Joshua Grigby, later member for Suffolk, and William Middleton. But the old members joined forces against them although one, Thomas Staunton, was an opponent of the North ministry, and the other, William Wollaston, supported it.[3] At Preston Sir Henry Hoghton and General Burgoyne stood jointly on the Derby interest against a candidate set up by the corporation, although they voted on opposite sides in parliament.[4] At Sudbury, a ministerial lawyer, Philip Champion Crespigny, chasing the fitful shadow of an old family interest in this most corrupt of constituencies, set himself up in conflict against two other friends of government, John Henniker, junior, and Sir James Marriott, the Judge-Advocate-General — to strengthen his chances he joined forces with Sir Patrick Blake, a West Indian who was an inveterate opponent of North's ministry.[5] All three candidates in the contest which took place at Evesham were hostile to the government. Similar diversity is apparent in the character of elections in the smaller open boroughs. Bridgwater, Hedon, Honiton, Windsor, and Stafford provide examples where the candidates at least were sharply divided in their politics, though it is doubtful if more than a small minority of electors thought in political terms : in contrast, at Barnstaple, Helston, Penryn, and Truro the rival candidates and the patrons who backed them were all supporters of the government.

declaring himself 'a firm friend to the distinguishing liberties of this excellent constitution', (*Canterbury Journal*, 11 Oct. 1774) : he retained his seat in 1780.

[1] George Aust to Hardwicke, 14 Sept. 1780, Add. MSS. 35617, f. 42.

[2] 'State, 1780', 20, Windsor MSS.

[3] Add. MSS. 25335, f. 18.

[4] W. Dobson, *History of the Parliamentary Representation of Preston* . . . (Preston, 1856), 25 ; *General Evening Post*, 16-19 Sept. 1780 ; *Leeds Intelligencer*, 3 Oct. 1780.

[5] Sir Jas. Marriott to C. Jenkinson, 4 Sept. 1780, Add. MSS. 38458, f. 121.

In general, politics did not enter at all into elections in the close constituencies, save in so far as a patron was guided in his choice of nominees by his attitude towards the government : from their nature no contest on political grounds was possible. But in 1780 strong currents of political opposition manifested themselves in at least two of the close boroughs regarded as under ministerial control. At Plymouth, where the franchise was restricted to the select body of the corporation and free-men, an independent candidate, J. Culme, stood forward on a platform of parliamentary reform and sought to establish by petition the electoral rights of the freeholders. Culme's agents polled 76 freemen (about a third of the whole) and claimed to poll on his behalf 127 other persons who were freeholders in the borough — had their names been admitted Culme would have secured more votes than any of the other three candidates.[1] At Portsmouth, a borough with a similarly restricted electorate, the corporation itself was divided over the American War. A dissident group led by the Carter family opposed the government's American policy and therefore challenged its control through the corporation of the election of members of parliament, setting up Sir Harry Fetherstonhaugh in opposition to the Admiralty nominees ; later this faction also declared its adherence to the Yorkshire Committee of Association's programme of shorter parliaments and a more equal system of representation.[2] Neither of these candidates was successful, but the mere fact that they could command a considerable measure of support was of some significance.

Certain tentative conclusions emerge from these examples. In 1780 the 'political election' was by no means an exception. Political considerations were undoubtedly canvassed and had some relevance to the course of elections in both the county constituencies and in the larger boroughs. But the political element in elections varied greatly in extent from place to place, and it was almost entirely absent from some open constituencies as well as from most of those commonly described as close.

[1] *General Evening Post*, 19-21 Sept. 1780 ; *The Canterbury Journal*, 19 Sept. 1780.
[2] Oldfield, *Representative History*, iii, 504-6 ; John Carter to C. Wyvill, 20 Jan. 1783, *Wyvill Papers*, iv, 255.

Disputes of a political character were most noticeable in the counties. This was to be expected, since, although elections were determined by a small minority of the voters — the educated and politically alert class of landed proprietors, with a sprinkling from the upper fringe of various professional groups — this minority was steeped in a tradition of public service and enjoyed the necessary leisure to attend to political affairs. Such political conflicts were far more numerous than is suggested by the comparative rareness of contested elections. Contests were few, partly because of the expense, partly because the existence of two-member constituencies offered a standing temptation to the Englishman's habit of compromise, especially where disagreements over national issues were inter-linked with rival local interests of fairly equal strength. But a major swing of opinion could readily be registered in the counties, by an uncontested change of the representation, such as occurred, for example, in 1780, in Kent, Bedford, Suffolk, and Yorkshire. The county elections were a political seismo-graph which no government could afford to neglect. This was not so fully the case with even the very large urban constitu-encies. The decisions registered by London and Westminster were clear and important — that this was fully realized by the government is evident from the effort and the money devoted to those contests. But elsewhere, even in the boroughs with over 1000 voters, local interests and considerations and personal rivalries affected elections to a much greater extent. True, local groups were influential in some counties also, but the heads of a municipal clique were less likely to have an informed opinion about questions of national policy, or any opinion at all, than members of such leading aristocratic groups as the Berkeleys in Gloucestershire or the Cavendishes in Derbyshire. Still, where members of a county electorate also had voting rights in a neighbouring borough they might give a consider-able political colour to its election affairs. The Beaufort and Berkeley factions, for instance, had their connections among the voters of Gloucester as well as of the county. On 3 September 1780 Nicholas Webb wrote to John Parsons, on behalf of 'many of the gentlemen of Gloucester' who supported the Beaufort candidate for the county, requesting his support for their candidates in the borough (George Selwyn and Sir Andrew Hamond), explaining: 'As friends of Government we support them which they have no doubt will make them acceptable to you'.[1] Fragmentary as the evidence is, it is sufficient to provide a warning against thinking of the next general election, that of 1784, as a new phenomenon in Georgian politics. Political partisanship played no small part in the elections of 1780. If the politics of the candidates only are considered, there were conflicts of a political nature, between avowed supporters and avowed opponents of the government, for some forty-five seats in over thirty English boroughs — about half the English borough constituencies and seats contested.

It is also evident that the eighteenth-century representative system was by no means entirely inadequate as a means of reflecting changes of public opinion at times of parliamentary elections. A swing against the government in the county constituencies was faithfully reflected in the returns of their representatives. No such trend was discernible in the big urban constituencies, and correspondingly there was little change in the political character of their representation. The instrument may not have been a very sensitive one by modern standards, but it is arguable on at least two grounds that it was sensitive enough. First, the political complexion of the House of Commons as shown by the votes cast in divisions was not fixed to any great extent by the results of a particular general election: the independent members, without whose support no government could stand and no policy involving legislation be pursued, responded readily, if sometimes, uncritically, to any clear upsurge of sentiment in the country. Second, public opinion had hardly yet been developed or organized to the point at which a more sensitive instrument for recording it was required. From early in the next century, the development of public opinion was to prove perhaps the most important factor in the reshaping of the British parliamentary system. Then, electoral reform could no longer be withheld. But in 1780 this

[1] Parsons MSS., Glos. Record Office.

development was only in its beginnings. The falling away of support for the Reform Associations after 1780 supports this conclusion, for it indicated that, except in the eyes of a few enthusiasts and of part of the 'middle class' of the metropolitan districts and in a few 'corporation boroughs', the representative system seemed to contemporaries to function satisfactorily.

(v)

THE RESULTS OF THE ELECTIONS

During September 1780 the comments of politicians and their friends upon the elections revealed a confusing diversity of views. On the opposition side, Fox, from the start, was optimistic: 'It is quite clear', he wrote, 'that we shall rather gain than lose'.[1] Correspondence among people on the ministerial side, reflecting gloom and dismay at various election results, seemed at first to bear him out. At an early stage Charles Jenkinson bemoaned the defeat of friends of government at Wallingford and Canterbury,[2] and the next day North noted that three more friends had been beaten in open boroughs: 'Our elections seem to go but ill', he wrote to Robinson. 'We are in a bad sort of way, unless we have some good events to set against these misfortunes.'[3] Inevitably North became the butt of complaints in ministerial circles. Charles Sackville, a connection of Germain, wrote to a friend on 21 September: 'Elections in general are not thought to go on as smoothly as they should do if proper steps had been taken in time, but indolence and procrastination have always been and will always be the characteristick of Government so long as Boreas presides over it'.[4] 'The elections in Westminster, Stafford, Yorkshire, and Surrey are mortifying enough', William Eden wrote that same day to Loughborough; but he was careful to point out that there were compensations: 'I can give you, however,

[1] *Memorials and Correspondence of Charles James Fox,* edited by Lord John Russell (4 vols., 1853-7), i, 257.
[2] To Robinson, 10 Sept. 1780, Abergavenny MS. 304.
[3] To Robinson, 11 Sept. 1780, Abergavenny MS. 305.
[4] To Sir Charles Hotham Thompson, 21 Sept. 1780, Hotham MSS.

a comfortable list of ousted politicians : Sir W. Howe, C. Brett, Admiral Keppel, T. Coventry, E. Burke, A. Popham, Sir W. Meredith, Governor Pownall, G. Rous, R. Pennant, Walsh, Lord Richard Cavendish, Sir George Warren, Crofts, Keck, Sir G. Robinson, Sir A. Hume, Sir J. Shelley, Goring, Meynell, Sir T. Frankland, R. Scott, etc., etc.'[1] At the end of the fray optimists on either side could equally draw some comfort from the results. 'Elections in general have passed off with less contest than could have been imagined and with little party violence', Lord Bathurst wrote to Lord Hardwicke on 27 September. 'It convinces me of the propriety there was in having the elections at this season, when faction was lulled to sleep or transported abroad ; so that we may expect the true sense of the people to be met with in the new parliament.'[2] But two days later Christopher Wyvill was rejoicing in a letter to Lord Mahon at the more favourable appearances for parliamentary reform created by the elections: 'From the success of the popular candidates in many elections, and from other recent events, there is reason to hope the plan will be supported not only by a respectable body of friends who have taken an early and active part in promoting it, but also by the united powers of opposition of every description and determination'.[3] And early in October Rockingham wrote in an optimistic vein to Edward Eliot :[4]

> By some of the returns of persons chose in Devonshire and Cornwall, and by the names of the disappointed candidates, it has occurred to me, that the Ministers, etc., have met with many unexpected checks, and that possibly some of those gentlemen who may formerly have given their interest according to the wishes of the Minister may have now in the calamitous state which this country has been brought into desisted. . . . I feel much hope — that the ballance of gain or loss in point of numbers — doth predominate on our side.

[1] Add. MSS. 34417, f. 207. However one or two of the opposition politicians in Eden's list, including Burke and Keppel, soon found their way back into the House for other constituencies.
[2] Add. MSS. 35617, f. 56.
[3] 29 Sept. 1780, *Wyvill Papers*, iii, 264.
[4] Draft, 8 Oct. 1780, Rockingham MSS., R. 140-92.

Such conflicting statements suggest what, in fact, was the case, that the results of the general election had been inconclusive.

Disappointment was perhaps most severe on the ministerial side. In July 1780 Robinson had forecast the political group-ings in the new parliament as likely to be *Pro* 252, *Hopeful* 47, *Doubtful* 70, *Con* 189; and he estimated the maximum possible voting strengths on either side as *Pro* 343 and *Con* 215.[1] But in February 1781 he drew up an 'Abstract and State' of the House of Commons, in which a very different picture is presented. (See page 160.) Fortunately a copy of the nominal roll from which he obtained these figures is preserved in his papers, and from this can be learnt the known or anticipated political behaviour of all but a few of the members at that date. This list of names was subsequently amended for use in November 1781, at the opening of the second session of this parliament, so the reliability of the data contained in it was tested over some months and would appear to be particularly trustworthy.[2] The survival of this list of names and of the abstract prepared from it makes possible a comparison of the new House of Commons with the old and also with Robinson's forecast of July.[3]

This comparison yields what is at first appearance the extraordinary fact, that the general election expected by Robinson in July to yield a possible absolute majority of 128 in favour of government produced, according to the data avail-able in the following February, a probable maximum working majority of six. The count of members absent and abroad on the abstract goes only part of the way to explain the discrepancy. With the inclusion of these members on each side the govern-ment apparently had a notional absolute majority of 26 in a House of 552 members (excluding the Speaker and five vacant seats), so that Robinson's estimate was out by more than a hundred. In fact the situation was not so bad as this, for in February 1781, in an excess of caution, Robinson classified as

[1] See pp. 36-8 above.   [2] Abergavenny MSS., bundle A2.
[3] No earlier lists for this parliament have survived, either in Robinson's papers or in those of George III in the Royal Archives at Windsor, though it is on record that at least one was drawn up and sent to the King before the parliament met at the end of October 1780.

ABSTRACT AND STATE, 14TH FEBRUARY 1781

Pro Pres.	Pro Abs.	Pro Abroad	Hopeful Present	Hopeful Absent	Doubtful Present	Doubtful Absent	Con Pres.	Con Abs.	Con Abroad
223	30	12	23	1	40	3	214	4	2

552
6
558

Add to these for Helston 2, Beeralston 1, Bristol 1, Aldeburgh 1 & the Speaker 1

To the Pros pres. add those who it is supposed may be got of the Pros abs.
14
237

Suppose also the Hopeful present
23

Total that can be hoped for, except some reckoned doubtful may be for
260

Add the doubtful to the Cons
40
254

which number they may possibly be.

'doubtful' or 'contra' several members, new and old, who turned out to be friendly. Still his calculations of the summer had been far wide of the mark. Even allowing for the corrections to his estimate which he could not but have seen were necessary as his preparations became more complete during the course of August, it is evident that he — and the ministers generally — were greatly deceived in their expectations. Far from the government having scored a triumph in the elections, it was — so far as can be stated with any precision — weaker as a result of the general election by five or six votes in the new House (making a difference of ten to twelve in a division). After allowing for the five vacant seats mentioned in the abstract (where no political change occurred) and excluding political changes appearing on the nominal roll as a result of old members being reclassified adverse (not always correctly), it is possible to draw up the following table of changes which had taken place as a result of the general election — the figures are stated in terms of gains or losses for the government:

	Gains	Losses	Net Gain	Net Loss
ENGLAND				
Counties		8		8
Open boroughs with over 1000 voters	7	6	1	
Open boroughs and open seats in 'mixed' boroughs, with electorates of less than 1000 *	15	16 †		1
Close boroughs, and seats under 'influence' in 'mixed' boroughs	19	18	1	
WALES	no political change			
SCOTLAND	3	1	2	
	44	49		

* By 'mixed' borough is meant one in which one seat was at the disposal of a patron, the other not.

† One of the new members so classed, Francis Basset (Barnstaple), later proved to be friendly to government.

As an operation undertaken for the purpose — and with the confident hope — of strengthening the government's position

in the House of Commons, the general election was clearly a
failure. True, as William Eden noted, a number of virulent
opponents and doubtful friends had been ousted — but only
at the cost of admitting other bitter critics returned for other
constituencies, among them Lord Mahon, Lord Surrey, John
Townshend, and R. B. Sheridan. The King and his ministers
could draw only this much comfort, that the actual voting
strength of the government in the House of Commons was
very little weaker than before.

Before the general election Sandwich, Rigby, and Eden, if
not others also, had pressed the importance of exploiting the
favourable turn of public opinion.[1] But ministers were disappointed in so far as they placed their reliance not on rotten
boroughs but on the popular constituencies to provide a better
majority. The opposition was perfectly justified in claiming
that those constituencies where a genuine popular voice existed
had given their verdict against the government,[2] though the
actual swing in number of such seats was only about ten. The
answer from the counties was decisive. Whereas twenty-six
county members had been reckoned as friendly or hopeful by
John Robinson before the general election, after it the number
had fallen to fifteen. This reflected a growing weariness and
dislike of the American War among the country gentlemen,
despite the recent successes of British arms in the southern
colonies. As a social group they were among the first to feel
the financial burden of war through increases in the land tax,
and those of them who wanted capital to develop their estates
or merely loans to support their extravagance found themselves
frustrated by the channelling of credit into government loans.
In the boroughs of over 1000 voters, the government, having
gained one seat, commanded much the same amount of support
as before, losses in some places being compensated by gains
in others. But only a minority of the representatives of these
boroughs — exactly one-third — voted ministerially in the new
House of Commons. The underlying bodies of opinion reflected

[1] William Eden to Loughborough, 5 Aug. [1780], Add. MSS. 34417,
f. 120.
[2] Speech of Richard Fitzpatrick, 6 Nov. 1780, Almon and Debrett,
The Parliamentary Register, i (1781), 30.

in these election results are difficult to gauge, especially since, as is indicated by examples discussed earlier in this chapter, public policy was not always the primary question at issue in the elections. Two great trading centres where the government made conspicuous gains were Bristol and Liverpool, places where commercial groups were more exclusively concerned than elsewhere with the colonial trade across the Atlantic. On the other hand, the commercial interests represented by the livery companies of London and the ratepayers of Southwark were largely hostile to the ministry, but it seems probable that many strands of opinion, not merely, perhaps not even mainly, commercial considerations lay behind the results — genuine radical sympathy with the constitutional claims of the Americans and discontent with the existing representative system, militant protestant dislike of pro-Catholic measures supported by the ministers, plus the perennial rivalry between the corporation of the City and the national government. In the open boroughs with electorates of medium size — between 1000 and 500 — the proportion of members returned who were friendly towards the government was little greater. The 24 boroughs of this type returned 47 members. In July 1780 only 17 of these were government supporters, and the general election made no change in the number. The government, therefore, remained, after the elections, as before them, with a relatively small absolute parliamentary majority (part of which was permanently non-effective through absences abroad), based mainly on the close constituencies and the cohorts of Scotland. Friends sat for two-thirds of the borough seats at the command of private patrons; the Treasury, Admiralty, and Ordnance contributed about 24 more; and 41 out of the 45 Scottish members voted with the ministers. The personnel of this new House of Commons, and its political organization, will be considered in the following chapter.

PART II

CHAPTER I

THE HOUSE OF COMMONS OF 1780

A QUESTION which arises at the outset of an examination of the relations between Lord North's ministry and the House of Commons elected in 1780 is, did this House differ in any way in its essential characteristics from the House elected in 1761 ? The House of Commons of 1761 has been analysed in detail.[1] But was that House, with its complex array of human types and its amorphous traces of group organization, a norm for the later eighteenth century, or had the course of events in the ensuing twenty years worked any change in parliament's structure and composition ? *Prima facie* some change might be expected, for the conditions in which these two parliaments were elected differed considerably. That of 1761 came into being at a period of national success in war and of relaxed political tension at home. But the elections of 1780 came at a time when the country had been humiliated by defeats, when the revived naval strength of the Bourbon Powers raised once again the scare of invasion, when informed political opinion was bitterly divided over the American question, and when, to sober reckoning, doubts might well be entertained whether real, substantial success would ever materialize from Cornwallis's military triumphs in the thinly populated southern colonies. In 1780 there were thus numerous reasons for discontent with the government, political tension was acute, and the circumstance that for over five years America had been the subject of a continuous great political debate had given a certain continuity to political groupings. In these circumstances, how far did the personal composition and the political organization in George III's fourth parliament conform to the pattern found in 1761 ?

[1] Sir Lewis Namier, *England in the Age of the American Revolution* (1930), 195-262.

The following survey of the House of Commons elected in 1780 is based, as far as practicable, upon a count of the men first returned for each constituency at the general election. But whatever course were adopted some minor anomalies would be bound to occur, and this case is no exception. Three of the members included died before parliament met : Anthony Chamier, under-secretary of state in the southern department, died on 12 October ; Captain Robert Boyle Walsingham, R.N., was lost with his ship in the West Indies during the great gales of October 1780, but his death was not reported at home until July of the following year ; John Kirkman died on 15 September — his death was not known until six hours before the close of the poll for the City of London, and his name, after some anxious consultation by the returning officers, was included on the return of the four members duly elected — a curious instance of a dead man returned to parliament! Another three yielded their seats during November 1780 to the prior claims of relatives or of more important politicians,[1] and thirteen others subsequently lost their seats on petition.[2] A further difficulty is presented by the fact that 558 members — the full complement of the House — were not synchronously elected : two men were returned, each for three constituencies, and eleven others for two.[3] As a statistical survey requires adher-

[1] Warren Lisle (Weymouth and Melcombe Regis), Savile Finch (Malton), Daniel Lascelles (Northallerton). As a result, Gabriel Steward, Edmund Burke, and Edwin Lascelles, are not included in the statistics of this parliament.

[2] Alexander Macleod, Honiton ; Sir Thomas Rumbold, Shaftesbury, elected for Yarmouth, Hants, a few days after the loss of his seat ; Benjamin Allen, Bridgwater ; Sir Patrick Craufurd, Arundel ; Sir Thomas Hallifax and Thomas Rogers, Coventry ; John Macpherson, Cricklade (not unseated till February 1782, several months after he had returned to India) ; John Lewis, New Radnor ; Major Hugh Montgomerie, Ayrshire ; Hugh Scott, Berwickshire, who secured his re-election ; William Miller, Edinburgh ; Peter Johnston, Kirkcudbright ; Robert Baikie, Orkney and Shetland.

[3] Lord Cranborne (Launceston and Plympton) vacating both on succession to the earldom of Salisbury ; John St. John (Lostwithiel, Midhurst, and *Newport, Hants.*) ; Lord Algernon Percy (Beeralston and *Northumberland*) ; Thomas Whitmore (Wenlock and *Bridgnorth*) ; Sir James Lowther (Haslemere and *Cumberland*) ; Lord Lewisham (Horsham, Malmesbury, and *Staffordshire*) ; Filmer Honywood (Steyning and *Kent*) ; William Lowther (Appleby and *Carlisle*) ; Philip Champion Crespigny (Aldeburgh, Suffolk, and *Sudbury*) ; William Eden (Heytesbury and *Woodstock*) ; Sir

ence to the full number, the course has been adopted of including the men subsequently elected for the seats from which these members withdrew as if they had been returned at the general election.[1] Double returns were made in 1780 from Helston and Lyme Regis. The two returns from Lyme were both declared void by the House, and in this case the members are included who were chosen at the ensuing by-election in December. In February 1781 the House confirmed the return for Helston of Philip Yorke and Jocelyn Dean, and they have accordingly been reckoned for statistical purposes as the members chosen at the general election — although Dean died in November 1780, three months prior to this determination of the House which thus brought on an immediate by-election. At Coventry, where a return of 'no election' was at first made, those counted as the members are the men who were named on the second return dated 29 November 1780.

(i)

ITS PERSONNEL

(A) AGE AND TENURE OF SEATS

After the general election of 1780 the House of Commons still included some twenty members whose boyhood memories

Richard Sutton (Aldborough, Yorks., and *Sandwich*) ; John Robinson (*Harwich* and Seaford) ; Lord Frederick Campbell (Dunbartonshire and *Argyllshire*). Italics indicate the seats for which these members elected to serve. Most of the vacancies being filled within a few weeks of the beginning of the session, the principle of synchronism is not seriously violated, save in two unavoidable cases. Crespigny and Lord Frederick Campbell deferred their choice of seat pending the determination of petitions against their returns for Sudbury and Dunbartonshire respectively. The petitioners were not seated until the next year, Sir James Marriott for Sudbury on 26 April, and George Keith Elphinstone for Dunbartonshire on 14 Feb. 1781.

[1] The men subsequently elected were : John Bullock (Steyning), Francis Burton (Heytesbury), John Calvert (Malmesbury), Christopher D'Oyly (Seaford), George Keith Elphinstone (Dunbartonshire), Lord William Robert Fielding (Beeralston), George Forester (Wenlock), Sir Sampson Gideon (Midhurst), George Johnstone (Lostwithiel), Sir James Marriott (Aldeburgh), Edward Onslow (Aldborough), Sir George Osborn (Horsham), Charles George Perceval (Launceston), William Pitt (Appleby), Walter Spencer Stanhope (Haslemere), James Stuart (Plympton). Lord Cranborne,

reached back to the days when a Stuart sat on the throne of England. The father of the House was William Aislabie of Studley Royal in Yorkshire, who had behind him an unbroken parliamentary experience of almost sixty years; whose father's parliamentary memories had gone back to 1695; who had been returned, when barely of age, for the family borough of Ripon, when his father, the John Aislabie of South Sea Bubble notoriety, had been expelled by resolution of the House; and who had seen the fires of old party animosities banked down to be replaced by faction squabbles in the golden days of Sir Robert Walpole. Nearly forty years after Walpole's fall, there were still a few members who could recall his presence in the House: apart from Aislabie himself, Thomas Noel (first elected in 1728), Charles Fitzroy Scudamore (1733), Lord Panmure (1735), and John Dodd (1740); whilst General Conway, Lord Nugent, Lord George Germain, Sir Charles Frederick, and Welbore Ellis, first returned at or just after the general election of 1741, entered it in time to witness his overthrow. Of the young men first returned to the House at, or not long before, the general election, over thirty survivors were to see the passing of the old unreformed House of Commons in which their political careers had been spent — though only one of them, Thomas Coke of Holkham, remained a member until its final demise after the passage of the Reform Act, at the dissolution of December 1832 — and nearly twenty of them lived to see the crown of Great Britain pass once more to a queen.

I have been able to discover the actual or approximate dates of birth of 536 of the members elected in 1780. I thus obtain the following table of age groups:

Men born before 1721			59
,,	between 1721 and 1730		115
,,	,,	1731 and 1740	125
,,	,,	1741 and 1750	137
,,	,,	1751 and 1760	100

returned for Launceston and for Plympton, succeeded as Earl of Salisbury on 19 Sept., before having chosen for which place he would serve. In this case, for which there seems no ideal solution, I exclude him altogether, and include his successors in both seats, this course appearing less anomalous than that of arbitrarily assigning one of these seats to him.

The parliament fated to deal with the closing stages of the American War was thus slightly, but not significantly, younger in composition than the parliament of 1761. The men elected in 1780 who were over forty, that is those in the first three groups above numbered rather under 56 per cent of the House, as against rather over 56 per cent in 1761. The members aged between thirty-one and forty formed, as in 1761, the most numerous group, but their predominance was not so marked, for they comprised only 25½ per cent, as against 28 per cent; and there was in 1780 a slightly greater number of younger men: members under thirty formed 18½ per cent of the House, whereas only 16 per cent were under thirty in 1761.[1] The group of members under thirty included 53 of the 144 who now sat in the House for the first time — two of these were under age when elected — and was distributed between the government and opposition benches in very much the same proportion as the House as a whole.

Similarly, the House of Commons of 1780 differed but little from that of 1761 in the measure of experience enjoyed by the members. Concentration of political power in the hands of a limited number of noble and gentle families made for length and continuity of membership. Long, unbroken service in the House was most easily ensured by command of a pocket borough, as in the case of William Aislabie, sixty years M.P. for Ripon, 1721–81, or Henry Bankes and John Bond, both new to the House in 1780, joint proprietors of Corfe Castle in Dorset and its representatives until 1826 and 1801 respectively. But even without this advantage a long parliamentary career was possible. Wealth and social status gave some country gentlemen a sure hold on that apex of local society, membership for the shire: of the eighty English county representatives in this parliament, thirty-seven — nearly half — held their seats for continuous periods of at least twenty years. Also providing a strong element of continuity in the House were the professional politicians, great and small. Lord North entered it in 1754 and remained a member for thirty-six years; the Younger Pitt sat for twenty-six years, his rival, Fox, for thirty-

[1] Namier, *England in the Age of the American Revolution*, 249-50.

eight. And there were lesser fry of this type — men such as Richard Rigby, first returned in 1745, and a member for Tavistock for thirty-four years in the Russell interest, in virtue of his position as man of business to the fourth Duke of Bedford; William Gerard Hamilton, who sat for six different boroughs in eight successive parliaments under the aegis of various patrons; or Charles Jenkinson who as a civil servant served successive governments, in or out of office, during his twenty-five years in the House of Commons, being provided with his seat first by his friend, Sir James Lowther, and later by the government. Reckoning from the total lengths of their service in the House, the average term in parliament of the men elected in 1780 was twenty-one years.[1] After the general election, there were sixty-eight men in the House who had served continuously for twenty-one years or longer; and twenty-two of these had sat uninterruptedly for thirty years or more. The parliamentary experience of the members in the early days of the new parliament was as follows:

79 entered parliament before the general election of 1761
29 at the general election of 1761
51 between April 1761 and March 1768
65 at the general election of 1768
49 between March 1768 and September 1774
72 at the general election of 1774
69 between October 1774 and September 1780 [2]
144 in 1780, at the general election, and at by-elections occasioned by the withdrawal of men returned simultaneously for two or three constituencies.

Just over one-fourth — 26 per cent — had not sat in parliament before. As earlier, so towards the end of the eighteenth century the proportion of new members entering the House at each

[1] Excluding heirs of peers, forty-two men under thirty, returned to the House for the first time in 1780, served for an average of under 17½ years, which is below the average for the whole parliament. Seven of them died in service before they were forty, and one — Pitt — at the age of forty-six. This group appears to have had less than average fortune; but fourteen of them sat in the House for over twenty years, and eight for over thirty.

[2] The parliament elected in 1774 was prorogued on the 8th of July 1780 and dissolved in September. Henry Simpson Bridgeman, returned at a by-election in August, although in this group, ranked as a newcomer in point of parliamentary experience.

general election remained fairly constant.[1] Of the 414 members
with previous experience, the average length of parliamentary
service, up to the opening of the new parliament, was twelve
years.

Deducting from the total of 224 members elected at or
before the general election of 1768, twenty-one whose careers
in the House were broken for substantial periods between 1768
and 1780,[2] there remain 203 — 36 per cent — who sat throughout most or all of the later developments of the American crisis.
A much smaller number — 114, or 20 per cent — were
members continuously, or almost continuously, from January
1765, and so could have direct parliamentary experience of the
American question from the time when the ill-judged policy
of George Grenville first made it acute.[3]

(B) INTERESTS AND PROFESSIONS

The new House of Commons contained sixty-nine sons of
British peers, two of them illegitimate;[4] nine sons of Scottish
peers, and four sons of former Scottish peers who had suffered

[1] G. P. Judd, *Members of Parliament, 1734–1832* (O.U.P., 1955), 28–9.

[2] The twenty-one include Robert Monckton, an army officer, M.P.
1751–4, March–September 1774, and 1778–82; Lord Macartney, M.P.
1768–9, 1774–5, and 1780–1; and William Woodley, M.P. 1761–6 and
1780–4; whose careers lay in government service rather than in parliament;
and John Lewis, whose elections for New Radnor were disallowed on
petition with unfailing regularity, in 1769, in 1775, and in 1781.

[3] Grenville's Stamp Act was introduced in the House of Commons in
February and became law in March 1765. I subtract from the total number
of the members who had entered the House before the end of January
1765:

> Seven of the men sitting before the dissolution of 1761, who
> were not members during the passage of the Act: Sir Thomas
> Clavering, George Forester, Lord Westcote, Robert Monckton,
> and Robert Vyner did not sit at all in this parliament, Lord Lisburne
> entered it later, in December 1765, and John Wilkes was expelled
> in 1764:
> One man — Keith Stewart — returned at a by-election in 1762,
> who resigned his seat a few weeks later:
> Nine men in parliament during 1765 who later ceased to be
> members for substantial periods (four years or more): John Bullock,
> Sir Merrick Burrell, Sir Edward Dering, Lord Adam Gordon, John
> Henniker, Thomas Medlycott, Edward Morant, Sir George Brydges
> Rodney, and William Woodley.

[4] Hugh Boscawen and Charles Fitzroy Scudamore.

attainder after the 'Forty-five ; twenty-four Irish peers and ten sons of Irish peers ; 114 in all. A great proportion of the remaining members belonged to the gentry. The landed interest, as always, predominated. But a survey of the various professional groups in the House indicates that these made up a slightly larger number of the members than in 1761.

About eighty members were fully qualified lawyers, though over twenty of these do not appear to have pursued careers in law, at least up to this date. Some qualified men never did so, having studied the law simply to complete their education. A career at the bar was unnecessary for the heir to a great commercial fortune like William Baker,[1] or for the heads of wealthy county families such as Thomas Berney Bramston or William Chaytor. Fifty-six of the members were, or had been, engaged in active careers. Of these sixteen had retired, for reasons of age, health, wealth, or the opportunity of advancement in politics and administration.[2] Nineteen of the remaining forty held legal employments in the service of government : the Law Officers of the Crown, James Wallace, Attorney-General, and James Mansfield, Solicitor-General, Henry Dundas, Lord-Advocate, and Alexander Murray, Solicitor-General for Scotland ; Andrew Stuart, Keeper of the Signet in Scotland (also a member of the Board of Trade and Plantations) ; Sir Charles

[1] Eldest son, heir and residuary legatee of Sir William Baker, M.P., Knight and Alderman, a merchant of London. I have not come across an estimate of Sir William's fortune at his death, but by his will (P.C.C. 41 Jenner) he bequeathed to each younger son £10,000 and £400 per annum in 'long annuities', plus cash sums of £25,000.

[2] Lawyers no longer pursuing their professions were : Richard Wilbraham Bootle, Isaac Rebow-Martin, and Thomas Staunton, all old or infirm ; Thomas Farrer, who made a sufficient fortune to retire in less than four years of practice at the Calcutta bar ; Sir Fletcher Norton, at this time extremely disgruntled to find that he had sacrificed his chance of professional advancement on becoming Speaker in 1770 ; George Dempster and Christopher D'Oyly, who gave up practice on inheriting fortunes sufficiently ample for retirement — public life claimed them both, and also Sir Grey Cooper, William Eden, Bamber Gascoyne, Thomas Gilbert (formerly land agent to Lord Gower, which I class as a legal pursuit), John Kenrick, John Robinson (also formerly a land agent), John St. John, and Lovell Stanhope ; and Charles Garth, who became a colonial agent in 1765. I have not included as practising lawyers men who merely held borough recorderships. These were posts often sought for political purposes : see, for instance, on the recordership of Devizes, Namier, 'Charles Garth and his Connections', *English Historical Review*, liv, 447.

Gould, the Judge Advocate-General, and Sir John Marriott, Judge in the Admiralty Court; the legal advisers attached to various departments; Francis Cockayne Cust, council to the Board of Admiralty, Francis Eyre, solicitor for Plantation Appeals, Richard Jackson, council to the Board of Trade, and Sir Richard Sutton, council to the Board of Ordnance; William Masterman, a London solicitor, officially a legal pluralist in the Duchy Court of Lancaster and unofficially election agent for the Treasury in Cornwall and Devon; Philip Champion Crespigny, King's Proctor; John Ord, Master in Chancery, Attorney-General in the Duchy Court of Lancaster (also Chairman of Ways and Means in the House of Commons); Thomas Orde, Recorder-General in the same Court; three Chief Justices in Wales, Archibald Macdonald, Lloyd Kenyon, and Abel Moysey, and the Attorney-General for North Wales, John Parry. Of rather similar standing, though not technically in government employment, was Charles Ambler, Solicitor-General to the Queen; and the sinecurist, John Yorke, Clerk of the Crown in Chancery, may also be classed as on the fringe of this group. In addition to these office-holders, there were at least nineteen other men in legal practice in 1780.[1]

While the length of parliamentary service of the fifty-six legal members was slightly below the average, they added considerable weight to the House of Commons in the way of age and general experience.[2] They included very few young men — only five were under thirty in 1780 — and thirty-seven, about two-thirds of the group, were aged forty or above. Whereas,

[1] *Browne's General Law Lists*, 1777, 1779, and 1782, give not very reliable lists of barristers in practice in London and on the circuits. These were — William Graves, Master in Chancery, Francis Burton, K.C., Thomas Davenport, Serjeant-at-law, and Edward Bacon, Barne Barne, John Bond, Lancelot Brown, Daniel Parker Coke, Charles Wolfran Cornwall (elected Speaker in 1780), John Dunning, Sir Gilbert Elliot, Peter Johnston, Edward Norton, William Pitt, Charles Robinson, Samuel Salt, and Clement Tudway; two more must be added — John Wilmot, who became a Master in Chancery in 1781, and John Baines Garforth, who appears in the lists of Attorneys in practice in London. The total number of practising lawyers both in and out of place was thus forty, corresponding closely with the figures for 1754 and 1761 (Namier, *Structure of Politics*, 44.)

[2] Sixteen out of the fifty-six had not sat in the House before. The average parliamentary service of the remaining forty was somewhat under twelve years, and only five had sat for over twenty years.

in the House as a whole, the men between thirty-one and forty formed the largest single group, among the lawyers the largest age-group was of those between fifty-one and sixty (eighteen out of fifty-six — almost a third). Their social origins were varied, but not one could be described as a self-made man. The legal profession was a well-established channel for entry into the highest ranks of society and politics; but the ascent was not always — or even usually — made in one generation, and it is not surprising that twenty-one of the fifty-six were sons, and two more, grandsons, of men who themselves had made careers in the law. The parents of six had been engaged in trade, and another six were children of men in various other professions. The rest came from families ranging in economic status from that of Lloyd Kenyon, son of 'a landed proprietor and farmer of good education but limited means',[1] to those of wealthy landowners like the Barnes of Suffolk or the Bonds of Dorset.

The greater part of the professional lawyers — about three-quarters — supported the government. Of those who had retired, only four were reckoned as in opposition in the period immediately following the general election (Bootle, Dempster, Sir Fletcher Norton, and Staunton), and several of the others ranked among the government's 'men of business' — Sir Grey Cooper and John Robinson, secretaries to the Treasury, John Kenrick, Clerk of the Deliveries of the Ordnance, William Eden, secretary to the Lord-Lieutenant of Ireland (three, including Eden, had served as under-secretaries of state). Of the nineteen active lawyers not in office, nine — a larger proportion — were hostile to the administration, among them two leading debaters, John Dunning and William Pitt. But including the twenty-one office-holders, forty-three of the lawyers were in the ministerial camp, most of them to be classified as members of the court and administration group.

The eighteen naval officers returned in 1780 included six Flag Officers, three of them in responsible situations: Vice-Admiral Darby had just become commander-in-chief of the Western Squadron and a member of the Admiralty Board;

[1] *D.N.B.* (1908–9), xi, 30.

Admiral Sir George Rodney commanded the fleet in the West Indies; and Vice-Admiral Lord Shuldham held the post of Port Admiral at Plymouth. In this professional group the younger men preponderated, among them the talented Captain Lord Mulgrave, the explorer, exceptional in the extent of his professional knowledge, a man whose abilities had made him the main support of Lord Sandwich at the Board of Admiralty. In this parliament the naval officers were the most aristocratic professional group. Half of the eighteen belonged to the aristocracy (two were sons and one a grandson of British peers, two sons of Scottish and six of Irish peers). The majority sat for counties or boroughs in their own or their families' interest. Only one had been brought in for a government borough, Darby at Plymouth — since at this general election, most of the Admiralty seats were retained by the First Lord for civilian placemen or for personal friends who had little or no connection with the naval service.

All but five of the naval members were government supporters, but owing to their professional duties the government could never count on the attendance of more than five or six in the House of Commons. Five were on foreign service at the time of the general election, of whom two, Walsingham and Lord Robert Manners, never returned to take their seats. Even those posted to duties in home waters could not always be got to Westminster.[1] Four who were attached to the parties in opposition were out of employment and frequently in the House — Rockingham's friend, Admiral Keppel, whose breach with Lord Sandwich was complete after his court-martial in 1779; Vice-Admiral Lord Howe, who had quarrelled with the ministers the same year about his conduct while in naval command in America; Vice-Admiral Pigot, whose personal antipathies for the First Lord of the Admiralty were aggravated by intrigues in the East India House centring upon the death at Madras of his brother, Lord Pigot, after deposition by members of his Council; and Captain Peregrine Bertie, brother of the radical peer, Lord Abingdon.

[1] Lord Sandwich to John Robinson, 21 Nov. 1781, Abergavenny MS. 396.

Only forty-six army officers were returned to the House of Commons in 1780. This figure is somewhat below the average of the previous twenty years, and, at first sight, unexpectedly low for a period of war-time military expansion. In 1761, towards the end of the Seven Years War, fifty-nine had been elected.[1] In the winter prior to the dissolution of 1774 — a year before the outbreak of war in America — the number was about fifty, and in the spring of 1780 it was nearer sixty.[2] Varying, often local, circumstances contributed to the reduction at this general election, but two general causes were at work. One was the increased incidence of foreign service: some men who would otherwise have entered the House either found this react unfavourably on their chances of election, or else they gave their whole attention to the immediate opportunities and responsibilities of service abroad. Secondly, ministers, though desirous that the army interest should be well represented, were anxious to avoid the election of absent officers whose votes would not be available in divisions.[3]

As a group the army officers of 1780 conformed to much the same pattern as those of 1761. The aristocratic element was still strong, though not quite so marked — twenty were sons of peers, six held court appointments, and over a quarter were serving in guards regiments. Not one of the guards officers was a Scotsman, although, as before, Scots formed a high proportion of the group, numbering thirteen — two of these, sons of the Earl of Bute, sat for English boroughs, the other eleven represented Scottish constituencies — almost a quarter

[1] Namier, *England in the Age of the American Revolution*, 254.

[2] The *Royal Kalendar* of 1774 identifies fifty-two members as holding military rank, some of them with regiments or other appointments. That of 1780 lists fifty-nine, of whom fourteen were abroad (including two in Ireland). (These figures include the two old soldiers turned diplomats — Sir Joseph Yorke and Sir Robert Murray Keith). While the lists in the *Royal Kalendars* are not absolutely accurate, they are usually approximately correct.

[3] Charles Jenkinson wrote to Robinson on 24 Aug. 1780: 'I have consulted my brother and we can think of no military man so proper for Bath as General Amherst, and I wish it the more, as it will contribute to strengthen the army interest in the House of Commons.' And to Lord Bute he wrote on 6 Sept.: 'I think you judged perfectly right in bringing Mr. Chas. Stuart in for Bossiney and in destining Mr. Jas. Stuart for the seat which Lord North is to find for you, as the latter from his absence in the West Indies would not have it in his power to attend during the whole of the next session of Parliament.' Abergavenny MS. 292; Add. MSS. 38308, f. 2.

of the Scottish members were in the army. In distribution of rank also, this group conformed closely to the pattern of 1761 — there were eight generals, nine lieutenant-generals, six major-generals, eight colonels, five lieutenant-colonels, three majors, five captains, and two ensigns. Of the twenty-three general officers all but two held colonelcies of regiments. Seven general officers were at this time in opposition to the government, but only one of them, Burgoyne, had no regiment, having seen fit to resign it after differences with the ministers over his conduct of the operations leading up to Saratoga. Nine of the twenty-three had military governments, and six or seven had commands or staff appointments, at home or abroad. Eleven out of the forty-six were in opposition, but only two of these, Burgoyne and Richard Fitzpatrick, had no military employment.

The term 'merchant' was used in the eighteenth century to cover a variety of business activities, and it includes here men pursuing careers in banking, finance, industry, and commerce. No absolutely clear line can be drawn to separate the landed class from those who engaged in trade, and the classification of one or two of the members returned in 1780 cannot but be somewhat arbitrary. Although the following had obvious connections with business, I do not include them : John Hanbury, owner of the Pontypridd iron works; Charles Boone, part proprietor (in the right of his first wife) of Crawley's iron forges, whose mother-in-law kept the business firmly under her own control; William Pulteney, one of the richest men in England, who had personal and financial connections with East India House, and, for a time, a banking partnership with the great entrepreneur, Sir Robert Herries; Edward Eliot of Port Eliot, who dabbled in banking as a partner of William Praed during the period of the American War; or George Dempster of Dunnichen, one of the 'improving landlords' of the western Highlands, who included banking at Aberdeen among his interests. But I have included Sir Herbert Mackworth, Bart., whose name appears in the London commercial directories as head of the Gnoll Copper Company with a city office in Monument Lane, and who corresponded in this capacity with the Board of Ordnance; and Sir Matthew White Ridley,

from 1778 Governor for thirty-five years of the Merchants'
Company of Newcastle-upon-Tyne, monopolist of the mining
and shipping of coal from the Plessey district and its outlet, the
port of Blyth, and a partner, from 1780, in the newly formed
Northumberland Glass Company which took over the glass-
making business built up at Wallsend during the past century
by the families of Tyzack and Henzell.[1]

As with the lawyers, so with the merchants: the number
of members who could speak in the House from first-hand
experience of their calling was appreciably greater than the
number then actually engaged in business, for fourteen retired
merchants were returned to parliament in 1780.[2] Some of
these, like John Pringle, John Strutt, or Lord Newhaven, had
been in business for a short period only before making or
inheriting a fortune on which they could retire, but others, such
as Sir George Cornewall, Nathaniel Newnham, or Martin
Fonnereau, had been for many years well-known figures in the
City. The number of men elected in 1780 who were still
actively engaged in business was seventy-two, rather higher
than in the previous parliament (there were sixty-five just before
the dissolution) and almost half as large again as the number
returned in 1761.[3] As was usual, London merchants formed
the majority of this group, sitting mainly for various small
corrupt boroughs in the south of England. But a substantially
higher proportion than in 1761 were local merchants, representing the boroughs or districts in which their own business
connections chiefly lay: Abraham and Henry Rawlinson
(Lancaster and Liverpool), Sir Matthew White Ridley (Newcastle-upon-Tyne), Sir Herbert Mackworth (Cardiff), Henry
Rosewarne (Truro), John Baring (Exeter), Sir John Duntze
(Tiverton), Sir Henry Lippincott (Bristol), Thomas Kemp

---

[1] On Ridley, see the *Gentleman's Magazine*, 1813, 671-2 ; *The History
of Northumberland*, ix (1909), 233-7, xiii (1930), 480-1.

[2] Matthew Brickdale, Anthony Chamier, Sir George Cornewall, John
Darker, Sir Lawrence Dundas, Martin Fonnereau, Thomas Halsey, William
Hussey, Lord Newhaven, Nathaniel Newnham, John Pringle, John Strutt,
Pinckney Wilkinson ; and George Graham, who had been in trade in India
— not, however, in the service of the East India Company, though he had
been in contract with its military organization.

[3] In 1761 there were fifty (Namier, *England in the Age of the American
Revolution*, 257).

(Lewes), George Gipps (Canterbury), Clement Taylor (Maidstone). With these may also be classed Giles Hudson, M.P. for Chippenham, representative of the London clothing firm of Fludyer, Marsh, and Hudson, which had strong connections with the cloth manufacturing district of Wiltshire; [1] William Praed, the Cornish banker who sat for St. Ives; Robert Smith, a member of the great banking family whose London activities were now expanding but which still remained based in his native town and constituency of Nottingham; and the horse dealer, Thomas Fitzherbert, whose business activities seem to have lain mainly in Hampshire and Sussex, and who bought his way into the rotten borough of Arundel. Nine of these fifteen had not sat in parliament before. Together with the five merchants returned for Southwark and the City of London,[2] no less than twenty business men in this parliament had genuine professional connections with their constituencies.[3]

As a group the merchants made for age and seniority in the House, but their contribution of political experience was less than that of other groups within it. Though there are a few exceptions, it was unusual for business men to enter parliament at an early age, and few of them served for long periods. In 1780 only four had unbroken parliamentary experience of over twenty years. The ages of sixty-three out of the seventy-two active merchants have been ascertained: only fifteen were under forty, and twenty-eight were over fifty; and, as in 1761, at least three-fifths of them were over forty-five. Twenty-seven had not sat in parliament before, and thirty-four did not re-enter the House at the next general election in 1784, owing to death, permanent retirement, or the defeat of their attempts to be re-elected. Eleven of the merchants returned in 1780 died while still members before the next dissolution.[4]

---

[1] Namier, *Structure of Politics*, 129.

[2] One of the members for London, Nathaniel Newnham, had retired from business by 1779, though he later resumed activity as a banker.

[3] In 1761 the number was eleven (Namier, *England in the Age of the American Revolution*, 257).

[4] The mortality rate for the merchants returned in 1780 (over one in seven) was double the rate for the whole parliament. Of the 558 members returned at the general election (including consequent by-elections), forty-two died members of the House — a rate of roughly one in fourteen.

In 1761 the commercial group in the House of Commons had stood in close relation to the government. No less than thirty-seven of the fifty merchants in the House had enjoyed such close business relations with the spending departments as to be classed as government contractors.[1] In this respect, the picture had changed considerably by 1780. Although there were more merchants in the House, a much smaller number had large-scale business connections with the government. War contracts made by the Treasury — the greatest of the spending departments — for the supply of specie abroad and for the victualling of troops on foreign service were distributed between some thirty business houses embracing about forty individuals.[2] Only twelve of these men were among the merchants returned at the general election.[3] A very few more members had connections with the Treasury through the distribution of government loans. The published lists of subscribers to the loans of 1780 and 1781 show that (apart from small individual allocations) amounts of scrip ranging from £20,000 to £240,000 were allotted to twelve banking houses of which one or more of the heads were in parliament after the general election of 1780.[4] These were:

John and Francis Baring	Robert Mayne
Robert Drummond and Co.	Sir Robert Herries
Staples, Dimsdale and Co.	Sir Thomas Hallifax and
Ladbroke, Rawlinson and	Co.
Co.	Sir Charles Raymond, Har-
Sir W. Lemon, Furby and	ley and Co.
Co.	Smith, Payne, and Smith
Crofts, Roberts, Devaynes,	Samuel Smith and Son
and Dawes	

In November 1780 fourteen men from these firms had seats in the House. But six of them belonged to the opposition

---

[1] Namier, *Structure of Politics*, 48-9.

[2] Minutes of the Treasury Board, 1779–81, P.R.O., T.29/48-50; Debrett, *The Parliamentary Register*, ii (1781), 119-26, vii (1782), 623-37.

[3] Thomas Harley and Henry Drummond (specie contract); Anthony Bacon, Adam Drummond and John Nesbitt, John Durand, John Henniker, Sir William James and Abel Smith, Robert Mayne, John Stephenson, and Sir George Wombwell.

[4] Almon, *The Parliamentary Register*, xvii (1780), 416-23; Debrett, *The Parliamentary Register*, ii (1781), 256-68.

(J. Baring, Dimsdale, Ladbroke, Sir W. Lemon, Sir T. Hallifax, and Robert Smith — two, however, Ladbroke and Smith, were partners of men who supported the government), and another four (Henry Drummond, Mayne, Harley, Abel Smith) had government contracts, so that only four friends of the Administration not otherwise connected with it commercially received a favour in this way.[1] Only one of the big London banks with a partner in parliament — Martin's — took no share in these loans, owing to the personal idiosyncrasy of its head.[2]

Contracts were also placed by the Victualling Office of the Admiralty and by the Board of Ordnance. Neither of these bodies seems to have acted with much regard to political patronage in the distribution of its orders. In the Treasury this was, of course, a constant preoccupation, and John Robinson, who handled patronage matters, also dealt with contracts. But the Victualling Board, despite its links with the Admiralty, the head of which, Sandwich, had a particularly lively interest in questions of patronage, nevertheless had only one contractor among the merchants in parliament, the notorious Christopher Atkinson, a London cornfactor, whose malversations eventually brought retribution in the criminal courts.[3] Two members of the House only had considerable contracts with the Board of Ordnance. Anthony Bacon manufactured and supplied cannon for the armed services in addition to his victualling business for the Treasury.[4] And Thomas Fitzherbert, at various times during the American War, held contracts for the supply of

---

[1] In 1782, when North as the result of parliamentary criticism decided to distribute the loan by a 'close subscription', allocations were made to ten banking houses. Only three of the heads of these firms were in parliament — Robert Child, Henry Drummond, and Thomas Harley, the two last already holding the specie contract. Had North been thinking of distributing scrip with an eye to political considerations, he might easily have widened the field and avoided giving offence to friends like Abel Smith, who protested vigorously in the House of Commons against his exclusion (Fortescue, v, no. 3531; Debrett, vi, 292-309).   [2] Ibid. 308.

[3] Minutes of the Victualling Board, 1780, P.R.O. Adm. 111/83-4. The Board also had dealings with John Blackburn, the partner of John Stephenson, one of the Treasury contractors. But, on the whole, they seem to have made a practice of distributing numerous small orders among many lesser business men — in particular, arranging supply contracts for the various naval bases with local merchants.

[4] On his contracts, see Namier, 'Anthony Bacon, M.P.', in the *Journal of Economic and Business History*, ii, 21-68.

gunpowder from Holland, for the importation of small-arms from Liège, and for the hiring of horses to the Board in connection with work on new fortifications at Portsmouth, with the artillery train, and for other services.[1] To these businessmen connected with the government there should perhaps also be added the printer, William Strahan, in virtue of his appointment as King's Printer: [2] the position was held by patent (of which Strahan had bought a share), but he may be included among the contractors rather than the placemen, since his service to the government was essentially commercial in type.

Here in all were fifteen merchants in contractual relations with the government — not a very remarkable proportion of the seventy-two elected to parliament. Inclusion of ten other members, who did not hold contracts but had extensive dealings with government loans, raises the number of business men with substantial government connections to twenty-five, but the significant reservation must be made, that six of these were in opposition to the North ministry, business relationship making no difference to their politics. It cannot be said that the merchant group as a whole was ministerial. In fact it was almost equally divided. Thirty-six of its members were supporters of administration, including the fifteen men with contracts; but the remainder were all more or less bitterly engaged in opposition. Far from the merchants as a group being at the beck and call of the government in the House, this, of all the professional groups, included the highest proportion of members in opposition.

(c) Placemen

By the beginning of 1780 the number of placemen in the House had fallen appreciably since the accession of George III.[3] It remained virtually unchanged after the general election.

[1] Minutes of the Board of Ordnance, 1775–82, P.R.O., W.O. 47/86-99.
[2] About him see R. A. Austen Leigh, *The Story of a Printing House; being a short account of the Strahans and Spottiswoodes* (London, 1912), 1-32.
[3] See my essay, 'Economical Reform and the Influence of the Crown', *The Cambridge Historical Journal*, xii (1956), no. 2, 144-54.

First, there were about fifty members of the administration, that is, the leaders of the government, junior ministers, and civil servants. They included two cabinet ministers, Lord North, First Lord of the Treasury, and Lord George Germain, Secretary of State for American affairs. Then there were eighteen members of the four departmental Boards — six from the Admiralty, four each from the Boards of Treasury, Ordnance, and Trade. Below these came six regular 'civil servants': two Secretaries of the Treasury, the Secretary to the Admiralty, one Under-Secretary of State, the Secretary-at-War, and the Commissary-General of Musters. Next come five financial officers: the Paymaster-General, his deputy, the Treasurers of the Navy and of the Ordnance, and the Paymaster of Marines. In this group may be classed also twelve men holding legal appointments: the Attorney and Solicitor-General, the Judge Advocate-General, the Judge of the Admiralty Court, three Welsh judges, legal advisers to two of the Boards, the Attorney-General for North Wales, and the Lord-Advocate and Solicitor-General for Scotland. There were two professional diplomats, both absent from England, Sir James Harris (Petersburg) and Sir John Stepney (Dresden); and, lastly, the Chief Secretary in Ireland. Here were forty-six men in the House holding efficient government posts under the Crown. As might be expected, the total is very close to that for 1761.[1]

[1] Namier, *England in the Age of the American Revolution*, 258-60, where the number is given as 43. The difference between 43 and 46 is partly due to my inclusion (*en bloc*) of four members of the Board of Ordnance. I conclude from a perusal of the Board's minutes from 1775 to 1781, and from reports of parliamentary debates, that none of the posts on this Board can be correctly described as sinecures in this period. All four junior members regularly attended the very frequent meetings of the Board, and all took part in conducting its business in the House of Commons. Accordingly I would class as a 'man of business' Sir Charles Cocks, an official of over thirty years' standing in this department, who as Clerk of the Ordnance was responsible for all its clerical and financial routine; and this description can, I think, also be extended to his juniors, Henry Strachey and John Kenrick. Each officer of the Board had his definite responsibilities; when Strachey attended as a new member on 10 July 1778, with his patent of appointment to the junior place, that of Clerk of the Deliveries, 'the Book of General Instructions was presented to him by the Clerk of the Ordnance, and he took his seat at the Board accordingly'. And a formal 'deputation' had to be signed by Cocks authorizing Kenrick to act for him, when Cocks intended a prolonged absence in 1781 (P.R.O., W.O. 47/92, p. 43 and 47/97, p. 363).

There is, however, no such conformity with the earlier figures in respect of other categories of placemen. It has been estimated that there were in 1761 about fifty members holding sinecures and between forty and fifty court officials.[1] By 1780 these numbers had been reduced by nearly half. After the general election there were not more than about twenty-seven members of parliament holding sinecure offices, nor more than thirty with court appointments — twenty-four in the King's household and six with places in the households of other members of the royal family. Allowing for one or two appointments which may have escaped detection, and one or two places that may have been held in trust, there were in round figures about 110 members holding efficient offices, sinecures, and positions about the Court.

The number of officers in the armed services not already included in previous categories was fifty-six: the figure was practically the same as in 1761, for although there were fewer army officers in parliament in 1780, only six (out of forty-six) held court appointments. Of the eighteen naval men two members of the Board of Admiralty are included in the total of government servants.[2]

Finally twelve men returned to the House of Commons were in receipt of pensions from the Crown, but only four of these had no place under government.[3] About three of the pensions there was no secret whatsoever. Sir Richard Sutton

[1] Namier, op. cit. 260-2.

[2] After the general election in 1780 not one naval member of the governing body of Greenwich Hospital was sitting in the Commons: Palliser, its Governor, entered the House at a by-election a little later. But there were three civilians, for Sandwich had disposed of part of this departmental patronage to his political friends — John Clevland, Martin Fonnereau, and Sir William James, whom I have included among the holders of sinecures.

[3] The pension lists for this date are well documented. A statement of pensions paid by the paymaster of pensions at the Exchequer was laid before the House of Commons in March 1780 (Almon, *The Parliamentary Register*, xvii, 216). This is supplemented by a list in a manuscript book relating to changes in the establishment in 1782, preserved among the papers of the Marquis of Rockingham (Fitzwilliam MSS. R. 219, Sheffield City Library). The secret service accounts of John Robinson for the period Jan. 1779 to Apr. 1782, with a statement of the position as at the end of Mar. 1782, are in the British Museum (Add. MSS. 37836, ff. 58-140), and those of Sir Grey Cooper for the greater part of the same period are in the Royal Archives at Windsor Castle. Also, some of Robinson's memoranda are in print (Laprade, 49-50, Fortescue, v, 467-9).

and Lovell Stanhope had both been granted pensions payable at the Exchequer on termination of service as under-secretaries of state : these were included in the list of pensions laid before the House in the spring of 1780. A similar grant, chargeable on the $4\frac{1}{2}$ per cent office, had been made to Henry Strachey when he ceased to be secretary to the Commission (held by the brothers Howe) for restoring peace in America. All three also had places — Stanhope a court office, the others efficient posts.

Ten members of parliament were in receipt of secret service pensions, but the additional number is nine only, for these include Lovell Stanhope, who appears in both lists, his secret service pension being held in trust by William Cory. Of the rest, payments to Charles Garth and to Thomas Johnes were in lieu of places, which were found for both within a few months of the general election; so was the pension to John Mayor, in consideration for services to the Treasury in connection with the excise duties on paper. The £500 per annum paid to John Ord was by way of salary in recognition of his services as Chairman of Ways and Means in the House of Commons. Thomas Bowlby's pension was in lieu of a loss of salary on changing employments. Sir James Cockburn's stood in the name of his wife and was a charitable grant. Only three of these pensions had a direct political significance to which the squeamish might take exception. John Dodd had begun before 1760 to prise large sums out of the Duke of Newcastle for the support of his interest at Reading ;[1] and no known contemporary account of him makes reference to any other service to the state or to the government of the day which would justify a pension of £750 a year in and after 1779. George Selwyn's pension was for his interest at Ludgershall, where he controlled both seats and habitually placed them at the disposal of the Treasury.[2] Finally James Macpherson was the hired scribe of the government.

Including with the 110 officials and sinecurists the 56 officers in the fighting services, 15 merchants with contracts, and

[1] Namier, *Structure of Politics*, 217, 220, 427, 429, 434, 439, 451, 457, 463, 470, 476, 480.
[2] Fortescue, v, 469.

4 recipients of pensions who had no other provision,[1] the aggregate total of placemen in the new parliament may be stated in round figures as about 180. The number was lower by about a quarter than the high peak reached about 1761. This circumstance certainly counsels caution about giving credence to the Rockingham party's insistence on the necessity for Economical Reform.[2] It is doubtful if placemen had any particular significance in relation to the working of the parliamentary system at the close of North's ministry. About 1780, as twenty years earlier: 'Not every one who held a place, office, commission, or pension was truly dependent on the Government, while among those who do not appear in this list, there were many men bound to it by the strongest ties and ever ready to serve it'.[3]

(ii)

ITS POLITICS

In 1780, as during the past five years, parliamentary politics were dominated by one issue, the American War. The campaigns for Economical or Parliamentary Reform were but by-products of this great argument. On one side or the other of this conflict the various parliamentary parties had taken their stand, and to it was subjoined the normal rivalry of 'Ins' and 'Outs'. The opposing sides ranged in the House of Commons appeared to have achieved a certain permanence — on the one hand, North's ministry pledged to the subjugation of the colonies, and on the other the groups of members who condemned the war as fratricidal and ridiculed its object as unattainable. This clash over high policy heightened the semblance to a two-party system in British politics. On the surface all was a struggle between two parties. But such an interpretation of parliamentary politics would be misleading, and would leave much unexplained regarding the organization

[1] On the contractors see pp. 182-4 above. The four pensioners were John Dodd, Charles Garth, Thomas Johnes, John Mayor.
[2] See my essay, 'Economical Reform and the Influence of the Crown', *The Cambridge Historical Journal*, xii (1956), no. 2, 144-54.
[3] Namier, *England in the Age of the American Revolution*, 262.

of the House of Commons and the springs of political power. How, then, was the House organized? What were the instruments of power within it?

The House of Commons of the fourth parliament of George III formed no exception to the normal eighteenth-century pattern. Certain slight and temporary modifications of the political structure had been induced by the stress of the American War, but it had suffered no basic change. The members, according to the general tenour of their political behaviour, fell broadly into the old, familiar groups — the independents, the circle of court and administration, and the political parties — each group fulfilling its proper and separate role in the working of the parliamentary system. Parties, if slightly more fixed and stable as a result of the prolonged controversy about America, still displayed something of the old kaleidoscopic quality: multiplicity and diversity remained their chief characteristic. Despite the clash of two bitterly opposed opinions in the House, there were not two parties but several, and they differed considerably in type and in aim.

Evidence about the political conduct of the members of this parliament is fairly abundant, not only in printed sources of biographical information but also in contemporary division lists and analyses of the House.[1] Still not every member can be neatly pigeon-holed under one or other political classification. It is easy to distinguish the main body of the independents, or of the court or the nuclei of the political parties. But the unevenness of the available information about individuals, the absence of papers, or such circumstances as a man not being a good correspondent and writing never or rarely to his friends and patrons, renders the picture inevitably incomplete. Furthermore, men on the borderlands between the various groups in the House are difficult to classify, and no finality can be claimed for some of the judgments made here upon particular individuals. Members who acted fairly regularly with leaders of the opposition or who gave constant support to the government were sometimes indistinguishable from independents; and the place-hunting followers of ministers

[1] See Appendix I, pp. 373-5 below.

overlapped with the men of the court and administration group, from whom, in type, they were often hardly dissimilar. But the broad lines of the picture are sufficiently clear. Generally speaking, of the members elected in 1780 about a third belonged to one or other of the various political parties. Here some change had indeed occurred over the last twelve years, though one of degree only rather than substance : the American War had hardened party divisions and had increased the number of members of rather independent type who voted with parties upon principle and conviction; twelve years before, not more than a quarter of the members had belonged to political parties.[1] About 220 of the members returned in 1780 — rather over a third — were independents, and the rest — about a quarter of the House — belonged to the court and administration group.

(A) THE INDEPENDENTS

The terms 'independent' and 'country gentleman' were often used interchangeably to describe this type of member. But the second description carries a suggestion of homogeneity of social type which is not really found, and for the sake of clarity the word 'independent' only is used below to describe the men in this category. County members were often independents *par excellence*, like Rolle of Devon, who, Robinson complained, was 'not to be depended upon in any trying question'.[2] But many independents sat for other types of constituency. Some — the Drakes of Amersham were an example — were returned for borough seats over which they had established a leading influence or complete control.[3] Others sat by negotiation with borough patrons.[4] The independents were never exclusively country gentlemen. They invariably included some townsmen — examples in this parliament were the four members for the City of London, and the representatives for Southwark and from two or three of the

---

[1] J. Brooke, *The Chatham Administration, 1766–1768* (1956), 386.
[2] 'State, 1780', 12, Windsor MSS.   [3] Laprade, 43.
[4] *E.g.* Charles Boone (Ashburton), P. C. Methuen (Great Bedwin), *ibid.* 44-5, 46.

larger provincial towns. Indeed, some of the merchants were among the most aggressively independent members in the House. James Martin, member for Tewkesbury, and head of one of the great banking firms in London, explained in debate in 1782 : 'He had never applied for any part of a loan, not wishing to add a penny to his fortune, by taking advantage of the public necessity, and being determined not to contribute any the least assistance towards carrying on the abominable, ruinous and wicked American War'. This self-denial was not due merely to temporary political considerations : a year later he refused, and with indignation, the offer of a share in the loan, made to him by Shelburne, head of a peace ministry of which he approved. 'He connected himself with no party', Oldfield wrote afterwards in his *Representative History*, 'but voted upon every question agreeably to the dictates of his own upright mind, except when he was instructed by his constituents, whose opinions he thought it his duty, most implicitly, to obey, in conformity with the constitutional practice of the purest times.' [1]   In an analysis of the members sitting in this parliament in 1783, John Robinson distinguished 104 'country gentlemen and persons unconnected', whose political conduct was unpredictable. These included thirty-five out of eighty English county members and eight out of the twelve Welsh county representatives — it is small wonder that contemporaries were inclined to equate independent with county member. But there were also among these members some twenty representatives of large and medium-sized open boroughs. There were eleven members sitting on their own family interest for close boroughs and a rather smaller number who had obtained seats for close boroughs by negotiation with the patrons.[2] Allowing for the exceptions in the last two categories, the independents were usually distinguished by being members for popular constituencies with sizable electorates and at least some element of active public opinion.

The essential characteristic of the independents was their detachment from both the Court and the political parties.

---

[1] Debrett, vi, 308 ; T. H. B. Oldfield, *Representative History*, iii, 491.
[2] Parliamentary List, Melville MSS.

But clear-cut distinctions can never be drawn : borderline and exceptional cases are always to be found in analyses of the eighteenth-century House of Commons. It is difficult, for instance, to class Sir Gilbert Elliot or John Sinclair, both members for Scottish counties, as other than independents at this early stage of their political careers. Although the first later became a regular associate of Fox and Portland, and the second would have liked, and eventually got, an opening in the government service, at this time they regarded themselves as tied neither to the Court nor to a party. In general, however, the independents were men who did not enter into the competition for honours and places of profit, the acceptance of which would have brought obligations binding them to the Court or to the train of some leading politician. Consequently, whatever the local interests and the social prejudices which helped to form their opinions, these were not tinged — or at least not greatly — by a limited party point of view ; nor were they biased by the corporate outlook developed by those who made their careers in the King's service, in the army, the navy, the court, or the civil administration. They kept their freedom of judgment intact, committed themselves to no leader, and accepted only the guidance of their own natural understanding. Deference was paid to them, partly because it seemed that, unswayed by such partial considerations, they could most effectively speak for what were regarded as the great abiding interests of the nation — land and trade — partly for the more prosaic reason, that their co-operation was essential if governments were to govern or oppositions to triumph. Their support in parliament was courted on all sides, and the most conservative politicians admitted their excellence, while not following radical reformers in a desire to increase their numbers.

The independents were never a party (this, indeed, would have been a contradiction in terms). But the idea of an organized group of independents strong enough to sway political events had, nevertheless, its attractions, especially for young members. Thus, in September 1780, William Morton Pitt, son of John Pitt of Encombe, the 'great commoner of the west', wrote in these terms to his intimate friend, Lord Herbert

— both young men were in their twenties, had only been elected within the past ten days, and had not yet entered the House as members : 'We are now both in Parliament. . . . I long much to talk with you further on the subject. I believe we shall agree that it is better as well as more prudent not to appear to come with a predetermined intention of siding uniformly with one or the other set. Surely it is possible to act an upright, independent and respectable part in Parliament : yet I am told not. I hope you feel yourself bold enough to try it : be assured of one thing that if a number, and even a very small number fall into that channel they must acquire consideration, and collect a greater force daily.' [1] Yet, by definition, the independent members lacked the qualities and outlook which would enable them to cohere in parties or to unite for practicable political objects. Only eighteen months later, when John Sinclair and other independents came together with the intention of preserving North's government while bringing the American War to an end, they succeeded only in helping to precipitate that minister's resignation.[2] Nor did subsequent attempts at constructive action by independents in 1784 and in 1788 bear much relation to political realities or prove productive in their effects.[3]

From this type of member variety in action might be expected, not combination. Among the 220 or so independents were men of many varying shades of opinion, ranging from association with one or other of the elements supporting the government to quasi-connection with groups in the opposition. In July 1780 Robinson found himself with an irreducible core of thirty-five members whom he was compelled to assign to his categories of 'hopeful' and 'doubtful'. Most of these continued to sit in the next parliament. 'Mr. Whitbread is a very doubtful uncertain man for either side,' he noted when drawing up his State prior to the dissolution, 'but if either way I think may be reckoned more hopeful to go in general with government, though certain in popular questions.' 'Lord Newhaven

[1] *Letters and Diaries of Henry, tenth Earl of Pembroke*, ed. Lord Herbert (Cape, 2 vols., 1939, 1950), ii, 42-3. [2] Sinclair, *Correspondence*, i, 80. [3] *The Annual Register*, 1784-5, 268 ; Sir Lewis Namier, *Personalities and Powers*, 31.

stands and expects to come in again, he is sometimes with, at others against, but he professes great friendship.' 'Mr. Darker shuffles, and is a doubtful man.'[1] One result of the general election was to double the number of 'uncertain' members, and in the State which he prepared in February 1781 Robinson put down some seventy as 'hopeful' or 'doubtful'.[2] In certain cases this was due simply to lack of knowledge regarding new men who had not yet taken their seats, but for the most part these members were otherwise unclassifiable, even by this experienced parliamentary manager. Thus most of these seventy may be regarded as independents *par excellence*. But they do not exhaust the examples of this type, which seems to have flourished in opposition. The independents noted by Robinson in February 1781 as hostile to the government numbered about a hundred and ten. Not more than about fifty of them appear from their voting habits or from other evidence to have had some sympathy with the Rockinghams. In a few cases this indeterminate association approached the fringe of party connection : examples are Filmer Honywood, M.P. for Kent, and the friends he brought in for Steyning ;[3] or George Hunt of Lanhydrock, member for Bodmin, about whom in 1782 Robinson was clearly unable to make up his mind.[4] According to Robinson, some forty of the independents were to be classed as friends of the government at the beginning of 1781, among them such county members as Bramston, Chester, and Sir Thomas Egerton, Brickdale and Henry Rawlinson from Bristol and Liverpool, and leading figures in Scotland like Sir Gilbert Elliot, John Sinclair of Ulbster, and James Wemyss, the member for Sutherland. Thus about 90 of the 220 independents inclined to one side or the other in the House of Commons. The rest, about 130, remained entirely unconnected — a total which corresponds reasonably well with the figures of 104 members placed in this category in 1783 and of 108 in 1788.[5]

[1] 'State, 1780', 3, 8, 21, 47, Windsor MSS.
[2] Abergavenny MSS.
[3] Laprade, 92.   [4] *Ibid.* 47.
[5] Parliamentary List, Melville MSS. ; Parliamentary List and analysis, Guilford MSS.

(B) The Court and Administration

By contrast with the independents, conformity in political conduct was the characteristic of the members in the court and administration group. These members were identified by their common readiness to give support to any ministry of the King's choice. Like the independents, men in this group did not compete for the highest offices in the state, and kept aloof from the strife of parties, but they differed from them in one important characteristic — their interest in places. And they sought permanence of employment by emphasizing their direct connection with the Crown.

Little space need be given here to discussing the members in this group. Generally it embraced two types — the professional men and the courtiers. These types were perennial, and it is not necessary to present more examples from this parliament to add to those described in the first section of Sir Lewis Namier's *Structure of Politics at the Accession of George III*. The group included a high proportion of the professional men in parliament. There were hard-working administrators like Sir Charles Frederick of the Ordnance, Philip Stephens, Secretary to the Admiralty, and Charles Jenkinson, the Secretary-at-War; the lawyers who held, or aspired to, government appointments; the officers of the fighting services, and the great merchants (a privileged minority of their class) whose business activities included government contracts. Side by side with these men, concerned as many of them were in one way or another with active work of government, were the members of slightly different social type who staffed the court. In general the latter came from a more restricted circle, but there was never any clear-cut distinction between these and the professionals. Thus Thomas Harley and Henry Drummond, the London bankers who held the American specie contracts, both came from aristocratic families, and Charles Jenkinson's origins and connections were among the gentry. If the courtier's work was of a different kind, it might be no less onerous, as appears from Fanny Burney's descriptions of life in the Queen's household a few years later. No distinction can be made on this ground : the courtier was not by definition a sinecurist. Sinecures indeed there were, held both by courtiers and by professional men ; but they were by no means always the perquisites of 'political parasites', being often awarded as a form of pension after a period of strenuous public service.

Although this section of the House had a certain cohesion, the description of 'party' can no more be properly used to describe it than to describe the independents. It lacked one important attribute of party — political leadership. This was provided by the factions associated together in the government —that is, in 1780, mainly by those led by Lord North, by the Earl of Sandwich, and by Earl Gower.

(c) THE PARTIES

The third section of the House of Commons embraced those members who belonged to the various political parties, large and small. At the heads of these parties were the great politicians (most of them in the Upper Chamber), whose ambitions and talents drew them to compete for the high offices of state. It was the interplay of the parties which created and constituted national politics, which gave dynamism and vigour to the parliamentary machine. Vehicles for the expression of wills and points of view, and for the healthy clash of opinions, they were also to some extent instruments of political power. True no eighteenth-century politician derived from his party following alone sufficient power to lay down government policy or to dictate to the King his choice of ministers. But the King on the other hand could not with impunity flout at the same time several leaders of major parties. Only by reliance on some of them could he free himself from the importunities of one whom he disliked and form a ministry congenial to his taste ; and if those whom he preferred failed him, this freedom disappeared. Thus, about 1780, the parties were not instruments of political power to the extent they afterwards became. They did not yet perform the function of furnishing alternative administrations; but they did provide the material for alternative ministerial combinations. The architects of eighteenth-century governments built in parliament on a triple basis. One element in the resulting structures was constant — this was the court and administration group. Another, changeable, was the body of well-disposed independents. The third, also a changeable element, was the party following. The essential condition for a parliamentary majority, without which a government could not stand, was the recruitment in combination of a sufficient force of party followers. In the lifetime of this parliament, the process was to be displayed to the full. Between 1782 and 1784 nearly every practicable combination of the major parties was to be tested in turn, before a stable successor was found to the war-shaken ministry of Lord North. And just as ministers could not stand by virtue of their party-strength alone and looked for other support to the court and the independents, so politicians in opposition sought other means of influence in the only part of the House where they might find it. They usually drew with them a fair proportion of the independents, and at a time of crisis their power depended on the extent to which they could influence still others to go with them.

What was the distribution of strength among the parliamentary parties in 1780 ? What were their characteristics and who their leaders, and what, if any, the political distinctions between them ?

THE GOVERNMENT'S FOLLOWING

Of the three major parties on the government side of the House of Commons, the largest was that attached to Lord North. This was as might be expected. Politicians, to be sure, might attain the leading place in administration without the advantage of party. George Grenville had done so in 1763 — but his abilities were outstanding, and he had been 'adopted' by Bute. North reached the same situation, not by connection, but by virtue of the parliamentary talents which brought him to the notice of the King. 'Though nobly born', Lord Dacre wrote in 1772 to the Earl of Guilford, 'he is as little indebted to connections or the powerful support of great persons as if he had been a Novus Homo.'[1] But in no circumstance did a First Lord of the Treasury hold office for long without attracting a substantial group of supporters.

Tracing the membership of this party presents a certain difficulty, for the ranks of a minister's following tended to merge into the main body of the court and administration, and were often not easily to be distinguished from it. This problem does not arise with the groups in opposition. A spell in opposition purged parties of their half-hearted associates and fair-weather supporters. Ministerial parties always included men of both descriptions, who regarded themselves as clients whilst their patron was in office, but, for one reason or another, were disinclined to go with him into opposition. Thus a minister's resignation provided a sort of acid test of his following, making clear which of them would adhere to him in adversity.

The connections North formed, like those of other First Lords of the Treasury, arose often out of some favour or service which he could perform in virtue of his official position. Others were created by association in office. Even if such friendships commenced over some material bargain, place or pension or contract, yet sometimes honour and respect prolonged them and set upon them a more worthy cachet : plentiful warnings against too cynical an interpretation of eighteenth-century faction politics are provided by the examples of members who, having once enrolled themselves in the service of a political leader, adhered to him through good and evil fortune. Edward Gibbon, after the fall of North's government, kept in mind the fact that North had given him a place at the Board of Trade. As he wrote afterwards, of the events of 1783 : 'From a principle of gratitude I adhered to the coalition : my vote was counted in the day of battle, but I was overlooked in the division of the spoils'.[2] William Jolliffe

---

[1] 21 June 1772, Bodleian Library, North MS. D. 14, f. 175.
[2] The Autobiography of Edward Gibbon, as originally edited by Lord Sheffield, with an introduction by J. B. Bury (O.U.P., 1907), 199.

similarly, in memory of favours received, adhered to North after his loss of power, although desertion might have paved the way to satisfaction of his hopes of a peerage founded upon the claims of his wife. Long afterwards, in an autobiographical memoir he recorded : [1]

> On his [Lord North's] junction with the Duke of Portland, he recommended me to the Admiralty. This I held until that connection were entirely dismissed, and tho' I was assured I might continue in my office if I chose to support the new government of Mr. Pitt and that my claims for my wife would be equally considered, I thought myself pledged to the other connection and therefore wrote to Lord North to desire he would take such steps as he thought proper to signify my resignation . . .
>
> On my arrival in London Mr. Robinson earnestly requested me to avoid going to the House, and I have no doubt was authorized to give me full assurances of the attainment of my wishes, but as I had always acted on principles of consistency, I determined not to depart from them on this occasion : I went immediately and gave my vote, as did my brother, with the Opposition. Soon after this it being understood that the Duke of Portland was to be the head of that connection, Mr. Keene [2] desired he might introduce me to his Grace (and he told me Lord North had in the fullest manner recommended me to him).

How slight might be the obligation that created such a bond of loyalty can be seen from the following example. One of the fortunate aspirants to a seat in parliament in 1780 was Charles George Perceval, a half-brother of the third Earl of Egmont. Robinson secured leave from North to recommend Percival to the Duke of Northumberland as a suitable friend of government to be returned for Launceston. From that time Perceval regarded himself as one of North's followers. Three years later Fox's East India Bill thrust upon him a conflict of loyalties. Unable in conscience to support this measure, he

[1] Hylton George H. Jolliffe (Baron Hylton), *The Jolliffes of Staffordshire and their Descendants* (1892), 56-7.
[2] Whitshed Keene, M.P. Montgomery, married to a stepsister of Lord North.

felt obliged to suggest to North that he resign his seat — a course from which he was only dissuaded by strong assurances, both from the Duke and from Robinson.[1]

Not long after North had gone out of office, in the summer of 1782, William Eden considered that, 'he could on *very* easy terms answer for thirty or forty, quite as personal friends and followers'.[2] Examination of the personnel of the House of Commons confirms this judgment.[3] This party was entirely the creation of North's years at the Treasury. Before 1770 little more than half of its members had been in the House, and they had not acted together. North's character is a sufficient explanation of this circumstance. Even though he had no great territorial power behind him, his family connections were not insignificant, and more might have been made of them had he been, what he was not, the type of man to fashion and lead a parliamentary party. In 1780 he had more or less close family connections with at least twelve of the men supporting his ministry, including his son, George; the son (Lord Lewisham) and the brother-in-law (Whitshed Keene) of his step-brother, the Earl of Dartmouth; and his cousin-german, Sir George Osborn. Through his wife he had connections with two other members, William Graves and Sir Richard Sutton. Through the family of his paternal grandmother, Alice Brownlow, he had links with the Custs, Francis and Peregrine, and with Lord Robert Bertie, M.P. for Boston. His father's third marriage, to Katherine, Dowager Countess of Rockingham, daughter of Sir Robert Furnese, Bart., gave him a family contact with Sir Edward Dering (whose first wife had been her sister), and with her nephews, Henry and John St. John, sons of Viscount St. John by her half-sister, Anne. Of these men, Bertie and the Custs belonged

[1] Add. MSS. 38567, ff. 165-6, 171.
[2] *Journal and Correspondence of William Lord Auckland* (4 vols., 1861-2), i, 29.
[3] The party of about this size must be distinguished from the larger mass of a hundred or more members who were reckoned to be acting with North in the winter of 1782-3 — a number which included independents and bewildered followers of the court and administration thrown out of office by Rockingham and uncertain as yet how best to return to the fold (H.M.C., *Carlisle MSS.*, 633-4; Buckingham, *Courts and Cabinets of George III*, i, 158).

to the court rather than to North's following, and Dering rather to the independents; but eight of them can be counted as of his party. North also had personal links with other groups in the Commons, though these had little or no party significance: his stepsister, Anne Legge, had married a Brudenell, member of a court family with extensive connections, and his cousin-german, Elizabeth Montagu, had been the first wife of Lord Hinchingbrooke, the son of his ministerial colleague, the Earl of Sandwich.

Eight relations constituted alone the firm core of a party following, but North's other friends in the House brought his party to a strength which made it one of the largest in parliament. First there were his particular friends and his professional connections at the Treasury — Charles Townshend of Honingham, an ex-Rockinghamite, had been brought on to the Treasury Board in 1770; Lord Palmerston and Lord Westcote had been promoted to it in 1777; and connections of a professional type which had become, or were in course of becoming political, existed with Sir Grey Cooper, one of the secretaries to the Treasury and with John Mayor, who had been employed in an advisory capacity. Then, obligation, though with less personal contact, drew in others. William Adam, at first a most unpredictable member of the House, finally attached himself to North in 1779, a connection welded the following year by the grant of a government post. P. C. Crespigny had obligations to North, and he carried with him his cousin, Martin Fonnereau, an independent 'but well inclined to government'.[1] William Jolliffe and Edward Gibbon had successively occupied a seat at the Board of Trade under North's auspices: the former had a promise of a peerage, and he drew into the party with him his brother, Thomas Samuel Jolliffe. Hans Sloane had been appointed to the Board of Trade by North in 1780. The Fane family was closely connected with North: Henry Fane had been given a court sinecure in 1772, and he brought into North's camp his wife's uncle, David Robert Michell. Lord Melbourne had received his peerage from North in 1770. Abel Moysey, made a Welsh

[1] Laprade, 43.

judge in 1777, 'owed his place to Lord North',[1] and the
Attorney-General and Solicitor-General appointed in 1780 —
James Wallace and James Mansfield — both recognized a
political obligation to him. The border between North's
following and the administration group is difficult to define,
but perhaps the following members also came within the ambit
of his party : John Buller, senior, for long a member of the
Admiralty Board and promoted to the Treasury in 1780 ;
Charles Greville, another of North's appointees to the Board of
Trade ; and Henry Penton, made a Lord of the Admiralty in
1774, whom North tried to push into a court appointment in
1780. Next, there were a number of men who stood on terms
of affection, obligation, and loyalty towards North in 1780,
but who found themselves unable to follow his coalition politics
in 1783 : Henry Dundas, the Lord-Advocate ; Adam Drummond, the banker, a government contractor, who, during the
American War, broke off his political connection with his
brother-in-law, the Duke of Bolton, in order to side with
North ; Lord Fairford, the son of one of North's political
associates, the Earl of Hillsborough ; C. G. Perceval, who felt he
owed his seat in parliament to North ; and John Robinson, the
junior secretary to the Treasury, whom North clearly regarded
as one of his followers right up to the moment of their breach in
January 1784. Between 1779 and 1785 William Eden was place-
hunting with North's group, but his was a sort of conditional
membership, and it is perhaps incorrect to class him as fully
a follower of North. Lastly, men of a more independent type
whose support for North had something of the consistency of
party attachment were John Campbell, Francis Charteris,
William Dickinson, Sir John Eden, and William Hanger. This
roll of members gives a total for North's party of nearly forty,
which accords well enough with Eden's estimate. It is hardly
possible to be more specific. No less than thirty-five other
members are identified as friends of North on both of the lists
prepared in February and March 1783, but their connection
with him was not so close as to justify their being classed as
members of his party. Four — Lord Lisburne, Lord Mul-

[1] *Laprade,* 45.

grave, Peter Delmé, and John Purling — belonged to other factions associated with North at this period. Five more — Francis Basset, William Clive, Sir Charles Farnaby, George Johnstone, and Lord Sheffield — were independents rather than party men. Most of the rest can be classed as of the court and administration group rather than followers of North ; [1] but a few of them, particularly Sir William Cunynghame and John Kenrick, are doubtful cases, and in the absence of other evidence, either positive or negative, possibly an allowance for two or three more members of North's party should be made.

Next to North's own following, the chief parties supporting the administration in 1780 were those of the Earl of Sandwich and Earl Gower.

Sandwich, formerly a member of the group of peers which headed the Bedford party, was by this time at the head of a separate parliamentary faction. His family connections in parliament were less extensive than those of North, and his own electoral influence was by no means considerable, being confined to three of the four seats in the county and town of Huntingdon (though he added to this, so long as he remained in office, the influence exerted by the Admiralty in various sea-ports). Nevertheless, despite these limitations, he had by assiduous labour built up a strong following in the House of Commons. No one understood better than himself that the continued existence of this group depended on his retention of his office and the control of patronage which that afforded. 'At present', he wrote to North on 26 March 1782, 'my parliamentary interest is very considerable. Your Lordship knows that it is so without my naming names, but if I am reduced by my circumstances to live in absolute retirement, that interest will soon sink to nothing, and my means of doing any service to this distressed country be utterly annihilated.' [2]

---

[1] Clearly belonging to the court group, judging by the general tenor of their careers, were Christopher Atkinson, Anthony Bacon, Sir James Cockburn, Nathaniel Curzon, Welbore Ellis, Sir Charles Frederick, Bamber Gascoyne and his son, John Halliday, John Henniker, Sir George Howard, Edward Lewis, James Macpherson, P. P. Powney, Lovell Stanhope, William Strahan, Sir Richard Worsley, and Nathaniel Wraxall.

[2] H.M.C., *Abergavenny MSS.*, 53, no. 463.

In establishing this interest, Sandwich employed two main channels — the Admiralty and the East India House.

Sandwich's connections with East India House went back at least to 1754, and before 1780 he had established there a personal position recognized as 'unique' — one created, however, for the purpose of strengthening his political position in general, not for that of inter-meddling in the affairs of the Company.[1] His friends in parliament after the general election included two leading directors, Sir William James and Sir George Wombwell (but the latter died a few weeks after the elections), a third director, John Purling, the son of another former director, John Pardoe, junior, and John Durand, a member of the East India shipping interest. He commanded also the support of George Stratton, a former servant of the Company who was under suspicion of complicity in the intrigues against Governor Pigot at Madras. Stratton was brought in, by the arrangement of Sandwich, for Lord Orford's borough of Callington, and may have looked to Sandwich for protection against further attack by Admiral Pigot and his friends in the opposition.[2] In this group also were Sir Walter Rawlinson, the brother-in-law of Wombwell, and John Stephenson, an old commercial contact of over thirty years standing, who had served him in the East India House in the seventeen-sixties. As a result of the efforts of John Robinson to extend government influence within the Directorate (which Sandwich loyally assisted), no less than four of these eight members — Durand, James, Stephenson, and Wombwell — were possessed of government contracts in 1780.

Sandwich's naval friends were less numerous. He could count among them Lord Mulgrave and his brother, Charles Phipps, and the unreliable Sir John Borlase Warren, whose wavering conduct in 1782 drew down imprecations on his head from both Robinson and Sandwich. Mulgrave was his leading assistant at the Admiralty until 1782, and other members whom

---

[1] L. S. Sutherland, *The East India Company in Eighteenth Century Politics* (Oxford, 1952), 125, 277-8.
[2] L. S. Sutherland, 318-20 ; *Parliamentary Characters, 1779-1781*, 56 ; Abergavenny MSS. 254, 269, 396, 461.

he selected to assist him on the Board were Lord Shuldham [1] and Sir Hugh Palliser,[2] both of whom he regarded as to some extent his followers. Apart from Sandwich's connections through the Admiralty and the East India Company, he could count on his son, Lord Hinchingbrooke, and three personal friends: Lancelot Brown, son of the famous landscape gardener, 'Capability' Brown, the retired diplomat, Sir William Gordon, and John Morshead of Trenant Park in Cornwall, all of whom owed their parliamentary seats to him. About 1780 he could thus call on seventeen friends in the House of Commons.[3] But not all the members of this group were equally attached to him, one or two of them sharing rather the outlook of the court and administration party. Sandwich himself, less than three years later, put his party strength in the Commons at no more than twelve.[4] As he foresaw, his following soon began to disintegrate after he lost office, and the process was hastened by his adherence to the Coalition, a course in which his own son eventually refused to support him. With the establishment of the Pitt ministry, his 'rats' began to slip away. Mulgrave accepted a place — though, as Sandwich evidently refused to re-elect him for Huntingdon, he had to wait till the general election, when he was offered a seat by the Duke of Newcastle.[5] Palliser, in a long and dignified defence of his conduct, in language reminiscent of that used by Robinson to North,[6] warned Sandwich, 'Your Lordship

[1] H.M.C., *Cornwallis-Wykeham-Martin MSS.*, 315; Fortescue, iv, 297; Abergavenny MS. 396.

[2] By arrangement with Robinson, Sandwich brought in Palliser for Huntingdon in 1780, vice Wombwell, in order to provide a counter-blast to Admiral Keppel (Add. MSS. 38214, f. 230). But Palliser did not resume his place on the Admiralty Board, which he had resigned in 1779.

[3] Robinson's list of March 1783 (Melville MSS) included as friends of Sandwich all these members except John Purling (omitted in error) and Sir John Warren who had by then parted with him. It adds one other, Admiral Darby, another of Sandwich's appointments to the Admiralty, who is, I think, more correctly classed as of the court and administration group.

[4] Sandwich to Hinchingbrooke, 16 Feb. 1783, Sandwich MSS.

[5] Mulgrave to Sandwich, 23 Dec. 1783, Sandwich MSS. By March 1784 Mulgrave had already found another seat, but he then accepted Newcastle's unsolicited offer of one at Newark (Mulgrave to Newcastle, 20 Mar. 1784, Newcastle MSS.).

[6] My essay, 'The Political Allegiance of John Robinson', *Bulletin of the Institute of Historical Research*, xxix (1956), 122.

knows my rule of conduct is not to oppose the King and his government', and resigned himself to exclusion from politics as Sandwich would not have him re-elected for Huntingdon : 'As to myself I do not mean to embarrass ministers with anything about myself . . . if I am to be driven down deeper into obscurity than I am I can't help it'.[1] Before April 1784 Hinchingbrooke, Pardoe, and Stephenson had quietly entered the ministerial ranks, the two last being provided with seats by Lord Mount Edgecumbe at the ensuing general election, probably by negotiation through the Treasury.[2] Two or three more of Sandwich's friends, Durand, Shuldham, Stratton, found themselves without means of securing re-election. Only four of his old followers who remained faithful to him — Brown, Morshead, Purling, and Rawlinson — survived the elections and continued to support him in opposition. This was the natural fate of a party composed largely of 'fair-weather friends' and of men who also had other connections with the government.

The party led by Earl Gower was very different in type. Professional or commercial connections played very little part in holding it together, family and electoral interest a great deal. At this time Gower headed a little junto of peers formerly associated with the fourth Duke of Bedford — his colleagues were his brother-in-law, the Duke of Bridgwater (who took only a small direct interest in politics and let himself be guided by Gower), and his close associate, Viscount Weymouth. Between them they controlled eight seats in the House of Commons. On the death of Bedford in 1771, Gower had virtually succeeded to the leadership of the 'Bedford Party' (of which his friends formed a large part of the rank and file), and this description of the group remained current for another decade. But he was able to hold together only part of it. Some of its members, the Fitzpatricks and John Bullock, broke away into opposition after the beginning of the American War.

[1] 7 Mar. 1784, Sandwich MSS.
[2] Parliamentary memo., Jan. 1784, Laprade, 54-5 ; parliamentary list, British Museum ref. 1850. d. 26(62) ; election memoranda, Laprade, 108, 124, 128.

So did Gower's sister, the Dowager Duchess of Bedford, who retained control of a substantial part of her husband's electoral interest and exerted it against the government in 1780, in Westminster, Bedfordshire, and elsewhere. Another of its leading men, Lord Sandwich, had proceeded to build up his own separate following. By 1780 Gower's group in the Commons numbered little more than a dozen — a substantial size, nevertheless, for an eighteenth-century party. Nearly half of these were connected with him by family relationship. His son, Lord Trentham, and his son-in-law, Archibald Macdonald, came in for his borough of Newcastle under Lyme, and his nephew, Sir John Wrottesley, sat for Stafford county with the aid of the strong Gower family interest there. There were his brother-in-law, Richard Vernon of Hilton, and John William Egerton, a distant relative of his first wife. By his second marriage with a daughter of the Earl of Galloway, Gower had developed a connection in Scotland, and his wife's brother, Captain Keith Stewart, R.N., was member for the county of Wigtown. The party was strong in 'men of business'. In addition to Macdonald, a professional lawyer, appointed a Welsh judge in 1780, there were Thomas Gilbert, the poor-law reformer, brought in by Gower for Lichfield, formerly for many years in his employment as land agent, and Richard Rigby, now paymaster, who had acted as secretary, factotum, and general agent to the Duke of Bedford. In addition to these members, Gower's brother-in-law, Bridgwater, and his ally, Weymouth, brought into parliament for their boroughs their friends, John St. Leger Douglas, Andrew Bayntun, and Timothy Caswall; while Rigby controlled the political conduct of his nephew — the heir to his estate of Mistley — Francis Hale. Gower's connection (as father-in-law) with the fifth Earl of Carlisle attached two more members in the Commons to his party — Carlisle's brother-in-law, Peter Delmé, and his friend, Anthony Storer.

Until a year before the general election both Weymouth and Gower had held cabinet office, but neither now had a place in the government. Gower had thrown up his post in October 1779. Ostensibly he did so because unwilling further to share responsibility for the weakness displayed by the administration with regard to the affairs of Ireland and the American War. But he was suspected of intending to force the King to give up North, whose nervelessness and inactivity were considered the chief causes of this weakness, though it never became clear what alternative arrangement, if any, he contemplated.[1] Weymouth had followed his lead. But when this 'Bedford conspiracy' (if such it was) failed,[2] its makers would have nothing to do with a formed opposition, and the division lists show that, with one or two exceptions, the members of the party voted regularly and consistently to the last on the side of North's ministry. A pillar of the group still remained in the cabinet in the person of Lord Chancellor Thurlow, and other followers of Gower continued to hold minor office.

These three main ministerial parties were backed by various minor groups, most of them of a family type. Of the other ministers, Lord Bathurst, the Lord Privy Seal, brought in his brother-in-law, James Whitshed at Cirencester. He had also a nephew in the Commons, John Buller of Morval — but Buller was no very reliable supporter, being offended at North's failure to satisfy his importunate demands for office.[3] Germain, the American Secretary, was a member of the Commons, and nominated with himself at East Grinstead his friend, Sir John Irwin. Lord Lisburne, a colleague of Sandwich at the Admiralty, carried with him his brother, General Vaughan, and his brother-in-law, Robert Shaftoe.[4] Then there were minor politicians among the great aristocratic patrons, whose

---

[1] H. Butterfield, *George III, Lord North and the People, 1779-1780* (1949), 117-38.

[2] A letter from Rigby to Lady Spencer, dated 26 Mar. 1780, referring to the events of October 1779, suggests that little credit should be given to the idea of a 'conspiracy' by Gower and Weymouth. Their resignations were not concerted with their political friends. After they had gone out, Rigby, thinking the ministry too weak and ineffective, would have liked to complete its destruction by further resignations, in the hope of securing a strong coalition government prepared to continue the American War. But he felt nothing could be done without the support of Thurlow, who refused to be a party to any such manœuvre. Spencer MSS.

[3] On John Buller, see my paper, 'Private Patronage *versus* Government Influence . . . at Saltash', *English Historical Review*, lxxi (1956), 249-55.

[4] *Journal and Correspondence of William Lord Auckland*, i, 29; Laprade, 46, 95.

ambitions were satisfied with court offices, sinecures, and favours. The Duke of Newcastle contributed four supporters. His brother, Sir Henry Clinton, absent as commander-in-chief in America, sat for Newark, and there were also his son, Lord John Clinton, and his friends, Anthony Eyre and Charles Mellish; for his other two borough seats, Newcastle accepted government nominees. The Earl of Hertford, Lord Chamberlain of the Household, had not yet attained what was perhaps the unique distinction of having five sons sitting at one time in the House (this occurred in 1784 and again in the years 1788 to 1790), but three of them were elected in 1780. Although Hertford had clung to his place through successive changes of administration for nearly twenty years, this brotherhood was on the whole a political group. His eldest son, Lord Beauchamp, for six years (1774–80) a member of North's Treasury Board, spoke fairly often in debates and comported himself as if having some pretensions to be considered an active politician and not merely a courtier; after 1783 he and his brothers adhered to North in opposition. Support for the administration came also from the Duke of Northumberland, Master of the Horse, who in 1780 opened most of his borough seats to government nominees, but returned his friend, John Coghill, for Newport in Cornwall, while his influence secured one of the county seats in Northumberland for his son, Lord Algernon Percy. The two Clives, and their friend, Henry Strachey — a member of the Board of Ordnance — also gave their votes to North's government. Altogether, these ministerial parties, large and small, included between eighty and ninety members of the House of Commons.

A second part of the government's following came from among the independents. This was partly due to North's popularity among some of the country gentlemen, an asset which he particularly valued; and there were others who regarded him less favourably but supported his ministry because they agreed with its policy. From the calculations made by Robinson in February 1781, it appears that North could depend on about forty of the independents, whilst another twenty or so were hopeful.

The rest of the government's majority came from the court and administration group. Excluding those members holding places who have already been enumerated among the followers of particular leading politicians, there remain about a hundred and forty who belonged to this category. Among these too, there were family groups and affinities. There were, for instance, five members connected with the Brudenells. Charles Jenkinson was related to the Cornwall cousins, Charles and Frederick, and had ties of friendship with the sons of Lord Bute. But it would not be profitable to pursue these connections further. No such importance attaches to them as to those which have already been discussed. The parliamentary significance of men like Jenkinson sprang not from such associations (however important these might have been to them individually in promoting their careers) but from their devotion to the King's service in court or in administration. In this group were to be found the civil servants, the lawyers whose careers were linked up with service to the Crown, many of the officers in the fighting services, the government contractors (though with some of these their personal connections with North or Sandwich counted for more), the courtiers and sinecure-holders; and most of the Scottish members, whose detachment from the leading English factions made it natural for them to support whatever government the King saw fit to entrust with his affairs.

THE OPPOSITION

The most numerous of the parties which constituted the opposition in the new House of Commons was that led by the Marquis of Rockingham. The core of this group is easily identified; the main difficulty arises in defining the penumbral zone where it merged into the amorphous body of the independents. One fairly expert estimate of its size was made by Richard Rigby about eighteen months after the general election. A few days after Rockingham's death, Thurlow told Gower: 'Fox . . . carries out with him the immediate friends of Lord Rockingham, all the Cavendishes, the Spencers, Keppel,

Burke, etc., to the number of about fifty or sixty, as Rigby computes it, in the House of Commons'.[1] As this description suggests, Rockingham's following was to some extent an agglomeration of squadrons rather than a single party: but its strength was here rather underestimated.

The three parliamentary lists extant in the Lansdowne, Melville, and Guilford papers, provide the primary evidence regarding the membership of this group. First there is the roll of forty members in Shelburne's list of about November 1782 who were then regarded as definitely hostile to his government. Thirty of these were returned at, or just after, the general election, and there is ample evidence from other sources, that almost all of these were members of the 'hard core' of the party.[2] Next, Robinson's list of March 1783 attributes to Fox's party seventy-seven of the men returned at or just after the general election.[3] Twenty-seven of these are as in the Shelburne list: eighteen of the remaining fifty appear again as followers of Fox five years later, in the list preserved in the Guilford papers.[4] Adding to Robinson's list the names of Sir George Savile, Lord Verney, and John Webb, who appear as members of this party in Shelburne's list, a total of eighty members is obtained. Some of these, however, can be set aside. One, John St. John, was a friend

[1] (C. 7 July 1782), H.M.C., *Fifth Report*, Appendix, 211.

[2] The thirty were: Lord Althorp, William Baker, Lord Edward Bentinck, John Bullock, Edmund Burke, George Byng, Lord John Cavendish, Lord G. A. H. Cavendish, Sir Robert Clayton, Lord Duncannon, Thomas Dundas, Charles Dundas, Richard Fitzpatrick, C. J. Fox, Booth Grey, W. H. Hartley, Dudley Long, Frederick Montagu, Sir J. Ramsden, Sir George Savile, R. B. Sheridan, Richard Smith, J. M. Smith, Lord Robert Spencer, Thomas Stanley, John Townshend, Lord Verney, Horace Walpole, John Webb, and William Weddell. The one doubtful case is Webb, who supported Shelburne's peace preliminaries, but he appears as a member of Fox's party in 1788.

[3] Seventy-three of these are in the list of eighty-nine names headed 'Mr. Fox's connections', plus three from the 'Army' list and one from the list 'Public Offices'.

[4] George Dempster, Henry Fletcher, Edward Foley, Andrew Foley, John Harrison, Thomas Lister, Lord Maitland, Edward Monckton, William Nedham, C. A. Pelham, William Plumer, St. Andrew St. John, John Sawbridge, Thomas Scott, John Scudamore, W. C. Sloper, J. S. Stewart, Edward Winnington. All these members except Stewart voted with Fox on the Regency question, six months after the compilation of this list. Unfortunately it is incomplete, thirty-four names beginning with the letters A, B, and C being on a page which has not survived.

of North rather than of Fox. Three more, John Courtenay, John Craufurd, and John Nesbitt, were not acting with Fox before 1782. Another, General Richard Smith (with whom went his son, J. M. Smith) often co-operated with the Rockingham party, but he was rather allied to it for the pursuit of his particular East India House interests than a member of it. A further seventeen members, from their general conduct and apparent lack of connection with any leader of the Rockinghams, are more correctly to be classed as independents. However, to the fifty-seven members who thus remain [1] there must be added another twenty [2] who in 1780 had an appreciable connection with Rockingham, but who were not so shown in Robinson's list owing to deaths, absences, miscalculations, and changes of political allegiance.

[1] The letters in brackets after each name indicate the list(s) in which it appears : L — Shelburne's list, Nov. 1782, Lansdowne MSS. ; M — Robinson's list, Mar. 1783, Melville MSS. ; G — North's list, May 1788, Guilford MSS. :

Althorp, Lord (LM)
Anderson, F. E. (M)
Baker, W. (LM)
Bentinck, Lord E. (LM)
Benyon, R. (M)
Braddyll, W. (M)
Bridgeman, Sir H. (M)
Bullock, J. (LM)
Bunbury, Sir T. C. (M)
Burke, E. (LM)
Byng, G. (LM)
Cavendish, Lord G. A. H. (LM)
Cavendish, Lord J. (LM)
Clayton, Sir R. (LM)
Coke, E. (M)
Coke, T. W. (M)
Coxe, R. H. (M)
Dempster, G. (MG)

Duncannon, Lord (LMG)
Dundas, C. (LM)
Dundas, T. (LMG)
Fitzpatrick, R. (LMG)
Fletcher, H. (MG)
Foley, A. (MG)
Foley, E. (MG)
Fox, C. J. (LMG)
Gascoigne, Sir T. (M)
Grenville, T. (M)
Grey, B. (LM)
Harrison, J. (MG)
Hartley, W. H. (LM)
Honywood, P. (M)
Hotham, Sir R. (M)
Lister, T. (MG)
Long, D. (LMG)
Maitland, Lord (MG)
Minchin, H. (M)

Monckton, E. (MG)
Montagu, F. (LMG)
Pelham, C. A. (MG)
Plumer, W. (MG)
Ramsden, Sir J. (LM)
Savile, Sir G. (L)
Scudamore, J. (MG)
Sheridan, R. B. (LMG)
Sloper, W. C. (MG)
Spencer, Lord R. (LMG)
Stanley, T. (LMG)
Stewart, J. S. (MG)
Tollemache, W. (M)
Townshend, J. (LM)
Verney, Lord (L)
Walpole, H. (LMG)
Walpole, R. (M)
Webb, J. (LG)
Weddell, W. (LMG)
Winnington, E. (MG)

[2] Barrow, C.
Bridgeman, H. S.
Burgoyne, J.
Cavendish, Lord R.
Clerke, Sir P. J.
Crewe, J.
Davers, Sir C.

Dundas, Sir L.
Gregory, R.
Keppel, Admiral A.
Keppel, General W.
Lucas, T.
Ludlow, Earl
Pigot, H.

Rawlinson, A.
Salt, S.
Thompson, B.
Upper Ossory, Earl
Vanneck, Sir G. W.
Walpole, T.

In this great phalanx of opposition, there was first the section of the party centred directly upon Rockingham himself. Family connection played little part in this formation, though two of its members, Sir John Ramsden and William Weddell, were related to Rockingham's wife and all three households were on terms of intimacy.[1] To a much larger extent, it was based upon a coalition of Yorkshire politicians, comprising (as well as the Weddells of Newby, the Ramsdens of Byram, the Cavendishes, the Lumleys and other local families), Sir Thomas Gascoigne of Partington, Beilby Thompson of Escrick, Savile Finch of Thriberg (who resigned his seat at Malton in favour of Edmund Burke soon after the general election), and Sir George Savile of Thornhill. Savile may be included, for although he was by no means dependent on Rockingham, stood high in his own right among the gentlemen of Yorkshire, often voiced opinions contrary to those of the Marquis, and in general formed views less coloured by partisan spirit and therefore often more balanced, nevertheless, on the great political questions of America and Economical Reform, he was in substantial agreement with Rockingham and was prepared — as a colleague, not as a subordinate — to co-operate with him. The three members of the Dundas family of Fingask, with their seat at Aske controlling the parliamentary borough of Richmond, were, in some sort, though mainly a Scottish connection, a part of Rockingham's Yorkshire group. This was an extremely new development in 1780. A family connection with Rockingham had been established in 1764, when Thomas, the only son of Sir Lawrence Dundas, was married to his niece, Charlotte, sister of the fourth Earl Fitzwilliam. But at that time, the marriage had no political significance. Sir Lawrence, formerly a government contractor, moved in ministerial circles and maintained a valued friendship with the Earl of Sandwich. For many years the Dundases acted with the Bedford party, in its train became supporters of the Grafton and North ministries, and in 1779 were still regarded as on

[1] Rockingham's mother-in-law married secondly Sir John Ramsden, 3rd Bt., and her children by him included Sir John Ramsden and the wife of William Weddell.

the fringe of the Gower group. Disquiet over the course of the American War, and perhaps also disappointment over a peerage, brought them into opposition in 1780. In addition to the connection with Rockingham, Sir Lawrence's nephew, Charles (through his mother, a daughter of the sixth Earl of Lauderdale), was first cousin to Lord Viscount Maitland, one of the able young men newly returned to the House, who attached themselves to Fox.

Outside Yorkshire, Rockingham's group included a number of individuals, some of them men of rather independent type, drawn by ties of friendship or political principle into the circle of the Marquis or of his friend and adviser, Edmund Burke. Rockingham returned for his borough of Higham Ferrers his Northamptonshire friend, Frederick Montagu (whom in 1780 he would have liked to see Speaker of the House). There were the Keppels: Admiral Augustus Keppel had been associated with Rockingham early in the reign, had refused to serve at sea against the colonists at the outbreak of the American War, and, though accepting command of the Channel fleet at the commencement of war with France in 1778, retired in high dudgeon, greatly incensed against ministers in general and Sandwich in particular, after the enquiry and his court martial which followed the battle of Ushant. His brother, General William Keppel, followed his political line. William Baker, the eldest son of Sir William Baker, Newcastle's business adviser, came into parliament under Newcastle's auspices in 1768, and continued thereafter on terms of friendship with Rockingham and Burke. He made parade at times of his 'independence': thus, in 1774, he sought advice or a recommendation from Rockingham for some borough where, 'at a price not exorbitant, I may be elected with certainty, and have the free use of my vote on all occasions. . . . These two conditions are with me indispensable, for I can never be reconciled to the idea of sacrificing my conscience in the support of measures I disapprove, nor my fortune in establishing interests in which I have no real concern.' But these protestations do not obviate the fact that he steadily and freely maintained a political association with Burke and Rockingham and later with

Portland.[1] George Dempster of Dunnichen, and the East India director, Robert Gregory, both, like Baker, protested their independence but were drawn by their convictions to act very consistently with the Marquis. Conviction, or personal esteem, would appear to have prevailed over the place-hunting appetites of Earl Ludlow and Sir Robert Clayton, who both pleaded years. of loyal service when requesting places of emolument after the Rockinghams came into office in 1782.[2] Charles Barrow and Ralph, Earl Verney, were friends whom Burke drew with him into the party.

Another substantial section of the Rockingham party was grouped round the Duke of Portland and the Cavendish relations of his wife, who was the only daughter of the fourth Duke of Devonshire. Portland himself had a wide, miscellaneous political connection. It included his brother, Lord Edward Bentinck ; Booth Grey, the brother of his brother-in-law, the fifth Earl of Stamford ; George Byng, the 'muster-master' of the opposition, whom Portland had provided with a seat for Wigan in the two previous parliaments ; Henry Simpson Bridgeman, whom he brought in there in 1780, and his father, Sir Henry Bridgeman ; and Henry Fletcher of Clea Hall, Cumberland, a director of the East India Company, an independent man but much associated with Portland, to whose influence and support he owed his tenure of a seat for his native county. Portland also maintained contact with various country gentlemen (some of whom at times represented their shires), whose political conduct placed them as party supporters rather than independents — John Bullock of Essex, Richard Hippesley Coxe of Somerset, William Plumer of Hertfordshire, and John Scudamore of Hereford. To Scudamore was due the entry into parliament in 1780 as a member of the party of Thomas Lucas of Lee in Kent, a South Sea Company director. Samuel Salt, a lawyer and also a director of the South Sea Company, was a regular supporter of the party, at least from

[1] Add. MSS. 32988, f. 44, 32989, ff. 7, 227 ; Rockingham MSS., R. 1-839, 913, 976 ; *Correspondence of Edmund Burke* (4 vols., 1844), ii, 44-6, 86-92, 205-7 ; 'Sketch of the Life of Mr. Baker', by his son, Robert George Baker, Bayfordbury MSS., Herts. R.O.
[2] Rockingham MSS., R. 1-1137, R. 109-8b, 8c.

about 1771, and his connection with it was probably due to his close friendship with William Plumer. General Honywood, brought in by Lord Thanet for Appleby, had connections both with Portland and the Cavendishes.

Portland's Cavendish friends and connections included two sons of the late fourth Duke of Devonshire, elected on the family interest for the county and town of Derby, and one of Devonshire's brothers, Lord John Cavendish, chosen for York with the assistance of Rockingham. Lord John's nephew, Viscount Duncannon, was returned for the Cavendishes' pocket borough of Knaresborough. The marriage of Lord John's sister, Rachel, to Horatio, second Baron Walpole of Wolterton, brought in another family connection, four members of which sat in the Commons in 1780 — Walpole's son, Horatio, returned for Wigan on Portland's interest, his two merchant brothers, Richard and Thomas, and their brother-in-law, Sir Gerard William Vanneck, the last three all sitting on their own or their family interest for East Anglian boroughs. Friends and associates of the Cavendishes were Abraham Rawlinson and Wilson Braddyll, who sat for Lancaster, and Dudley Long of Saxemundham in Suffolk. Lastly, William, fifth Duke of Devonshire — now head of his house but not active in politics — had married in 1774 Georgiana, a daughter of John, Earl Spencer, and her brother, Lord Althorp, headed a further group of four members in the Commons. These included, besides Althorp himself, Lord Spencer's friends, Humphrey Minchin, and W. C. Sloper, returned on his interest for Okehampton and St. Albans, and Althorp's cousin Wilbraham Tollemache — who, although returned by Shelburne's arrangement for one of Edward Eliot's Cornish boroughs, acted not with Shelburne but with the Rockinghams. Minchin nursed pretensions to be considered a man of business, to judge from the frequency with which he intervened in debates and the special attention he devoted to questions of naval and military administration — efforts which brought their due reward in a place at the Board of Ordnance in the Coalition Government of 1783.

The other main constituent group of the Rockingham party

was the circle of Charles James Fox. Here was a formation of a different type, based neither on family relationship nor on territorial interest, but largely on personal attraction. Fox carried with him into politics the friends he made among the young men of fashionable society, whom his dazzling talents and unruly, uninhibited behaviour drew to his side. Several, like Admiral Pigot, shared with him the bond of slavery to the gaming tables at Brooks's. John Crewe and his wife had early been drawn into Fox's intimate circle and provided funds to help meet his gambling debts. His brothers-in-law, the Fitzpatricks, John, Earl of Upper Ossory and his brother, Richard, originally members of the Bedford party, were won over by Fox to the opposition as early as 1775. Three years later Fox was active in securing the adherence of Burgoyne. And, at the beginning of 1781, he carried over another friend, Lord Robert Spencer, although Spencer's brothers, Lord Charles and the Duke of Marlborough, remained firm supporters of the government. Coke of Holkham attached himself to Fox from the time of his first entry into parliament, and with him went his brother, Edward, a new member in 1780. Among the other new members, Sheridan was already Fox's boon companion, and the young men, Lord Maitland, St. Andrew St. John, and John Townshend, were either in his circle or gravitated rapidly towards it about the end of 1780, modelling their parliamentary conduct upon his example. Before long the youthful Thomas Grenville was also drawn into his following. On the fringe of the group was Edward Monckton, Sheridan's colleague at Stafford. By marriage he was nephew to Pigot, and both men had bones to pick with Lord Sandwich and with his East India friends about naval affairs and the late events at Madras. Fox's friends thus already numbered over a dozen in 1780, and formed a substantial addition to the opposition.

Furthermore, the Rockingham party received consistent support from various individuals and minor groups. Three peers who gave support to the leaders of the opposition, the Duke of Bolton and the Earls of Derby and Bristol, each had a member in the Commons attached to their interest and brought

in with the aid of their electoral influence — Sir Philip Jennings
Clerke (Totnes), Thomas Stanley (Lancashire), and Sir Charles
Davers (Bury St. Edmunds). Another, Lord Foley, had two
brothers, Andrew and Edward Foley, and a brother-in-law,
Edward Winnington, in the House. Thomas Lister brought
to Rockingham's support his own vote and that of his brother-
in-law, John Parker, his fellow-member at Clitheroe, whose
seat he made available when the Rockinghams wished to bring
John Lee, as Solicitor-General, into the House in April 1782.
Another magnate who cast in his lot with Rockingham was
Charles Anderson-Pelham, 'one of the richest commoners' in
England, who represented the county of Lincoln. With him
went his brother, Francis Evelyn Anderson, and his friend,
John Harrison, brought into parliament on his interest for
Beverley and Great Grimsby.

Adding together these various groups a total is obtained
of seventy-two members constituting the main mass of the
Rockingham party in the newly elected parliament of 1780.
This still leaves out of account four or five of the men named
in Robinson's list of March 1783, who stood somewhere on
the fringe of the party. Richard Benyon had been brought in
at Peterborough with the assistance of Rockingham's nephew,
Fitzwilliam. Sir Thomas Bunbury was an uncle by marriage
of Fox and maintained an occasional correspondence with
Burke. W. H. Hartley was drawn into the party in the wake
of his half-brother, David, who was at this time temporarily
without a seat in Parliament: David Hartley was a protégé of
Sir George Savile and active in the counsels of the Rockinghams.
Letters in Rockingham's papers show that Sir Richard Hotham
was regarded as one of his connections about 1780. John Shaw
Stewart was a friend of Fox, Burke, and Sheridan. Roughly
speaking, the strength of the party at this time was about
eighty, but it is impossible to state a precise figure, for there
were some men on its fringe whose exact relationship with it
defies definition.

Recruited rather more exclusively than the House as a
whole from the wealthy landed gentry and aristocracy, the
Rockingham party included roughly one member for every

seven in the House of Commons, a proportion which nearly held good for its complement of serving officers and merchants, but which did not obtain in one important respect. It boasted only one practising lawyer in the House, Samuel Salt, and in relation to its size it was comparatively weak in 'men of business'. As to parliamentary talent, it included three men of the first rank, Burke, Fox, and Sheridan. Despite the remarkable gifts of the first and last of these men, Fox stood supreme, by virtue of his sheer capacity for business, his abounding vitality, and his ability to present a party case. Fox had not a tithe of the stability of character of such leading figures of the party as Sir George Savile or Lord John Cavendish. But though men of the highest integrity, they were by comparison with him mediocre and inarticulate : his talents made him indispensable to the party.[1]

Such a party was not easy to lead. Some of its members were in no way dependent upon the magnates associated with Rockingham. They acted with them in free association, based on common hostility towards North's government and its policies, but they were not amenable to direction, and their erratic attendance and behaviour were the despair of a thorough party man. Burke noted in December 1782, in a letter to Burgoyne : 'On paper we are strongest of all, but we never can appear with true numbers. Our people act from principle, and, of course, very irregularly, and many of them very feebly. Some do not come to town at all, some will not appear early ; and as the principle is formed with a firmer or weaker tone of understanding there is more or less system.' There was, however, he noted, one consolation : 'Among the disadvantages of our party, which arise from their general integrity, and they are very very many, we have this one advantage, equal indeed to almost all the others, that very few of the corps are disposed to betray us for their interest'.[2]

Still, despite the rather heterogeneous composition of the party, it had a strong cohesion. With one or two exceptions

[1] Fitzmaurice, *Life of Shelburne* (2 vols., 1912), ii, 70.
[2] E. B. de Fonblanque, *Political and Military Episodes . . . from the Life and Correspondence of . . . John Burgoyne* (1876), 419-20.

(and allowing for changes due to deaths and electoral defeats), all these members accepted Fox and Portland as their leaders after the death of Rockingham, and held firm in their allegiance until the party was broken in two by the impact of the French Revolution a decade later. Mere family relationship could not bind so large a formation. Family connections within it were, indeed, not negligible, but they played less part in its structure, and the ties of personal and political loyalty more, than in most of the other parties. Ambition also can be a party bond, and there were ambitious men in this party as in others — but there were also men who, like William Plumer, sought no place or favour from the Crown, or who, like Coke, aspired to peerage, but desired no office or other honour. So many men of diverse outlook and independent cast of mind could only be drawn together by more general factors — especially admiration and affection for their leaders and agreement on great issues of policy. In their different ways, both Fox and Rockingham exerted a personal attraction upon their following. It was in tribute to the magnetism of Fox in these years, that the cold, self-possessed William Pitt spoke of 'the wand of the magician'.[1] With none of Fox's ability or *élan*, Rockingham had a patient sweetness of disposition, which brought him many friends, and a considerable capacity to placate and conciliate men. 'As to getting various persons to give way and agree to one opinion', Richmond once wrote to him, 'that is your forte, and very far from mine'.[2] As for policy, unity grew out of the fact that many of the men in this group thought or felt alike, deeply and bitterly, on the question of the American War. The resulting sense of common purpose generated a momentum and a conserving force which held the party together for years after the achievement in 1782 and 1783 of its main objective. In 1770 Burke's political associates had fallen far short of his famous definition of a 'party': there was little trace among them of its essence, devotion to an agreed set of principles of policy. By 1780 a party in this sense had

[1] Stanhope, *Life of Pitt* (4 vols., 1861–2), i, 133.
[2] Albemarle, *Memoirs of the Marquis of Rockingham* (2 vols., 1852), ii, 268. See also Horace Walpole's judicious assessment of him, letter to Sir Horace Mann, 1 July 1782.

come into being, and, once established, survived the principles and circumstances which had first given it life.

In 1780 the members of the party had a precise programme before them. The fratricidal war against the colonists must be wound up, even if the price were the recognition of American independence. And a judiciously selective measure of Economical Reform was intended to reduce the centripetal pull exerted in politics by the Crown and to facilitate — as critics of the party never wearied of pointing out — the tenure of office by an aristocratic clique. Indeed, driven by mind and heart to defend the constitutional rights of Englishmen in America, many of the opposition were led into strange and hardly orthodox positions regarding that British Constitution which they claimed to be defending. But it was left to Charles Fox himself to boast in March 1782, 'that this revolution which he brought about was the greatest for England that ever was; that excepting in the mere person of a King, it was a complete change of the Constitution'.[1]

No other organized parties on the opposition side of the House could compete with the Rockinghams in point of voting strength or extent of interest. The remaining active politicians who devoted their energies to attacking North's administration were divided amongst various small groups and connections, or acted independently.

There were, first, two factions so closely associated at this time with Rockingham as nearly to form constituent parts of his party. These were the friends of the Duke of Rutland and the Earl of Abingdon. But neither of these groups belonged so intimately to the Marquis's following as those which have previously been considered.

Rutland was good-natured and convivial, but had no claim to distinction except the fact that he commanded about six members in the new House of Commons. From his father, the Marquis of Granby, he had inherited a legacy of co-operation with Rockingham; and letters to him from the Marquis suggest that the latter regarded him as one of his following.[2] But no place was found for Rutland or his relations when the

---

[1] H.M.C., *Carlisle MSS.*, 604.
[2] Albemarle, ii, 186; H.M.C., *Rutland MSS.*, iii, 10, 14, 34.

second Rockingham administration was formed in March 1782, and his group was soon to shift its ground and seek office under the auspices of the younger Pitt. Six members of Rutland's connections were returned to the House at the general election. In addition to his family interest at Scarborough, and a controlling influence over three other borough seats, he had sufficient weight in the counties of Cambridge and Leicester to carry one seat in each. All but one of the six were relatives — this was indeed a perfect example of the family group in politics. They included his brother, Lord Robert Manners, his brother-in-law, Lord Tyrconnel, his uncle, Lord George Sutton, and his cousin, George Sutton. A fifth, Thomas Thoroton, was married to a great-aunt of the Duke born out of wedlock. William Pochin, M.P. for the county of Leicester, was unique in the group in not standing in any degree of relationship with its leader.

To this section of the opposition a distinguished addition was made shortly after the general election, when Rutland procured from Sir James Lowther a seat at Appleby for his close friend, William Pitt. In so doing he was to find, in a year or two, that he had recruited not a follower but a leader. His circle was to form the core of Pitt's own party, into which various young independents were soon attracted — Lord Camden's son, and Eliot's, Henry Bankes and Robert Smith. Within eighteen months, Dundas was urging that Pitt's group should be recruited to support the tottering North administration; and about the same time, George Selwyn described Pitt as 'at the head of a dozen young people . . . a corps separate from that of Charles; so there is another *premier* at the starting post, who, as yet, has never been shaved'.[1]

Lord Abingdon's faction was smaller and less coherent. Two of his close relatives sat in the Commons, his brother-in-law, Lord Wenman, for Oxfordshire and his brother, Peregrine Bertie, for Oxford city. In addition, he returned two clients for Westbury, John Whalley Gardiner, and the West Indian planter, Samuel Estwick, and his interest at Wallingford helped to secure the election there of another West Indian,

[1] H.M.C., *Abergavenny MSS.*, 50, no. 440A; H.M.C., *Carlisle MSS.*, 518, 593.

Chaloner Arcedeckne, and of John Aubrey, an independent who inclined towards Shelburne. An intimate friend of Rockingham, and, like him, utterly opposed to the American policy of the government, Abingdon co-operated zealously with the Marquis until his death, but broke away when Rockingham's political heirs entered into the coalition with North. Radical in his opinions, reputedly eccentric, and not, so it seems, ambitious for office, Abingdon stood in many respects near to the independents, and is more appropriately classed as such than among the great political groupings. On the whole, the same was true of his associates. Only two of them had, or accepted, official ties. Bertie held the naval rank of post-captain, but declined a command until 1782, when the war against the Americans was plainly over. Estwick accepted a minor post under Shelburne in 1782, and a little later also obtained from him the place of Searcher of the Customs at Antigua, a West Indian sinecure. Gardiner also later became associated with Shelburne, and appears to have been too independent in his conduct to suit Abingdon, who refused him re-election in 1784. But the Earl made no claim to command the votes of Gardiner, or of Estwick or Arcedeckne : he answered only for his two relatives when called upon for support by Rockingham.[1]

Rockingham was less happy in his relations with the Shelburne set. From Abingdon he received the help due from a close friend. Rutland he regarded as a youthful protégé. No such circumstances eased the contact between himself and Shelburne. While both men agreed that the American war was a disaster, their attitudes towards empire deepened the breach between them. Rockingham would hurry on a peace, even though it involved American independence. Shelburne foresaw that this independence might be inevitable, but, inheriting Chatham's principle that the loss of the colonies would spell the end of British greatness, he sought to postpone the evil day to the last possible moment. Under the influence of Burke Rockingham hesitated to have anything to do with parliamentary reform. Shelburne, partly in deference to Chatham's shade, partly owing to genuine interest, took up this

[1] Albemarle, ii, 437, 444.

idea with enthusiasm, and lost patience when he found the Marquis unresponsive.[1] Thus there were ample causes for misunderstanding, added to which both Shelburne and Rockingham nursed high political pretensions, and were potential rivals for the leadership of the government they hoped to form.

As Shelburne himself admitted in March 1782 — though later in the year the fact seems to have escaped his memory — if co-operation with North were ruled out, he and his following could never be more than an auxiliary to the massive Rockingham party.[2] He never had more than about ten supporters in the House of Commons, and the general election of 1780 reduced them for a time to six or seven. This group had no basis of family connection. It was held together by the various ties of personal friendship, or a tradition of attachment to the late Earl of Chatham, and of a common interest in political radicalism. There were Barré and Dunning, members for Shelburne's borough of Calne, his two inseparable friends ; Lord Mahon, an enthusiastic Genevan convert to democracy, who accepted his nomination for Wycombe ; and John Baring the City banker and west country woollen merchant, drawn into the party by his sister's marriage with Dunning. As a magnate in Buckinghamshire, Shelburne had also recruited some support among his neighbours of the country gentry. He had developed an 'intimate' connection with William Clayton of Harleyford,[3] whose third wife was related to his wife through the Fermors. And he had also entered into a firm friendship with the Aubreys of Dorton, John Aubrey, the heir of the house, being consequently numbered among his following.[4] Possibly

---

[1] Fitzmaurice, *Life of Shelburne*, ii, 13-15, 17, 67-72 ; *Political Memoranda of Francis fifth Duke of Leeds,* ed. O. Browning (Camden Society, 1884), 30, 35, 39 and note, 41 and note, 48-9.

[2] Fitzmaurice, *Life of Shelburne*, ii, 88.

[3] Wm. Baker to Burke, 30 Sept. 1774, Burke papers, 1-348 (Sheffield). Cf. list, Melville MSS., under 'Lord Shelburne'.

[4] In Sept. 1779, Shelburne, corresponding with Lord Temple about a by-election for the county of Buckingham, advised him that he would support the candidature of Temple's brother, 'so far as consists with a particular regard and more than political friendship, which I have had from early days with Mr. Aubrey . . . I must be directed by him in every matter regarding the county of Bucks' (draft, 18 Sept. 1779, Lansdowne MSS.).

one other member should be included in Shelburne's party, Sir George Yonge, a former Chathamite, who took office under him in July 1782 as Secretary-at-War. On the fringe of the group stood Richard Jackson, a member of Shelburne's intimate circle, sharing his keen interest in colonial matters, and subsequently, in July 1782, a member of his Treasury Board. Yet the position of Jackson defies exact political definition about 1780. Though sympathizing with the claims of the colonists to independence, he continued to hold office and to associate with the ministers who were engaged in attempting to subdue them, behaving, that is, more like a member of the administration group than a follower of Shelburne.[1]

Roughly similar in size, but not in other features, was the party headed by Sir James Lowther. In 1780 Lowther commanded three county seats in Cumberland and Westmorland, won one in a contest at Carlisle, and had also expanded his electoral influence by the purchase of Haslemere. He thus controlled nine parliamentary seats, but at this general election two of them were made available to men in opposition who were not of his own following — to Pitt at Appleby, and to a son of Sir Fletcher Norton at Haslemere. The occupants of the remaining seven seats constituted the Lowther party. Four of them were Lowthers, and a fifth, Garforth, was the baronet's legal agent. All of them came from the north. Family and local association formed the bases of the group. Lowther looked to peerage (which he received in due season), as did many another so-styled independent country gentleman. But he nursed no high political ambitions, and did not otherwise engage in the scramble for office and rewards. Consequently, although his party — much more coherent than that of Lord Abingdon — had to be reckoned with in any analysis of the House,[2] politically it stood, like that of Abingdon, on the fringe of the independents. The course Lowther set for his following was largely determined by two factors. He was

[1] *Letters and Papers of Benjamin Franklin and Richard Jackson, 1735–1785*, ed. Carl Van Doren (Philadelphia, 1947), introduction.
[2] As it was, for instance, in 1782 by Dundas (H.M.C., *Abergavenny MSS.*, 50, no. 440A), and in 1788 by the independents (Sir Lewis Namier, *Personalities and Powers*, 31-2).

utterly opposed to the American War, which he had condemned from the beginning. But the clash of interest between himself and the Duke of Portland in Cumberland was an obstacle to cordial relations with the main body of the opposition — later he was to make it clear that he could not support a government in which his rival was Premier, declaring (in July 1782) that he would not support unless Shelburne went to the Treasury.[1] Probably, too, as his views on America had coincided with those voiced by Chatham in the last years of his life,[2] he preferred Shelburne since he claimed to follow Chatham's principles. However, he was never intimately connected with Shelburne, and his friends in the Commons formed a group quite distinct from Shelburne's party.

None of the other prominent politicians in opposition commanded more than two or three votes in the Commons. The Duke of Grafton returned a relative and a client for Thetford. He also brought in his friend, General Conway, for Bury St. Edmunds, but Conway had the standing of an independent in the House rather than of a member of a faction.[3] The Duke of Richmond could count on his brother, Lord George Lennox, member for Sussex, and his client, Thomas Steele, brought in for Chichester. Thomas Townshend, the future Lord Sydney, carried with him his brother-in-law, Lord Midleton. A voluble and vehement debater in opposition, Townshend held a leading place in his own right. He acted sometimes with Rockingham, at others with Shelburne, but cannot be classed as in the train of either.

In addition, the opposition in 1780 included a few politicians normally in the court and administration group, who had, for the time being, turned against the government. Edward Eliot of Cornwall, disagreeing with its American policy, opened his borough seats to Rockingham and Shelburne but gave no particular adherence to either. Sir Fletcher Norton, the Speaker in the late parliament, seems to have been actuated mainly by disappointment at not receiving advancement in the

---

[1] *Political Memoranda of Francis fifth Duke of Leeds*, 70.

[2] Stanhope, *Life of Pitt*, i, 46-7.

[3] As Conway's friend, Horace Walpole, was constantly pointing out, *e.g.* to Sir Horace Mann, 7 July 1782.

legal profession.[1] According to Robinson, some similar motive, a material disappointment, was also the cause of Sir George Warren's voting against the ministry, a defection which involved also Warren's son-in-law, Lord Bulkeley, and Bulkeley's associate, John Parry, member for the county of Carnarvon.[2] By 1784 all these men had returned to the government fold.

The active party politicians in opposition thus numbered rather more than a hundred. But according to the analysis of the parliament made by Robinson early in 1781,[3] more than half the potential voting strength of the opposition consisted of independents. Of these, adding Robinson's 'doubtfuls' to his 'cons', there were nearer a hundred and fifty. Among these were many familiar county names — Anson, Astley, Cornewall of Hereford, Salisbury Cotton, Duncombe, Forester, Goddard, Guise, Hanbury, Hill, Lambton, Lygon, Marsham, Medows, Noel, Powys, Rolle, Rous, Tempest, Thorold, and Trevelyan. But there were also less familiar names — those of representatives of the City of London and of a large proportion of the local merchants returned from commercial centres in the provinces. Among these independents were a small number of 'urban radicals', mainly from London and its immediate environs: John Wilkes, member for Middlesex, with his brother-in-law, Hayley, and his friend, Frederick Bull, representatives of the City; Sir Joseph Mawbey, the Vauxhall distiller, member for Surrey; and Richard Beckford, Thomas Scott, and John Sawbridge (who were classed by contemporaries as on the fringe of the Rockingham party). Yet another distinct type among the independents in opposition to the government was to be found in the small circle of East Indians, whose special interests brought them into conflict with it, and who found able spokesmen in C. W. Boughton-Rouse and the redoubtable Richard Smith.

[1] See his speech in the Commons, 13 Mar. 1780, Almon, *The Parliamentary Register*, xvii, 330-3.

[2] Laprade, 44, 96. Bulkeley's conduct may also have been partly determined by his friendship with Lord Temple and his dislike of a government proposal of early 1779 to enquire into encroachments of private landowners in the royal domain in Wales (*The Last Journals of Horace Walpole*, ed. A. F. Steuart (2 vols., 1910), ii, 213 ; Robinson to Jenkinson, 5 Mar. 1779, Add. MS. 38210, f. 324).   [3] Abergavenny MSS.

As might be expected, the independents in opposition included some of the most individualistic personalities in the House — as, for instance, William Hussey of Salisbury, a financial expert, with a passion for economy which calls to mind the Gladstonian liberalism of a later century; the upright William Pulteney, one of the greatest landed proprietors in England, of whom John Sinclair once wrote: 'I believe that he never gave a vote in parliament without a thorough conviction that it was right'; [1] or Powys of Lilford, member for the county of Northampton, later leader of the St. Alban's Tavern group which tried to reconcile Fox and Pitt in March 1784, an excellent example of 'the cross-bench type of mind'.[2] Men of this stamp were by nature critics of any ministry, and by 1780 a good proportion of the independents were inclined to opposition from a conviction that the American War was a mistaken policy. Dislike of a policy did not always, however, imply hostility to the ministers.[3] Many independents opposed to the war distrusted the factions in opposition even more than they distrusted ministers, and had no wish to remove the North administration from office.[4] Consequently, though the independents were potential voting material for the opposition, it was by no means easy to bring them into action in the way desired. Only at a time of crisis, or on a popular question, could the leaders of the opposition parties hope to mobilize these auxiliaries, as they did in the spring of 1780, and again after the disaster of Yorktown, in the winter of 1781–2. Only at such times could they hope for parliamentary victories over the government.

[1] Sinclair, *Correspondence*, i, 367.
[2] E. C. Forrester, *Northampton County Elections and Electioneering* (Oxford, 1941), 86.
[3] Robinson, for example, observed this distinction in his notes about the Drakes of Amersham in the summer of 1780. Classing the father as 'doubtful' but the son as a clear opponent, he minuted: 'Mr. Drake senior is oftener with government than against: in ministerial questions he may be against, but in the great constitutional points he will always be with, if the questions are to effect the government or constitution. Mr. Drake junior is not of such sound principles' ('State', July 1780, 1, Windsor MSS.).
[4] Sinclair, *Correspondence*, i, 480; Philip Yorke to his uncle, Lord Hardwicke, [23 Feb.], 1 Mar. 1782, Add. MSS. 35380, ff. 188, 194.

The cause of government and opposition alike in the House of Commons thus turned upon combinations of parties assisted by independents; and the parties of 1780 offered a rich diversity of pattern. Various factors contributed to their creation and their continuity. Personal friendships carried into political life played a considerable part, and one which, to some extent, was indispensable. Leaders were essential who were 'place-worthy', either by right of their own abilities or in virtue of the weight of their connections, for a leader who could not hope to reach high office, and so share in the dispensation of royal patronage, could exert little attraction upon a political following. Heads of parties might build up their groups from a core of relations and personal connections. They might exploit their electoral influence by offering seats to recruits who in return would give them political allegiance. Some, like Pitt or Fox, attracted support by the transcendent splendour of their abilities and the wisdom or popularity of the policies they adopted. Others gained a party through tenure of office, or by their prospects: a First Lord of the Treasury, actual or potential, possessed a high power of attracting a following. In most parties a combination of these various factors and processes might be traced, though one or another often predominated and set its stamp upon the resulting formation. Examples of every kind are to be seen among the diverse parties existing, forming, or dissolving, in the parliament elected in 1780. There were family groups — the Rutlands, the Gowers, the Lowthers — and parties created by the attraction and influence inherent in tenure of office — those of North and Sandwich — or in the prospect of office — which was partly the case with the Rockinghams. Shelburne's party and the circle of Fox were based partly on personal friendship, partly on political accord. In some of the parties, especially the family groups, the electoral influence of the leader was a useful ancillary; but this was largely accidental, and borough influence was never more than an ancillary, and certainly not indispensable. Much borough interest was in the hands of minor politicians such as Eliot, Edgecumbe, or Northumberland, who had no wish to create parties of their own, but were content to dispose of their seats to the government or to some faction leader. And on the other hand, leaders of parties often had little or no electoral influence — Fox, for instance, had no borough seats at his own disposal, and North but one.

The power and the influence which these party associations conferred upon their members were limited, a circumstance due to their multiplicity and their restricted size. Excluding the little family groups of twos and threes to be found on both sides of the House, there were still no less than seven major party formations, three of them on the government side and four on the side of the opposition. Group organisation usually achieved a membership of from six upwards to about fifteen, a limitation which reflected its essentially personal character (this general rule can be traced in operation through the component sections of the exceptional Rockingham party). Formations of over fifteen were unusual. The remarkable size of the Rockingham-Cavendish-Fox combination, which commanded some seventy to eighty votes, made it at this time uniquely formidable. It was, however, a confederation rather than a single party. Not even this group, with all its strength, could alone dictate policy or the choice of ministers, except at the period of national crisis in 1782.

NORTH'S GOVERNMENT AND THE NEW HOUSE OF COMMONS, 1780–1781

ON 31 October 1780 the new parliament assembled for the usual short autumn sitting made necessary by the routine of financial business. On 6 December, having passed the votes of supply, it adjourned for the Christmas recess. No crucial political issue arose during these weeks. Only events extremely unfavourable to the government, and to the fate of the country, would have drawn the independent members to Westminster and so encouraged the opposition to press attacks in the hope of achieving some decisive effect. But in October the administration was still basking in the glow of American triumphs, making the most it could in the gazettes of the victory of Cornwallis at Camden — a 'brilliant' affair, so it appeared from the public prints to that bitter critic of the American War, Lord Pembroke [1] — and the independents, unstirred by any sense of crisis, continued in their country pastimes and pursuits.[2]

This brief period of parliamentary activity thus provided no decisive test of party strength. Rockingham, as leader of the opposition, saw no chance for an immediate onslaught upon the government. True, he felt that the election results were encouraging, and in a long letter to Edward Eliot, early in October, he revealed some of his hopes for the future. From the returns of members chosen in Devon and Cornwall and from the names of the defeated candidates he drew the conclusion that the government's support in those districts was declining, and results elsewhere also inclined him to take an

[1] *Letters and Diaries of Henry, tenth Earl of Pembroke*, ii, 47.
[2] As only 342 members voted on the two sides in the division upon the Address on 6 Nov. 1780, over 200 were absent from the House, and it is probable that all but a few of these had declined travelling up to Westminster before the Christmas recess.

optimistic view. 'I feel much hope', he wrote, 'that the
ballance of gain or loss in point of numbers doth predominate
on our side. . . . There are several persons elected — who
undoubtedly at present must be considered — as doubtful
persons — but I think in the apparent state of this country —
the majority of those who are not chose by actual ministerial
influence — are more likely to join [in] destroying the ruinous
system of His Majesty's Ministers etc. — than to become supporters of it.' [1] His ideas regarding the mode of the parliamentary attack and the appeal to these potential allies had been
outlined somewhat earlier in a letter to Sir George Savile.
Attention, he thought, was to be focused not on the American
War but on the already tested programme of Economical Reform.
In his view one of the most important considerations was to
restore and maintain the unity of the parties in opposition.
Action should follow the lines upon which all were agreed.
For this reason he deprecated any entanglement with the
proposals of parliamentary reform put forward by such of the
committees of association as were inspired by Wyvill. Nothing
in the circumstances of the elections suggested to him that
these proposals had any widespread approval or that members
from popular constituencies felt obliged to support them : 'I
have not as yet seen one advertisement either from a county
or from any candidate — which points at — or still less —
specifically names — the two objects [of] the Association as
terms to be made or offered'. Rather, he considered, the
opposition should try the line which had already been attempted
with some success the previous spring : 'I should think —
some tried proposition whereon great numbers have voted in
the former parliament — might be the *best* on which to try
the new parliament. Everyone may have *a crochet* : I will
hazard mine — which would be — to take early the sense of
parliament on Dunning's motion . . . depend upon it the
generality of the old stagers will vote it — and the new commons
who have either been chosen on popular ground — or who
indeed are not the abject tools brought in by government will

[1] Rockingham to E. Eliot, 8 Oct. 1780, copy, Rockingham MSS.,
R. 140-92.

cheerfully concur.' Such a course appealed to him as the best means of drawing all sides of the opposition together on the limited ground upon which agreement was possible. 'Surely', he ended his argument, 'the great object is — to obtain a great union on principle.' [1] There was no word in this letter of attacking the policy of the American War; on this point, for the present, success had made the government invulnerable.

The tactics foreshadowed in this correspondence, which were adopted by the opposition, required the full attendance of the country gentlemen. The decision to follow them thus postponed until after the Christmas recess the crucial test of strength between opposition and government. In the meantime the ministers might face the session before Christmas with confidence, but they had little ground for complacency about the parliamentary situation, and their anxiety was not allayed until that decisive test had been surmounted. The general election had given them little comfort and provided no basis for a firm forecast of their strength.

In the absence of parties, membership of which was practically co-extensive with that of the House, no eighteenth-century government could reckon with confidence, that an absolute majority of the House was on its side. Between the Acts of Union of 1707 and 1800, the absolute minimum of votes required to guarantee a majority was 279. No ministry at that time could count on mustering so many votes in a division. The North administration was fairly typical of most eighteenth-century governments in being able to reckon upon the support of about a hundred and forty members of the court and administration group and of about another eighty belonging to its constituent parties and factions. These were its disciplined troops, in number far short of an absolute majority, and always somewhat below full strength in the House owing to the incidence of illness, service abroad, and other circumstances. For further votes it had to rely upon well-wishers among the independents. The opposition was in a similar case. The two rival groups of politicians were

[1] Rockingham to Sir G. Savile, n.d. (late Sept. 1780), draft, Rockingham MSS., R. 1-1073.

obliged to bid for the support of those members who were bound to neither side, but who judged ministers by results and issues on their merits as they heard them expounded by able and eloquent speakers. Neither could forecast far ahead what success they might have. There were always some members of the House whose conduct defied prediction. Attendance fluctuated violently. And the first session of a new parliament involved the additional difficulty, that the probable future conduct of some of the new members was completely uncertain. However, in the contest for independent votes, other things being equal, the government had a natural advantage. It was the King's government. Its members, the ministers, were the chosen agents of the head of the state. As such their wishes and actions commanded respect and support — which was one of the reasons why oppositions, in the Unreformed Parliament, so very rarely succeeded in converting themselves into governments.

From the diverse materials which lay to hand in the House, eighteenth-century governments obtained their majorities in divisions, and these majorities might, or might not, remain satisfactorily steady. This was the position of the North ministry in 1780 and in 1781. How large a working majority there might be, or even whether such a majority existed at all, these were points regarding which the Treasury experts had no precise knowledge in October 1780, and which would only be revealed by actual trial in the course of parliamentary business.[1]

Proceedings in the House before the Christmas recess did little to clarify the situation.

An initial clash over the choice of the Speaker caused public embarrassment rather than parliamentary difficulty to the government. Before the opening of parliament, George III had made known his wish, that the former Speaker, Sir Fletcher Norton, should not be chosen again.[2] During the months before the general election, Norton's health had been

---

[1] In the absence of any parliamentary state for the opening weeks of the parliamentary session, there is no direct evidence for this conclusion, but the circumstantial evidence noted in the following pages is ample to justify it.

[2] North to George III, 24 Oct. 1780, Fortescue, v, no. 3164.

poor and had caused some interruption in the Commons' proceedings. Ministerial spokesmen now sought to justify his supersession upon this ground. But, undoubtedly, Norton's politics rather than his health were the reason for his rejection, and it is unnecessary to look so far back as his outspoken exhortation to George III to practise economy in 1777, which opposition speakers, seeking the most popular ground for their attack, alleged to be the pretext for the ministers' action.[1] More recently, during the spring of 1780, abandoning that principle of impartiality which theory already firmly associated with the chair,[2] and to which all Speakers after Onslow paid lip service but not always due observance, Norton had expressed strong approval of parts of the programme of economical reform brought forward by the opposition.[3] Now, in consequence, in October no approach was made to him to ascertain his feelings about continuing in the chair.[4] This would have been the natural and courteous step to take had Norton's health been the sole point in consideration, and its omission by the ministers is hardly to be accounted for otherwise than by the political motive behind their desire for a change—North would not risk the possibility, however unlikely, of Norton's accepting renomination.

In October North cherished a plan, first mooted in the previous April, of replacing Norton by Frederick Montagu. This choice would in many respects have been admirable and would have eliminated all party dispute. Montagu, a man of equable temper and outstanding probity, whose character was praised by all about him, had a foot in both camps, was friendly with both North and Rockingham, and was the one political associate of the Marquis whom North would have trusted to discharge the duties of the chair with complete impartiality.[5]

[1] Speeches of Townshend and Fox in the debate of 31 Oct. 1780, Almon and Debrett, *The Parliamentary Register*, i, 8, 11.

[2] In proposing Norton's successor, Lord George Germain, listing the various qualities required of the Speaker, came finally to — 'that, which he considered as a Speaker's most important duty, . . . his conducting himself with the strictest impartiality on every occasion'. *Ibid.* 4.

[3] Almon, *The Parliamentary Register*, xvii, 319-29.

[4] Almon and Debrett, i, 9-10.

[5] 'There seemed to be considerable propriety in the plan of Mr. Montagu being put into the Chair, not only from his being a man of honour, candour, and integrity, but because he is the personal friend of the Minister, and

North and Rockingham both pressed him strongly to accept nomination. However, after some hesitation Montagu declined, on the ground that his health would not stand the strain, and also feeling it impossible, in view of his association with Rockingham, honourably to accept a position involving some connection with the government.[1]

Montagu's refusal made a compromise over the Speaker impossible. In the absence of any other agreed candidate, the two sides, government and opposition, contended for possession of the chair. North fell back reluctantly upon his second choice for the Speakership, Charles Wolfran Cornwall, one of his junior colleagues on the Treasury Board. 'He may, probably, succeed, but Lord North can not answer for his success, as he would have done for Mr. Montagu's', he told the King.[2] Cornwall, a placeman since 1774, was clearly a party nominee. This made his candidature far less suitable than that of Montagu : Henry Dundas, then in Scotland, after hearing the news and listening to comments made by his Scottish acquaintances, told Robinson there was a general complaint, that the dignity of parliament had been much let down.[3] Moreover, Cornwall's family connection with Charles Jenkinson (to whom he was both first cousin and brother-in-law) made him obnoxious to any members of opposition who might give credence to Burke's legend about the 'double cabinet'. Consequently, when the session opened on 31 October and Germain proposed Cornwall's election, the opposition attacked the nomination of a ministerialist and moved for the re-election of Sir Fletcher Norton. Their spokesmen contended that Norton had done nothing to deserve censure, and that, as the ex-Speaker, he was the natural choice; and they lavished

because in his person both sides would concur in maintaining the decency, dignity, and order of the House. I recollect Lord North once talking with me upon the subject, and these reasons had then decisive weight.' Henry Dundas to John Robinson, 3 Nov. 1780, Abergavenny MS. 321.

[1] Montagu to Rockingham, with copy of a letter from North to Montagu, Rockingham to Montagu, Montagu to Rockingham, all undated, and Rockingham to Montagu, 22 Oct. 1780, Rockingham MSS., R. 162 ; North to George III, 24 Oct. 1780, George III to North, 25 Oct. 1780, Fortescue, v, nos. 3164, 3165.

[2] 24 Oct. 1780, Fortescue, v, no. 3164.

[3] 3 Nov. 1780, Abergavenny MS. 321.

praise upon his impartiality.[1] Private correspondence suggests, however, that it was not his impartiality that they valued. On 22 October, a week before the opening of the session, Rockingham wrote to Montagu : 'I had a letter yesterday from Weddell, who had seen Sir Fletcher Norton. I think by the account Mr. Weddell sends me, Sir Fletcher *at present* has no communication with the ministers, and is inclined to be warm in opposition : at this same time I conceive from some circumstances that Sir Fletcher is not *decided* to refuse the chair if proposed to him by either side of the House. Perhaps he wishes that our friends would propose him.'[2] In fact, once Montagu had declined, though leaders on either side would not admit it, government and opposition were alike in wanting a party man of their own in the chair. After many evasive speeches had been made, it was left to the forthright Rigby to flout the pointed references of other ministers to Norton's health, and to declare roundly that it had nothing to do with the question, but that 'the true cause of moving for a new Speaker by one side of the House, and supporting the old Speaker by the other . . . was reducible to a very simple fact, and when put into plain English, and stripped of the dress of eloquence . . . was no more than this. "We'll vote for you, if you'll be for us." '[3] Despite Norton's insistence during the debate that he had no wish to be Speaker again, the opposition insisted upon a division against Germain's motion. In what had become a clear party question, the ministers had the satisfaction of seeing Cornwall's election carried by the substantial majority of 203 to 134.

A week later, on 6 November, the government secured an even more decisive victory in the division upon the Address. Opposition leaders were hard pressed to hold together those of their friends who had come up for the opening, and bemoaned the counter-attractions of the countryside. Rockingham wrote to Portland on 3 November : 'I will send to Charles Turner but I don't know that he can persuade Sir John Thorold to stay, General Honeywood and Sir John Griffin I find are

[1] Almon and Debrett, i, 3-17.   [2] Rockingham MSS., R. 162.
[3] Almon and Debrett, i, 14-16.

both gone into the country — I have wrote to General Honeywood and shall write to Sir John — It is sad work.'[1] On the
6th ministers carried their address by 212 to 130, congratulating
the King upon the successes of British arms in the southern
colonies and pledging the full support of parliament for the
further vigorous prosecution of the war. The debate on this
occasion drew in few but the regular party speakers. The only
two interventions by independents both indicated that, in view
of the recent military successes in the Carolinas, the opposition
could not have hoped at this time to push attacks against the
war with any effect. Both William Pulteney and Sir Horace
Mann expressed the view that the situation in America was
now much more favourable, and they agreed with the ministers'
contention, that a large proportion of the Americans — Mann
was prepared to put the number at more than half — were
'the friends of this country', in support of whom the war
must be continued.[2] No independent rose to express a contrary
opinion. Except for an attack upon the Admiralty by one of
the members for London, the opposition side of the debate
was sustained solely by its regular party supporters.

After the 6th the level of attendance in the Commons fell
rapidly, and the government had no further serious challenge
to face before the recess.[3] On 4 December, in the division on
the navy estimates, the opposition were able to muster only
seventy-three votes. To some pessimists in their ranks it
seemed as if the ministry were completely masters of the
situation, and that the estrangement between Shelburne and
Rockingham made their triumph secure. Aloof Shelburne
sulked in his galleries at Bowood, rejecting all the Duke of
Richmond's efforts to reunite the opposition.[4] In the Commons
his friends took little part in the proceedings : neither Barré
nor Dunning spoke in the debate on the Address of 6 November,

---

[1] Portland MSS.   [2] Almon and Debrett, i, 32, 47.
[3] On 16 Nov. 1780 Edward Eliot wrote from Cornwall to Shelburne :
'My friend Mr. Salt, whom I have consulted, writes me word that immediately after the first two divisions many gentlemen returned into the
country, and that no question of moment is proposed to be brought on till
after Christmas.' — Lansdowne MSS.
[4] Fitzmaurice, *Life of Shelburne*, ii, 70-2.

a fact duly noted by the political observers.[1] Some of Rockingham's own supporters appeared but half-hearted. The Duke of Manchester, having declined to come up to Westminster, told Rockingham he could see no point in attending parliament: 'The unfortunate riots last summer, and the violence of some of our friends on the occasion, added to the breach in the opposition, convinced me that any parliamentary measure now attempted by us would do more harm than good'.[2] In Cassandra tones Lord Camden gloomed in his letters: 'Lord Rockingham hardly condescends to return my salutation, and does not open his lips upon business: but he appears discontented, and finds his own party dropping off from him. By the end of the session he will be deserted.'[3] 'The new parliament is more devoted to the court than the former. What is called opposition is at variance with itself, and the whole nation abandoned to luxury, avarice, and rapine.'[4] On 5 December Shelburne's Wiltshire neighbour, friend, and political associate, Lord Pembroke, summed up the situation from the opposition point of view in colours equally dark in a letter to his friend, Carmarthen:[5]

That silly negotiation, by which Lord Rockingham was so completely led by the nose, has discomposed and divided everything, more I verily believe than all other causes put together. No one knows any longer, upon whom or upon what they can depend, even giving the greatest latitude possible for integrity and well-meaning. The folly of the negotiation may very probably have had a strong effect also on the Chancellor, Lord Gore, and Lord Weymouth, and have determined them not to co-operate with ropes of sand. The mischief of it, I am sure, will show itself more and more every day. Lord Shelburne is a very sensible man and will, no doubt, now look upon himself as disengaged from anybody and perfectly free . . . The Duke of Richmond, I believe feels himself equally free, though his

[1] Charles Sackville to Sir Charles Hotham Thompson, 7 Nov. 1780, Hotham MSS.   [2] 22 Nov. 1780, Rockingham MSS., R. 2-159.
[3] To Shelburne, 13 Nov. 1780, Lansdowne MSS.
[4] To Thomas Walpole, 25 Dec. 1780, Lullings MSS.
[5] *Letters and Diaries of Henry, tenth Earl of Pembroke*, ii, 86-9.

personal private friendship for Lord Rockingham is, I make no doubt, as great as ever. Charles Fox's sensations must be the same . . .

However, these prophecies of gloom were not entirely justified. Such opposition complaints suggest that the government's position was unassailable. This was not clearly the case. Though North had proved the House of Commons and found himself supported by large majorities, the size of these majorities was neither decisive nor reassuring, for the opposition's full strength had not yet been exerted. In mid-November, when the members of the House of Commons were already dispersing, the Treasury was still uncertain about the probable future conduct of many of them — 'realy people, except the old set, have so little aranged themselves yet, that it is hard to say what line they will adhere to', Robinson complained to Jenkinson on the 17th.[1] The parliamentary events of February 1781 were to give North more cause for acute anxiety than he had yet encountered since the general election.

When eighteenth-century governments provoked a powerful opposition in parliament, the part of the session between Christmas and Easter was likely to prove the period of their greatest trial. At other times, ministers could usually count on adequate majorities, owing to the absence or irregular attendance of independents whose votes the opposition might attract. But the main business of the session came on after Christmas, and then full parliamentary attendance was expected, and was, indeed, enforced by means of the call of the House. The call of the House meant the actual calling over, name by name, of the roll of members, on a day which the House had previously determined. A member who failed to attend either this roll-call or a call of defaulters fixed for a later day made himself liable to penalty (in theory, but scarcely ever in practice), unless he could plead some valid excuse, such as illness, employment in the King's service, special permission, or some other reason which had been declared sufficient by the House. It was not unusual for a call to be ordered more

[1] Add. MSS. 38458, f. 141.

than once in a session, but the practice was not popular.[1] The call was a device of which the government had little need to make use. Members of the ministerial phalanx were schooled to regular attendance. But to the opposition the call of the House was clearly advantageous. Its intended purpose was to ensure that after the Christmas recess there should be a full attendance of the country gentlemen. As it was upon the votes of these members that the opposition leaders depended, if their campaigns against the government were to be of any effect, the period between Christmas and Easter provided them with their most favourable opportunities and was correspondingly regarded with apprehension by the ministers.

No action of the government, nor change in the general political situation between the general election and the re-assembly of parliament on 23 January, had led the Rockinghams to suppose that any other plan of attack upon the government would prove more effective than their favoured programme of Economical Reform. On no other issues did the ministers appear to be particularly vulnerable.

Ireland for the time being was quiescent. The main Irish forum of agitation was temporarily silenced, for the Dublin parliament had been prorogued on 2 September 1780. Owing to the Irish custom of making biennial financial provisions, it would not meet again till some time in 1782. Shortly after the prorogation Lord Buckinghamshire had formally requested his recall. His successor, Lord Carlisle, who took over his charge on 23 December, was sociable and agreeable, and in William Eden he had a secretary with some pretensions to skill in the arts of political management. As represented to ministers by the politicians of Dublin Castle the outlook seemed set fair for Carlisle's lieutenancy. The Duke of Leinster's agent, Lees, so Robinson reported early in November, had brought over 'for Lord Carlisle and Mr. Eden a bed of down with the pillows before prepared for them, if they know how to rest upon it'.[2] The first impressions gathered by the new Lord-

[1] John Hatsell, *Precedents of Proceedings in the House of Commons* (4 vols., 1818), ii, 100-1 ; Almon and Debrett, i, 482.
[2] To Jenkinson, 5 Nov. 1780, Add. MSS. 38567, f. 85.

Lieutenant and his secretary on their arrival confirmed that the situation in Ireland was much less critical than it had been in the previous summer. In a lengthy letter to Hillsborough, Eden reported with guarded optimism on 9 January : [1]

> In this moment there does appear among a variety of men of the greatest weight and consequence in this kingdom, otherwise differently inclined and differently connected, a conviction that the aristocratic part of the government has lost its balance ; that there is an evident necessity of regaining from the people that power, which, if suffered to continue in their hands, must end in the general ruin of the whole ; that, for their own security and happiness English government must be supported ; that the wild notions of republicanism become every day more the objects of contempt and derision, that in short the national fever is subsiding, unless unfortunately again called forth, in which case the return of the disorder may be too strong for the best endeavours of the well-intentioned.

Nor had the situation in America yet reached a stage affording ground for damaging attacks upon the ministry, though it was clear before the reassembly of parliament, how unreal had been the high hopes set by the government upon the outcome of the southern campaign. Throughout the autumn optimism had been kindled among the ministers by Cornwallis's reports of loyalists ready to rise in North Carolina, by the opportunity to rally them which seemed open after his victory at Camden, and by Clinton's despatches concerning the preparation and departure of a diversionary force sent into Virginia in support of Cornwallis's campaign.[2] The defection of the rebel general, Benedict Arnold, together with other intelligence reaching Germain's office, seemed to Germain to indicate that the rebellion was 'evidently declining fast'.[3] It was a shock to the ministers to learn, just at the end of the year,

---

[1] S.P. 63/474, ff. 20-1.
[2] Cornwallis to Clinton, 30 June 1780, forwarded to Germain, Cornwallis to Germain, 20, 21 Aug. 1780, H.M.C., *Stopford-Sackville MSS.*, ii, 169-71, 174-82 ; Clinton to Germain, 30 Aug., 3, 20 Sept. 1780, C.O. 5/100 (1), 30 Oct. 1780, C.O. 5/100 (2).
[3] Germain to Clinton, 28 Nov. 1780, *ibid.*

that the failure to materialize of the anticipated massive loyalist support in North Carolina, and outbursts of rebel activity cutting across the British lines of communication further south, had obliged Cornwallis to retire, destroying all hope of an immediate recovery of the southern provinces.[1] But as yet he had not suffered any decisive defeat, and the opposition's virtual neglect of the American War during the debates in the early part of 1781 seems to show that they felt no purpose would be served by discussing it.

The deteriorating diplomatic situation did draw fire from the opposition, but this caused the government comparatively little parliamentary difficulty.

On 25 January, two days after the reassembly of parliament, the ministers took the first opportunity to give formal notice in both Houses of the outbreak of war with the United Provinces. Selections of documents illustrating the course of events up to the breach were submitted, and addresses were moved pledging support for the government. On this question the ministers had a fairly good case, but they were in the unfortunate situation of being unable to disclose it owing to the possible repercussions on Russian policy.

Of the difficulties created for the British government in the previous months by the development of the Russian Empress's pet scheme for an 'Armed Neutrality', those arising from the position of the Dutch were the most acute. Russia's own merchant fleet was so relatively insignificant, that deference to the Empress's objections to interference with her ships meant little sacrifice of the efficiency of the British weapon of blockade.[2] The Danish loophole had been partially closed by an Anglo-Danish agreement, made after the Danes' adherence to the Armed Neutrality, amending the Anglo-Danish trade treaty of 1670, so as to include weapons and timber as contraband goods [3] — 'the article respecting counterband is favourable to us, and

---

[1] Lord Rawdon to Alexander Leslie, 24 Oct. 1780, to Clinton, 28 Oct. 1780, H.M.C., *Stopford-Sackville MSS.*, ii, 185-6 ; Clinton to Germain, 12 Nov. 1780, enclosing Rawdon's letter to him, received in London, 28 Dec. 1780, C.O. 5/100 (2) ; Germain to Clinton, 3 Jan. 1781, C.O. 5/101.
[2] Sir James Harris to Stormont, no. 160, 13/24 Dec. 1780, S.P. 91/106.
[3] C.O. 5/143, ff. 217, 221 *seq.*

R

has that extension which in reason and justice such treaties ought to have to include maritime wars', Stormont reported with satisfaction.[1] But the activities of the Dutch merchant marine were in another category. The basic principle of the Armed Neutrality was that any hostile goods might be freely transported under a neutral flag unless defined as contraband by treaty between the neutral and the blockading power. For this same principle the Dutch had been contesting in the interests of their carrying trade. Only limited definitions of contraband were laid down in the treaties between Britain and the United Provinces, and the Dutch maintained they had the right under the Anglo-Dutch treaty of 1674 to transport naval stores and other supplies without interference to the ports of Britain's enemies. During the latter part of 1780 the British government had simply subjected Dutch shipping to the full rigour of the blockade, declaring Dutch privileges under the treaty of 1674 suspended since the Dutch for their part had withheld the armed assistance due to Britain under the Anglo-Dutch treaties of 1678 and 1716.[2] But if the Dutch acceded to the Armed Neutrality, this course of action would become impossible without risking war with its united forces. In September 1780 Stormont viewed the situation with concern but was nevertheless determined to maintain the weapon of blockade. On the 19th he expressed to Sir Joseph Yorke the opinion that if the Dutch were to publish a declaration of neutrality and then, 'attempt to give real and essential assistance to France . . . by sending out convoys to protect merchantmen laden with naval stores for the ports of France and Spain', it would be necessary 'to consider them as real, though not declared enemies and act accordingly'.[3] For the time being he nursed the hope that the Dutch proposal to join the Armed Neutrality would break down entirely owing to the Russian refusal of their demand for a general guarantee of all their territories.[4] But next month a stroke of good fortune re-

[1] To Sir Joseph Yorke, 15 Aug. 1780, S.P. 84/571, f. 166 ; to Harris, no. 54, 22 Sept. 1780, S.P. 91/105.   [2] Pp. 12-13 above.
[3] No. 51, 19 Sept. 1780, S.P. 84/572, ff. 42-4.
[4] E.g. Stormont to Harris, no. 51, 19 Sept. 1780, S.P. 91/105.

lieved the British government from dependence upon this unreliable circumstance. The capture of Henry Laurens with his papers brought to light the existence of a negotiation between the authorities of Amsterdam and the American Congress. Stormont was thus placed in a position to demand satisfaction and a full clarification of Dutch intentions without reference to the Armed Neutrality. In a letter forwarding copies of the captured documents to Yorke at The Hague, he tersely analysed the new turn which they gave to the situation. If the Dutch, by lowering their demands upon Russia for guarantees, were able to negotiate their entry into the Armed Neutrality, Britain would have 'no alternative'. The United Provinces would have to be treated as a hostile power. 'In such an event these papers will furnish to the whole world an ample justification of every measure we may find it necessary to pursue; and give the properest direction to the war, by making it a particular quarrel between Great Britain and Holland, in which no neutral power has any concern.' [1]

For a little longer Stormont hoped to avoid an armed clash with the United Provinces. Laurens's papers were not made an immediate pretext for a declaration of war. It was even hoped that disclosure of them to the States-General by the channel of the Stadtholder might give a check to the Amsterdammers and lead to the adoption by the Dutch of a policy less damaging to British interests.[2] In the meantime Stormont also set on foot a new and more positive attempt to gain Russian good-will, which, had it succeeded, would have drawn the teeth of the Armed Neutrality and made the accession of the Dutch to it immaterial. On 20 October he instructed Harris to make careful enquiries if there was any substantial concession by means of which Britain might buy Russian support in the war against the Bourbons.[3]

[1] No. 59, 11 Oct. 1780, S.P. 84/572, ff. 101-3.
[2] Stormont to Yorke, no. 62, 31 Oct. 1780, S.P. 84/572, ff. 116-7.
[3] Stormont to Harris, no. 61, 20 Oct. 1780, S.P. 91/106, referred to, but with incorrect date, *Malmesbury Corr.*, i, 345 note. This dispatch, received at Petersburg on 3/14 Nov., elicited a first reply in Harris's brief dispatch no. 150 of 24 Nov./5 Dec. 1780, stating that 'the only cession' which might induce the Russian Empress to become the ally of Britain was that of Minorca — S.P. 91/106, printed complete, *Malmesbury Corr.*,

On the same day, however, as this dispatch was sent to Harris, Yorke wrote from The Hague reporting that the estates of Holland had decided to give up the demand for a general guarantee from Russia as a condition of the Dutch entry into the Armed Neutrality.[1] The Dutch question immediately assumed a new urgency, and British diplomatic measures at The Hague were henceforth timed to ensure that, if the Dutch did not repudiate their unfriendly conduct, a rupture could be forced before their accession to the Armed Neutrality was complete. On 4 November, having secured the approval of the rest of the cabinet, Stormont forwarded to Yorke a strong memorial, demanding a disavowal of the negotiation between Amsterdam and the Americans and the punishment of those responsible. Yorke, however, was not to present it if the refusal of the other Dutch provinces to adopt the decision of Holland made it clear that there was no immediate likelihood of the United Provinces adhering to the Armed Neutrality.[2] When it became clear the Dutch were proceeding with the intention of acceding without the guarantee, Yorke on 10 November presented the memorial to the States-General. Immediate compliance with it would have averted the crisis, but the political situation at Amsterdam put this out of the question: compliance would only have been possible after a 'palace revolution' and a complete reversal of policy in the province of Holland. Neither Yorke nor Stormont had any real hope of such an outcome, and Stormont's sole concern was to force a breach over the American negotiation before the Dutch entry into the Armed Neutrality was completed at Petersburg. No satisfaction to the first memorial being forthcoming, a second, demanding an immediate reply, was for-

i, 345 — and a fuller answer in his no. 158 of 13/24 Dec. 1780, S.P. 91/106, *Malmesbury Corr.*, i, 363-6. On this see also cabinet minutes of 3 and 7 Jan. 1781 (Fortescue, v, nos. 3232, 3233) arising from the first of these answers, and Stormont's to Harris, no. 5, 19 Jan. 1781 (F.O. 65/1, partly printed, under date, 20 Jan. 1781, *Malmesbury Corr.*, i, 373-5). The offer of Minorca was declined by the Empress (Harris to Stormont, no. 38, 13/24 Mar. 1781, F.O. 65/2, *Malmesbury Corr.*, i, 398 (last line)-402).

[1] No. 100, 20 Oct. 1780, S.P. 84/572, f. 151.

[2] Cabinet minute, 3 Nov. 1780, Fortescue, v, no. 3171; Stormont to Yorke, no. 64, 4 Nov. 1780, S.P. 84/573, ff. 14-17; Almon and Debrett, i, 323-5.

warded and delivered by Yorke on 11 December.[1] By the 15th further dispatches received from Yorke gave the affair still greater urgency; and Stormont wrote to the King:[2]

> Your Majesty will see by Sir J. Yorke's dispatches that the Dutch business must now be brought to an immediate crisis. The intention of hastening the communication of the Accession of the Republic to the Northern League is very insidious, and every step taken after this Declaration might be attributed to resentment for it. To obviate this the best thing that has occurred to me and which I mean to propose to the Cabinet this evening is that orders should be sent instantly to Sir Joseph Yorke to quit Holland without taking leave, repair to Antwerp and wait there for further orders and that Count Wilderen should be informed in a friendly manner of the orders sent to Your Majesty's ambassador, which will prevent him, Wilderen, from attempting to make any communication.

The same day Stormont wrote to Yorke asking for advice regarding a final memorial and pressed him for an immediate answer, observing: 'It would be a very awkward thing to have the declaration of the Republic's accession to the Northern League notified to us before this business is drawn towards a decided point'.[3] By the next day he had secured the cabinet's consent, and Yorke was instructed to withdraw to Antwerp immediately. 'His Majesty', Stormont wrote, 'can no longer look upon the Republic in any other light than that of a secret enemy, whose hostile designs he has providentially discovered, and must act accordingly.'[4] On the 18th the cabinet agreed upon the form of a manifesto, breaking off relations with the United Provinces, but ministers decided to defer the publication until the 20th: 'The publishing it before the *possibility* of receiving an answer to the last memorial might appear too

---

[1] Cabinet minutes, 6, 7 Dec. 1780, Fortescue, v, nos. 3197, 3198; Almon and Debrett, i, 325–6 — the memorial is here dated 12 Dec., but Yorke stated it was delivered on the 11th (to Stormont, no. 122, 11 Dec. 1780, S.P. 84/573, ff. 188–9).

[2] [15 Dec. 1780], Fortescue, v, no. 2935 (undated and misplaced by Fortescue).

[3] No. 75, 15 Dec. 1780, S.P. 84/573, ff. 196–7. [4] *Ibid.* f. 223.

precipitate and might lead to a discovery of that reason which it is meant to conceal', Stormont wrote late that evening to the King.[1] By the next day this obstacle had been removed, for Yorke's dispatch of 15 December had arrived, reporting that the States-General declined an immediate answer and that the memorial had been referred to the provincial estates for consideration.[2] 'The answer from the States or rather the no answer will remove every difficulty and make the immediate publication of the manifesto highly proper', Stormont told the King.[3] On the 20th the British manifesto was published and diplomatic relations with the United Provinces sundered.[4]

The particular course of these events, and, more especially, the secret motive of the government underlying them, materially affected the course of the debates in both Houses on 25 January. The manifesto was the main *pièce justificative* submitted to parliament by the ministers. It retailed a long series of complaints : the Dutch refusal to break off relations with the powers which had attacked Great Britain and the assurances of neutrality given to those powers, contrary to Anglo-Dutch treaty engagements ; the assistance given to the Americans in the Dutch West Indies ; the refuge given to Paul Jones ; intrigues concerted with the French against the British in the East Indies ; and the drafts and correspondence concerning the projected Dutch-American treaty of amity and commerce, which was represented as final and clear proof of hostile intention. However, it was not these grievances, genuine as they were, which had led to the war, but the threat that the Dutch would obtain the support of the Armed Neutrality to destroy the British weapon of blockade — this is clear from Stormont's instructions to Yorke of 4 November and from stray remarks in their subsequent correspondence. But this real motive for the war could not be disclosed. The least official admission of it might cause exactly what the government's manœuvre was intended to avoid — a Russian intervention on the Dutch behalf. In

[1] 11 P.M., 18 Dec. 1780, Fortescue, v, no. 3210.
[2] Yorke to Stormont, no. 136, 15 Dec. 1780, S.P. 84/573, ff. 210-12.
[3] 19 Dec. 1780, Fortescue, v, no. 3211.
[4] Almon and Debrett, i, 315-18.

the first weeks of 1781 the Dutch persistently sought Russian armed support, on the ground that the British declaration of hostilities was due to their accession to the Armed Neutrality, and Harris at Petersburg strove successfully to avert a war with Russia by rebutting this argument.[1] Consequently the debates on the war had a marked air of unreality. The ministers could not explain that they thought this grave step to be essential, as the only way of maintaining the power of blockade without incurring the hostility of the whole Armed Neutrality. Thus they could not satisfy the demand immediately put forward by Burke, for ample proof that the war was either 'prudent' or at any rate (as they really believed) 'unavoidably necessary'.[2] They were obliged in parliament to justify the war on grounds which they, in ministerial council, had certainly not regarded as justifying it at the beginning of the previous November,[3] and on grounds some of which were manifestly weak. Their argument that the Dutch ought to have taken part in the war on the side of Great Britain in fulfilment of their treaty obligations was legalistically correct, but it was open to the very pertinent objection made by Thomas Townshend, that as an ally exposed to French attack the United Provinces would have become not an asset but a very considerable military and naval liability.[4] None of the pretexts which the ministers advanced to justify the outbreak of hostilities with the Dutch demonstrated that the war was 'unavoidably necessary'. But their majority in the Lords was assured, and in the Commons their position was at the moment equally safe, since many of the country gentlemen had not yet come up.

[1] Harris to Stormont, no. 171, 30 Dec./10 Jan. 1780/1, no. 2, 1/12 Jan. 1781, no. 13, 19/30 Jan. 1781, no. 19, 5/16 Feb. 1781, no. 38, 13/24 Mar. 1781, F.O. 65/1, all save the second printed in part from Harris's copies, *Malmesbury Corr.*, i, 372-3, 379-82, 385-6 (misdated 2/13 Feb.), 402-3 ; Harris to Sir Robert Murray Keith, 10/21 Jan. 1781, *ibid*. i, 376-7. The question whether Harris's success was so great as he claimed — whether the Empress really might have allowed herself to be entangled in a war in the west on any pretext whatsoever — is a problem of Russian policy which I do not attempt to go into here.

[2] Almon and Debrett, i, 341.

[3] Cf. Stormont's instruction to Yorke not to present the first memorial to the States-General unless he anticipated an early Dutch adherence to the Armed Neutrality, p. 246 above.   [4] Almon and Debrett, i, 351.

Nor was a future parliamentary onslaught on this question likely. As Richmond admitted in the debate in the Lords, the Dutch war was popular.[1] It was not, therefore, a promising subject for the opposition to use to harry the government later in the session. At the end of the debate in the House of Commons North carried by the substantial majority of 180 to 101 the ministerial address pledging parliamentary support for this 'just and necessary' war.

During these proceedings the government not only withheld vital information from parliament: they further deceived the two Houses by concealing the fact that they were doing so — a course of action for which, on diplomatic grounds, they had ample justification. So far as appears from the printed debates not one of the government's critics in the Commons detected the secret motive of their action — or if any did, they considered discretion advisable. In the Lords only Camden seems to have perceived what truly was, as he said, 'the real drift and tendency of the present measure'; that the ministers thought they might, 'under the pretence of detecting the Dutch in having entered into a treaty with the American Congress, deprive them of that security and protection which they would, but for this circumstance, be clearly entitled to as a member of the armed neutrality'.[2] His speech appears to have ended the Lords' debate, or else the gallery of the House was then cleared of reporters: at any rate, there is no record that the Dutch war was debated on its real merits.

The debates on the Dutch war were the most important event of the first week of the resumed parliamentary session — a week which went well for the government. On the first day, 23 January, ministers had carried a very partisan resolution, contrary to the spirit of the Grenville Act regarding controverted elections, that the petition of two staunch government supporters respecting the election at Coventry should be taken on 15 February instead of waiting its turn until 26 June.[3] The next day further business was dealt with without difficulty, which had caused North considerable previous anxiety. On

[1] Debrett, iv, 39.   [2] *Ibid.* iv, 123-4.
[3] Almon and Debrett, i, 245-54.

14 January he had informed the King, that the extraordinary supplies for the army might exceed £3,000,000, and that he could not 'but confess his apprehensions of very great uneasiness in parliament on that head'.[1] On the 24th, however, the long (but apparently unrecorded) debate produced no difficulties which North thought of sufficient importance to explain to the King, and the extraordinaries were voted by a majority of 180 to 57: George III was delighted and looked forward somewhat prematurely to a quiet parliamentary session.[2] On the 25th the question of the Dutch war was successfully surmounted. This parliamentary success was maintained on 1 February — the day after the call of the House — when an attempt by Fox to censure the ministers for the appointment of Sir Hugh Palliser as governor of Greenwich Hospital was defeated in a fairly full chamber by 214 to 149.

But the government's most difficult days were now approaching. The call of the House had been set down for 31 January, and the Rockingham party began to prepare for its grand attack. The call presented various opportunities. By careful management it was sometimes possible to arrange for a major onslaught upon the ministry to take place on the day when the call obliged all available members to be present. If used contrary to custom — postponed from week to week, or discharged and renewed for a future day — it could become a threat hanging over the heads of members in order to enforce attendance. Very much more use was to be made of the call in 1782. In 1781 its potentialities were by no means overlooked, but the opposition was worsted in its attempt to exploit them.

Management of this tactical weapon was left by the opposition leaders in the hands of Sir Joseph Mawbey, member for Surrey. This may have been done to avoid the imputation

<hr />

[1] Fortescue, v, no. 3243.
[2] North to George III, [24 Jan. 1781], George III to North, 25 Jan. 1781, *ibid.* v, nos. 3253, 3254. The extraordinaries occasioned a prolonged debate, lasting, so North reported, till nine o'clock, but no report of it is given in either the ministerial *Political Magazine* or in the opposition record, *The Parliamentary Register* — nor apparently did Cobbett find any report of it to include in the *Parliamentary History*.

that the call was being used for party purposes, for Mawbey
was a staunch independent, though at this time in full sympathy
with the policies of the Rockingham group. On 31 January
Mawbey made a first attempt to enforce future attendance, by
putting off the call to a later day — 'seeing', he said, 'the
House was tolerably full, and in order to comply with the
request of several gentlemen, he should now move to discharge
the former order, and renew the order for a call on the 8th'.[1]
On this proposal being rejected, the call took place, and it was
ordered that the list of defaulters should be read a fortnight
later, on 15 February. There can be little doubt that the
coincidence of the reintroduction of Burke's Establishment
Bill with this call of defaulters was a deliberate arrangement on
the part of the opposition to exploit the full attendance of
country gentlemen. On the 15th, probably with further stages
of the Economical Reform programme in mind, Mawbey again
tried to ensure future attendance, this time by a motion for
another call in four weeks' time; but on a division his proposal
was rejected, Sir Thomas Clavering declaring that it was
unusual to call the House over twice in one session.[2]

On 15 February Burke 'rose about half past six o'clock'
and moved, as a preliminary step, that the entry in the Journals
recording the passage of Dunning's resolutions should be read;
which was accordingly done. He then reintroduced, in exactly
the same form as before, his bill for the reform of the royal
establishment.[3] With this revival of the Economical Reform
programme, the Rockinghams played their strongest card.
Ministers might well fear, and opposition nurse high hopes of
the concern of the country gentlemen at high taxation and
increased expenditure and of the preoccupation of county representatives with the gathering hostility among their constituents to both these inevitable accompaniments of war.[4]

---

[1] Almon and Debrett, i, 377.   [2] *Ibid.* i, 482.   [3] *Ibid.* i, 482–99.
[4] On 10 Feb. 1781, Lord Hardwicke wrote to his nephew, Philip Yorke,
member for the county of Cambridge : 'I presume there will be no opposition to the bringing in of Burke's Economical Bill, tho' if it is much the same
with that of last session it will not be suffered to pass. You will do well to
consider your own conduct in it. The taxes may be so heavy that your
constituents may expect from their member some popular complaisance,
and provided it does not run to extravagant lengths there is no harm in an

Twice in the previous year opposition had defeated the government on this question.[1] Now, at the Treasury, in preparation for the crucial struggle in the House of Commons, Robinson was set to con his parliamentary lists. On the 14th, the day before Burke reintroduced his bill, he completed a state and abstract of the House which gave North very little reassurance.[2] 463 members were by now in regular attendance. Of these the government could count for certain on 223, the opposition on 214. But there were over 60 members whose conduct was unpredictable, 23 reckoned as hopeful, 40 as doubtful. On these figures the government might well be beaten. There were, however, by Robinson's calculations, 30 supporters absent from the House, and if 14 of these, whom he hoped to muster, could be got to attend, the ministry might just carry the day. He concluded that the total of 'pros.' that might be hoped for was 260, unless some of those marked 'doubtful' voted for the government, and that if all the 'doubtful' voted with opposition, they might divide 254 strong.

This estimate showed the opposing forces as almost equal. Without further assurances regarding the uncertain members, a ministerial victory could not be guaranteed. Events were soon to prove that these figures were, from the government point of view, too pessimistic. But, for the moment, confronted with them, North hesitated. Now, and for some days to come, the threat of defeat or near-defeat loomed like a

independent member like yourself showing that he does not strictly set his watch by the court dial. Your predecessor . . . hurt his interest in the county by following Administration too implicitly. I would at least vote for bringing the bill in and seeing what can be made of it.' (Add. MSS. 35379, f. 301). Yorke voted in the minority for the second reading of the bill on 26 Feb. (Yorke to Hardwicke, 27 Feb. 1781, *ibid*. ff. 322-3).

[1] On 8 Mar. 1780, on the clause in Burke's bill for abolishing the Board of Trade, and on 6 Apr., with the passage of Dunning's resolutions.

[2] Abergavenny MSS. The first of these documents, a full nominal roll of the House analysed under different columns, is contained in a wrapper dated November 1781, but it gives the detailed information which is summarised in the abstract dated 14 Feb. 1781. The full list, although annotated November 1781 contains the names of the members sitting in February and no corrections to correspond with changes of membership between February and November were made to it. This is the only list I have yet been able to discover for the period between the general election of 1780 and the division of 12 Dec. 1781 (for which a list was published), giving information about the voting habits of members.

nightmare. 'On this question of Burke's we shall be very hard run', Robinson remarked a week or so later, 'and the effects of losing the question or a small majority will in my opinion *now have bad effects indeed.*' [1] If the opposition were to win one division, waverers might turn towards them, and even if no greater disaster befell, the weary harassing round of the previous winter and spring might be repeated. North dared not at first risk a division. When Burke, on the 15th, moved for leave to bring in his Establishment Bill, he found that the ministry declined to oppose it.[2]

During the next few days North and Robinson were hard at work in an attempt to recover mastery of the situation. From Charles Jenkinson came encouragement and counsel. On the 17th Jenkinson returned Robinson his lists with the remark: 'It appears to me to be very well done and I think it is not too favourable to our side of the question. The whole depends on the conduct which the *hopeful* and *doubtful* will hold; I should think that with attention and industry many of these may be got, so as to make our majority secure.' And he added, with a reference to the disheartening effect of the recent refusal to do parliamentary battle, 'as soon as this was done, I would lose no time in trying a question, for we are at present rather in a state of humiliation'.[3] His advice was soon followed. On the 19th, what seems to have been a snap division was forced by the ministry. After Burke's bill had received an unopposed first reading in a thinly attended House, and Burke had proposed the 22nd for the second reading, Earl Nugent for the government moved an amendment putting off the second reading for a week instead of three days. His arguments suggested a concern with tactics rather than with considerations of substance. There were, he declared, 'many young members who could not be conceived to be in possession of the plan, large and comprehensive as it was, and who could

---

[1] Robinson to Lord Sandwich, 22 Feb. 1781, Sandwich MSS.
[2] Almon and Debrett, i, 502-5. On 19 Feb. 1781, Lord Camden wrote to his daughter, Fanny Stewart: 'Burke has renewed his famous Bill, and has leave to bring it in. Lord N. intended to have rejected it upon the first motion, but he was afraid of losing the question.' Camden MSS.
[3] Abergavenny MS. 349.

not make themselves masters of it in so short a time. Gentlemen would consider that there was not one day before Thursday
on which they could read it with the attention which it deserved,
since it could not be printed before Wednesday morning, and
Wednesday was the Fast Day.' Burke, in reply, very justly
'ridiculed the idea of the House being unacquainted with the
principle or the tenor of his bill'. The project had been fully
discussed the year before in public as well as in the House.
'There was not a member in the House, new or old, who did
not know its nature and tendency at this moment as well as
they could possibly do if the reading of it again was put off
for months.' He concluded by trying to dismiss the motion
as a frivolous attempt to keep the House free from business
on the evening on which a benefit performance was to be given
by the celebrated French dancer, Vestris; but Nugent carried
his motion by 89 to 77.[1]

By the 24th, at latest, North was sufficiently confident about
the ministry's parliamentary strength to have determined upon
a division on the second reading of Burke's bill,[2] and on the
26th he secured its defeat by 233 to 190. Perhaps because his
speech at the first appearance of the bill, on the 15th, had
suggested he was prepared to consider it clause by clause in
committee, he did not speak on this occasion. The attack on
the bill was introduced by two of his young friends in the
House, Thomas de Grey, a member of the Board of Trade,
and C. G. Perceval, and the Lord-Advocate wound up the
debate for the government. Several county members and
other independents normally friendly to the ministry voted
against it in this division. 'Mr. Keene, Sir Horace Mann,
Sir H. Gough, and others who almost always vote with Lord
North were part of the minority last night', Philip Yorke, M.P.
for the county of Cambridge, who was in the same case himself,
reported to his uncle, Lord Hardwicke. 'Mr. Pelham member
for Sussex was on the same side, and his brother, who sits for
Lewes, voted with the Court. Lords Lewisham, Hinchingbrook

---

[1] Almon and Debrett, i, 507-9.
[2] 'On Monday next, Burke's Bill is to be fought.' Lord Hillsborough
to Wm. Eden, 24 Feb. 1781, Add. MSS. 34417, f. 316.

and a few more were the only county members that voted against the second reading of the Bill.'[1]   In view of these defections on this 'popular' question, the exceptional size of the government vote had all the greater significance as an assurance of ministerial ascendancy in the House of Commons, and it was an undoubted triumph for North and Robinson. Extremely reassuring to them also was the fact that the opposition could only secure 190 votes, a total well below that mustered by the government and far less than was to be expected from Robinson's estimates of a fortnight before.

The division of 26 February was, in fact, the turning-point in this parliamentary session.   Hitherto (probably without much justification) North had been diffident, lacking in confidence in his ability to carry government business through the House of Commons.   In October, and again in December, he had flinched at the prospects and had harped on his old theme of resignation,[2] and in mid-February his hesitancy was marked. But after the 26th there was little further sign of hesitation on his part, and the King ceased to be troubled with reminders that his Minister's powers were failing — save for one occasion at the end of March, on the eve of a particularly unpleasant attack by the opposition on the management of the government loan.[3] The conduct of members and the mustering of majorities was no longer an anxiety to John Robinson and ceased for some months to be a topic of correspondence between him and his friends.[4] In the weeks following 26 February the government's financial business was carried through with dispatch: 'The whole business of the supply has gone through in the most satisfactory manner', Lord Hillsborough wrote on 21 March to William Eden. 'The opposition is at present if not dead

---

[1] 27 Feb. 1781, Add. MSS. 35379, ff. 322-3. Yorke's mention of Lewisham and Hinchingbrooke, both sons of ministers, was clearly meant to emphasize that only county members closely associated with the government voted against the bill.   [2] Fortescue, v, nos. 3164, 3206.
[3] North to George III, 25 Mar. 1781, Fortescue, v, no. 3289.
[4] The complete absence of any letters on this subject in the papers of either Robinson or Charles Jenkinson during the period mid-February to October 1781 contrasts very remarkably with the spate of correspondence upon it during the long crisis from the arrival of the news of Yorktown at the end of November 1781 till the fall of the North ministry in Mar. 1782.

at least asleep : since I have been in parliament, I do not recollect a session half so quiet.' [1] That same day the government also gave the quietus to the other outstanding items of the Economical Reform programme. The opposition leaders, by their failure to rally a full measure of parliamentary support, seem to have admitted beforehand that the game was lost. The order of the day for the commitment of the contractors' bill was defeated by 120 to 100, and Crewe's bill for the disfranchisement of revenue officers was refused second reading by 133 votes to 86.[2] The next day, 22 March, Humphrey Minchin could obtain no more than 45 votes in support of motions preparatory to a proposed enquiry into the effectiveness of the Admiralty's efforts to provide ships for the navy.[3]

Although by the end of February the main anxiety of the government with regard to the House of Commons was ended, the opposition was not quite dormant, and one more major parliamentary attack was launched before Easter. During March the opposition leaders made the most of an opportunity to pursue the Treasury with accusations of mismanaging the loan for £12,000,000 raised by North as part of the financial provision for the year. Their two main charges were, that North had made an extremely bad bargain for the Treasury, which could only be for the purpose of corruptly favouring political friends, and that gross political partiality had been shown in the distribution of stock. The loan came before the House on 7 March. On the 8th Sir Philip Jennings Clerke suggested that the report of the previous day's committee of ways and means should be rejected till a further enquiry into the circumstances of the loan had been made. On the 12th George Byng unsuccessfully moved for papers to enable the House to examine into the management of the loan. During the next fortnight the opposition's case was worked up in detail, and on the 26th all their friends were brought up for a final attack in support of a motion by Sir George Savile for a committee of enquiry.[4]

In the full-dress debate on 26 March, assertions and counter

[1] Add. MSS. 34417, ff. 325-6. [2] Debrett ii, 284-97.
[3] Ibid. 364. [4] Ibid. 204-5, 224-6, 320-31.

assertions regarding the first of the opposition's charges were freely bandied across the floor of the House, but nothing was established beyond mere statements of opinion. It was put forward by Henry Dundas as to North's credit, that he had, by delaying negotiations with the bankers until the arrival of mails from the Continent which gave some slight ground of hopes for a pacification, secured better terms than at first were offered.[1] William Ewer, deputy governor of the Bank of England, had given his assurance, in the course of the debate of 12 March, that none of those present at the negotiation of the loan had anticipated the further appreciation of government stock which had since occurred, and on which the opposition rested this part of its case.[2] North maintained from start to finish of the proceedings, that the bargain he had made, un-favourable as he admitted it to be, was the best that could have been obtained at the time.

Circumstances relating to the second charge tend to strengthen the suspicion, that the opposition was provoking a factious debate for little good reason. Their complaint notice-ably originated in matters of mere rumour. On 8 March Jennings Clerke stated that North's business adviser, Richard Atkinson, of Muir and Atkinson, had £3,300,000 of the loan to his own share, which he professed to regard as scandalous. On the 12th, Byng, rather more cautiously, stated that Atkinson was 'reported' to have £600,000. With the publication of the list of subscribers, it became apparent that Muir and Atkinson, not Atkinson himself, were included for the sum of £200,000, and that the opposition were no longer prepared to voice more than the tentative suspicion, that a sum set down against the names of the men who acted as Atkinson's attorneys might really be intended for Atkinson himself.[3] On 26 March Byng produced evidence, with a precision of detail which suggests that it was probably correct, to show that the list of subscribers to the loan was misleading. The firm of Gurnel, Hoare and Harman, despite strong protests made by Harman at the Treasury, were set down as subscribers for £560,000 although

[1] Debrett, ii, 345.   [2] *Ibid.* 329.   [3] *Ibid.* 205, 225, 328.

the £60,000 was really intended for a ministerial agent, Paul Wentworth. Noting that the firm of Muir and Atkinson were allotted £200,000, Byng observed, 'that he could scarce think this was all they had as he found the names of Messrs Smith and Sill, attorneys to Mr. Atkinson, were set down for £67,000, and which he knew was not for themselves'. He produced a list of the clerks in Messrs. Robert Drummond and Co. (the King's bankers), to whom allocations of stock had been made of from £15,000 to £41,000 and totalling over £400,000, which could hardly be regarded as on their own account. The clerks to Drummond's broker had each £25,000. All this concealment, Fox added later in the debate, was to facilitate parliamentary corruption.[1] Government spokesmen answered that this was nothing to cause alarm, since concealment of this kind was often practised and was a matter concerning the holders of stock, not the government. North, while not acknowledging any personal responsibility in this connection and stating his ignorance of some of the arrangements mentioned, admitted they might well have been made, and he expressed the belief that it was a perfectly normal proceeding: 'so long as he could recollect any thing of loans, it had been invariably the case. In his apprehension, it made very little difference, and no industry or caution could prevent it, if gentlemen chose to conceal their names. They might come in under another name, or for a part of another person's subscription, and at all events there was a risque attending managements of this kind, for which the ostensible subscriber was always responsible.' But while not controverting this part of Byng's assertions, North repudiated utterly the suggestion that various names in the list of subscribers provided cover for members of parliament whom he had favoured for political reasons with secret allocations of stock, and nothing appeared in the evidence paraded by Byng to shake his denial.[2]

An incident towards the close of the debate also fosters the impression, that the attack was a political stunt on the part of the opposition, and that they hoped to gain by sharp tactics the success which was otherwise beyond their grasp. John

[1] *Ibid.* 327–9, 357–8.   [2] *Ibid.* 364, 366.

Dunning made a last major contribution to the debate for the opposition ; then, 'when the learned gentleman had concluded, a number of members, who through the greatest part of the debate had been in the coffee rooms adjacent, now crowded in and called with loud and continued uproar for the question'. The Speaker, however, refused to be rushed into calling a division, and a further speech on the government side was delivered by the Attorney-General — perhaps to give the Treasury managers time to ensure that their majority in the House had not been swamped by an inrush of opposition supporters. When, after two further short speeches, the House divided, at about one o'clock in the morning, there were more members present than had attended at any division since the defeat of Burke's bill just a month before ; but the opposition fell far short of their strength on that occasion, the government defeating Savile's motion for an enquiry by the comfortable majority of 209 to 163.[1]

After Easter the opposition attempted one more blow in connection with Economical Reform. On 8 May Sir George Savile moved for a committee on a petition presented to the House five weeks before by thirty-two leading freeholders of various counties, praying for some remedy 'against the extensive and unconstitutional influence of the Crown', and for 'some stop . . . to the lavish expenditure of public money'.[2] But the country members upon whom the opposition relied were now deserting the House, and Savile could only secure 135 votes against 212 in a division. Two or three members, at least, who had supported Burke's bill, opposed his motion through dislike of the committees of association.[3] In general, from Easter onwards, the ministry seemed quite secure, regularly measuring its majorities on important questions by fifty or more. On 10 and 11 May, North continued his own counter-stroke against Economical Reform. On the basis of the first four reports of the Committee upon the Public Accounts, which he had set up the previous year, he initiated

---

[1] Debrett, ii, 370-1.　　　　　　　[2] *Ibid*. iii, 212-15.
[3] *Ibid*. 232, 276 ; Philip Yorke to Lord Hardwicke, 9 May 1781, Add. MSS. 35379, f. 373.

two bills, one to speed up the flow of the land tax from the hands of the receivers into the Exchequer, the other to facilitate the immediate transfer to the Exchequer of the balances outstanding on the accounts of former paymasters-general. With these he coupled a third bill renewing the Committee for a further session.[1] These measures encountered no serious opposition. On the 14th an attempt by Burke to embarrass the government by a call for papers regarding the seizure of private property by the British commanders who had occupied the Dutch island of St. Eustatius, was defeated by 160 to 86.[2] Ten days later, on the 23rd, when the government began to frame measures regarding the East India Company, it triumphed over an opposition amendment by 151 to 52.[3] Thus strongly situated, it was able by 24 June to reach an agreement with the Company for the renewal of its charter, which was carried through parliament without difficulty before the end of the session.[4]

As the session drew near its close, North had the further satisfaction of proof that the House was still fairly content to support the ministry's continuance of the American War. Twice during the spring the government was challenged on this question. As the news of march and counter-march in the southern colonies filtered into the newspapers, evidence of the continuing capacity of the Americans to mount operations in North Carolina cast a first cloud over the high hopes raised in 1780 by the British successes at Charleston and Camden. It began to be apparent that the victories claimed by Cornwallis were such only in the sense that the British forces could more than hold their own in set battles. But control of territory in the interior was beyond their power, and the reports of large bodies of loyalists ready to assist in the restoration of royal authority, with which Cornwallis had revived the hopes of the ministers in the previous autumn, were now seen to be without foundation. The ministers were reluctant to accept these

[1] Debrett, iii, 212-15.
[2] Ibid. 299, 342; North to George III, 14 May 1781, and encl., Fortescue, v, no. 3325.   [3] Debrett, iii, 378, 395, 397, 410.
[4] Ibid. 656-8, 699; L. S. Sutherland, *The East India Company in Eighteenth-century Politics*, 359-61.

unpleasant facts. One or two of them at least turned a deaf ear to all unfavourable reports, and continued to nurse hopes which bore increasingly less relation to the real situation. George III was not the only person in the circle of government who clung stubbornly to the idea that the loyalists were numerous and that with their aid America could and must be recovered. In the light of the depressing information reaching London from the commanders in America,[1] Germain's dispatches in the early part of 1781 present an almost incredible picture of deluded optimism. Early in February he thought that, such 'beyond doubt' was the 'low condition of Congress authority and finances', and 'so weak the state of Washington's army', that little opposition to British operations was to be expected in either Pennsylvania or Maryland. On 7 March he was writing to Clinton : 'so very contemptible is the rebel force now in all parts, and so vast is our superiority everywhere, that no resistance on their part is to be apprehended that can materially obstruct the progress of the King's arms in the speedy suppression of the rebellion'.[2] About the same time, Stormont was writing to Keith in Vienna of 'that disposition, which is now so manifest in a large majority of the Americans, to return to the Mother Country'.[3] It may be surmised that conversations on these lines, in the committee rooms and coffee rooms of the House and also at less purely political gatherings, helped to sustain the morale of the government's parliamentary following. It does not appear from the speeches of ministers that these illusory hopes were damped by the gloomy accounts of disaffection and defeat in the northern part of South Carolina which reached London towards the end of April,[4] nor by the unpropitious circumstances which accompanied Cornwallis's

[1] P. 241 above. On 26 Jan. 1781 Germain's office received Rawdon's dispatch to Clinton of 29 Oct. 1780, reporting further on the unpromising appearance of affairs in North Carolina and the failure of the loyalists to give any assistance. About the same time Cornwallis was describing South Carolina as 'most exceedingly disaffected' (to Leslie, 12 Nov. 1780). C.O. 5/101.
[2] To Clinton, no. 77, 7 Feb., no. 81, 7 Mar. 1781, C.O. 5/101.
[3] No. 25, 16 Mar. 1781, F.O. 7/1.
[4] Rawdon to Cornwallis, 5 Dec. 1780, Cornwallis to Clinton, 18 Jan. 1781, forwarded under cover of Clinton's to Germain, no. 119, 27 Feb. 1781, received in London, 25 Apr. 1781, C.O. 5/101.

victory at Guilford Courthouse, news of which was published in the Gazettes during May and June.[1]

Even the published information, however, provided leaders of the opposition with ample ammunition with which to renew their attacks upon the war policy of the government. On 30 May Henry Winchcombe Hartley, member for Berks, unsuccessfully moved for leave to bring in a bill to vest the Crown with sufficient powers 'to treat, consult, and finally to agree, upon the means of restoring peace with the provinces of North America'.[2] In this debate Germain took it upon himself to reaffirm his faith in the loyalists: 'He still believed as he had always done, that a great proportion of the inhabitants were inclined to a compromise with the mother country on the ground of allegiance'. If they had not sprung forth in support of Cornwallis, it was because they were unarmed and kept down by force and subjected to intensive surveillance by revolutionary committees.[3] In a thinly attended House Hartley's motion was defeated by 106 to 72. A fortnight later, on 12 June, further dispatches from Cornwallis having meanwhile appeared in print, Fox launched a more direct onslaught. He moved that the House should resolve itself into a committee to consider the American War, declaring his intention that, if this were carried, he would then move, 'that

---

[1] Cornwallis to Rawdon, 17 Mar. 1781, printed *London Gazette*, 11 May 1781; Cornwallis to Germain, 17 Mar. (2), 18 Apr. 1781, Lieut.-Col. Balfour to Germain, 1 May 1781, printed, *ibid.* 5 June 1781. Cornwallis to Germain, 18 Apr. 1781, *Correspondence of Charles, first Marquis Cornwallis,* ed. Charles Ross (3 vols., 1859), i, 89-90. This last dispatch, which ministers did not think fit to make public, would have given considerably more effect to Fox's parliamentary attack on 12 June (pp. 263-4 below). Cornwallis wrote: 'The principal reasons for undertaking a winter campaign were — the difficulty of a defensive war in South Carolina and the hopes that our friends in North Carolina, who were said to be very numerous, would make good their promises of assembling and taking an active part with us in endeavouring to re-establish his Majesty's government. Our experience has shown that their numbers are not so great as had been represented, and that their friendship was only passive. For we have received little assistance from them since our arrival . . . not above two hundred have been prevailed upon to follow us, either as provincials or militia. This being the case, the immense extent of this country, cut with numberless rivers and creeks, and the total want of internal navigation, which renders it impossible for our army to remain long in the heart of the country, will make it very difficult to reduce this province to obedience by a direct attack upon it.'

[2] Debrett, iii, 429-30.   [3] *Ibid.* 446.

His Majesty's ministers ought immediately to take every possible measure for concluding peace with our American colonies'.[1] On this occasion Fox had a worthier subject for his talents than the alleged parliamentary corruption, about which he had poured forth so much nonsense in the debate on Savile's motion at the end of March. In two speeches of very great force, he had no difficulty in showing that the campaign in North Carolina had completely failed in its object, and that government intelligence had grossly over-estimated the extent of support to be expected from loyalists in the province.[2] He based his attack on the last *Gazette*, 'from which on the authority of Lord Cornwallis, the impracticability of conquering America was plainly deducible', and declared that, 'on that alone', he would rest his argument. From Cornwallis's dispatches it was plain, he said, that geographical conditions and a disaffected people, 'timid friends and inveterate enemies', put any hope of success out of the question. As for the victory at Guilford Courthouse: 'Had our army been vanquished, what course would they have taken? Certainly they would have abandoned the field of action, and flown for refuge to the sea-side; now these are precisely the measures we were obliged to adopt after the action at Guilford, the victorious army leaving the field, abandoning the future object of its expedition, and retiring to the fleet.' Fox concluded his comments on the *Gazette* by observing: 'Though Lord Cornwallis had done everything he proposed, by penetrating into North Carolina; though he had been fortunate enough to come up with General Green, engaged, and defeated him, he had found no one good consequence of his success, not being joined by any body of Americans as he expected, nor even retaining the ground upon which he had conquered. . . . It was undeniable that the project was a vain one, similar to all the other enterprizes we had formed, during the course of the war.' Germain's reply to this onslaught was unconvincing. He devoted much time to the argument, that to pass the motion would be a confession of despondency highly encouraging to Britain's enemies. On the main point he was obliged to admit,

---

[1] Debrett, iii, 518.   [2] *Ibid.* 483 (511)-519, 575-90.

that the rebels had gained a decided advantage in North
Carolina through so terrorizing loyalists that they would not
rise for the King. This was in fact saying, though he did not
admit it, that even when supplies of arms and the protection
of a professional army were at hand, such loyalist sentiment as
existed was so half-hearted that its professors were not prepared to risk life and property in the royal cause. The speech
merited the taunt of Sir George Savile, who declared : 'The
noble lord had said more in favour of the motion made by his
honourable friend than he had urged in the course of the
debate'.[1]

The debate was not without disquieting features for the
ministers. Sir Thomas Clarges, an independent country
gentleman representing the city of Lincoln, announced his
defection from the government side, declaring his conviction
that the reconquest of America was no longer practicable.[2]
Two members of the ministerial phalanx, George Onslow and
Richard Rigby, confessed that, while they opposed Fox's
motion, they now saw little chance of any substantial success if
the war was continued.[3] But the immediate issue in parliament
was not in doubt. Many of the independents upon whom the
opposition relied for support had now dispersed, the ministerial
cohorts massed as usual at the summons of the Treasury, and
Fox's motion was defeated by 172 votes to 99.

The interactions of the government and the House of
Commons on the more salient occasions during the first
session of this parliament have been reviewed here because
they set the background for the critical period between the loss
of Yorktown and the fall of the North ministry. North bore
the main responsibility for the management of the Commons,
and his confidence in his power to discharge the task successfully
came only some months after the general election. In the first
months of the session he was far less sure of his power to
command majorities than has, perhaps, sometimes been
assumed. Confidence came with the decisive triumph of
26 February — which proved, among other things, the base-
lessness of his previous fears. In the absence of parliamentary

---

[1] *Ibid.* 536-42. [2] *Ibid.* 525-6. [3] *Ibid.* 530-1, 561.

states or of division lists for the period March to July 1781, it is impossible to deduce fully to what extent John Robinson had been able to add to the number of 253 dependable members (present and absent) recorded in his state of 14 February. But some measure of the way in which the government had attracted votes can be seen if that list is compared with the information regarding members' voting habits contained in his later parliamentary states and in the published division lists for the winter of 1781-2. If one of his 'pros.' and three 'hopefuls' had proved adverse or had deserted, as many whom he had counted as 'con' might sometimes be found voting with the government. Twelve of his 'hopefuls' had proved firm friends, another eight remained 'hopeful'. Of most consequence in this connection, at least eleven of those whom he had listed as 'doubtful' — assigning them in his abstract to the opposition — had come to vote regularly on the government side.[1] It seemed that, so long as the ministry could avoid disaster in the war, its position in the House of Commons was secure, and that, for a time at least, it would not fail to carry the House with it in continuing the struggle to reduce the colonies to obedience, in enacting burdensome financial provisions, and in defeating the wrecking moves of the opposition. But on 25 November, two days before parliament reassembled, news reached London that Cornwallis with the last army available for offensive operations in America had surrendered to Washington at Yorktown.

[1] This statement rests upon the known voting of the 'doubtfuls' on and after 12 Dec. 1781, but the number of them voting at least occasionally with the government between Feb. and July 1781 may have been greater than eleven.

CHAPTER III

YORKTOWN AND THE CRISIS WITHIN THE MINISTRY

(i)

YORKTOWN AND THE HOUSE OF COMMONS

IN the light of subsequent events, there was a certain irony in the contrasting attitudes of mind with which government and opposition looked forward to the commencement of the parliamentary session in the autumn of 1781. Little suspecting the blows which were about to fall, North and Robinson made plans for a short and quiet sitting of parliament before the Christmas recess. During August Robinson drafted a scheme of financial arrangements which would enable the recall of parliament to be postponed till 27 November,[1] and the decision to abide by these proposals was taken early in September.[2] As the end of November approached he took routine precautions to ensure an adequate attendance of government supporters, by the dispatch of circular letters and by applications to the leaders of political groups. Sandwich's answer of 21 November to a request for help in securing the attendance of naval officers and of his personal friends illustrates these proceedings : [3]

> I learn from Lord Lisburne's servants that he has written word that he shall set out from Mamhead on Saturday. I have however forwarded your letter to him by a messenger who is this day gone to Plymouth. Lord Shuldham has leave of absence and is on his way to town.
> It is utterly impossible to call Commodore Stewart from

---

[1] Robinson to George III, 3 Sept. 1781, Fortescue, v, no. 3401.
[2] Charles Jenkinson to Frederick Cornwall, 7 Sept. 1781, Add. MSS. 38308, f. 167b.   [3] Abergavenny MS. 396.

his duty, as this is the very moment when the Dutch convoy will push down the Channel if they mean to try that experiment; and the calling him from his station in the Downs where he is placed to watch them, would be highly unjustifiable. I have written to Lord Mulgrave who is at Lord Bristol's at Ickworth, but I think a letter to him from Lord North would not be misplaced.

I shall enclose your letter with one from myself to Mr Morshead, but I fear he is in the west of England.

I shall allso enclose your letter to Mr Stratton with every argument I can use to bring him to town, which I should hope will have the desired effect.

In contrast with this air of quiet confidence and competent management, opposition leaders viewed the political prospects at home with dejection and apathy, and made little preparation for the opening of the session. 'You may be anxious to know whether I shall take any part in the House', Camden wrote on 8 November to Thomas Walpole. 'I protest I do not know. Our opposition is scattered and runs wild in both houses under no leader. God knows how all this will end.' [1] Burke took comfort from the growing difficulties of Cornwallis in Virginia : 'As to North America, things there begin to operate their own cure. At least it looks as if that war was in a state of swift decay.' [2] But three weeks later he could see no promise in the state of affairs at home. Without a great change in public opinion, he felt, parliament could never be got to abandon the war. A change had begun to set in in Yorkshire, so Rockingham had informed him, but elsewhere he could perceive little sign of it. 'I saw very few symptoms of any such thing in London', he reported to Portland, 'and on the best enquiry I could make into the temper of Lloyd's coffee house, I had no reason to think the merchants were made a whit more reasonable, or better disposed, either by their alarms or their security. I am sure that if there be not a very signal change in the national temper, this people cannot be saved.' As for action in parliament, he had no suggestions, observing only, 'the session

[1] Lullings MSS.
[2] Burke to Portland, Oct. 1781, docketed 'received 24th', Portland MSS.

promises to open very oddly'.[1] About the same time, Frederick
Montagu had no idea whether the opposition was to attend in
strength or not.[2] And a week later Rockingham himself penned
a confession, which starkly reveals the feebleness of his leadership in adversity, and confirms Camden's impression of the
demoralized and shattered state of the opposition.[3]

> I go [to London] with much reluctance. I do not expect
> that the account of the decision of the attempt to relieve
> Lord Cornwallis's army, or the fate of that army, will be
> arrived at by the time of the meeting of parliament. I make
> no doubt, that His Majesty and his ministers will hold out
> and encourage various idle hopes, and I make as little doubt,
> that a majority in parliament composed of some credulous
> fools, and many corrupt knaves, will assent to whatever is
> desired to be re-echoed in the Speech.
>
> I do not know what line our friends will wish to take in
> both Houses of Parliament. I don't know who are likely
> to be in London, but *I should think several would.*

As for a programme, he had little to offer:

> My own idea would be to lament that there was no
> symptom of contrition or happy conviction *apparent* in His
> Majesty's Speech — that I also saw with concern, that there
> was no indignation arising among those who had long com-
> posed a majority in parliament — and who I should have
> thought by this time must have seen and been ready to
> resent, the gross deceptions by which they had been led to
> give support to measures, which have proved so ruinous to
> this country — that it was *in vain to contend* at present
> against such wilful blindness. The most calamitous events
> were perhaps upon the eve of happening, that even a victory
> at sea, and the being able to extricate Lord Cornwallis's
> army (which would almost be miraculous) would probably
> only *postpone* our final extirpation from the continent of
> America.

Thus, on the eve of events which were to transform the situation in their favour, furnish them with abundant ammunition,

---

[1] Same to same, 12 Nov. 1781, *ibid.*
[2] F. Montagu to Portland, 11 Nov. 1781, *ibid.*
[3] Rockingham to Portland, 19 Nov. 1781, *ibid.*

and expose the government to direct attack, the opposition leaders remained irresolute and inactive. The news of Cornwallis's defeat at Yorktown arrived too late for them to revise their counsels of despair and to solicit a fuller attendance of their friends before the first major business of the session, the debate upon the Address. The division upon the Address on 27 November, 218 to 129, reflected the contrasting results of Treasury zeal and opposition apathy.[1] But it was empty triumph for the ministers: already the news from Yorktown was stirring up uneasiness in the ranks of its followers. Opposition observers now regretted their party's lack of resolution. Lord Frederick Cavendish wrote that same evening to the Duke of Portland: 'It is a pity we had not a general muster, for I never saw so much dismay, and many of the followers of administration seem to dislike the Speech'.[2] Hastily repairing their mistake, opposition leaders were roused to summon up a greater number of supporters than had been seen in the House before Christmas in any year since the beginning of the war.

The session before Christmas, which lasted from 27 November till 20 December, was too short and insufficiently well attended, for the opposition to cause any serious embarrassment to the government. Nevertheless, in the well-founded belief that Yorktown would cause perturbation in the ranks of government supporters, the opposition leaders provoked five debates in which the future of the American War was the primary issue. Their first attack was focused upon the Address. Though this had been carefully worded to contain no direct reference to the war in America, from two general references to the struggle in which the country was engaged, they deduced the conclusion that the ministers still intended to attempt the subjugation of the revolted colonies. They devoted the debates of 27 and 28 November to denouncing this supposed intention, while the ministers, very much on the defensive, protested that the Address had been carefully framed to avoid any commitment on this point, and declared

---

[1] The attendance compared remarkably closely with that at the opening of the session the previous year, when the voting upon the Address on 6 Nov. 1780 had been 212 to 130.   [2] Portland MSS.

that they would defer till a future occasion any statement of the policy they proposed to adopt with regard to America. Two days later, on the 30th, Thomas Pitt opposed the order of the day for going into a committee of supply — the first time this had been done since 1689 — and a good deal of the same ground was covered in the debate which followed.

After this there was a pause for some days in the opposition's campaign. But the American issue was raised again in a more direct form on 12 December, when Sir James Lowther interposed with a previous motion before the House could comply with the order of the day for a committee of supply to vote the army supplies. Lowther put before the House the motion 'that it is the opinion of this House, that the war carried on in the colonies and plantations of North America, has proved ineffectual either to the protection of His Majesty's loyal subjects in the said colonies, or for defeating the dangerous designs of our enemies'. This fact was so notoriously true that the ensuing debate hardly touched upon it: attention was concentrated upon the second proposition with which he intended to follow up the first — 'that it is the opinion of this House, that under the present circumstances of the country, all further attempts to reduce the revolted colonies to obedience are contrary to the true interests of this kingdom, as tending to weaken its efforts against its ancient and powerful enemies'.[1] This motion would, if passed, have amounted to a parliamentary directive to the executive, not to take further military action against the colonies except such as might be necessary to defend bases still required for the conduct of operations against the Bourbon Powers. Also it carried at least the implication that if the colonists — not further to be coerced — insisted upon their independence, it would perforce have to be conceded. The subsequent debate centred entirely upon this second motion, although formally it was not before the House; and when the House at last entered into the delayed committee of supply on the 14th, much of the debate was a continuance of the same discussion.

The division of 12 December took place, not on Lowther's

---

[1] Debrett, v, 117-18.

motion, but on the order of the day to proceed to a committee of supply: but in casting their votes members did in fact indicate their support or their disapproval of the motion. The opposition made great efforts to bring up members for this debate: [1] in this they had considerable success, dividing 179 strong against the government's 220. As an indication of the movement of parliamentary opinion and of the balance of strength in the House, the debate and division were the most important of those which took place between the commencement of the session and the Christmas recess: the votes cast by 399 members are known from the published lists.[2] The purpose of the rest of this section is to show how opinions in the House were shaping during those weeks, how far the voting on either side might be said to be indicative of particular political views, and what light the division throws upon the state of the government's relations with the House.

Sir James Lowther's propositions of 12 December elicited from North a statement of policy remarkable for its vagueness and for what it left unstated. North felt bound

to speak more out upon the design of the future mode of the prosecution of the war than he was generally accustomed to do, or indeed than it was either wise or politic for a man in a high and responsible office to do, at any time, unless the urgent necessity of the case rendered it impossible for him to make any other election of conduct. He was willing to declare his sincere and honest opinion, 'that it would not be wise nor right to go on with the American war as we had done, that was to say, to send armies to traverse from the south to the north of the provinces in their interior parts, as had been done in a late case, and which had failed of producing the intended and the desired effect'. He was ready to say so much . . . as no farther supply of men was asked for the service of the current year, it could not possibly be the intention of Government to proceed in the war with America on the same scale, and with the same plan, as they had done hitherto. This he thought should satisfy gentlemen who were dissatisfied with that method, since it shewed

---

[1] Lord J. Cavendish to Portland, 29 Nov. [1781], Portland MSS.
[2] Debrett, v, 149-58.

them to a certainty, or next to a certainty, that it was to be conducted on a less extensive scale.

In the remainder of his speech he condemned Lowther's motions on the ground that they would, if passed, necessitate the complete abandonment of military assets in America (which ought, as later government spokesmen pointed out, to be retained if Britain was to secure an honourable peace) : for 'by the clear and expressive words of the motion, they could not carry on even a war with the other powers in that part'.[1] But what North left unsaid was perhaps more significant than what he said. The war was to go on, but he gave no indication what were to be its objectives, and he said nothing about the retention of authority over the colonies.

North's declaration would appear to have arisen from two considerations — his own changing conviction, and the parliamentary situation.

On 27 November, in the debate on the Address, North stated that the question in respect to the war was, whether members were inclined to resign their rights as a parliament or give such support 'as might, in the end, procure a peace consistent with the legislative powers over the colonies' [2] — by the wording of the Address, government stood by the policy of securing the submission of the colonists to imperial authority. But in little over a week after the debate on Lowther's motion, his mind had moved full circle, to the view that peace must be made with them, even at the price of American independence. On 21 December, in a conversation with the King, he represented the situation in the blackest terms. In a draft letter to Stormont George III indicated that North had hinted at complete surrender : [3] his language

was so extraordinary that I almost suspected that he painted his opinion in a stronger light than he felt in hopes of staggering mine . . . on this serious point he might throw off the mask ; he assured me that he had not said an yota that was not dictated by the strongest conviction ; on which

Ibid., v, 123-4, 128.   [2] Ibid. 34-5.
[3] 22 Dec. 1781, Fortescue, v, no. 3475.

I told him there were many unpleasant but intermediate steps to what I must ever deem *irrecoverable destruction* and to which I would never consent; that I by no means wanted him to open his mind to the whole Cabinet, but that now he . . . ought to fix a meeting with you and your collegue to whose province negotiations of Peace must fall: he eagerly seized the idea and said he would very much wish to open himself entirely to both of you.

In a last paragraph, which the King struck out of his draft, he revealed even more clearly his disquiet at the yielding attitude of his chief minister : [1]

> I desire Lord Hillsborough may know that I think after what I have stated he can no longer suppose it is in my power to bring Lord North right on this *essential* point. I owne I am a great enemy of persons mooting the same point and much more so when by it not the smallest ground is advanced.

George III continued to insist upon his own point of view, much to the exasperation of his Minister. On 26 December North forwarded for Robinson's information a letter in which the King had written that, if Germain retired, this must in no way be held to indicate that he was prepared to accept a separation from America; [2] and North's comment placed his own views beyond doubt: 'You see that there is no great objection to changing men, but a very great one to changing measures, and that it will be expected from me *alone* to carry on that plan which appears to me in our present circumstances ruinous and impracticable'. [3]

To what extent did other members of the cabinet agree with North? This remains obscure. The King's letter to Stormont cited above shows that he did not regard Stormont or Hillsborough as in North's camp. But if the ministers, as some believed, were afraid to press their convictions upon him, [4] how could he know? Surrender was so abhorrent to him

[1] Windsor MSS., omitted by Fortescue.
[2] Fortescue, v, no. 3485.
[3] H.M.C., *Abergavenny MSS.*, 46, no. 405.
[4] C. Matheson, *Henry Dundas, Viscount Melville* (Constable, 1933), 74.

that he closed his mind to the mere idea that any minister might be considering it. His view, therefore, is not a reliable one, and there is some evidence at least, that it was incorrect. On 12 December Germain boldly declared in the Commons that ministers were unanimous for continuing the war on the restricted plan hinted at by North.[1] But an account of the next debate, on 14 December, received by Hardwicke, hints at a clash of views between Germain and North which does not appear in the versions of their speeches printed by Debrett: 'Lord George . . . continued to hold his high language, that this country would be ruined unless America were subject to the same sovereign. He seemed to differ with Lord North who declared the war to be impracticable, and professed his design of not persisting in it any longer.'[2] North did not stand alone, for Germain thereafter regarded himself as isolated in the cabinet. On 16 December Germain wrote to the King:[3]

> In the present circumstances of affairs, there seems little probability that Your Majesty may find it convenient to continue the Seals much longer in Lord George's hands; the general dislike to the American War among the real friends of Government; the earnest desire expressed for accommodation, or rather for yielding up the rights of Sovereignty by many in Opposition and by others high in office and of great connections in the House of Commons convince Lord George that measures are taking to bring about some change in Administration. The Meeting of the Cabinet yesterday confirms this opinion, for though the conversation would naturally have tarried upon the later transactions in the House of Commons, and the measures to be pursued in North America, yet a total silence was observed upon those subjects, which marked diffidence at least in each other.

If, as appears from this letter, most of the ministers had become convinced by mid-December of the need to capitulate over America, their failure to insist upon the King's immediate acceptance of their views redounded neither to their credit nor

[1] Loughborough to W. Eden, 13 Dec. 1781, Add. MSS. 34418, f. 213.
[2] Philip Yorke to Hardwicke, 15 Dec. 1781, Add. MSS. 35380, f. 134.
[3] Fortescue, v, no. 3470.

to their wisdom. It is conceivable that they might thereby have avoided their ignominious expulsion from office three months later.

How far North himself had reached this position as early as 12 December is not certain ; but two circumstances suggest that his conversion was by then very nearly complete. He did not oppose Lowther's motions on the ground that they involved the surrender of the colonies (as Germain did), nor did he commit himself, either on the 12th or on the 14th, to any statement about the ultimate fate of America. And on the 14th, when Germain insisted that he could not agree to surrender sovereignty over the lost provinces, North made the most explicit gesture of disagreement by retiring to a seat behind the Treasury Bench, leaving Germain there alone to face the sniping of the opposition.[1]

Most probably then, by the 12th, North believed that the independence of America might have to be conceded. But he could not say so. A public announcement of opinions fiercely reprobated by the King would have made untenable his situation as the King's confidential minister. So long as there were hopes of salvaging anything from the war against the Bourbons, the effects of such an admission upon diplomacy and war operations would have been disastrous. Also it would have disrupted the government and broken in pieces the ministerial majority in the House of Commons — that is, North's declaration was, in part, a product of the parliamentary situation, not only the outcome of his own conviction. His task was to produce a statement of policy which would comprehend the views of die-hards and of those who now wanted peace. His declaration represented, so to speak, the highest common factor of American policy acceptable at that moment to the various individuals and groups on the government side of the House.

The debates between 27 November and 17 December, and especially the discussion of Lowther's motions, reveal the divergence of views which it was politically necessary for North to reconcile. In general, supporters of the government adhered to one of three main opinions. Some insisted that the war

[1] Wraxall, ii, 159-60.

must go on, with the return of the colonists to their allegiance as the object — though how this object was to be gained they did not suggest, for they admitted that the system of conducting the war hitherto adopted had proved a failure. These members took their stand — as the King himself did — refusing with blind die-hard obstinacy to accept the realities of the situation. Others (perhaps the greater part) considered that the war effort must be switched against the Bourbon powers, in the hope that Britain might attain a sufficiently strong bargaining position to salvage something of her imperial authority in America by negotiation. But these could see more or less clearly that America might have to be surrendered, and so, in varying degrees, they approached the stand taken by holders of the third opinion, who were already prepared to abandon America at once. Between the first group and the rest lay a fundamental cleavage of opinion. But holders of the second view might readily be converted to the third by the course of events.

The first of these opinions was voiced — practically alone — by Germain. He declared on 27 November that he would never give up 'the dependence' of America, for if this were done 'we should sink into perfect insignificance', and he added on 12 December that, whatever the consequences, 'he would never be the minister to sign any instrument which gave independence to America'.[1] No one else declared himself in this camp in the course of these debates, except George Daubeny, member for Bristol, who, on the 27th, spoke 'with great heat' for the continuance of the American War, stating that his constituents were prepared to sacrifice half their fortunes in the prosecution of it;[2] and Sir John Wrottesley, who would not hear of an abandonment of bases still held in the colonies, 'since the moment they were withdrawn, we effectually gave up the dependency of America'.[3] The second opinion was held, but stated only by implication, by North himself, by Welbore Ellis,[4] and by the Lord-Advocate, Henry Dundas.[5] The observations of two independents and of two

[1] Debrett, v, 43-4, 145.
[2] *Ibid.* 44.   [3] *Ibid.* 198.   [4] *Ibid.* 130-1.
[5] *Ibid.* 52-3, 143-4; Dundas to his brother, Robert Dundas, 29 Nov. 1781, cited Matheson, 74-5.

members of the court and ministerial circle may stand as representative of the third. On 12 December, Sir William Dolben declared he was 'heartily tired of the American war'; [1] and Sir John Hussey Delaval said he hoped 'every gentleman would resolve to give his best assistance to the putting an end' to it. [2]   On the 14th Richard Rigby, the Paymaster, admitted that in his view the reconquest of America was impossible and therefore the time had come to consider granting independence; [3] and Earl Nugent, holder of a sinecure as Vice-Treasurer of Ireland, 'expressed his surprise, that any man should now hesitate to grant the independence of America'. All parties, he said, 'were agreed that we could no longer carry on the war; was not this strange logic, to renounce the war and yet boggle at granting independence'. [4]

Men in the first group accepted North's declaration of 12 December, because it might be interpreted as expressing an intention to fight on for the recovery of America by other means than 'continental' campaigns (the declaration was fiercely attacked by the opposition for this reason). Those in the third group accepted it for the diametrically opposite reason, that it appeared a first step towards the abandonment of America and the ending of the war. But all sections of the government following concurred in welcoming it, on the ground that further extended operations in America, of the kind which had led to Saratoga and Yorktown, would be futile, wasteful, and tragic. On this point, for instance, the views of Wrottesley were as emphatic as those of Dolben or of Dundas.

As a move in parliamentary tactics the declaration made by North was essential. Without it the government might well have been beaten, for at least a part of its following would have deserted. Three members declared in debate that they would otherwise have voted for Lowther's motions — Sir Edward Dering, Sir William Dolben, and Henry Dundas: [5] Dundas's views were especially important, for he was building up a political connection in Scotland, and if he deserted the ministry,

[1] Debrett, v, 139-40.   [2] Ibid. 148.   [3] Ibid. 178.
[4] Ibid. 179.   [5] Ibid. 133, 140, 143-4.

others might follow his lead.[1] Two other members, Wrottesley and Delaval, indicated that it was North's declaration which decided them to support the government instead of abstaining.[2] Sir Walter Rawlinson, a close political associate of Lord Sandwich, who on the 12th voted with the ministry, had given notice privately a fortnight before that he could no longer vote for the continuance of the American War.[3] Here were at least six potential deserters, whose anxieties North managed to allay. But the number won over was substantially greater than this. The next day Lord Loughborough estimated it at about twenty ;[4] but it was probably somewhat larger, for Philip Yorke — whose information should be fairly reliable since he and his uncle John were among a group of members whom North felt it necessary to reassure in private before the debate — declared afterwards that had not North taken the steps he did, he would have been left in a minority.[5]

Tribute must be paid to North's skill in devising a formula which would comprehend all the various and conflicting views of government supporters. This formula could not provide any real basis of compromise among them, but it could suffice to gloss over differences for the moment and so to ensure a united front in the critical division of 12 December. The ministerial side was thus able to muster 220 votes. But it is simpler to state what this majority did not stand for than what it did. It was certainly not a majority for the continuation of the American War. True, members of it voted against the immediate discontinuance of 'attempts to reduce the revolted colonies to obedience'. But in many cases this was done simply in the belief that making peace should be left to the discretion of the executive, and that ministers would get better terms if their hands were not tied by parliamentary directions.

Similarly, on the opposition side, support for Lowther's propositions cloaked a considerable diversity of views. The

[1] In 1781 about twelve Scottish M.P.s had political connections with the Lord Advocate (Holden Furber, *Henry Dundas, Viscount Melville* (Oxford, 1931), 194).   [2] Debrett, v, 148.

[3] H.M.C., *Abergavenny MSS.*, 46, no. 398A.

[4] Add. MSS. 34418, f. 213.

[5] Add. MSS. 35380, ff. 130, 132-3.

actual purport of his motion was strictly limited : it demanded no more than that the resources of the country should be concentrated on a war against the Bourbons — a step which the existing state of affairs made urgently necessary. It could thus obtain general approval from independents who by no means agreed with the ulterior ideas of leaders of the opposition. It stated an opinion undoubtedly held by a number of members on the government side of the House — a fortnight previously Dundas had written to his brother: 'It is said and by me believed, that the greater part of [the] ministers are satisfied of the madness of any other proposition, but that of directing the whole remaining resource of the state to naval operations and endeavouring in some corner to beat the French'.[1] The motion did not touch upon various important issues, particularly the two questions of the future of the colonies and the retention of bases still held by British forces ; and the course of the debate showed that there were important divergences of opinion about these matters among the members who voted with the minority.

Thomas Powys of Lilford, M.P. for Northamptonshire, one of the ablest of the independents, a man with an exceptional capacity for adhering to essentials, declared that Lowther's motions 'went no further than to say that among the operations of the war America should not be the theatre'.[2] He avoided entering upon larger and more controversial points. But both Burgoyne [3] and Fox [4] took up the question of British bases in America and argued that these ought to be abandoned. Burgoyne advanced the rather debatable assertion that their retention was justified only if further offensive operations were intended : since the motion postulated an end of such operations, the bases should be surrendered. But in common with Fox he also employed the more cogent arguments, that British resources were urgently needed elsewhere and that without mastery of the seas such bases could not be held. This turn of the discussion revealed a divergence of opinion between the main body of the opposition and the Shelburne party. Like

[1] H. Dundas to R. Dundas, 29 Nov. 1781, cited Matheson, 74.
[2] Debrett, v, 122. On the character of Thomas Powys, see E. G. Forrester, *Northampton County Elections and Electioneering* (1941), 85-6.
[3] Debrett, v, 137-9.   [4] *Ibid.* 142-3.

many members on the government side, Shelburne and his friends were not yet reconciled to the idea of American independence. They shrank from steps which would strengthen the hands of the Americans in negotiation. New York and Charleston were at least bargain counters to set against American demands for independence. Isaac Barré conceded that ministers might still need to retain posts on the American coast, and evidently considered that Lowther's proposition would not preclude them from doing so.[1] Dunning agreed with him, but he also raised the more general question of the future of America, in a way which Fox and others had been careful to avoid. He thought that British troops should not be withdrawn 'without great consideration', and that 'we should be cautious how we decided upon a measure so big with the fate of the Empire'. 'He was not ready . . . to give up the dependency of America. He thought that the ruin of this country was accomplished when America was acknowledged to be independent.'[2] This language might have been used by many members of the government. But Dunning concurred in the immediate objects of Lowther's motions, and he and Barré both voted in the minority, as did three other members of Shelburne's party.[3]

Lowther's motions did not, directly, constitute a motion of no confidence in the North ministry. The existence of the government was not at that moment in question. They signified an intention to direct the activities of the executive, not an immediate desire to turn out the ministry. All the same, a majority for Lowther's motions would have brought this nearer. The attitude of the opposition leaders was that, after Yorktown, government policy must be changed and the idea of reconquering America must be abandoned, but that they could not trust ministers to make these essential changes in the direction of affairs.[4] To the independents, however, the question of confidence was not at this time raised so acutely as it was in the debates on Conway's motion in the following

[1] *Ibid.* 141.   [2] *Ibid.* 148.
[3] John Aubrey, Lord Mahon, and Sir George Yonge.
[4] Speeches of Sir Fletcher Norton, John Townshend, and Burke on 12 Dec. and of Fox and Pitt on 14 Dec., Debrett, v, 128, 131-2, 144-5, 167, 172-5.

February. At this stage, in December, the government had barely had time to appraise the situation and revise its policies, let alone to give effective indications that its intentions were changed. Accordingly, opposition arguments about no-confidence carried less weight than they were to do later, and a number of independents continued to support the government, who in February deserted it.[1]

As expected, therefore, an analysis of the lists of the division of 12 December [2] reveals little serious decline in the government vote and only a limited increase in that of the opposition. The pattern of the government majority was, approximately, court and administration following — 50 per cent, ministerial factions and family groups — 30 per cent, independents — 20 per cent. Of men classed the previous February by Robinson as 'pro' or 'hopeful', only six now voted against the government.[3] About 45 independents voted with the ministers. These included, however, only twelve representatives of English counties : [4] the greater part of the county members were now opposed to the ministry and 49 voted with the minority. The voting of independent members for London and the larger out-ports corresponded with the geographical division between west and east. The two members for Bristol, Henry Rawlinson, the merchant member for Liverpool, and his cousin, Abraham Rawlinson, also a merchant, who sat for Lancaster, voted with the government : members representing the metropolis and the east coast ports supported the opposition.[5]

---

[1] The evidence for this statement is presented in detail in the discussion of the divisions on Conway's motions, pp. 327-34 below.

[2] Debrett, v, 149-58.

[3] Henry Bankes, A. R. Bowes, Sir Thomas Clarges, James Dutton, Thomas Farrer, Lloyd Kenyon.

[4] The number may only have been eleven. The published list of the majority gives 222 names, which is two in excess of the number stated to have voted in the division. Two names which seem particularly out of place, and which were, perhaps, inserted in error, are those of Charles Penruddock, M.P. for Wilts, and Sir Patrick Blake, M.P. for Sudbury : it is not likely that either would have cast a vote so inconsistent with their usual behaviour.

[5] London, Nathaniel Newnham and Sir Watkin Lewes ; Southwark, Sir Richard Hotham ; Colchester, Christopher Potter ; Hull, William Wilberforce ; Newcastle, A. R. Bowes. The absent members for these constituencies, Hull excepted, were regular opponents of the government.

The government's majority of 41 over the opposition was not overwhelming, but this did not seem to portend any serious challenge to its parliamentary position. The ranks of the absentees appeared to promise an adequate reserve of support. 63 of them, according to their past record, were friends, and another 21 were inclined to be friendly.[1] Over 30 of these 84 members belonged to the court and administration group, and might be presumed to be reliable supporters.[2] Against these were to be set just under 70 members, whose opinions were doubtful or known to be hostile to the government. They included 14 members of opposition parties (four of whom were abroad), about 40 independents who acted at this time fairly constantly with the opposition, and another 14 who might be expected to do so.

This situation was such that the opposition could only hope to defeat the government, if three conditions were fulfilled — if it reduced its own absenteeism to a minimum, if it secured the support of absent and wavering independents, and, above all, if there were serious defections from the ranks of the government supporters. The history of the North ministry's relations with the House of Commons during the remainder of its existence is, largely, the story how these three conditions were secured.

(ii)

HENRY DUNDAS DEMANDS A 'HUMAN SACRIFICE'

From the rising of parliament on 20 December until the resumption of the session on 21 January, North was relieved from the thankless task of defending the government in the House of Commons. But parliamentary responsibilities continued to pursue him, and he was far from free of anxiety about the state of the ministerial majority. This burden was thrust

---

[1] Possibly some of them were already faltering in their loyalty to the Government; a number were among the deserters in Feb. 1782.

[2] However, 13 or 14 of these were out of England in the government services, and their votes were not therefore available.

upon him by the Lord-Advocate. Before the beginning of the recess, Henry Dundas had made up his mind that Germain and Sandwich must be dropped from the ministry. This demand he was prepared to enforce by the threat of a secession of himself and his friends from the House of Commons.

At this time Dundas was an able and active parliamentarian of some seven years' experience, vigorous, forceful, and something of a character in the House by virtue of his dogged refusal to anglicize his speech in the manner commonly adopted by the Scottish members. Hitherto — though by no means uncritical in private [1] — he had acted as a steady supporter of North's ministry, and he had been a firm opponent of American pretensions, even opposing the conciliation attempt of 1778 on the ground that it would appear an act of weakness and encourage the Americans.[2] Natural ability and his professional training as an advocate had brought him forward into prominence as one of the parliamentary spokesmen of the government.[3] By assiduous application and by exploiting his family connections, he had established the nucleus of a party among the Scottish members of the House.[4] Both in his own right, and as the leader of a political faction, he was now a man whose wishes North could not afford to ignore. A realist to his fingertips, he had, as he soon revealed to the House, no illusions about the military significance of the disaster at Yorktown. His further conclusions he kept to himself, probably in order to avoid disclosing too openly the dissensions within the government; but by Christmas at latest he was clear in his own mind, that any claim to imperial authority over the revolted colonies would have to be abandoned.[5] And while others hesitated, he felt the need for immediate action: if the ministry was to survive, both measures and men must be speedily changed.

His object in pressing for the removal of Sandwich is made clear in a letter to Robinson of March 1782. By then the ministry was on the brink of defeat, and he referred tartly to

---

[1] *E.g.* Dundas to John Robinson, 3 Nov. 1780, H.M.C., *Abergavenny MSS.*, 38, no. 321.   [2] Debrett, iii, 568-9.
[3] George III to Robinson, 2 July 1779, Add. MSS. 37834, f. 101.
[4] Furber, 194.   [5] Matheson, 75.

the rejection of his advice, which, he was sure, would have saved the situation if it had been followed: 'A few changes two months ago would [have] left us all upon our legs. But Lord Sandwich was a favourite with too many of you, and by that partiality we are reduced to what we now are.' [1]

In the opinion of Dundas, Sandwich was a dangerous political liability, and the sooner the ministry was relieved of his presence the better. There was much to commend in his administration of the navy, but it was by no means without fault, as even his friend Robinson admitted, [2] and there were many things which his enemies could attack. Moreover he was in the mortifying and vulnerable position of directing a navy inferior in numbers to the forces opposed to it. To patriotic Englishmen who, in Pitt's time, had been filled with pride at their country's oceanic supremacy, it was irritating in the last degree, to see hostile fleets venture boldly into the mouth of the Channel, and to know that Cornwallis's defeat in Virginia was in large measure due to the loss of naval supremacy in American waters. Unfortunately for Sandwich and for the government, further naval humiliation followed hard upon the news of the defeat at Yorktown. On 12 December, in accordance with plans drawn up by the Admiralty and approved by the cabinet, Admiral Kempenfelt, stationed off Ushant, intercepted the French fleet and military convoys outward bound from Brest for India and the West Indies. That evening he succeeded in taking a number of transports, but next day he found the superiority of the French ships of the line greater than he had been led to expect, and he dared not hazard an action. [3]

To the opposition this mishap was a golden opportunity. A long succession of defeats and withdrawals, rarely relieved by any victory, had lost the Head of the Admiralty any popularity he might have had, and made him the most vulnerable member of the government. An attack upon him was sound political

[1] H.M.C., *Abergavenny MSS.*, 51, no. 445.
[2] To Jenkinson, 30 July 1781, Add. MSS. 38216, ff. 316-17.
[3] Kempenfelt to the Secretary of the Admiralty, 14 Dec. 1781, Debrett, v, 354-5; *The Sandwich Papers*, edited by G. R. Barnes and J. H. Owen (4 vols., 1932-8), iv, 16.

tactics: it offered the most likely chance of forcing a first breach in the ranks of the ministry, which might lead to its final collapse. Such a move was already being contemplated by the opposition. Since the beginning of the session on 27 November, their leaders in the Commons had been vilifying Sandwich for failure to produce an adequate navy or to use effectively what forces he had. In the debate of 20 December, after news of Kempenfelt's retreat had been made public, their spokesmen set off like a pack of hounds in full cry. The expedition was 'a disaster', cried Byng; 'ignominious and disgraceful', thundered Fox.[1] A demand was made for an immediate enquiry. When parliament rose that evening for the Christmas recess, the ministers knew that their first political battles after the holidays must be fought on the least favourable and less popular of issues, a defence of Sandwich against opposition charges of mismanagement and incapacity.

Dundas — and Thurlow also — held Sandwich to be incompetent; on this point there was much stubborn wrangling with Robinson during the winter. 'I hope the Advocate will not be so hostile as you expect', Robinson wrote to Sandwich on 14 January. 'I have argued the point with him about you many and many times and never given up, either to him or to the Chancellor, that you was the properest man in this kingdom for the head of the Admiralty, with proper assistants . . . when I come to state facts to the Advocate from your instructions, I have some confidence in convincing him as to the civil department. The military he often raves about, and says that even Scotland grows dissatisfied about this part. . . .'[2] Holding such views, and believing that the naval enquiry would be a personal attack upon Sandwich, Dundas felt that the rest of the ministers should hasten to dissociate themselves from him as quickly as possible. By this means they, at least, might survive in office. But few others in ministerial circles believed that the opposition's move was aimed at Sandwich alone, and Robinson doubtless reflected their ideas when he stressed the contrary view in his talks with Dundas. 'I am truly sensible',

---

[1] Debrett, v, 202, 205.
[2] Robinson to Sandwich, 14 Jan. 1782, *The Sandwich Papers*, iv, 276.

he wrote to Sandwich on the 14th, 'that the consequences of Opposition carrying their point in this enquiry goes high indeed, and most certainly would affect the peace, comfort, and happiness of the highest: nay perhaps form a change in the Constitution.'[1] 'My attack upon the Advocate', he explained a fortnight later, 'to get him to attend and to take a favourable part in the naval enquiry, is on the public ground that it is now become a general attack on the King's government, not a personal one, that his professions to support His Majesty and the Constitution against the violent attacks of Opposition which endanger both, call upon him to exert himself on this occasion'.[2] At the beginning of February, with reluctance and without conviction, Dundas yielded to Robinson's arguments. His surrender may have been partly due to the fact that on this point his ally, Rigby, refused to support him. In mid-December Rigby had taken part in the baiting of the Admiralty.[3] But a few days later he was professing 'the warmest friendship' for Sandwich,[4] and, after being furnished with a copy of the Earl's memorandum drawn up in preparation for the enquiry,[5] he wrote to him on 28 December in terms of cordial satisfaction: 'My dear Lord, I have read over with all possible attention the inclosed paper, which very clearly evinces great attention on your part to the augmenting the naval forces of this country'.[6] What is certain, is that Dundas gave up the less reluctantly over Lord Sandwich, because he had at last got his way over the dismissal of Lord George Germain.[7]

Dundas considered Germain as an even heavier political liability than Sandwich, for the American Secretary now stood as the symbol of an unpopular and impracticable policy. In the hard reassessments of policy which must now be made the less part played by his influence the better. There was enough difficulty to be encountered from the stubborn resolution of the

---

[1] *Ibid.* 277.
[2] Robinson to Sandwich, 31 Jan. 1782, Sandwich MSS.
[3] James Hare to Carlisle, 1 Jan. 1782, H.M.C., *Carlisle MSS.*, 560-1.
[4] Sandwich to George III, 23 Dec. 1781, Fortescue, v, no. 3481.
[5] *The Sandwich Papers*, iv, 281-301; another copy, Fortescue, v, no. 3510. [6] *The Sandwich Papers*, iv, 274-5.
[7] Charles Jenkinson to George III, 3 Feb. 1782, Fortescue, v, no. 3511.

King. At the first news of the disaster to Cornwallis, George III, according to Wraxall's report, had written to Germain: 'I trust that neither Lord George Germain nor any member of the Cabinet will suppose that it makes the smallest alteration in those principles of my conduct, which have directed me in past time, and which will always continue to animate me under every event in the prosecution of the present contest'.[1] The same evening Germain was instructed to draw up new war plans for submission to the other members of the cabinet,[2] and the King wrote in the same unyielding spirit to North: 'I have no doubt when men are a little recovered of the shock felt by the bad news, and feel that if we recede no one can tell to what a degree the consequence of this country will be diminished, that they will then find the necessity of carrying on the war, though the mode of it may require alterations'.[3] The King's attitude was public knowledge. On 30 November Lord Fitzwilliam wrote to Portland: 'Your Grace will have seen with astonishment His Majesty's gracious speech: it is believed that it was made so strong in consequence of his own peremptory command: one much less violent was read to the Boards on Sunday night, but His Majesty summoned the wisdom of his Counsellors to Buckingham House at twelve o'clock that night, when he commanded them to animate it to a pitch of strength, worthy the firmness of his own great mind'.[4] It was evident to Dundas, as to many other observers, that a tug-of-war was now developing between the King and those of his advisers who appreciated that the old policies could no longer be pursued. The idea that the King should prevail appalled Dundas, for that way he foresaw in America only further military disaster and at home the early defeat of the North ministry. On 29 November he wrote to his half-brother, Robert Dundas, that affairs at Westminster were in a 'very extraordinary state'. According to rumours, which he thought were correct, most of the ministers saw the utter foolishness of any other course but that of directing all

[1] Wraxall, ii, 141-2.
[2] George III to North, 8.40 A.M. 28 Nov. 1781, Fortescue, v, no. 3449.
[3] 8.8 P.M. same date, *ibid.* no. 3450.   [4] Portland MSS.

remaining resources against the French. But it was also said that they were afraid to press their conviction upon the King : 'If this is so it is equally disgraceful to themselves as wicked to the public'. He thought parliament would probably reject any proposal for raising a new army to be sent to America and declared that he himself would oppose any such measure, regardless of the loss of present preferments and future prospects.[1] As he saw the situation, it was essential that some lead from below should be given to the ministers, which would strengthen their hands in their dealings with the King and with any colleagues who held the same obstinate opinions; and he came forward to provide it without a moment's delay. His speech on 28 November was 'a political event'.[2] 'I spoke in a manner last night in the House of Commons which must soon compel Administration to take their ground one way or another', he told his brother. 'I believe they felt it as the severest bomb ever thrown among them. . . . All I contended for . . . was that Administration should immediately take the state of the country under their serious consideration, that they should go with the result of their deliberations to His Majesty, and that those who staid in his service if their opinion was not adopted were traitors both to him and to the public.' If he had any doubts about the advisability of his action, they were soon dispelled by the approval of many of his parliamentary colleagues : 'Although nobody will take the courage or have the public virtue to hold the same line of conduct towards them, there were fifty people came to see me in private afterwards, and thanked me for what I had done'.[3] On the other side of the House also his speech attracted attention, and opposition leaders had little difficulty in guessing his aim. 'For my part', Lord John Cavendish wrote to Portland, 'I have no doubt but the Advocate, the Chancellor and most likely Rigby and his friends see the impracticability of going on with the American War, and wish to force him [North] to tell the King that it must be abandoned, or to break with him on that point.

[1] Matheson, 74.
[2] George Selwyn to Lord Carlisle, 28 [Nov. 1781], H.M.C., *Carlisle MSS.*, 538.   [3] Matheson, 74-5.

Whether they will have the resolution to go through with this purpose is more than I can guess.' [1] But there was no justification for his doubts. Once undertaken, Dundas's object was pursued with determination; and as Germain, once and again, reaffirmed his extreme views upon the American question, so the more he became the target of the Lord-Advocate's campaign. So long as Germain remained in office, it would be generally believed, however much the other ministers might deny it, that the government was bent on continuing the war for the recovery of America; and peace could never be obtained upon such terms. His retention would be politically disastrous. Nothing would more quickly provoke the disapproval of the now war-weary independent country gentlemen, and without their support the government would meet immediate and inevitable defeat in the House of Commons. Germain, therefore, must go. On this point Dundas had the whole-hearted support of Rigby, and the two men worked in the closest collaboration to secure Germain's removal.

Their campaign began during the second debate on the Address, on 28 November. From then on, now one, now the other, rose in debate, with broad hints that government policy must be reconsidered, and that those ministers whose views were overruled by their colleagues should resign. They criticized Germain's die-hard declarations and enlarged with barbed comments on discrepancies between his professions and those of Lord North. 'A minister', said Dundas on the 28th, 'who, to preserve his situation, could submit to concur in measures that he condemned, must be one of the meanest of mortals; he betrayed his trust, and deserved the execration of his country . . . the minister who would sacrifice his opinion to preserve his situation was unfit for society.' [2] Rigby on 14 December declared, 'there was something dark in the manner of acting of the two noble Lords; something obscure, of which the House had certainly a right to call for an explanation'.[3] These shafts were aimed as much at North as at Germain, implying that North ought to threaten resignation if he could not make his views prevail in the closet over those of

[1] 29 Nov. [1781], Portland MSS. [2] Debrett, v, 55. [3] *Ibid.* 177.

the American Secretary (and of the King). 'I see plainly', wrote Philip Yorke to his uncle, describing the debate of 14 December, 'that all Lord North's friends are desirous to reduce Lord G. G. to a necessity of going out ; . . . The Lord Advocate said that the noble lord had acted a very manly part in declaring his opinion with openness, and that if he still continued in the same sentiment, he would have an opportunity of acting a still more manly part than before — by which he meant that he ought to resign if his opinion was overruled in the Cabinet.'[1] After parliament rose the Lord-Advocate continued to press upon North the necessity for Germain's retirement, 'because while he remained everybody must believe it to be the resolution of His Majesty's servants that this country never was to have peace except upon terms which never could nor would be obtained'.[2]

In this task Dundas unwittingly acquired a strange associate — the King himself. At first sight, this fact is astonishing, for Germain was, by mid-December, perhaps the only member of the cabinet who still proclaimed as stubborn a veto on American independence as George III himself.[3] But the King's state of mind was such that this mattered nothing. He insisted that ministers must follow the line he laid down and eschew any move towards conceding independence :[4] what their own convictions were on the question was, in his view, entirely

[1] Philip Yorke to Lord Hardwicke, 15 Dec. 1781, Add. MSS. 35380, ff. 134-5. The force of these speeches appears only very imperfectly from the printed report of the debates, which requires to be read in conjunction with descriptions of the proceedings in private letters. Evidently some of the most telling verbal gestures made by Dundas and Rigby were missed by the reporters in the gallery, or else they were omitted by Debrett, whose version is here closely followed in the *Parliamentary History*. References to the speeches are : Dundas, 28 Nov. — Debrett, *The Parliamentary Register*, v (1782), 52-6 ; C. Matheson, *Henry Dundas, Viscount Melville* (1933), 74 ; George Selwyn to Carlisle, 28 Nov. 1781, Anthony Storer to Carlisle, 1 Dec. 1781, H.M.C., *Carlisle MSS.*, 538, 541-2 ; Rigby and Dundas, 14 Dec. — Debrett, *op. cit.* 177-9, 182-3 ; Philip Yorke to Hardwicke, cited above ; James Hare to Carlisle, 1 Jan. 1782, H.M.C., *Carlisle MSS.*, 560-1.

[2] Dundas to Robert Dundas, cited, without date, C. Matheson, 75. Cf. *The Last Journals of Horace Walpole*, ed. A. Francis Steuart (2 vols., 1910), ii, 396.

[3] Germain to George III, 16 Dec. 1781, Fortescue, v, no. 3470.

[4] George III to North, 15, 26 Dec. 1781, 21 Jan. 1782, to Stormont, 22 Dec. 1781, Fortescue, v, nos. 3469, 3475, 3485, 3501.

secondary. In consequence he set no particular value on the presence of Germain in the cabinet, and a circumstance had arisen which made him ready to dispense with his services. Sir Henry Clinton insisted upon resigning. As his successor-in-command at New York, the King wished to employ Sir Guy Carleton.[1] Carleton was an excellent choice for the appointment, but he had previously, while in command at Quebec, had personal altercations with Germain, which made Germain unwilling to re-enter into any official correspondence with him.[2] To get Carleton's services George III was prepared to pay the price of the removal of Germain from the American Department,[3] but he wished that Germain's retirement should be publicly understood as arising from his quarrel with Carleton, and not as signifying any change in his (the King's) opinion on what was for him 'the essential point . . . a peace at the expense of a separation with America . . . a step to which no difficulties shall ever get me to be in the smallest degree an instrument'.[4]

North thus found himself pressed from two sides, by men acting from very different motives, to effect a change in the composition of the government which he thought neither necessary nor desirable. During the recess he made one rather half-hearted attempt to find a successor for Germain. About 3 January he offered the American Department to Charles Jenkinson.[5] But when Jenkinson refused it, for three weeks thereafter he made no attempt to comply with the wishes of the King or the demands of Dundas. North in fact wished to keep Germain as a colleague, hoping to win him over to his own views about the necessity for an early peace even at the price of American independence.[6] His primary concern was to have a capable spokesman to answer for American affairs in the House of Commons. Himself he could not and would not

[1] Fortescue, v, no. 3468. [2] Ibid. no. 3470.
[3] Ibid. no. 3478. [4] Ibid. no. 3485.
[5] Add MSS. 38309, f. 22 ; Fortescue, v, no. 3504.
[6] This conclusion was reached, for instance, by James Hare — Hare to Carlisle, 1 Jan. 1782, H.M.C., Carlisle MSS., 561. A contrary view, that North wished to get rid of Germain, was recorded in his memoirs by Wraxall (ii, 160) and has sometimes been followed by later writers : the evidence cited below shows that this view was incorrect.

do it in addition to his other responsibilities. Jenkinson would have fitted the bill; but if Jenkinson would not act, then Germain must stay, for North could see no one else suitable for the post.[1] If Germain would only come round on the American question, Dundas might yet be satisfied and all would be well: in mid-January North told Germain's under-secretary, William Knox, that 'it was an alteration of measures, not of men, that was wanted'.[2] In the meantime he could see no advantage in getting rid of Germain on account of his American views, so long as the King maintained his veto on independence. 'I never suggested to Your Majesty', he wrote in a long explanatory letter,

> that the removal of Lord George Germain would prove of permanent benefit to your service, nor do I think it will, because, although many of my principal friends will become very lukewarm if he continues in office, I apprehend their objections are stronger against his system than against his person. . . . If General Carleton were appointed Commander in America, and Lord George Germain removed in an honourable and distinguished manner into the Upper House, and either Mr Jenkinson or Lord Advocate placed in a situation that would put it in their power to answer all American points, Your Majesty's affairs would certainly go on with greater ease for some time. But I am afraid that the difficulties we are under will not be entirely removed by this measure. Peace with America seems necessary, even if it can be obtained on no better terms than some federal alliance, or perhaps even in a less eligible mode.[3]

Until the King should give the cabinet *carte blanche* to work for a peace, North saw no reason to incur the crippling inconvenience of losing Germain's services as American minister in the Commons. If the King gave way, then would be the time to settle the question of Germain's situation if he should continue firm in his die-hard attitude. As for the King's desire for Carleton's appointment, North attached less importance to this

---

[1] Fortescue, v, no. 3503 ; Add. MSS. 38217, f. 265.
[2] Knox's Memorandum, H.M.C., *Knox MSS.*, 274.
[3] [21 Jan. 1782], Fortescue, v, no. 3503.

than to his own concern for a strong Treasury Bench in the House of Commons. Accordingly he put off the question of Germain's resignation to the very last possible moment — until, on the reassembly of parliament, the Lord-Advocate forced him to give way.

Germain's removal at the end of January was due, finally, to an ultimatum from Dundas. The Lord-Advocate wasted no time. Parliament reassembled on the 21st. On the 22nd he reached London on his return from Scotland. The same day he and Rigby made an appearance in the House of Commons, but then went away, declaring their intention not to attend, so long as Germain remained in office.[1]

The situation of the government in relation to the House of Commons was too vulnerable for North to dare to stand out against this threat. The political support of the Lord-Advocate was essential, alike for his personal talents and in view of the extent of his connections. As a debater, Dundas was outstanding. North regarded him, next to Germain and Jenkinson, as one of the most able and valuable supporters of the government in the House of Commons. 'Ability, spirit, eloquence, he has in perfection', he wrote.[2] And not only would the defection of Dundas leave a gap in the ministry's all-too-thin line of defence ; there was the question, how many others might he carry with him ? Two or three of the Scottish members were his particular friends. Andrew Stuart, M.P. for Lanarkshire, was bound to the Dundases of Arniston by close ties of friendship, and their political connections in Lanark were placed at his disposal in alliance with the Hamilton interest.[3] Both he and Sir Adam Fergusson, M.P. for Ayrshire, were members whose interests the Lord-Advocate sought to promote.[4] Hew

---

[1] Sir Grey Cooper to W. Eden, 29 Jan. 1782, Add. MSS. 34418, ff. 310-11 ; H.M.C., *Knox MSS.*, 276 ; W. Knox to W. Eden, 1 Feb. 1782, Add. MSS. 46490-1.

[2] To George III [21 Jan. 1782], Fortescue, v, no. 3503.

[3] Andrew Stuart to the Duchess of Argyll, 9 Oct. 1773, *Intimate Society Letters of the Eighteenth Century*, edited by the Duke of Argyll (*c.* 1910), i, 181-2 ; *The Political State of Scotland*, ed. Sir Charles Elphinstone Adam (1887), 212-3.

[4] H. Dundas to Robinson, 26 Dec. 1780 and 6 July 1781, Abergavenny MSS. 337, 368 ; H. Dundas to W. Eden, 20 July 1781, Add. MSS, 34417, f. 398.

Dalrymple, M.P. for Haddingtonshire, was another protégé: a 'steady friend' Dundas called him on more than one occasion.[1] Alexander Garden, Lord Graham, and Peter Johnston were other Scotsmen reckoned by Dundas as followers not long afterwards.[2] Including Dundas, here were seven members whose support would probably be lost if Germain were not dropped from the government. And possibly there might be other defections. Owing to Dundas's close political alliance with the Duke of Buccleuch, his connections with the Gordons, and his extensive family relationships with other leading Scottish families whose members exerted strong influence in parliamentary elections, he could count in 1782 perhaps another five or six Scottish members who were beholden to him for assistance during the elections in 1780 and to whom his help might be valuable again in the future.[3] The Duke of Buccleuch, who followed Dundas 'blindly', had much the leading interest in the county of Selkirk, and the member, John Pringle, was indebted to their good offices.[4] The Duke of Gordon's group included his brother, Lord William Gordon, his stepfather Staats Long Morris, his uncle Lord Adam Gordon, and Lord Adam's brother-in-law Adam Drummond; and, less certainly, his cousin Francis Charteris. On 12 December 1781 the Scottish members voting for the government had numbered more than half the ministerial majority of forty-one. North could not afford to risk desertions in this quarter.

Rigby was of less political consequence than Dundas; still, the threat of his defection was serious. He had been connected with the old Bedford party, and there was no telling how his example might react upon members of that set now gathered in the train of Earl Gower. It might also have some effect on the loyalty of one or two of the members from eastern Essex,

---

[1] Dundas to Robinson, 23 Mar. 1781, Abergavenny MS. 354; to George Rose, 5 Mar. [1783], Lansdowne MSS.; parliamentary list, Melville MSS., under 'Connections of Lord Shelburne's Government'.

[2] *Ibid.*

[3] G. W. T. Omond, *Arniston Memoirs* (Edinburgh, 1887), 212; Furber, 194.

[4] *Ibid.* 191, 195; *The Political State of Scotland*, 315.

where he had large estates and some influence. Furthermore, Rigby had his own little clique in the House [1] — his nephew and heir, Francis Hale; Robert Mackreth, the ex-waiter from White's turned financier, who borrowed sums from the funds which lay in Rigby's hands as paymaster to reinvest them in loans to his clients; and John Dawes, a banker and the son of a stockbroker, whose profession suggests that his connection with Rigby was also of a financial character.

Only the roughest estimate can be made, but it seems likely that had North stood firm over Germain, Dundas and Rigby might have deprived the government of somewhere between ten and twenty regular ministerial supporters in the House of Commons. But to these defections there would have had to be added the desertion of many independent country gentlemen, now inclined to peace at any price, who would not have supported a government which seemed pledged by the presence of Germain to continue the war. In these circumstances there would quite certainly have been no ministerial majority. North had to give way. A conference with Germain on 22 January showed him that while the American Secretary had come round so far as to contemplate seeking a truce on the basis of the *uti possidetis*, he was as adamant as ever on the subject of independence.[2] Dundas proved equally firm. The last week of January was spent by North discussing and planning various new arrangements for the American Department, trying once again, it would seem, to secure Jenkinson's services, and perhaps also delaying in hopes that Dundas or Germain would change their minds.[3] On the 31st, at last, he reconciled himself to the replacement of the stubborn Germain by the willing nonentity, Welbore Ellis — an appointment which provoked from Horace Walpole the scornful comment: 'Nay what may [England] not recover with the semblance of a new Secretary, who has all the activity of an Aulic counsellor, the circumstantial minuteness of a churchwarden, and the

[1] Parliamentary list, Melville MSS.
[2] Knox's Memorandum, H.M.C., *Knox MSS.*, 275-6.
[3] Hillsborough to Robinson, 27 Jan. 1782, H.M.C., *Abergavenny MSS.*, 47-8, no. 413.

vigour of another Methusalem'.[1] It was a poor arrangement, but Jenkinson persisted in his refusal, Dundas would not do,[2] and none better was to be had.

Charles Jenkinson wrote to the King on 3 February : [3]

> I understand that a great deal has passed between Lord North and the Lord Advocate, through Mr. Robinson, which as I apprehend, Lord North has never communicated to Your Majesty, nor Mr. Robinson to me. The purport, as I am informed, was that Lord George must be dismissed before the Lord Advocate would consent to come into the House of Commons, and I suspect that Mr. Robinson has consented to give up Lord George in order to save Lord Sandwich, for I am now told that the Lord Advocate will be satisfied with *one human sacrifice*. This is the expression that was made use of. The whole transaction is very strange and humiliating.

The breach in the ranks of the government's following was now hastily closed. It seemed likely, however, that Dundas's stroke had succeeded too late. Loughborough wrote on 31 January that Germain's impending retirement, 'whenever it happens is supposed to imply that our American pretensions are lowered'.[4] But this impression was not general in less-well-informed circles. Charles Townshend wrote to William Cornwallis on 6 February: 'The only public news which I have to send you is that Lord G. Germain is retired, and a peer. His removal does not yet appear to be attended with any change of measures, if we can credit reports. Arnold is to go out with a considerable command, and the American war is to [be] carried on with great vigour.' [5] The delay in getting rid of Lord George had doubtless helped to foster these rumours. They were damaging to the government, and certainly anathema to Dundas, whose main concern had been

[1] Knox's Memorandum, H.M.C., *Knox MSS.*, 276 ; Walpole to the Countess of Upper Ossory, 9 Feb. 1782.
[2] Hillsborough to Robinson, 27 Jan. 1782, H.M.C., *Abergavenny MSS.* 47, no. 413.
[3] Fortescue, v, no. 3511.
[4] To W. Eden, 31 Jan. 1782, Add. MSS. 34418, f. 312.
[5] H.M.C., *Cornwallis-Wykeham-Martin MSS.*, 327.

to dissociate the ministers as completely as possible from the unyielding policy which Germain had symbolized. It was thus under auspices far less favourable than Dundas had hoped for, that the government faced its impending parliamentary battles.

CHAPTER IV

THE PARLIAMENTARY CRISIS

(i)

ATTENDANCE IN THE HOUSE AND THE DIVISION LISTS OF FEBRUARY AND MARCH 1782

HENRY DUNDAS'S coup against Germain ushered in the parliamentary crisis. Between the beginning of February and the middle of March the opposition challenged the government in six major divisions. On 7 and on 20 February Sandwich's naval administration came under attack. On the 22nd and again on the 27th the opposition expressed distrust of the government's American policy, carrying the House with it at the second attempt — a first outright defeat for the ministers. On 8 and 15 March it brought motions of no-confidence against them. During all these proceedings the organizers on both sides of the House were acutely concerned with the attendance and voting of members and made exceptional efforts to promote the one and keep record of the other.

Throughout the period covered by these divisions, the leaders of opposition laid the greatest stress upon the enforcement of attendance by the call of the House. Acutely conscious that success depended upon the votes of the independents, they showed complete disregard of the convention that a call, followed by a call of defaulters, should take place once only during a session. At first, George Byng, the 'whip' of the Rockingham-Portland group, even intervened himself in the arrangements; afterwards, they were left, as was more usual, in the hands of friendly independents, more especially in those of Sir Joseph Mawbey, the Southwark distiller, M.P. for Surrey, who regarded this as one of his special cares.

On 5 December, in anticipation of the critical business to be discussed after the recess, the House had resolved that a call should be held on 31 January. On the last day before the recess, after vain demands that the length of the vacation should be reduced, Byng secured the passing of a resolution fixing a call of the House for the first day of reassembly after the Christmas adjournment, 21 January, and he declared his intention that it should be rigorously enforced.[1] There had thus arisen the rather unusual situation, that orders for two calls of the House subsisted at the same time. Even more unusual use of the procedure of the call was to follow. When the House met after Christmas, this second, but earlier, call duly took place, and defaulters were ordered to attend on the 31st, the day for which the original order for a call was still outstanding.[2] On the 31st, with the call-over of defaulters, the taking of the remaining call, and the usual summons to defaulters arising therefrom, these proceedings, in a normal year, would have come to an end. But Byng and his friends were determined to hold the threat of the call over the heads of members in order to keep the independents at Westminster and to ensure attendance at critical divisions. On the 24th, to exploit the full attendance which the call would bring, Fox fixed for the 31st his committee of enquiry into Sandwich's naval administration.[3] He and his colleagues in opposition were therefore all the more indignant, when, on the 28th, with the plea that information could not be provided so soon, the ministry decided to postpone the enquiry till the following week. George Byng complained: 'It had an ill appearance, that the Admiralty should wish to put off the enquiry for Thursday next: on that day the House was to be called over: and it was only in a full House that so important an enquiry should take place'.[4] On the next day, the 29th, Mawbey wished to adjourn the call from the 31st until 7 February, so that it could coincide with the new date fixed for the naval

---

[1] Debrett, v, 203, 205, 224; *Commons Journals*, xxxviii, 610, 628.
[2] *Commons Journals*, xxxviii, 630.
[3] Debrett, v, 248(228)-248, 258: proceedings incorrectly dated as 23 Jan. 1782.   [4] *Ibid.* 268.

enquiry. Byng supported his proposal, declaring that, 'He wanted the attendance of the independent gentlemen; and he was determined not only to do his duty himself, but also, as far as in him lay, to make others do theirs'.[1] This suggestion was not accepted; but on the 31st the call was adjourned until 11 February.[2] By that date, when Mawbey moved that the call be adjourned yet again for a fortnight, discontent began to be voiced, and there was a 'tedious conversation' between those who wished to have the House called over forthwith and others who wished to have the order adjourned, 'that it might be still kept hanging over the heads of members, in order to enforce attendance'. Finally a further call was fixed for 21 February.[3] When, on the 20th, the House sat so late that there was no prospect of a sitting on the 21st, this order was discharged before the House rose, and a new order made for a call on the 27th.[4] This, in its turn, was superseded by an order for a call on 7 March;[5] but before this day had arrived, an alteration in the government's parliamentary programme was made the excuse for yet another deferment. On 6 March Sir Joseph Mawbey, observing that the First Lord of the Treasury had put off his tax proposals until the following Monday, while the call of the House stood for the morrow, declared: 'It would be exceedingly proper that the call be put off until a proper day, that gentlemen might not leave town at a time when such material business was likely to come on'. On motions put by him, the order for the call on the 7th was discharged and a new one made for the 14th.[6] Similar tactics and similar arguments were used again by Mawbey on 14 March, to the annoyance of John Rolle and one or two other independents. Rolle 'as usual' opposed the call of the House being deferred unless it were put off entirely and moved to postpone it for six months.[7] This aroused a storm of protest from Mawbey and from Sir

[1] *Ibid.* 281-2.
[2] *Ibid.* 283; *Commons Journals*, xxxviii, 659.
[3] Debrett, v, 420; *Commons Journals*, xxxviii, 779.
[4] *Ibid.* 809, states that the call was put off till the 28th, but this appears to be an error, for the call was treated as an order of the day on the 27th (*ibid.* 861). [5] *Ibid.* 861.
[6] Debrett, vi, 374; *Commons Journals*, xxxviii, 874.
[7] Debrett, vi, 446.

Philip Jennings Clerke, who declared 'there never was any time so critical as the present, or which so forcibly called for the attendance of the House; and therefore they thought where gentlemen would be so regardless of the interest of the nation, they ought to be compelled to pay that duty, which they owed their constituents and their country'.[1] After this outburst the deferment of the call was approved, and fixed for Tuesday 26 March.[2] Before that day North had announced the resignation of the ministry.

Whether because of these unorthodox tactics of the opposition, or because of the independents' concern at the state of the country's affairs, attendance at the House reached a remarkable level, and it appears to have been maintained with greater consistency than during the previous crisis in 1780. Robinson's states and the printed division lists reveal that (excluding the Speaker) only forty-two members did not vote at all in any of the five great divisions from 20 February to 15 March, and the reasons for the absence of most of these members are known. Fourteen friends and four opponents of the government were abroad, including three serving naval officers,[3] one diplomat,[4] three men serving in civil or military employment in India,[5] two in Ireland,[6] three in America,[7] one at least who had gone for the sake of his health,[8] and one at least who had gone to escape his creditors.[9] Two members, Sir John Eden and Charles Dundas, who were on opposite sides of the House and had a permanent arrangement to pair during their absence, were away on their private affairs.[10] Eight members, two of whom died before the end of the crisis, are shown as ill in one or more of Robinson's lists,[11] but to these there must also be

[1] *Morning Post*, 15 Mar. 1782, 2.
[2] *Commons Journals*, xxxviii, 894.
[3] Captain Elphinstone, Captain Lord Robert Manners, and Admiral Rodney.   [4] Sir James Harris, at Petersburg.
[5] Benfield, Lord MacLeod, Sir Hector Munro.
[6] W. Eden and Colonel Luttrell.
[7] George Damer, Sir Henry Clinton, Harry Burrard.
[8] Sir Charles Cocks.   [9] Thomas Walpole, then living in Paris.
[10] *Commons Journals*, xxxviii, 683, 697.
[11] A. Bacon, Lord Robert Bertie, Sir Merrick Burrell, General W. Keppel, General Robert Monckton, Sir Hugh Owen, C. F. Scudamore, and Lord Wenman.

added Charles Ambler and R. Hippesley Coxe, making ten in all. Ambler was granted leave by the House for the recovery of his health on 12 March.[1] Coxe had informed Portland before Christmas that convalescence after a severe illness had taken him into the country.[2] Absence was deliberate, and for political reasons, in at least four cases : Anthony Eyre ignored repeated applications for his attendance ;[3] John Fownes Luttrell and James Luttrell, so Robinson noted on 8 March, would not attend ;[4] and William Woodley kept away from the House because his obligation to Lord Ailesbury for his seat prevented him from voting against the government.[5] This leaves seven absences for which I have not found an explanation. John Acland may have been kept away by private affairs, for he had leave of absence from the House,[6] and illness may have been the reason for the absence of three others : T. P. Legh and Lord Robert Manners, senior, whom Robinson noted on 8 March as not able to attend — Manners died a few weeks later ; and Thomas Noel, M.P. for Rutland, noted by Robinson 'never attends', who was in his seventy-seventh or seventy-eighth year.[7] The reasons for absence of George Dempster, Sir James Lowther, and Sir Herbert Mackworth are unknown.

Apart from these absentees, and although not more than 468 members appeared in the House at any one division, there were about five hundred members at Westminster during the weeks from 20 February to 15 March, all but fifty or so being present throughout that period. Certainly in this time of crisis the attention of members of parliament to their business gave little ground for complaint.

The same close preoccupation with numbers which led the opposition to make such use of the call of the House produced also an exceptional abundance of printed and manuscript division lists. The production of this material — which greatly facilitates study of the relations between government and House

---

[1] *Commons Journals*, xxxviii, 886.
[2] R. H. Coxe to Portland, 1 Dec. 1781, Portland MSS.
[3] Fortescue, iv, no. 2580, v, no. 3560 enclosure.
[4] 'State, 8 March 1782', Abergavenny MSS.
[5] See pp. 64-5 above.   [6] *Commons Journals*, xxxviii, 679.
[7] 'State, 8 March 1782', Abergavenny MSS.

of Commons during the last four weeks of the North ministry
— was a work partly of the parliamentary organizers, partly
of the now rapidly expanding London press. From these
sources, and from other scattered information, it is possible to
construct complete lists for the divisions of 20 and 27 February
and of 8 and 15 March, and a list of the government majority
on 22 February.[1]

(ii)

THE NAVAL ENQUIRY: MINISTERS WITH THEIR BACKS TO THE WALL

Henry Dundas had scarcely time to congratulate himself upon
forcing the government to jettison Germain, or Lord North
time to arrange the appointment of Germain's successor, before
the onset of the first of the parliamentary shocks, which, within
six weeks, were to sweep away the ministry. The opposition
leaders, as they had threatened before Christmas, aimed their
first stroke at the weakest point in the government's armour:
they demanded the resignation of the First Lord of the
Admiralty. Many considerations combined to fix them on this
course: the bitter feelings engendered by Keppel's court-
martial in 1779; the failure of the Admiralty to produce, as if
out of a hat, a three-power navy; the string of recent naval
failures and humiliations; the knowledge or suspicion that
elements within the government itself were hostile to Sandwich; and, not least, the hope that the removal of another
minister would bring the whole government edifice tumbling
down — 'an administration', Bamber Gascoyne, a Lord of the
Admiralty, told John Sinclair about this time, 'is like a set of
nine-pins. If you knock one down, the others are very apt to
follow in succession.'[2]

The attack gave rise to two crucial debates and divisions in
the House of Commons. On 7 February, in a Committee of the
Whole House, the ministers defeated a motion of censure by

[1] For these division lists, see Appendix II, pp. 376-405.
[2] *The Correspondence of the Right Honourable Sir John Sinclair, Bart.*,
. . . edited by himself, 2 vols., 1831, i, 77.

205 to 183. On the 20th, in an ordinary sitting, they quashed a second vote of censure, this time by the slightly reduced majority of 236 to 217. On neither occasion were these slender majorities reassuring to the government. On the whole, its voting strength was fairly well maintained; but the increase of the minority in the second division was formidable, for whenever opposition could find over 200 supporters in the House, the ministry was hard-pressed indeed.

There are no lists showing the voting of members in the division of 7 February, though some information is available concerning government supporters and friendly independents who failed to attend.[1] For the division of the 20th, there are lists drawn up by both sides — the government lists compiled by Robinson for official use and the lists published by printers connected with the opposition. These reveal the alignment of forces in the House of Commons soon after the commencement of the crisis, and they also make clear the first stage in the undermining of the parliamentary foundations of the North ministry.

The call of the House of Commons on 21 January revealed an attendance of 443 [2] — the independent members were up in force, a circumstance that augured well for the opposition. Three days later, on the 24th, Fox moved for an enquiry into the naval administration.[3] At the commencement of a long speech, after some preliminary tilts at Sandwich, he indicated that the proposed enquiry would be confined to the conduct of recent naval operations. Setting aside any question as to what naval forces the First Lord might have mustered by proper exertions, it would be limited to examining whether he 'had employed the forces which he really had . . . with wisdom and ability'. Fox excluded from the enquiry any investigation of the First Lord's efforts to provide adequate fleets: this, he declared, would make it too tedious and perplexing; it would also, he insinuated, be of little avail, as it would 'bring forward

---

[1] Sandwich to George III, 20 (should be 19) Feb. 1782, Fortescue, v, no. 3521, and accompanying list of members, Fortescue, iv, no. 2580 (misplaced by the editor).
[2] George Aust to Lord Hardwicke, 24 Jan. 1782, Add. MSS. 35619, f. 45.   [3] Debrett, v, 248-52, 233-48 (duplicated page numbers).

so many office witnesses, witnesses all under the patronage of the noble lord himself'.[1] Fox's speech reflected his grasp of the essential point, that, for the opposition to gain any advantage, their onslaught must be brief, sharp, and easily understood; above all, the country gentlemen, whose support they hoped for, must not be bored or frightened away by tedious detail. He and his friends would exhibit a few outstanding examples of failure on the part of the Admiralty, backed by simple evidence, and the country gentlemen would be invited to condemn Lord Sandwich on these grounds. Having thus defined the general scope of the proposed enquiry, Fox, for good measure, launched out upon a general catalogue and survey of naval failures and deficiencies since the beginning of the American War. He concluded by moving 'that it be referred to a committee to inquire into the causes of the want of success of His Majesty's naval forces during this war, and more particularly in the year 1781'.[2]

This motion was not opposed by the ministers. At that moment they were in no position to cry defiance, for the revolt of Rigby and Dundas had not yet been dealt with. In any case it would have been unadvisable to refuse an enquiry. This would have suggested that Sandwich had something to hide. In fact, he was confident from the start that his work at the Admiralty could be fully vindicated,[3] and his colleagues pinned their hopes on his ability to clear himself when the enquiry should come on. The motion therefore passed without a division, one member only, John Luttrell, expressing dissent. Fox then moved, without opposition, for the enquiry to be undertaken in a Committee of the Whole House on the following Thursday (31 January). He followed this step with various motions for papers, which he wished should be laid before the House, and by the evidence of which he intended to justify a motion of censure against Sandwich; and further papers were moved for on the following day.[4]

As the debate proceeded, Sandwich awaited with anxiety

---

[1] Debrett, v, 233.   [2] *Ibid.* 248 duplicate.
[3] Sandwich to Robinson, 13 Jan. 1782, H.M.C., *Abergavenny MSS.*, 47, no. 408.   [4] Debrett, v, 258-61, 262-4.

news of the direction of the attack to which he must make answer, and Robinson sent him word of Fox's first motion as soon as Fox had finished speaking. The First Lord was somewhat disturbed. In the written and verbal messages he returned to Robinson, he expressed a dislike of the possibility of a secret or a select committee: 'My wish is that by all means it should be a Committee of the Whole House that the enquiry may be as publick as possible, and that every member in the House may have an opportunity of making what enquiry he thinks proper'.[1] However, the ministers in the House were not required to fight for this point, as Fox sought the same object with his second motion.

Sandwich was also disconcerted at Fox's decision to omit any investigation into his alleged failure to increase the country's naval strength. Before the recess he had been subjected to sweeping denunciations on this score by opposition speakers in the Commons,[2] and he feared the effects of these diatribes (if they remained unanswered) upon the independent supporters of the Government. 'Surely', he wrote in his scribbled message to Robinson, 'your country gentlemen will not be satisfied with a partial enquiry upon the military operations; I understand that they were uneasy on an apprehension that the Admiralty had not used proper exertions to augment the fleet.' Anticipating that the main weight of the opposition attack would be directed upon this part of his administration, he had taken particular pains to amass evidence to refute such charges.[3] Now the enquiry, as shaped by Fox, would deprive him of the chance of using what was perhaps the most effective

[1] An unaddressed note in Sandwich's hand, endorsed by Robinson · '24th January 1782, Lord Sandwich's minutes of his wishes on Mr. Fox's motions. Received at the House on my sending the motion to him. J.R.' On first receiving the paper, Robinson pencilled on it two messages: 'Mr. B. says Lord Sandwich has no objection to the motion, but fears under the word Committee a secret or select committee by ballot'; and, at the foot: 'Read this and then put it into the hands of Lord North which I cannot do as Lord Mulgrave is speaking'. — Abergavenny MS. 411. I have been unable to identify 'Mr. B.' Probably he was North's private secretary, William Brummell.

[2] Debrett, v, 21-3, 26, 57, 66-8, 98-101, 112.

[3] Richard Rigby to Sandwich, 28 Dec. 1781, Sandwich MSS., cited p. 287 above; 'State of Naval Affairs, Jan. 1782', Fortescue, v, no. 3510.

part of his defence. However, the ministers in the Commons could not alter the form of the enquiry to Sandwich's liking; and it was of little use for them to hint at a wish that Fox would do so, as Lord Mulgrave, Sandwich's chief adjutant at the Admiralty, did in his reply to Fox's opening speech.[1] Fox had chosen the ground which, from the point of view of parliamentary tactics, suited him best, and gave the least advantage to his adversary, and it was his decision that determined the course of proceedings.

On the morrow Sandwich was in better spirits, writing to Robinson: 'I hope yesterday was a good day for administration as well as for the Admiralty, and I flatter myself that we shall none of us be idle between this and Thursday next in ransacking every quarter to secure attendance on that day; . . . We are preparing and digesting . . . a narrative of everything that seems necessary as materials to answer the several heads of enquiry.' But one cloud still darkened his horizon. 'I understand', he added in a postscript to his letter, 'that neither the Lord Advocate or Lord Howe was yesterday at the House.'[2]

His anxiety was fully justified. By this time the conciliation of the Lord-Advocate was, indeed, as essential a preliminary as any other preparations to the holding of the naval enquiry. His vote, and those of his friends, could not be spared. It was possibly this circumstance which gave rise to the decision of the ministers on 28 January, to secure postponement of the enquiry for a further week, until 7 February. Their ostensible reason was that more time was needed for the copying of documents to be laid before the House:[3] but it is not unlikely that North also wanted more time to try and win over Dundas, who had declared 'without reserve in many places that he would not defend Lord Sandwich, nor even attend the enquiry'.[4] Until very near the eleventh hour, the ministers remained uneasily uncertain about his intentions.

---

[1] Debrett, v, 254: this was presumably the speech which Mulgrave was in the course of making when Sandwich's message reached Robinson.

[2] Abergavenny MS. 412.

[3] Debrett, v, 264-6.

[4] James Hare to Lord Carlisle, 11 Feb. 1782, H.M.C., *Carlisle MSS.*, 575.

Robinson was still wrestling with him in argument on the 31st,[1] and about 3 February his attitude was still doubtful : 'I think', Sandwich wrote that day to Robinson, 'it is absolutely necessary you should see the Lord Advocate without delay, as it is very material to know whether he is adverse or not'.[2] Four days later Dundas grudgingly attended the enquiry — exposing himself in consequence to the taunts of Fox — but he declined to speak in Sandwich's defence.[3]

The correspondence between Sandwich and Robinson, incomplete though it is, makes it possible to observe two other phases in the parliamentary preparations for the naval enquiry — the organization of a group of spokesmen ready to take the lead in the debate, and the last-minute briefing of a more general meeting of members of the Commons, whose support was expected or hoped for. Sandwich was quite confident that he could produce a defence against any attack which might be made upon him, but for its presentation in parliament he felt himself entirely dependent on North and Robinson. This was their responsibility in their special field, and Robinson applied himself to the task with his usual zeal. In a conversation with Sandwich on or about 13 January, he first suggested a meeting between Sandwich, North, and some of the principal government supporters in the House of Commons. Sandwich concurred eagerly with the suggestion. 'A meeting of the kind you mention', he wrote, '. . . seems to me absolutely necessary, and should that not be obtained with cheerfulness on the part of the friends of Government, I should not augur very well of the event of the enquiry. With that kind of support I fear nothing, but am inclined to flatter myself that Government as well as myself will gain credit from the enquiry.' He urged that it should take place before the meeting of parliament on the 21st. Ellis and Jenkinson, he believed, could be relied upon to attend and give assistance, and he welcomed Robinson's

[1] Robinson to Sandwich, 31 Jan. 1782, Sandwich MSS. ; Sandwich to Robinson, 1 Feb. 1782, Abergavenny MS. 416.
[2] Abergavenny MS. 417.
[3] James Hare to Lord Carlisle, 11 Feb. 1782, H.M.C., *Carlisle MSS.*, 575. Debrett's report of Fox's speech in this debate makes no reference to Fox's attacks upon Dundas mentioned by Hare.

idea of recruiting a promising young member of the court circle, Thomas Orde. 'You desire [me]', he went on, 'to give my opinion how the motion for the enquiry shall be treated, and that you will talk to Lord North as I shall fix; in answer to this I can only say that this is a question utterly impossible for me to decide, or to give an opinion on in writing; the meeting of the gentlemen of the House of Commons can only decide that measure; they know the disposition of the House and how it is to be managed.'[1]

Robinson replied next day proposing the following Saturday (the 19th) for the meeting.[2]   At this time he envisaged the brunt of the debate being borne by the members of the Admiralty in the House of Commons: 'It will be right in my opinion not only to have Lord Mulgrave present at the meeting on Saturday, but also all the other Lords of the Admiralty and Mr. Stephens;[3] and so I mean to propose to Lord North unless you shall disapprove of it. . . . I am for having the whole Admiralty because I think it will lay with them chiefly to speak first on what I apprehend will be the first motion of Opposition'.[4]

There is no other reference to this meeting in the correspondence of either Sandwich or Robinson, though it may be presumed from later developments that it took place. The subject recurred in letters at the end of the month, when a note from Robinson mentioned that it had been decided to add C. G. Perceval — son of a former head of the Admiralty and a political client of North — to the 'panel' of government speakers. Papers had been supplied both to him and to Orde, and Sandwich displayed anxiety to brief them; his office was then hard at work preparing copies of a précis of his defence to be distributed among 'our leading friends'.[5]

A letter from Sandwich to Robinson of 3 February dis-

---

[1] Sandwich to Robinson, 13 Jan. 1782, Abergavenny MS. 408.
[2] Robinson to Sandwich, 14 Jan. 1782 (first letter of this date), *The Sandwich Papers*, iv, 276.   [3] Secretary to the Admiralty.
[4] Robinson to Sandwich, 14 Jan. 1782 (second letter of this date), *The Sandwich Papers*, iv, 277.
[5] Same to same, 31 Jan. 1782, Sandwich MSS.; Sandwich to Robinson, 1, 3 Feb. 1782, Abergavenny MSS., 415, 417.

closes that the next preparatory step — a large rally of government supporters at Lord North's house in Downing Street — had already been provisionally fixed for the day before the debate on the naval enquiry.[1] The decision to adopt this arrangement — one comparable to the established practice of disclosing the government's declaration of policy in the King's Speech to a large gathering of friends at the Cockpit at the opening of the session — is a reminder that eighteenth-century ministries did not confidently rely on their majorities following them blindly : in a manner somewhat similar to modern party practice, they felt it necessary, from time to time, to lay their measures before their supporters, and explain and justify them. This larger meeting duly took place on 6 February. For many days previously Robinson had devoted his time to parliamentary arrangements. Now the task was done, and for a brief moment he could relax. In a family letter of that evening to his son-in-law and to the daughter whom he dearly cherished, he noted briefly that the meeting was in progress and that the attendance was considerable. 'I have been, and am, so very much taken up with the public business', he wrote 'that I have lately been a very bad correspondent, and indeed I am now stole out from a great meeting of the gentlemen of the House of Commons here consulting on the business of the naval enquiry to hastily' scrawl this to you.'[2] He had gathered in the members : the direction of the morrow's debate was a task for others.

The next day, the 7th, the opposition made the first of their two attempts to pull down Sandwich. Fox, skilfully weaving as damning an indictment as he could from the evidence which had been laid before the House, condemned Sandwich for failure on four specific counts — letting de Grasse slip away with reinforcements for the French naval force in American waters ; not preventing the loss of the St. Eustatius convoy ; despatching misleading information to the civic authorities at Bristol ; and mismanaging the naval war against the Dutch. For good measure he added a condemnation of

[1] Abergavenny MS. 417.
[2] Robinson to Mr. and Mrs. Henry Neville, 6 Feb. 1782, Abergavenny MSS., packet 18.

the Kempenfelt expedition. He concluded by moving, 'That it appears to this committee that there was gross mismanagement in the administration of naval affairs in the year 1781'.[1]

Fox failed to carry his motion; but this attack was beaten off by the government by the rather disturbing majority of 205 to 183. North was severely shaken. 'Lord Sandwich's majority of 22 makes Lord N horrid sick', Colonel Edward Smith reported next day to William Eden. 'In short we all seem going to pieces as fast as the opening confusion will enable us.'[2] 'Lord North is worried to death,' wrote Hillsborough, 'and things wear a very uncertain aspect.'[3] True, on this occasion, Sir Thomas Dundas and his cousin, Charles, both voted with the government,[4] although, on other questions they were by now firmly in the Rockingham camp:[5] their conduct was undoubtedly due to ties of personal friendship with Sandwich dating back to earlier association in the ranks of the Bedford party.[6] But this assistance from the other side of the House merely emphasized the plain fact, that an unexpected number of regular friends had voted adversely or had declined to make their appearance at what was, beyond doubt, a critical division for the government.

The identity of thirty-five of these defaulters is revealed by a list, forwarded on 19 February by Sandwich to George III, of persons who did not vote on the 7th, but who were expected to attend in support of the ministry on the 20th.[7] Two-thirds of the men named in this list were either personal friends of North or of other ministers, or were members of the court and administration circle. They were confirmed supporters of the government, and their absence must have been either accidental

[1] Debrett, v, 406-12.
[2] 8 Feb. 1782, Add. MSS. 34418, f. 323.
[3] To W. Eden, 12 Feb. 1782, *ibid.* f. 324.
[4] James Hare to Lord Carlisle, 11 Feb. 1782, H.M.C., *Carlisle MSS.*, 575.
[5] On their connection with the Rockinghams, see pp. 213-14 above.
[6] Sir Thomas's father, Sir Lawrence, who died in 1781, was a friend of Sandwich for over thirty years (Sir Lawrence to Sandwich, 27 Nov. 1779, Sandwich MSS.). Robinson expected four members of the opposition to vote on the government side: two were clearly the Dundases, but I cannot place the identity of the other two (List and Calculations on the Call, 21 Jan. 1782, Abergavenny MSS). [7] Fortescue, iv, no. 2580.

or the result of some mismanagement on Robinson's part. But this explanation does not apply to the remainder. There seems to have been something like deliberate abstention on 7 February by Lord Lincoln, heir of the Duke of Newcastle, and by three other members connected with the Duke, Anthony Eyre, Charles Mellish, and Sir Samuel Brudenell Fludyer: 'none of [them] voted in the former division', Sandwich reported in his covering letter to the King.[1] Eyre, a friend of Lord Lincoln, also declined to turn up on the 20th, although his vote had been promised, and Lincoln himself gave up attending the House after the 22nd; Fludyer ended by voting against the government. Almost certainly in the same case were Christopher Potter, a government contractor, and Paul Cobb Methuen, a Wiltshire country gentleman, who both stayed away on the 20th; the very independent Derbyshire barrister, Daniel Parker Coke, who voted on the 20th with the opposition; and Robert Vyner of Lincolnshire, another independent country gentleman, who in the House used 'strange language', about which Sandwich felt something should be done.[2] The absence of John Peach Hungerford and of Thomas Gilbert, who both voted with the ministry on the 20th, may also have been deliberate, in view of their later hostility in divisions.

One other independent supporter of the ministers, Sir William Dolben, is known, from his own confession in debate, to have voted against them in this division.[3]

It is impossible, from this very fragmentary evidence about the lists of the division, to reach any firm conclusions about the extent of any weakness in the government majority which it revealed. All that emerges clearly is the desertion of the Newcastle faction, one government contractor, and half a dozen independents, eleven in all, of whom more than half returned to the fold on the 20th. But weakened it was: North was dismayed, and Fox was emboldened to try a second fall.

On 20 February Fox introduced in the House a motion of censure against Sandwich couched in practically the same

[1] Fortescue, v, no. 3521.
[2] Sandwich to Robinson, 14 Feb. 1782, H.M.C., *Abergavenny MSS.*, 49, no. 423.　　　　　　　　　　[3] Debrett, vi, 258.

terms as that moved before the Committee of the Whole House a fortnight before.[1] This time the opposition leaders made an all-out effort, summoning up every vote they could possibly muster. One adherent was sent for, so it was believed, even from Paris.[2] 'Lord Robert Spencer and Lord Ossory . . . tell me they suppose that we shall carry the question by ten, if the question is put; but it is imagined rather by them that the ministers will give it up'; so Selwyn reported the views of two of Fox's close friends. 'I hear', he went on, 'that all the different parties in opposition are determined to draw together in this question, how much soever they may differ afterwards, in hopes, I suppose, by their united force to destroy this Administration.'[3] The great size of the minority in the division — 217 — testifies to the correctness of his information and to the determination with which Fox and his allies pursued their object.

On the other side, the flurry of activity into which the announcement of Fox's intention threw Sandwich and Robinson in their anxiety to secure a safe majority for the government, is revealed in the many staccato messages with which Sandwich in the intervening days bombarded his friend.[4] On the 14th the two divided the lists of known and supposed friends between them,[5] and during the next two days they penned urgent messages to patrons and to members, till they were, as Robinson described himself, 'quite spent'.[6] They were both acutely aware of the urgency of their task — Sandwich was now fighting for political survival — and it is fair to conclude that the 236 votes cast for the ministry on the 20th represented the absolute maximum of support that could be got by every possible form of appeal.

[1] Debrett, vi, 247.
[2] Sandwich to Ailesbury, 15 Feb. 1782, H.M.C., *Ailesbury MSS.*, 238.
[3] George Selwyn to Lord Carlisle, 19 Feb. 1782, H.M.C., *Carlisle MSS.*, 580.
[4] Sandwich to Robinson, Abergavenny MSS., 14 Feb., no. 423, 15 Feb., nos. 424, 425, 426, 427, 428 (docketed by Robinson, 'answered immediately near midnight') 16 Feb., nos. 430, 431, 432, 433.
[5] Same to same, 13 Feb. 1782, Abergavenny MS. 422; Robinson to Charles Jenkinson, 14 Feb. 1782, Add. MSS. 38217, f. 315.
[6] Sandwich to Robinson, 16 Feb. 1782, Abergavenny MSS., 431, 433; Robinson to Charles Jenkinson, 16 Feb. 1782, Add. MSS. 38217, f. 326.

The efforts of both sides to bring up supporters made this division, far more than that of the 7th, a major test of their respective strengths. Rarely were so many members to be found in the House. One provincial newspaper, extremely warm in support of the opposition, exulted, with perhaps pardonable exaggeration, that the attendance of 458 members present at the division was unprecedented since the beginning of the reign.[1] This was not the case — 467 members had been present, for instance, at the last crucial division of the Economical Reform crisis, on 24 April 1780 — still, not often can the attendance of the 20th have been exceeded.[2] But on 24 April 1780 the ministers had carried their point by 50 votes, the division demonstrating that, at a supreme parliamentary crisis, North had been able to bring up over 250 supporters. Why was he now unable to repeat this success ?

His failure can be seen to have been due to the first waverings among the ranks of the government supporters. On the 20th the government was able to assemble almost all of its party followers, about 75 in all ; and also about 100 members of the court and administration group — about another 25 members of this group were abroad, or ill, so the number not secured was very small. The core of its majority thus remained firm. As yet, too, it still kept most of its essential following of independents : about 60 of these voted with the majority.

But already the 'rats' were beginning to appear. Among the members who did not vote in the division were at least 16 who were generally regarded as friendly, and whose absence was — in view of the strenuous 'whipping in' of Sandwich and Robinson — probably deliberate. With one or two exceptions, they were present in the House on other occasions, no notes of their being ill or abroad appear in Robinson's lists, and in some cases at least, there is evidence that they had been applied to by either Robinson or Sandwich.[3] They included five English county representatives — Thomas Pelham, George Pitt, Sir

[1] *The Canterbury Journal*, 26 Feb. 1782.
[2] These figures include the Speaker and the four tellers.
[3] Sandwich to Robinson, 15-16 Feb. 1782, Abergavenny MSS., 425, 427, 431 ; Sandwich's list sent to the King on 19 Feb., Fortescue, iv, no. 2580.

John Wrottesley, Philip Yorke, and Lord Charles Spencer, the last-named noted by Robinson as having gone away before the division; four independents sitting for boroughs — Lord Hyde, P. C. Methuen, George Philipps, and Sir Herbert Mackworth; John Campbell, Sir John Henderson, John Dawes, and Anthony Eyre, who were connected by personal friendship or by political interest with Lord North, Henry Dundas, Richard Rigby, and the Duke of Newcastle respectively; and Hugh Boscawen, Christopher D'Oyly, and John Nesbitt, who belonged to the court and administration circle.

Still worse, from the point of view of the ministers, a handful of the members who usually supported the government decided on this occasion to vote against it. Among these was Thomas Grosvenor, M.P. for Chester, who had some reputation as a leader among the country gentlemen who favoured administration.[1] They included also three other independents, D. P. Coke, Samuel Whitbread, and the Liverpool merchant, Henry Rawlinson, and two lawyers belonging to the court group, Francis Burton and Abel Moysey.

Altogether, these defections included eleven independents, five party men, and six members of the court and administration following. The desertion of the five English county representatives left only ten county members voting on the government side. The loss of the six members who went over to the opposition was sufficient in itself to prove the force of Dundas's later complaint about the retention of Lord Sandwich:[2] had these six abstained from voting, the government's majority would have been, at twenty-five, fairly respectable, and had some of them supported the ministers, it would have approached thirty, a figure which was regarded as a safe margin.[3]

[1] In a letter to the King four weeks later — 18 Mar. 1782 — North reported Grosvenor as having approached him as spokesman for a number of independents (Fortescue, v, no. 3566). In 1784, Grosvenor took the chair at the meetings of the St. Alban's Tavern group of independents who wished to bring about a union between Fox and Pitt (*Annual Register*, 1784-5, 268).

[2] In his letter to Robinson of 9 Mar. 1782, H.M.C., *Abergavenny MSS.*, 51, no. 445.

[3] George Selwyn wrote to Lord Carlisle, just before the last critical division on 15 Mar.: 'We reckon upon a majority of from twenty to thirty; if it approaches the latter number the old ministry and their friends will hold up their heads'. — H.M.C., *Carlisle MSS.*, 593.

The list of the minority in this division can be analysed into four groups, two very large, and two very much smaller, but nevertheless in some ways the most important.

There were, first, about a hundred members belonging to the opposition parties : as Selwyn had told Carlisle, the party leaders had brought up every friend they could muster, and only about eight or nine of the members in this category were absent ; in two or three cases, at least, illness was almost certainly the reason,[1] and this proportion of absenteeism was, perhaps, not far from the normal ; examination of the division list for 12 December 1781 shows that then, also, eight party followers from this side of the House (a different eight) were absent.

Secondly, there were about a hundred independents who were confirmed opponents of the government : since the commencement of this parliament, if not before, they had shown themselves consistently hostile to the North ministry. This group, too, was now mustered in force : it included about thirty members, who had not been present at the division of 12 December 1781, being perhaps not sufficiently zealous in their politics to come up to Westminster for the short sitting before Christmas.

These two groups, both deployed at almost full strength, accounted for 204 members of the House.[2] Together, they included 46 of the English county representatives, 29 of them independents, the other 17 connected more or less closely with one or other of the parties in opposition. Constituting the regular phalanx of the opposition in the House of Commons, nevertheless they were not sufficiently strong, without other assistance, to break down the government's hold upon the House : in this division the ministerial vote was thirty-four in excess of their numbers.

Other assistance, however, was forthcoming. What turned the scale, and made this division virtually a defeat for the

---

[1] Robinson noted Sir George Savile and C. F. Scudamore as 'very ill', and Lord Wenman as 'ill, can't attend', in his State for the division of 8 Mar. 1782. Neither Wenman nor Scudamore voted at all during these weeks.   [2] This figure includes the two tellers.

government, was the behaviour of fifteen members in the two remaining small groups referred to above. One of these groups was formed by the six deserters, who, as already noted, went over to the opposition on this question. The other was made up of seven independents — Noel and Richard Hill, the two members for Shropshire, Sir Thomas Clarges, Drake of Amersham, Thomas Farrer, Arthur Holdsworth, and William Morton Pitt — and two men connected with the court — Colonel Adeane, who was an aide-de-camp to the King, and Lloyd Kenyon, a lawyer associated with Lord Chancellor Thurlow. The voting of these nine men distinguishes them from the main body of opposition independents, though from now on they became merged with it. None of them were identified with it a year previously. In February 1781 Robinson still counted Adeane, Clarges, Farrer, and Holdsworth as friends.[1] Kenyon at that time had been rated 'hopeful', and in November he was still regarded as enough of a supporter to be admitted to the select ministerial gathering held at Lord North's on the 25th (the day before the larger meeting at the Cockpit) for a preview of the Speech and Address.[2] Drake, Richard Hill, and W. M. Pitt were classed by Robinson in February 1781 as 'doubtful'; Noel Hill, the only one whom he then described as 'con', later proved himself not hostile to the ministry to the point of wishing to bring it down, for he alone out of the nine abstained from voting against it on 15 March.[3] The nine are, on the other hand, also distinguished from the six deserters (all of whom subsequently cast votes in favour of the government) by their consistent opposition during the next four weeks. Thus, in this division, the opposition benefited by the temporary support of one set of six members, and by the more or less recent, but now permanent accession of another nine, all of them men who had formerly given votes

---

[1] 'State', February (docketed November), 1781, Abergavenny MSS.

[2] *Ibid.*; Kenyon's diary, Kenyon MSS. I am indebted for this information from the Kenyon papers to Mr. Colin Shone.

[3] 'Persons who staid away . . . Hill, Noel, staid away at request.' — Robinson's notes on the division, 16 Mar. 1782, Fortescue, v, no. 3560, enclosure. Kenyon, also, did not vote on 15 Mar. 1782, but he was in a different case, as he had left London to go on circuit.

to the government. It was thus enabled to secure 217 votes in the division, and to clip three off the ministry's previous majority of 22.

Between the 7th and the 20th February the opposition vote against Lord Sandwich increased by 34. This was the most significant feature of the division on the 20th and, from the ministers' point of view, the most dangerous. The minority of 183 on 7 February had been hardly any greater than that on Lowther's motion of 12 December — at an initial glance, apparently not large enough to cause the government any serious concern. But now it began to seem as if the maintenance of an adequate majority was beyond its power, and without loss of time the leaders of the opposition pressed forward their next assault.

(iii)

THE HOUSE OF COMMONS REPUDIATES THE AMERICAN WAR

On 22 February, almost without a moment's breathing space, the opposition leaders switched the direction of their parliamentary attack from the government's naval administration to its American policy. General Conway moved for an address to the King requesting that the war on the American Continent should 'no longer be pursued for the impracticable purpose of reducing the inhabitants of that country to obedience by force'.[1] This proposition being lost by one vote only, Conway in the following week returned to the charge, encouraged by the assurances of support he had received from members not present at the division.[2] On the 27th he moved the following lengthy resolution : 'That it is the opinion of this House, that the further prosecution of offensive warfare on the continent of North America, for the purpose of reducing the revolted colonies to obedience by force, will be the means of weakening the efforts of this country against her European enemies, tends under the present circumstances dangerously to increase the mutual enmity, so fatal to the interests both of Great Britain

[1] Debrett, vi, 262.   [2] *Ibid.* 310.

and America, and, by preventing an happy reconciliation with that country, to frustrate the earnest desire graciously expressed by His Majesty to restore the blessings of public tranquillity.[1] This motion was carried in a crowded House by nineteen votes, and the opposition immediately followed it up with a second, which was passed without a division, for an Address to the King, to lay before him the sentiments of his faithful Commons.[2]

Votes for this motion were labelled at the time votes 'for peace with America',[3] and the misleading impression was created even during the debate that here was a simple issue — peace or war: William Pitt, for instance, maintained, that if the ministers were not prepared to accept Conway's motion without demur, they ought to admit openly that they intended to continue the American war.[4] But Conway did not himself intend his motion to be taken this way; indeed, in his introductory speech on the 27th, he was careful to explain that his motion did not mean an immediate military surrender; the real issue which it raised was the question of confidence in the ministers. The motion, he said, 'went to advise His Majesty to order his ministers to renounce the war on the continent of America, for the impracticable object of reducing the colonies by force. The object of the motion was, in his mind, very clearly expressed; it was to give up the idea of conquest, and, consequently, of an offensive war.' This did not mean that the government would be obliged to withdraw immediately all troops from the colonies and abandon New York and other bases on the American coast still in British possession: these could, perhaps should, be held, and defensive operations to maintain them would not be precluded.[5] Conway thus had no intention of striking bargaining counters out of the ministers' hands. He made it clear that his motion had no other object than to bind the ministry to the line of policy announced by

---

[1] Debrett, vi, 316-17.   [2] Ibid. 330.
[3] E.g. Stockdale's broadsheet list of the division of 27 Feb. 1782, B.M. ref. 1881, c. 7.   [4] The Political Magazine, iii (1782), 201.
[5] Debrett, vi, 313-4. Afterwards, in the debate upon the Address which followed the passing of his motion, Conway insisted again, that his meaning was 'not that peace should be made with America as soon as possible; but that the offensive war with America should immediately cease' (ibid. 349).

North on 12 and 14 December, when North had declared that attempts at military reconquest would be abandoned. But in his final speech at the close of the debate he raised openly the question of confidence, saying that he preferred the clear declaration of the House to the vague promises made by ministers.[1] His case was that the ministers were not to be trusted, and that they were evading the assurances they had given before the Christmas recess.

What in February was the ministerial policy regarding America? Were they really evading their assurances?

Since Yorktown the formulation of an American policy had proceeded by fits and starts, with all the hesitancy which bespoke divided counsels in the cabinet. On 8 December the ministers had reached the decision 'that under the present circumstances it would not be expedient to send to North America any more force than what is necessary to recruit the regiments there';[2] and they had thus given up the idea of offensive warfare in the interior, a decision announced by North during the debate on Lowther's motion. About this time they had before them a memorandum drawn up by Germain, in which he discussed the possibilities of the unfavourable situation produced by Cornwallis's surrender, but were loath to deal with it and put off discussion of it for 'three cabinets'. At length, on 22 December, they talked about it 'in general terms' and referred it to a further meeting for more detailed consideration.[3]

No minute of the further cabinet meeting on this subject survives in the papers of the King, Germain, or Sandwich; but on 2 January 1782 Germain dispatched two important sets of instructions to America, the contents of which indicate that some at least of the ideas in his memorandum had been adopted.

Sir Henry Clinton at New York was advised that Cornwallis's army would not be replaced, but that existing establishments would be maintained. With that force it was hoped to

---

[1] *The Political Magazine*, iii (1782), 204.
[2] Cabinet Minute, Fortescue, v, no. 3462.
[3] H.M.C., *Stopford Sackville MSS.*, ii, 216-20; H.M.C., *Knox MSS.*, 272-3; Stormont to George III, 22 Dec. 1781, Fortescue, v, no. 3477.

retain possession of all remaining posts and garrisons on the Atlantic coast : also, wrote Germain, 'such detachments may occasionally be spared for such joint operations with the navy against the ports and towns upon the sea-coasts of the revolted colonies, for destroying their shipping and stores, and obstructing their trade, as may be necessary to prevent them from acting offensively against us'. The main object of retaining the bases was to provide rallying points in hope that loyalist movements might yet turn the tide against Congress : on this point Germain and the King, at least, still deceived themselves. Clinton was informed that, 'although it is not the King's intention that any operations should be carried on within land, with the view of reducing any of the revolted provinces or countries to His Majesty's obedience by force, it is nevertheless his purpose that you should give all possible encouragement to the loyalists in every province to persevere in their attachment to this country, and if any number of them shall think themselves sufficiently strong to effect a restoration of the constitution with the assistance of a small force, it is His Majesty's pleasure that you do furnish them with arms and ammunition, and send them such a force as you can afford to protect them in embodying themselves and disarming the rebels, and making such establishments as may enable them to resist any attempts of the Congress to subdue them'.[1]

In his other despatch, to Haldimand at Quebec, Germain commended Haldimand's approaches to loyalist leaders in Vermont and his concentration of troops on the Canadian border where they might be used to intervene in that quarter. He expressed the hope that Haldimand might be able to employ a force greater than Washington could detach to oppose him, and concluded by repeating his recommendation 'to make the recovery of Vermont to the King's obedience the primary object of your attention'.[2]

Steady the loyalists ; harass the rebels till they grew sick of resisting : this was how Germain now envisaged the conduct of the war. Even on the eve of the resignation which had been

[1] Germain to Clinton, 2 Jan. 1782, C.O. 5/263.
[2] Germain to Haldimand, 2 Jan. 1782, ibid.

forced by opponents of his policy, he wrote in a letter to Major-General Robertson, who had been designated as Clinton's temporary successor in the American command: 'I am persuaded you will omit no opportunity of promoting His Majesty's service by such military operations as may best tend to defend our present possessions, or distress the rebels in that manner which may most incline them to peace, as His Majesty's great object is to restore legal government'.[1] Moreover, for a week or so after, his successor in the American Department, Welbore Ellis, still held forth in similar strains. In a letter to Robertson of 18 February, notifying him of Sir Guy Carleton's imminent departure from England to take up the American command, he exhorted him 'to take every proper occasion of assuring the King's loyal subjects of the continuation of His Majesty's regard and attention to their happiness, and encourage them to persevere in their attachment to the constitution; and, with a due regard to their own safety, to prepare themselves to act in concert with His Majesty's forces for the restoration of their liberties and deliverance from the tyranny of the rebel rulers, at such times and in such manner, as they shall be directed by the Commander-in-Chief'.[2]

These bellicose strains, however, did not accord with the views of other ministers. North, for instance, had declared in private conversation with Germain on 22 January, that it was impossible to continue the war, 'that America was lost, and that it was vain to think of recovering it'.[3] But it was another thing entirely to make such admissions in public: such an action would simply be playing into the hands of the enemy. He did not wish, he said, during the debate of 27 February, 'to make declarations in that House, because he did not think he was speaking to that House alone; he was speaking to America, to Holland, to France, to Spain, and to all the world . . . it would not be proper for him to say what orders might be given, what alliances were in agitation, or on what conditions peace might be eventually obtained; for then France might say to

---

[1] C.O. 5/245.　　　　　　　　　　　　　　[2] 18 Feb. 1782, *ibid.*
[3] Knox's memorandum on the removal of Lord George Germain, H.M.C., *Knox MSS.*, 275.

America, you are sure at all events of peace ; I have held out for your success, now hold out a little while for mine'.[1]   In fact, he could not both maintain what he felt was essential secrecy about ministerial policy and at the same time effectively refute the charges that he still wished to reconquer America. All he could do was to repeat the assurances he had given in December, and then appeal to members to trust the government.   If they would not trust it, then they should demand its removal.   An adverse vote, he told them, would be tantamount to a withdrawal of confidence, and would make it incumbent upon him to resign.[2]

Moreover, behind North stood Dundas, who was firmly convinced that hopes of recovering the American colonies must be abandoned and that the war must be brought to an end.   As a junior minister, Dundas could speak in slightly less guarded terms than North, and in the debate of 22 February on Conway's first motion he made a forthright declaration of the government's conversion to this view.   Germain's resignation, he explained, was not due to personal quarrels and personal intrigue :   his retirement signified also a repudiation of his policy.[3]   Dundas pointed out, that

before the holidays, the noble lord, then American Secretary, had declared in his place, that he would never subscribe to the independency of America . . . the very reason that induced him [Dundas] now to stand up and confess he wished for peace with America, was the very reason that made the noble lord's retreat necessary, viz the very important and essential change in the affairs of the country. He was extremely happy to find, when the noble lord's retreat became necessary, that the Crown had been advised to render it honourable and dignified.   It was right to shew to the nation at large, that the noble lord's conduct in office was approved, and that it was not from any sense of incapa-

[1] Debrett, vi, 323.
[2] *Ibid.* 321-2 ;   North to George III, 28 Feb. 1782, Fortescue, v, no. 3535.
[3] *The Political Magazine*, iii (1782), 202-3.   This important pronouncement is not even hinted at in the brief notice of Dundas's speech in Debrett (vi, 280), which is repeated verbatim in *The Parliamentary History* (xx, 1047).

324

city, neglect, or error in any part of it, that his services were dispensed with, but merely because, such was the unfortunate situation of our affairs, that the noble lord's principles were no longer practicable.

In view of his Scottish following in the House of Commons, and in virtue of the high value North set upon his services (the King was told later that they had been indispensable),[1] Dundas, though not a member of the cabinet, was in a position to insist that his views be accepted. His continued support for the government itself refuted the suspicions of the opposition, that the ministers still nursed offensive designs against the colonies.

Even Welbore Ellis, despite the tone of his dispatch of 18 February, did not share the obstinate convictions of Germain. A week or two later, referring in the House to the division of 27 February, he declared that he and North 'did not at all differ from the majority of the House on that day in the principle of the question; it was merely on the expediency that he had differed from the majority'.[2] His dispatch undoubtedly reflected the King's views rather than his own; and here it is necessary to set these debates in their proper constitutional perspective.

George III remained adamant on his 'essential point' of no independence. The ministers, bound by their loyalty to the head of the executive, and believing in any case that, if he would let them, as surely he soon would, they could get a better peace than the Rockingham party, would not try to coerce him by collective resignation: they thus rejected the only weapon they might have used against him. In these circumstances, despite the growing realization that the colonies were lost, no more yielding statement of policy could issue from the American Department, unless either George III changed his mind or the House of Commons imposed a change of policy upon him. In the last week of February the ministers were in an impossible situation, since the King, while accepting the cabinet minute of 8 December,[3] declined to accept its implications, that the recovery of America by force was no longer feasible and that

[1] North to George III, 19 Mar. 1782, Fortescue, v, no. 3569.
[2] Debrett, vi, 390.   [3] P. 321 above.

therefore independence might have to be conceded to obtain peace. On this point the King's unreasoning obstinacy was seen at its worst. His servants were obliged to bear the brunt of an attack which they did not deserve. Far from evading the assurances they had given before Christmas, they had no intention of pursuing further offensive operations in America. They knew America was lost. But until they could bring round the King to their opinion, they could not openly show themselves ready to negotiate for peace. This, however, was what members of parliament in general now desired; and the ministers, unwilling to extricate themselves by threats of resignation, suffered a fatal decline in their political credit. Possibly this might have been avoided, had they stood out resolutely in December for the abandonment of the King's American pretensions and the jettisoning of their symbol, Germain. Still it is not easy to blame them for not taking this course: duty to the King apart, such a move would have been a public admission of defeat calculated to make the Bourbon Powers stiffen their terms. However, in the end parliament forced this public admission. The opposition preserved the constitutional decencies by directing their attack against the ministers, but in reality it was aimed at the King; and indeed, if the road was to be cleared quickly for peace negotiations, this was the only way in which it could be done. On 27 February the House of Commons exercised a legitimate parliamentary right, in imposing a check upon the policy of the executive. Not only confidence in the ministers, but policy also, were questions at issue in these debates.

The passage of Conway's motion affirmed, then, a policy which some members of the government already fully accepted, and to which the rest were prepared to conform. The reconquest of America was abandoned. Royal obstruction, and any hesitation among members of the ministry, about this point were now perforce ended.[1] But the motion did not in any way prescribe how the war was to be brought to a con-

[1] The decisions of the House of Commons were notified to the authorities in America on 6 March — W. Ellis, dispatches to Sir Henry Clinton, to Major General Leslie, and to Major General Robertson, C.O. 5/245.

clusion. On this point the ideas of the opposition and those current in ministerial circles differed considerably : they ranged from Fox's view that 'the idea of sovereignty over America ought to be totally renounced' and an *entente* sought with the new American state, to that of the King, that present possessions should be held and the inducement of independence held out to different provinces to detach them from the French alliance, provided they remained separate states.[1]

In the House of Commons the debates and divisions of 22 and 27 February did not make any clear separation between those who on the one hand might wish to continue the American war and others who wished to see it ended. As at the time of the debate on Lowther's motion on 12 December, the government ranks contained a variety of opinions, some of which came very close to those of men who voted with the opposition. If there were any who still thought the war should be pursued, none of them rose to their feet to express this conviction ; whereas, apart from the declaration of Dundas, already cited, the Attorney-General admitted on the 27th that peace was necessary,[2] and Rigby, having on the 22nd described the war as impracticable, confessed on the 28th that 'he did not entertain an idea of preserving the sovereignty over America ; he gave that up for the same reason that he gave up the war — because he could not help it'.[3] Friends of North, Rigby, and Dundas, desired peace as did the members of the opposition. But they preferred the existing ministry to any formed by the opposition, they thought it more likely than any such new ministry to obtain reasonable peace terms, and they considered it would fare better in negotiation if its hands were not tied by parliamentary directives.

What the divisions did reveal, however, was the waning confidence of the House of Commons in the government. Certain elements in the House now declined to support the government, or even voted against it in plain disregard of the assurances given by ministers. For a few of these deserters the breach was final : having withdrawn their support from

[1] 28 Feb. 1782 ; Debrett, vi, 342 ; Fortescue, v, no. 3537.
[2] Debrett, vi, 325.   [3] *Ibid.* 280, 342.

the government on this question, they decided to abandon it altogether. The decisive demonstration was furnished by the division on the 27th. That of the 22nd was inconclusive — the day was a Friday, some members had gone out of town, and neither side was able to muster in full force. But by the 27th members had had nearly a week to consider or reconsider their views, and both sides had summoned up every friend they could hope to bring to the House.

On the 22nd the government mustered for the division the hard core of its following — most of its party supporters and members of the court and administration circle, and about thirty friendly independents. On the 27th it was able to add thirty votes from members who had been absent on the 22nd, and also four from men who had voted for the first of Conway's motions. Most of the thirty were party supporters or members of the court group — their absence on the 22nd seems to have been partly due to Robinson's oversight in failing to send out messages to members to attend the division.[1] The four repenting deserters were two independents — Sir William Dolben and Philip Rashleigh — Francis Burton, a client of the Duke of Marlborough, and Abel Moysey, holder of a legal appointment under the Crown. Even with these accessions of strength, however, the ministry could muster only 217 in the division. As North had foreseen, desertions and abstentions were numerous: 'Lord North . . . will take every means to secure an attendance', he informed the King on 25 February, 'but he is apprehensive, that many persons whom he may send for may vote against him, so little can he depend upon the House in any question of that nature'.[2]

On the 27th the course taken by the division fully confirmed North's pessimistic forecast. Three independents, John Fuller, John Rolle, and Lord Fife, and one member of the court group, Sir Frederick Leman Rogers, reversed their votes of the 22nd and now went into the lobby against the ministry.

[1] G. Selwyn to Carlisle, 25 Feb. 1782, H.M.C., *Carlisle MSS.*, 583. If Selwyn's report was correct, Robinson bore a heavy responsibility for what followed, for it may well be doubted if the opposition would have scored their later successes had they not come so close to defeating the government on 22 Feb. [2] Fortescue, v, no. 3533.

Ten members who had voted with the government on the 22nd were now absent — one or two of these absences were involuntary or accidental — John Purling was ill,[1] and the same perhaps may have been the case with John Halliday — but most of them were undoubtedly deliberate : two independents, Lord Galway and John Sinclair, and three men with court or government connections, Sir Samuel Fludyer, John Frederick, and Henry Pelham, were seen by Robinson to leave the House before the division ;[2] a member of the Duke of Newcastle's group, his son, Lord Lincoln, declined to turn up for this, or for any subsequent division ; and the absence of Andrew Bayntun was probably also intentional, for three other leading members of the Gower party (to which he belonged) either abstained or voted against the government. The abstaining members, it may be concluded, agreed with the proposition that attempts to reconquer America should be abandoned ; but they were, for the most part, too loyal to the government — or too mistrustful of the opposition — to express this by voting for a motion which the ministers opposed (only in one case, that of Fludyer, who later voted for the government's dismissal, did abstention indicate a complete withdrawal of loyalty). Also contributing to the defeat of the government was the absence or abstention of another seventeen members normally regarded as friendly who had not been present at the division on the 22nd. Sir Charles Frederick and Giles Hudson both appear as 'ill' in one or more of Robinson's lists for this period. But the absence of the others was probably intentional. They included Earl Gower's son, Lord Trentham; three Scotsmen, John Craufurd, Sir John Henderson, and John Pringle, the first a member of the court group, the other two connected with Henry Dundas; John Buller and Peregrine Cust, connections of North; two ministerialists, Hugh Boscawen and Richard Jackson; and five independents, the first two being county representatives — James Dutton, George Pitt, A. R. Bowes, William Clayton, and George Philipps.

These abstentions partly explain why the government vote

---

[1] J. Purling to Sandwich, 13 Mar. 1782, Abergavenny MSS, 448c.
[2] 'State of Division, 27 Feb. 1782', Abergavenny MSS.

fell well beneath its normal maximum on 27 February. Independents predominated among the absentees, but they also included regular members of the government following, party supporters and men of the court and administration circle. Even so, however, the ministry might not have been defeated, but for the loss of other deserters whose votes went to swell the opposition majority.

In the division on Conway's second motion on 27 February, the opposition vote reached the highest point it attained during the whole crisis. It is not possible to ascertain completely which members voted that day who had not voted on the 22nd. Robinson's state for the division on the 22nd gives an imperfect list of the minority, naming 211 members, 16 of whom must have been absent. Still this state does identify as absent 34 members who afterwards voted for Conway's motion on the 27th. Nine of these were regular party supporters of opposition, whose previous absence was probably due to illness or some other non-political reason.[1] Another 14 were country gentlemen and independents who usually voted fairly regularly against the government.[2] But the addition of these 23 expected votes would not alone have given victory to the opposition: what tipped the scales in its favour was the behaviour of members formerly loyal to the government, who, on this occasion, voted against it.

These, numbering over twenty, can be divided by the manner of their voting into three groups.

In the first come the four men, already noted, who voted with the government on the 22nd, but decided to support Conway's second motion on the 27th — John Rolle, John Fuller, Lord Fife,[3] and Sir Frederick Leman Rogers.

---

[1] John Crewe, Richard Hopkins, James Lowther, Thomas Lister, Lord Ludlow, C. A. Pelham, Lord Surrey, Lord George Sutton, Sir George Savile.

[2] Richard Benyon, William Bouverie, Sir Geo. Cornewall, Lord Howe, Lucy Knightley, Sir Watkin Lewes, William Lygon, Crisp Molineux, H. W. Mortimer, Sir Fletcher Norton, W. M. Owen, Humphrey Sturt, Sir William Wake, Sir R. S. Cotton.

[3] Lord Fife, however, was more an opponent than a friend of the ministry and does not rank as a deserter in the sense in which that word applies to the other twenty-one members here mentioned.

The second is made up of eight members who are shown by Robinson as voting with the opposition on the 22nd, and who therefore opposed the government in both these divisions. Although Robinson's list was imperfect, it is improbable that he made mistakes over these men — he was likely to have his eye most particularly on deserters — moreover their voting is, in four cases, independently attested.[1] The eight included three English county members, Philip Yorke (Cambs.), Thomas Pelham (Sussex), Sir John Wrottesley (Staffs.), and two Scottish members, Sir Gilbert Elliot (Roxburgh), and James Hunter Blair, merchant and banker, a leading figure in the commercial and civic life of the city of Edinburgh, which he represented in parliament; Lord Graham, son of the Duke of Montrose; John Peachey, son of a Sussex baronet; and Thomas Gilbert, who, like Wrottesley, was connected with Gower.

The third group consisted of ten men, who were absent from the division on the 22nd, but attended and voted against the government for Conway's second motion. They included two government contractors, Christopher Potter and John Nesbitt (only eighteen months before, North had informed George III that Nesbitt was 'likely to be a very good friend in the House of Commons',[2] but now he turned his back on the North ministry for good); Robert Child, the banker, 'with a million of the loan in his pocket', who had been one of the successful negotiators with the Treasury just three days previously; [3] and several country gentlemen representing constituencies geographically scattered and of very differing types: John and Charles Morgan, county representatives, magnates of South Wales; Richard Myddleton of Denbigh in the north of the Principality; R. A. Neville, heir to one of the richest landed estates in Berkshire, lately returned to parliament by

---

[1] Philip Yorke, writing to Hardwicke on 23 Feb. noted 'many of those who generally support Government deserted them on this occasion, amongst the most remarkable were . . . Lord Graham, Sir Gilbert Elliot, Mr Pelham, . . .' and informed him that he himself had voted for the motion, Add. MSS. 35380, f. 188. Elliot's desertion is also mentioned by Loughborough in a letter to William Eden of the same date, Add. MSS. 34418, f. 331.   [2] North to George III, 1 Sept. 1780, Fortescue, v, no. 3127.
[3] Loughborough to W. Eden, 1 Mar. 1780, Add. MSS. 34418, f. 337; Fortescue, v, no. 3531.

the rather tumultuous, 'popular' constituency of Reading — Robinson noted of him, 'friendly but called on at Reading on his election to vote against the American war'; [1] Sir Henry Gough and Francis Fownes Luttrell, returned on their own interests for pocket boroughs in the south and west of England; [2] and John Pennington, sitting for a pocket borough which was at the government's disposal.

A comparison of the voting of these twenty-two deserters with their conduct regarding the rather similar motion proposed in December by Lowther shows how the government had lost ground since before the recess. In December only two of them — Pelham and Potter — had voted against the ministers, and no less than eleven had voted with them against Lowther's motion. [3] Similarly, of the twenty or so friends of administration who abstained from voting on 27 February, nine (including three Scotsmen) had voted in December on the government side. [4]

In brief, on 27 February the government fell victim to a combination of adverse trends of opinion on both sides of the House. On the one hand, practically all the independents who were inclined to oppose it, but whose attendance was usually somewhat haphazard, were sufficiently roused to act in unison against it. [5] On the other, some forty to forty-five of its friends decided to desert it — about half of these abstaining from the division and the other half voting for Conway's motion. The combined effects of these two developments produced what

[1] 'State of Division, 27 Feb. 1782', Abergavenny MSS.

[2] Bramber (Sussex) and Minehead (Somerset).

[3] Sir Gilbert Elliot, John Fuller, Thomas Gilbert, Lord Graham, F. F. Luttrell, John Nesbitt, John Pennington, John Rolle, Sir F. L. Rogers, Sir John Wrottesley, and Philip Yorke. Two other independents, William Drake senior and H. W. Mortimer, also altered their voting in the same way.

[4] William Clayton, Sir John Coghill, John Craufurd, Sir S. B. Fludyer, John Frederick, Lord Melbourne, Henry Pelham, John Pringle, and John Sinclair.

[5] Six independents who had voted against the government on the 22nd, did not vote on the 27th: Sir Patrick Blake, John Darker, Alex. Garden, Thomas Farrer, Lloyd Kenyon, and Chas. Ross. Darker, Garden, and Ross appear marked with a cross in Robinson's state for the 22nd, which indicates that approaches were made to them by the government before the 27th, and they may have abstained from voting at North's request. But this was not sufficient to save the day for the ministry.

neither of them singly could have done, a decisive defeat for the ministry.

The majority of the members who had parted from the ministry on the American question returned immediately afterwards to their allegiance. Thirty of them voted against the opposition motions of censure, twenty both on 8 and 15 March, the other ten in one or other of these divisions. (Seven only — Child, Elliot, Fludyer, Nesbitt, Pennington, Rolle, and Wrottesley — now turned definitely against the government, voting in March for its dismissal).

The most noticeable defections among the party supporters of government were those of Gower's group, Lord Trentham, Sir John Wrottesley, and Thomas Gilbert. Although Gower and Weymouth, in 1779, had withdrawn from the ministry, their followers in the Commons had continued fairly consistently to support the government, Wrottesley and Gilbert, however, adopting a quasi-independent stand on Economical Reform. Now, the desertion of Gower's son, his cousin, and his former land agent and legal adviser may well have aroused some speculation in the House and led to other desertions; but it did not presage the immediate withdrawal of all support for the ministry on the part of the Gower party.

But, while some defections occurred among party followers, and among members of the court and administration circle, it was the independents who were mainly responsible for the defeat of the ministry. In no way is this more plainly demonstrated than by the behaviour of county representatives. Six English county members were among the forty-odd men who deserted on this question. Out of sixty-six who took part in the division, ten only voted for the government — and six of these cannot properly be described as independents, since they had some connection or other with the court or the ministry. Fifty-six county members voted with the opposition and yet another acted as one of the opposition tellers.[1] The dislike of the war was even more marked among the twelve

[1] Of the remaining thirteen members for English counties, two were abroad, eight (of whom three or four were ill) voted regularly with the opposition, and only three were friendly towards the government.

Welsh county members: nine of them voted for Conway's motion, and only one with the ministers — Thomas Johnes of Radnor, a placeman connected with Thurlow. A motion such as Conway's was, of course, well chosen to appeal to the independents. Their own personal experience of growing financial stringency (through taxation and the decline of rents), the representations of their constituents, the only too obvious story of failure by land and by sea — all these inclined them to protest against further waste of the country's resources and to press for an early peace. It attracted support even from some of those who had no wish to replace North's ministry by one drawn from the opposition side of the House. Sir William Dolben, Thomas Pelham, John Sinclair, Philip Yorke, may be cited as examples of this class. They supported the government, either because it was the King's government, or because they had a personal respect and regard for North — and none for that king of the faro table, Charles Fox — but they felt it was time ministers gave some definite sign of their intention to make peace, and were disquieted at their failure to do so. An example of this state of mind is furnished by Philip Yorke. 'I perfectly agree with Sir Joseph [Yorke] in detesting the views of some of the faction leaders in opposition, and in wishing to support the King's government', he avowed in a letter to his uncle, Hardwicke. Nevertheless he voted for both of Conway's motions, to the great embarrassment of his other uncle, Sir Joseph, to whom Hardwicke hurriedly passed on his excuses. 'I told him [Sir Joseph]', Hardwicke wrote next day to his nephew, 'had the Attorney's Bill [for clearing away legal obstacles to a negotiation] been proposed the first day, I was sure you would have voted against Mr Conway's motion, but the appearance was that the Ministry were evading their assurances before the holidays, of not continuing an effective American war.'[1]

It was a further factor in the opposition's favour, that such independents, not being used to nice calculations about ministerial credit in the House, tended to close their ears to

[1] P. Yorke to Hardwicke, 1 Mar. 1782, Hardwicke to P. Yorke, 2 Mar. 1782, Add. MSS. 35380, ff. 194, 190.

North's argument that a vote for Conway's motion was tantamount to a vote of no-confidence. Philip Yorke, for instance,
could see no good reason for spurning what seemed to him a
good motion just because it originated with the opposition.[1]
Sir Gilbert Elliot professed to see no distinction between the
purpose of the motion and the declared intentions of the
government — 'certainly', he concluded, 'they both went to
one and the same point' ; [2] accordingly he gave his vote to
Conway.   Such men overlooked, or underestimated, the effects
of defeat on such an issue upon the parliamentary position of
the ministry.   'Is not Sir G's. conduct very provoking, and
Burton's and Moysey's,' Loughborough fumed in a letter to
William Eden after the division on 22 February, 'but there
would be no end of the list of sensible men who are silly enough
to vote a proposition without taking into consideration what its
tendency is, and who are commonly thought to be shabby
when they mean to be very sincere.' [3]

At least one rather half-hearted attempt was made (outside
the ministerial circle) to draw together some of the more critical,
independent supporters of the government, in order to bring
concerted pressure to bear upon it.   One of the moving spirits
in this manœuvre was John Sinclair of Ulbster, the youthful
member for Caithness.   Sinclair was as pushing and ambitious
as any of his Scottish compatriots in the House.   In November
1781, when he had been but a year in Parliament, he volunteered
to second the Address at the opening of the session.[4]   Even
earlier than this, he had tried to forward his fortunes with
Sandwich, offering at the end of January 1781 to speak in
defence of the appointment of Sir Hugh Palliser as Governor
of Greenwich Hospital, and enclosing the heads of a speech
for Sandwich's approval.   'Permit me to add', he went on in
characteristic vein, 'that as there is likely to be soon a vacancy
at your Board, your Lordship would have an opportunity of
filling it with one who would neither be useless nor ungrateful,

[1] P. Yorke to Hardwicke, 1 Mar. 1782, Add. MSS. 35380, f. 194.
[2] Debrett, vi, 329.
[3] 23 Feb. 1782, Add. MSS. 34418, f. 331.
[4] Sinclair, *Correspondence*, i, 75.

whose principle object is, to get into the line of public business, and whose fortune is sufficient to enable him to bestow any share of the emoluments upon any proper object that might be pointed out.'[1] Like Dundas, Sinclair wished to preserve the North ministry (or most of it) and hoped that political services would bring him advancement; but his actions at this time confirm the conclusion that, though imaginative and energetic, he was deficient in foresight and in staying-power. At this time he was just as eager as Dundas to make sure that the government adopted a policy of peace, but, being connected with one of the Scottish cliques hostile to the growth of the Lord-Advocate's influence in Scotland,[2] did not enter into co-operation with him to attain this object. Long afterwards, when preparing some of his own correspondence for publication, he recorded :[3]

> I had always been of opinion that the Americans would give better terms. to Lord North and his colleagues than they would to any Administration composed of those who had befriended the cause of America in parliament, and on whom consequently they had some hold. I had about this time formed a party of independent members of the House, among whom were Sir William Dolben, Sir H. Hoghton, Mr Gilbert, member for Lichfield and others, who were all anxious to put an end to [the] war.

Sinclair engaged in discussions with the captured President of the American Congress, Henry Laurens, who was then a prisoner on parole in London, and disclosed the substance of these conversations to his friends, who 'immediately resolved publicly to declare their wishes for peace'. In acting upon this decision he — and they — entirely overlooked the damage which a parliamentary defeat would inflict upon the reputation of the government, which they wished to preserve, and upon the morale of its following in the Commons. Sinclair thus bore some appreciable responsibility for the defeat of the government on 27 February. But the haphazard way in which his

[1] Sandwich MSS., undated, but written a day or two before 1 Feb. 1781, the day of Fox's motion of censure upon Palliser's appointment.
[2] Furber, 193.   [3] Sinclair, *Correspondence*, i, 80.

idea was put into effect is strikingly demonstrated by the fact
that no two of these four men — Sinclair and the three associates whom he named — followed the same line of conduct
through the two divisions on Conway's motions : in the second
division, Dolben and Hoghton voted with the government,
Gilbert with the opposition, and Sinclair went away from the
House. Co-operation was achieved within the group only in
the loose and imperfect manner characteristic of most attempts
made by independents in the age of the unreformed parliament
to 'form a party'.

Some, perhaps more, responsibility for the government's
defeat must be laid to the charge of Sir Gilbert Elliot. There
were many independents who, on the 27th, took their lead
from him, although their later conduct showed that they were
not in agreement with the political line which he was now
beginning to follow. From his first entry into parliament six
years before, Elliot had, up to this moment, given loyal support
to the government and had believed in the justice of its
American policy. Now he turned against it, and his speech
reflects the trend among one section of hitherto friendly
independents which was least favourable to the survival of the
ministry. Elliot declared [1]

> that he now plainly saw that the nation, the House of
> Commons and the ministers had been for a long time in
> the wrong; and he could no longer, with justice to his
> constituents, support their measures. Why gentlemen
> should make a distinction between the motion as proposed
> by the honourable General, and that mentioned by the
> Attorney General, he could not see, for certainly they both
> went to one and the same point; he should, therefore, give
> his hearty assent to the present motion.

This speech was thoroughly damaging to the government's
cause. Loughborough reported to Eden on 1 March : [2]

> Sir Gilbert Elliot's speech did much mischief, for Sir
> William Dolben had declared himself satisfied with the
> ministers' declaration and that he should *therefore* vote

[1] Debrett, vi, 329.   [2] Add. MSS. 34418, f. 337.

differently from the vote he had given on Friday, for which he was as you may imagine, exposed to much attack and pelted as an example to deter others, after which Sir Gilbert got up professing himself unsatisfied, though a hearty friend in general to administration — the effect of the comparison between the two was to fix all the wavering well-wishers in the same line with Sir Gilbert. I have no patience with him, for he cannot be the dupe of his own reasoning so much as to convince himself that a vote in the House of Commons is an expedient for making a peace.

Thus the friendly independents, having hearkened to the partisan arguments of both sides, acted in the division according to the lead given by one of the more vocal and forceful personalities in their own section of the House ; and in so doing rejected the pleas of the ministers. For the government this spelt the beginning of the end.

Not out of place here is a comment on the conduct of the Scottish members, especially as two of their number had played no small part in producing the defeat of the government. Popular propaganda continued to represent them as ministerial hirelings. In Stockdale's broadsheet list of the division of 20 February it was noted, for instance : 'Of all the Scotch members, two only [1] voted against Government. It would be useless to distinguish them [the Scots] by their ostensible places.' On that occasion thirty-two of them had rallied to the defence of Lord Sandwich. But on the 27th only twenty-four — little over half — turned out to support the government against Conway's motion. What John Robinson thought of the two Scotsmen whose manœuvres had played havoc with his calculations is not on record.

The significance of the division of 27 February was clear to both sides. The opposition was encouraged to press on its attack without respite. As for the government, the defeat was far more decisive than North had expected. He told his followers while they were in the lobby for the division : 'Probably we shall lose this question : if so they will move to go up with the resolution in an address to the throne, and upon that ques-

[1] In fact only one seems to have done so. Appendix II, pp. 404-5.

tion I mean to divide, because I apprehend they will not have a majority upon that, though they may have one upon this'.[1] But on discovering the size of the majority against him, he decided it was useless to oppose the address. The immediate reaction of the ministers was to admit that parliament had withdrawn its confidence. North pressed upon George III the urgent necessity of widening the basis of the administration by some sort of coalition, in order to recruit further parliamentary support. It might, he thought, 'be feasible to divide the opposition, and to take in only a part', but some move of this kind seemed 'almost absolutely necessary'.[2] The King reluctantly accepted his advice. During the following days attempts were made to construct new governments round Gower and Weymouth, Shelburne, or Grafton, or to enlist their support for a reformed ministry headed by North.[3] All these schemes had, as their object, the transfer of about ten or so votes — if possible more — from one side of the House to the other: this, if it were possible, would re-establish an assured ministerial majority. The accession of Gower and Weymouth would bring back Wrottesley, Gilbert, Trentham, and one or two other deserters of their party, and, if Grafton joined them, as was hoped at one time, he would add two or three more. Shelburne, if he joined forces with North would bring with him seven or eight votes. The same idea inspired Dundas's hints at the expediency of attaching Sir James Lowther, the Duke of Rutland, and Pitt and his friends, by offers of honours and junior ministerial posts.[4] Lowther commanded six votes besides his own. Pitt and Rutland between them could muster nine or ten.

By 8 March, however, all these proposals had proved abortive. 'Indeed, Sir,' North wrote to the King, 'I am afraid, it will be very difficult to form a mixed system, and I am

---

[1] *Morning Chronicle*, 28 Feb. 1782.

[2] 2 A.M., 28 Feb. 1782, Fortescue, v, no. 3535.

[3] George III to North, 28 Feb. 1782, Thurlow to George III, 6 Mar. 1782, Jenkinson to George III, 6, 7 Mar. 1782, Fortescue, v, nos. 3537, 3542, 3543, 3544.

[4] H. Dundas to Robinson, 3 Mar. 1782, enclosure, H.M.C., *Abergavenny MSS.*, 50, no. 440A.

perfectly convinced that, whatever may be the event of today, the present Ministry will not go on.'[1] That afternoon in the House of Commons, the opposition commenced the last phase of its attack upon a government which was already tottering, and which, under steady pressure, was bound very soon to collapse.

(iv)

THE LAST PHASE: THE FAILURE TO RESTORE THE GOVERNMENT'S MAJORITY

During the first week of March, while frantic efforts were being made behind the scenes to secure additional support for the North administration, ministers continued to present a bold front in the House of Commons. North gave more than one assurance that the government would adhere strictly to the instructions voted by the House on 27 February : no further attempt would be made to recover America by offensive warfare.[2] Meanwhile, he declared, he would remain in office, until either the King instructed him to resign or else 'the sense of that House, expressed in the clearest manner, should point out to him the propriety of withdrawing'. This decision he justified by the apparent absence of 'any settled system or agreement' among the leaders of opposition and by the fear that they intended changes in the constitution — 'therefore it would be for the good of the public that he himself should stay in, and continue in office to prevent, as he had hitherto done, confusion in the state, and the introduction of principles which might not be constitutional'.[3] What these principles were he did not specify ; but it is clear both from a letter he wrote to the King on 8 March, and from a remarkable speech made later that day by William Adam (of which more below) that there was serious concern about Charles Fox's enthusiasm for parliamentary reform.[4]

On 28 February, as a first token of the ministers' intention to wind up the war in America, the Attorney-General moved

[1] Fortescue, v, no. 3545. [2] Debrett, vi, 348, 349-50, 367.
[3] *Ibid.* 368. [4] Fortescue, v, no. 3545.

for leave to bring in a bill to enable the government to conclude
a peace or truce with the revolted colonies.[1] The effect of this
step was somewhat spoiled next day, 1 March, when the King
received the Speaker and leaders of the opposition and returned
his reply to the Address voted on the motion of Conway on the
27th. The ministers, at their preliminary discussions and at
the cabinet which met on the morning of 1 March to approve
the form of this response,[2] had tried to limit the House's
invasion of their executive responsibility by claiming as wide
a latitude as possible in dealing with the situation. In the final
draft of the reply the King told his faithful Commons : 'You
may be assured that, in pursuance with your advice, I shall
take such measures as shall appear to me to be most conducive
to the restoration of harmony between Great Britain and the
revolted colonies, so essential to the prosperity of both ; and
that my efforts shall be directed in the most effectual manner
against our European enemies, until such a peace can be
obtained as shall consist with the interests and permanent
welfare of my kingdoms'.[3]

When the House met again on Monday, 4 March, and
received from the Speaker the text of the King's reply, opposition spokesmen declared themselves dissatisfied with both these
gestures. Intent on discrediting North and his colleagues,
they argued that, since the King's answer did not specifically
acknowledge the request of the House that offensive warfare
for the reconquest of America was not to continue, therefore
ministers still harboured such designs. Conway, once again
taking the lead, declared 'he could not resist the impulse he
felt to rivet, if possible, those fetters, which he hoped the
Address voted on Wednesday had put upon the American
war'.[4] Accordingly, he moved another motion, as expressive
as his previous one, of distrust in the ministers, to the effect

---

[1] Debrett, vi, 341.

[2] 'I was kept [at Lord North's] until between 12 and 1 o'clock and I am
this instant going out to the Chancellor's about His Majesty's answer which
I sent two sketches of to him at midnight for his consideration. From the
Chancellor I am to return to Lord North's, where there is to be a Cabinet on
it at 11°,' Robinson to Jenkinson, 9 A.M., 1 Mar. 1782, Add. MSS. 38218,
f. 3.   [3] Debrett, vi, 343-4.   [4] *Ibid.* 345.

that 'after the solemn declaration of the opinion of this House
in their humble address . . . this House will consider as
enemies to His Majesty and this country, all those who shall
endeavour to frustrate His Majesty's paternal care for the ease
and happiness of his people, by advising, or by any means
attempting, the farther prosecution of offensive war on the
continent of North America, for the purpose of reducing the
revolted colonies to obedience by force'.[1] In a speech in support of this motion Fox went so far as to declare that the vague
nature of the Reply, coupled with the language recently used
by ministers in the House, made it manifest that the government intended to continue the war and that the Attorney-
General's bill was mere window-dressing to conceal their
designs: 'This answer of the Ministry, coupled with their
language in that House, was perfectly intelligible: for here
they declared, and particularly the Minister of the American
Department, the best way to conclude a peace with America
was to make them feel the calamities of war. This expression
the new Secretary of State had made use of but a few days
before. His Majesty, he sincerely believed, wished to conclude
peace with America, as his faithful Commons had advised
him; but his Ministers undoubtedly meant no such thing,
for their language was different.'[2]

This speech was a sound stroke of political tactics, but it
did not represent fact. It did the ministers grave injustice.
They knew peace was necessary. North, on the 27th, had
opposed Conway's motion not because he wished to continue
the war but because he did not want to have Britain's craving
for peace advertised to the world. He and his colleagues did
not wish to make an unconditional surrender to the terms
required by the American Congress if anything better could
be obtained by unfettered negotiation: some of the lines on
which their thoughts were running were revealed by part of the
instructions with which the King briefed Thurlow before
Thurlow sounded Gower on the possibilities of a coalition:
'the basis of public measures . . . [was to be] founded on
keeping what is in our present possession in North America,

[1] Debrett, vi, 347.   [2] Ibid. 354.

and attempting by a negotiation with any separate provinces or even districts to detach them from France, even upon any plan of their own, provided they remain separate states'.[1] The ministers' intentions were in general conformity with the resolutions of the House on 27 February, though not going so far as the unconditional concession of American independence demanded by the sections of opposition headed by Fox and Rockingham. North, however, saw no point in a trial of strength upon Conway's motion, which was allowed to pass without a division. He pleaded merely that a little time should be given, in which it would become clearly apparent that ministers were acting in accordance with the directions of the House.[2]

The next day's debate (5 March) showed that the opposition had no intention of letting the ministers recover their place in the saddle. The Attorney-General duly introduced his bill in a previous committee and explained its provisions. The draft bill provided 'that it shall and may be lawful for His Majesty to treat, consult of, agree, and conclude, with any body or bodies corporate or politic, or any assembly or assemblies or description of men, or any person or persons whatever, a Peace or Truce with the said colonies or plantations. . . . And in order to obviate any impediment, obstacle or delay . . . His Majesty shall have full power and authority, by virtue of this act, by his letters patent under the Great Seal of Great Britain, to repeal, annul, and make void, or to suspend, for any time or times, the operation and effect of any act or acts of parliament, which relate to the said colonies or plantations.'[3] Wallace expressed his hope for the unanimous support of the House for a measure which would promote the peace now so generally desired. But the opposition was not

[1] George III to North, 28 Feb. 1782, Fortescue, v, no. 3537.
[2] Debrett, vi, 350. Contemporary evidence does not support but disproves the claim made nearly forty years later by T. W. Coke of Holkham to have carried the decisive motion against the American War by 178 to 177 and to have then taken up the Address founded upon it to the King. His biographer's highly colourful account of the episode, resting only on his faulty memory, is entirely unfounded (Mrs. A. M. W. D. Stirling, *Coke of Norfolk and his Friends*, 2 vols., 1908, i, 207-10).
[3] *The Political Magazine*, iii (1782), 142.

thus to be disarmed. Fox, rising to reply, 'assured the Committee that nothing but the personal respect he bore the learned gentleman had prevented him from treating the proposition before the Committee just as it deserved to be treated ; and that was to burst out a laughing when he had heard it, and then to walk out of the House ; for nothing could be so ridiculous and farcical as to hear such a proposition from that side of the House, and from a member who, on Wednesday last, had combatted, as far as he was able, a resolution, the obvious tendency of which was that very peace with which the learned gentleman seemed at present enamoured ; the supporters of the present administration entertained at present a wish for peace, but they had been beaten into it ; and nothing but flagellation and correction could drive them to think of peace : — pity it was that so much correction should be necessary!' How far was it probable, he went on, that ministers were inclined to make peace, and then proceeded to pour scorn on the suggestion that they were so inclined.[1]

This contumelious reception of Wallace's Bill bespoke the opposition's intention to destroy the credit of the government by every means in their power. 'The Honourable Member', North remarked, 'seemed to be in a great hurry to get the places of the ministers.'[2] In fact, from now onwards, the conflict in the House of Commons was, openly, not a struggle over war or peace, but a struggle for power, between the opposition covetous for office and the ministers intent on keeping their places. Each side felt it could best secure the interests of the country ; but North and his colleagues were weighed down by their past record. To those members of parliament who stood detached from the strife of parties, the question at issue was becoming one of confidence in the capacity of the ministers to extricate the country from a dangerous and humiliating situation ; and the opposition leaders had much justification for arguing that the government's incompetence was such that the way should be cleared for a new administration. Unfortunately for the ministers, their prestige was

[1] Debrett, vi, 365-6. [2] *Ibid.* 368.

further reduced during the first week of March by the loss of Minorca and St. Christopher. The great debates and crucial divisions of 8 and 15 March showed that the marginal votes in the House of Commons were turning against them, as independent members became convinced, by opposition arguments, that they were incapable of saving anything from the wreckage of defeat.

The opposition's first direct proposal for the removal of the ministers was put forward on 8 March. Lord John Cavendish moved the first of a string of resolutions, three of which were statements of fact about the unhappy situation into which the country had been brought in the past six years, whilst the fourth laid all the blame for misfortunes and reverses upon want of foresight and ability on the part of the ministers. He proposed that, if these resolutions were carried, the House should then address the King requesting him to make such arrangements in his councils as should prevent the total ruin of the country.[1] Although only the first of these motions was officially before the House, it was with all of them, and especially the last, in view, that members on both sides carried on the debate, and the intention of the motions was plain to all. Immediately after the debate, North told the King: 'It was moved by the Opposition that they meant by their motions to remove, in as little offensive a manner as possible, all the administration. This was likewise understood by the friends of Government, so that the question was, in fact, whether the ministry should be immediately removed or not, and yet they were saved only by ten votes.'[2]

Ministers carried the day by 226 to 216. Their position was not a strong one, for it was difficult to refute the accusation that they had not spent to the best advantage the vast sums which had been voted for the war. Moreover Jenkinson's defence, that the triumphs of the Seven Years' War had brought down upon Great Britain the jealousy and hostility of all the other powers, was open to Pitt's pertinent comment that, if relations with foreign powers were so unfavourable, war should

[1] *Ibid.* 380.
[2] North to George III, 3 A.M., 9 Mar. 1782, Fortescue, v, no. 3546.

not have been begun, or at least not continued : [1] this perhaps was the most damning criticism which could be brought against the government, a trenchant indictment of the wisdom and judgment of its members, pointing inexorably to the conclusion that they should no longer be trusted with the direction of affairs. It was clear to ministers that some counter-attack was necessary, and William Adam and Henry Dundas endeavoured to win votes for the government by representing to the House the undesirability of dismissing the North ministry only to make inevitable the replacement of it by one drawn from the opposition.[2] Adam drew a powerful picture of Fox as the destroyer of the constitution :

> Mr Fox had said, in a former debate, That that man would be infamous, who, on coming into office, should forget or retract his former principles. The honourable gentleman having been so candid, as to make this declaration, previous to his coming into power, it would, he presumed, be allowed fair, and he trusted, it would be felt necessary for that House, called on, as they were, to vote a removal of the present ministers, to pause for a few minutes, in order to recollect and consider, what had been the principles and the doctrines of the men who were to form the new ministry, if a new ministry was to be formed. And first the honourable gentleman had more than once declared, that the voice of the people was to be collected without doors from the people themselves, and not from their representatives — a position that went not only, to what he thought, a breach of the constitution, but was an express reprobation of the majorities of that House, not withstanding that the honourable gentleman had found it convenient to hold up a late majority, as an authority of the first importance ; a doctrine which he was ready to subscribe to, though not more than to the authority of majorities in general. The honourable gentleman had also repeatedly told them, that he was an advocate for annual parliaments, in opposition to the wisdom of their ancestors, who, after the maturest consideration, adopted septennial, as the most serviceable to the common weal, and the most useful to government,

---

[1] Debrett, vi, 388, 411-12.   [2] *Ibid.* 398-9, 402-5.

at the same time that they infringed not on the right of the people, so as to injure those rights in the smallest degree. The honourable gentleman had likewise expressed a desire to alter the representation of the people ; a measure, gentlemen would see, that would be a violent alteration of the constitution, which had for so many years been looked up to and admired as the most perfect system of political arrangements and distribution of power that human wisdom could frame. He then adverted to the plan of Mr Burke for reducing the civil list, and declared that he should consider it as a direct violation of national faith, and a measure to which he was sure many gentlemen of that House could not agree.

This was hitting back with a vengeance! When Fox had replied to Adam, Dundas followed with much more in the same strain, and also with a more telling presentation of arguments which Charles Jenkinson had already employed. Their theme drew some response among a few at least of the country gentlemen, one or two of whom had already expressed their preference for North. Sir John Delaval declared early in the debate, that 'he should vote against the motion, . . . because he saw not where a better administration could be found than the present', and Sir Henry Hoghton followed him with a similar declaration.[1] Dundas's speech, less vividly reported than Adam's, seems to have been the more noteworthy of the two. Rigby declared, 'he was sure the learned Lord's was by far the best speech that day, because he perceived it had given most offence'.[2] Dundas himself felt that he had excelled on that occasion ; and it was doubtless not just flattery that made North attribute to the Lord-Advocate's speech the government's slender majority of ten.[3]

Robinson's state of the division shows that the government was just saved from immediate defeat by the return to its ranks of a substantial number of members who had deserted it over Conway's motion on 27 February. There now voted with it 11 out of the 27 members, formerly reckoned as friends or as

[1] *The Political Magazine*, iii (1782), 294.   [2] Debrett, vi, 408.
[3] H. Dundas to R. Dundas, 9 Mar. 1782, cited Matheson, 79.

hopeful, who had voted with the opposition on 27 February,[1] and 17 out of the 22 or 23 men who had deliberately abstained from that division.[2] Among these it secured now the support of three independents who had abstained from voting on and since 20 February, George Pitt (Dorset), James Dutton (Glos.), and George Philipps (Carmarthen). It was also supported by five other independents, all of whom had voted on the 20th for the dismissal of Sandwich — Thomas Grosvenor, Henry Rawlinson, Whitbread, Farrer, and Dimsdale: the last two had voted fairly steadily against the ministry since before the recess, so that their votes were an unexpected *volte face* in its favour. It would appear that most of these members found themselves in a position similar to that of Philip Yorke,[3] ready to vote for resolutions tending to an end of the war, but unwilling to see the North ministry destroyed and a new one formed from the opposition set up in its place.

The government was thus able to muster 226, comprising 72 party men, 93 members of the court and administration circle and 61 independents. The alignment of members in its favour was nearly, but not quite restored to the situation of 20 February, when ten more votes than this had been cast in support of Sandwich. The slightly lower majority on 8 March was mainly due to casual absences of regular friends, but there were now one or two new desertions, notably John Peach Hungerford (Leics.), who had hitherto given steady support to the government but now voted against it. Three barristers, D. P. Coke, Francis Burton, and Thomas Davenport, now left Westminster to go on circuit:[4] of these, Coke was a very independent member, but the other two were counted as firm friends by Robinson — there is no evidence on the point, but

---

[1] J. H. Blair, Sir G. Elliot, J. Fuller, Lord Graham, F. F. Luttrell, Charles and John Morgan, J. Peachey, T. Pelham, Sir F. L. Rogers, P. Yorke.
[2] A. Bayntun, A. R. Bowes, W. Clayton, Sir J. Coghill, J. Craufurd, P. Cust, J. Frederick, Lord Galway, Sir J. Henderson, R. Jackson, Lord Melbourne, H. Pelham, J. Pringle, J. Sinclair, James Dutton, Geo. Philipps, Geo. Pitt.
[3] See p. 334 above.
[4] *Commons Journals*, xxxviii, 874, 875, 877; 'State, 8 Mar. 1782', Abergavenny MSS.

their decision, at such a moment of crisis, to put professional business before political obligation seems to suggest that their friendship was cooling. There were also a few ominous abstentions among former friends of the government who had voted against it on 27 February — three independent country gentlemen, Sir Henry Gough, Richard Myddleton, and R. A. Neville; two business men, Robert Child and John Nesbitt; and the more independent associates of Gower, Thomas Gilbert, and Sir John Wrottesley.

On 8 March the opposition vote dropped back to the level of 20 February. With one or two exceptions, all those members who had swung over to the opposition on the division of 27 February declined to support it on a direct vote of censure against the government; some, as has been shown, reverted to their ministerial allegiance, others abstained, and only John Rolle, Abraham Rawlinson, and John Pennington voted against the ministers again on the 8th. There were one or two new recruits — Hungerford, and the very independent Scotsman, William Pulteney, who, although not particularly friendly to North's ministry, both in December and in February opposed motions which might embarrass the government in peace negotiations. Otherwise the minority was made up of men whose hostility to the ministry was either of long standing or had become fixed by the end of the Christmas recess. Except for nineteen persons, its composition was the same as the minority of 20 February. There were now present rather over a hundred members of parties in opposition, at most two or three more than there had been in the division of the 20th. This confirms the conclusion to be deduced from a comparison of the lists for this and the next division that, allowing for pairing and an irreducible minimum of absentees, the leaders of the opposition had, by 8 March, scraped up their very last reserves of regular supporters. Any member absent on the 8th, whose attendance was secured for the 15th, would count in that later division not as an extra vote but merely as a replacement for one who had voted on the 8th but was then lost owing to illness or some other accidental cause. About 12 or 13 March Robinson had a list of eleven 'cons' 'sent to and expected' by the opposition.[1] On the 15th nine of them paired or voted, but, owing to the absence of other members previously present, the opposition made a net addition of one only to its numbers from this group. Once again it had reached the point at which further success was only possible if it could attract the votes of still more government supporters. This its leaders were confident they could do, and the event proved them right.

The near-defeat on the 8th confirmed ministers in their belief that the existing government could not last for many days without further support.[2] But the attempts of the previous week to form a coalition had by this time come to nothing, George III, to his great regret, finding 'every description of men equally unwilling to stand forth'.[3] The King, acting through his Lord Chancellor, was therefore obliged to approach the main party of opposition. Apparently on Rigby's advice, Rockingham was approached directly in preference to Shelburne, but Shelburne was informed of the step being taken.[4] On 11 March Thurlow commenced an exchange of views with Rockingham, sounding him on his willingness to form an administration on a 'broad-bottom'. But this attempt to salvage some part of the North ministry came to a standstill on the 14th, when Rockingham disclosed his terms — no veto on American independence, enactment of the full programme of Economical Reform, and full power for the Marquis to form an administration excluding all 'persons who had been considered as *obnoxious Ministers*, or of those who were deemed as belonging to a sort of secret system'.[5] Although discussions dragged

[1] Notes in preparation for the division of 15 Mar. 1782, Abergavenny MSS. They had been drawn up by the 13th, on which day Robinson forwarded them to Jenkinson for his information, Add. MSS. 38218, f. 26.

[2] North to George III, 3 A.M., 9 Mar. 1782, Jenkinson to George III, 13 Mar. 1782, Fortescue, v, nos. 3546, 3553 ; H. Dundas to Robinson, 9 Mar. 1782, H.M.C., *Abergavenny MSS.*, 51, no. 445 ; H. Dundas to R. Dundas, 9 Mar. 1782, cited Matheson, 79.

[3] George III to Thurlow, 10 Mar. 1782, British Museum, Egerton MSS. 2232, f. 45.

[4] Jenkinson to George III, 13, 14 Mar. 1782, Fortescue, v, nos. 3553, 3556 ; memorandum by William Adam, *Memorials and Correspondence of C. J. Fox*, ed. Lord John Russell (4 vols., 1853-7), i, 294.

[5] The King's account of this negotiation is summarised in his letter to Thurlow of 18 Mar. 1782, Fortescue, v, no. 3564. This agrees very closely with the rather more detailed account set down by Rockingham, Rockingham

on until the 18th, no further progress was possible. Such a defiance of the royal prerogative of choosing ministers was wholly revolting to George III, nor could he see any advantage to be gained to the country by a total change from one group of politicians to another.[1] The one definite result of the negotiation was to confirm the opposition leaders in the belief that the destruction of the ministry and their own succession to office were imminent. 'You must soon see all at your feet in the manner you would wish, and with the full means to do what is right', Richmond wrote on the 12th to Rockingham. '. . . by firmness all will come right yet, and you will carry the nation with you with such *éclat* as to ensure you the means of doing what you wish.'[2] In the same spirit of expectant optimism, Burke's wife wrote the same day to a friend : 'Here we consider the Ministry as gone, they die hard, however they are in great confusion, and look on themselves as dead men. Never was there so great a change in the appearance of things in so few days. Their last majority of ten is looked upon as a death struggle. . . . They talk of a dissolution of Parliament, but it is thought they will be afraid of such a step.'[3] With every confidence Rockingham's friends in the Commons prepared for their second onslaught on the government on 15 March.

However, during the week leading up to 15 March, one or two men in the inner circle of the government still nursed some hopes of success. Even on the 15th Sandwich expressed the view that, 'if Lord North did not despond and talk of giving the thing up matters would not be yet irretrievable'.[4] Robinson, carefully conning his lists, embarked with some confidence on

---

MSS., R. 1-1124; this document is reproduced with several errors in transcription — which render one passage completely unintelligible — in Albemarle, *Memoirs of the Marquis of Rockingham*, ii, 451-3. Thurlow's first letter to the King concerning the negotiation was dated as 13 Mar. by Fortescue, on the strength of the King's endorsement, but was clearly written on the 12th, Fortescue, v, no. 3551.

[1] George III to Thurlow, 15, 18 Mar. 1782, Fortescue, v, nos. 3563, 3564 ; correspondence between Thurlow and Rockingham, 15-18 Mar. 1782, Albemarle, ii, 457-60.

[2] *Ibid.* 446.

[3] Jane Burke to (?) R. Champion, 12 Mar. 1782, draft, Burke MSS. (Lamport).   [4] H.M.C., *Abergavenny MSS.*, 52, no. 454.

preparations for a further division: on paper he still had a fair reserve of supporters on whom to draw, noting, about the 13th, a list of twenty-three 'pros.' and one 'hopeful' all absent on the 8th who were now 'sent to and expected'. This, he thought, was nearly twice as many as the opposition could possibly bring up, finding in his lists only eleven 'cons.' and three 'doubtfuls' previously absent who might be expected to vote on the other side. Completing his calculations he concluded, 'It is possible to divide 252 and 231'.[1] These figures betokened a better majority than on the 8th, and a message to this effect was duly relayed to the King through Jenkinson.[2] Independent computations made about the same time by Lord Denbigh corresponded closely with those of Robinson, putting the probable majority at between eighteen and thirty.'[3] But these forecasts both proved to be wildly optimistic.

On 15 March the opposition made what proved to be the last effort required in the House of Commons to dislodge the ministry. This time a prominent independent, not a party leader, was chosen to deliver the attack. As the primary object of the debate was to appeal to wavering independents, the choice was apt, and Sir John Rous, member for Suffolk, who opened the debate on the motion of no-confidence, was careful to stress his own independent status: [4]

> No one could suppose that he was actuated, in any degree, by a spirit of party; it was well known, and he was not ashamed to confess it, that he was descended from a Tory family, and had been bred up in Tory principles: this circumstance alone, he hoped, would screen him from any imputation of being devoted to a party adverse in general to administration. From the first dawn of the American war, he had felt the injustice and impolicy of it; and he came into that House its declared enemy on principle: but at the same time that he was an enemy to the war, he had

[1] Notes in preparation for the division of 15 Mar. 1782, Abergavenny MSS. The final figures included tellers.
[2] Robinson to Jenkinson, 13 Mar. 1782, Add. MSS. 38218, f. 26; Jenkinson to George III, 13 Mar. 1782, Fortescue, v, no. 3553.
[3] Selwyn to Carlisle, 13, 15, 16 Mar. 1782, H.M.C., *Carlisle MSS.*, 592-4.   [4] Debrett, vi, 447-8.

come into parliament highly prepossessed in favour of the noble Lord in the blue ribband; and he had felt such a respect for his character, that he would have gone great lengths to support him; but when he found that the noble Lord persevered blindly to pursue measures, which had already reduced the country from a state of glory and prosperity to calamity and disgrace, he should deem himself an enemy to his country, if he did not exert every faculty to remove him.

Rous concluded by moving a resolution of no-confidence which implicitly blamed the ministers for all the misfortunes of recent years : [1]

That this House (taking into consideration the great sums voted and debts incurred, for the service of the army, navy, and ordnance, in this unfortunate war, to the amount of upwards of one hundred millions; and finding that the nation has, notwithstanding these extraordinary exertions, lost thirteen ancient colonies belonging to the crown of Great Britain, the newly-acquired province of West Florida, and the islands of Dominica, St. Vincent, Grenada, Tobago, and Minorca, besides several valuable commercial fleets . . . and that we are still involved in war with three powerful nations in Europe, without one single ally) can have no further confidence in the ministers who have the direction of public affairs.

In this motion of censure, and in the arguments which were used to support it, were woven together both threads of the opposition's previous attacks upon the ministers : they could not, it was alleged, be trusted to carry out the wishes of the House respecting the war in America — North, so Rous declared, still 'persevered blindly' — and their lack of success proved them thoroughly incapable of conducting either war or foreign policy, or even of extricating the country from the war without further disaster.   Other independents, who normally voted on the opposition side, re-echoed the belief that ministers were incapable of dealing with the situation.   Charles Marsham, member for Kent, declared that 'the honour of the country had

[1] *Ibid.* 448-9.

been tarnished in the hands of the present administration, and its naval empire had been lost; this was sufficient reason for him to wish to have the present ministers removed; for from the measures of those by whom so much had been lost, he could not hope that anything could be recovered . . . if those who were out should pursue the measures of those who were in, he would be as great an enemy to them as he was now to the present ministers'.[1] General Smith 'disclaimed any party spirit or resentment . . . he had in that House always opposed the measures of Government; but in another situation (at the India House) it was well known he never had endeavoured to clog the wheels of government. The measures of the present ministers were in general . . . weak and impolitic.'[2] Richard Hill, member for Shropshire, told the House that 'if the time was come, when the safety of the state required new men, that consideration must, with him, absorb every other . . . he certainly would vote for the motion; though at the same time he should rejoice if a coalition could take place among those who were out, and such of those who were in, as he thought amiable, worthy, and deserving characters'.[3]

The idea of a coalition — of a combination of all the country's talents to extricate it from its dangerous situation — had an irresistible appeal to the independent members in the House of Commons. Once introduced by Hill into the debate, it was taken up again at least twice, by Dolben and by Gilbert, and it seems apparent from the observations of Henry Dundas towards the close of the debate that other members whose speeches were not reported also favoured it. In a simple view of the political situation, the capitulation of the ministry over the American question, whether forced or voluntary, seemed to clear the way for co-operation between men from all sides in politics. 'The grand principle of distinction and separation between parties (the American dispute) is now removed', Sir Gilbert Elliot wrote to his brother on 5 March, a few days before this crucial debate. 'There is at least an opportunity, therefore, for coalition, without the sacrifice of former principle on either side. . . . *All* the ability of the country united to

[1] Debrett, vi, 457.   [2] *Ibid.* 461.   [3] *Ibid.* 462.

direct *all* the resources of the country to one good end, is a prospect which I hope is not quite out of sight.' But he was too much a realist not to know that exclusive party ambitions, 'the damned intricacies of arrangements, private interests and personal considerations', were more than likely to destroy any chance of such a union.[1] In fact the Rockinghams, intent on an exclusive party ministry, were resolutely opposed to any such scheme. But they were prepared to exploit its popularity in the House, and they appear to have done so successfully despite the counter-demonstrations of Henry Dundas. Dundas, speaking towards the end of the debate, concluded that 'a coalition of parties seemed to be the general desire of the House', and confessed that he himself was of that opinion. But he felt it urgently necessary to try and curb enthusiasm for the motion by pointing out that it would not in the least guarantee a coalition, 'for it went to the immediate discharge of the present ministry, and put the government into the hands of the opposition alone. . . . A Coalition could only be formed by the substantial union and connection of all parties, and not by driving out one half of those who ought to compose it.' A vote for the motion, he went on, would be a vote for an opposition party administration. If a coalition were desired, the present ministry should be retained until it was formed.[2] Lord John Cavendish hastened to dispel these unfavourable representations, disingenuously declaring, 'that by agreeing to the present motion, the House by no means placed the opposition in power, and thereby prevented the coalition so ardently desired. They did no more than take the executive government from the present hands, and leave it to His Majesty to frame the new administration as His Majesty should think most proper.'[3] His quick intervention probably had some success, judging by the action of independents in the division. In mentioning the King's right to rearrange his ministry, he was paying lip-service to familiar, accepted constitutional doctrine, and reassured independents who would have been shocked had they known with what scant regard for it the

[1] Countess of Minto, *Memoir of Hugh Elliot* (1868), 235.
[2] Debrett, vi, 472.   [3] *Ibid.* 473.

Rockinghams had already decided to act. Judged in the light of the discussions going on behind the scenes, Cavendish's statement was unscrupulously deceitful : lured by the imminent prospect of office and power, he seems, for a moment, to have abandoned that outstanding probity for which he was, on the whole, justly extolled.

The division proved that the arguments of the opposition had just sufficient success to put the game into their hands. Their loss of the division by nine votes was a virtual victory, for it proved that the government could not keep the allegiance of its friends and was certain very soon to be defeated outright. 'The rats were very bad,' complained Robinson, 'I fear they will increase before Wednesday, when Mr Fox has given notice they will again attack.' [1]

What, then, had gone wrong with Robinson's forecast of the 13th ? In his calculations, which, however, presupposed no desertions from either side, the ministry was expected to have a majority of about 21, with a maximum vote in the division of 250 against 229 for the opposition. On the 15th the opposition, with 227, almost exactly fulfilled this forecast : but the government, with 236, fell well short of it, this although four votes were secured which Robinson had not expected, those of Hugh Boscawen, Thomas Gilbert, Lord Hyde, and P. C. Methuen.

Robinson's estimate of 250 for the majority was a possible target which it was unlikely the government would achieve. The theoretical maximum of votes was always reduced by illness and other causes of involuntary absence. This alone would not have invalidated his calculation of the government's margin of votes over the opposition, for both sides were equally exposed to losses of this kind, and, as shown above, they had occurred among the opposition ranks.[2] But the evidence shows that such losses on the 15th would not have brought the government vote down by more than five or six below Robinson's estimate : his figure of 250 would have been nearly achieved but for the deliberate action of a few members, who refused

[1] Robinson to Jenkinson, 16 Mar. 1782, Fortescue, v, no. 3560, enclosure.
[2] Pp. 317, 349-50 above.

to support the ministers, some of them, by their adverse votes, raising the opposition vote above the figure it might otherwise have been expected to reach.

Four members who might have voted with the government declined to attend the House. Two of these had supported it on the 8th — Richard Jackson, counsel to the Board of Trade, and Lord Melbourne, a follower of Lord North who now yielded to the pressure of Fox's friend, the Prince of Wales.[1] The others who would not attend were Newcastle's son, Lincoln, who had retired to Bath and 'would not come up though his father wrote to him', and Archibald Douglas, recently elected member for the county of Forfar, who for the past five weeks had put off taking his seat and continued to do so till the North administration was no more.[2]

Another six, who came up for the debate, declined to support the government, and went away before the division. These included Rigby's friend, John Dawes, the banker; Christopher D'Oyly, a member of the administration circle; Gower's son, Lord Trentham; two independents, R. A. Neville and John Sinclair;[3] and Sandwich's client, Sir John Borlase Warren.[4] Three of these, Dawes, Sinclair, and Warren, had voted with the government on the 8th. Warren, at least, was being strongly pressed in his private circle to desert the ministry: he wrote next day to Sandwich to excuse himself, on the ground that the motion seemed pointed at North, not at any other person (*i.e.* not at his patron), and that, had he stayed for the division, all his friends and relations would have forsworn his society.[5]

Four more members — Dimsdale, Farrer, Whitbread, and Sir Gilbert Elliot — who had voted with the government on the 8th, now changed their minds and voted against it.

'Your Lordship will see', Robinson wrote the following day

[1] *The Last Journals of Horace Walpole*, edited by A. Francis Steuart, 2 vols. (1910), ii, 420; Selwyn to Carlisle, 18 Mar. 1782, H.M.C., *Carlisle MSS.*, 597.
[2] '15 March 1782, Remarks', Abergavenny MSS., copy in Fortescue, v, p. 390.   [3] *Ibid.*
[4] Robinson to Jenkinson, 19 Mar. 1782, Add. MSS. 38567, f. 93.
[5] 16 Mar. 1782, Sandwich MSS.

to Sandwich, 'that if our old number of friends who before voted had kept up, the new ones added whom we got and the hopeful come to us, our majority would have been handsome.'[1] For his part every effort had been made to ensure success. Finding attendance slack at the beginning of the debate, he had spent much of the evening routing up government supporters, being forced meanwhile 'to send to Sir James Marriott, who was up, to keep talking by the hour',[2] — a circumstance which had its entertaining side, for Marriott, forced into desperate improvisations, diverted the House considerably with his inadvertent remarks about ships not being built in ninety-five hours, and with legal fantasy about the representation of the American provinces in parliament by the members for Kent, in virtue of their charters making them part of the manor of Greenwich.[3] It cannot be doubted that Robinson had secured every available vote. But by these defections, the ministry was deprived of the votes of fourteen members, nine of whom had previously sided with it, and upon whose votes North and Robinson might for the most part have fairly counted. Otherwise it might well have secured between 240 and 245 votes in the division,[4] instead of 236.

The opposition, having reached previously, on the 8th, the point where further success depended upon winning over to its side in divisions still more former friends of the government,[5] found its hopes adequately if not amply fulfilled on the 15th. In addition to the four members who now changed sides, it was also supported by five men, hitherto generally friendly towards the government, who had abstained from voting on the 8th. These were Robert Child, John Nesbitt, and Sir John Wrottesley, who had voted against the ministers for Conway's

---

[1] [16 Mar. 1782], Sandwich MSS. [2] *Ibid.*

[3] Debrett, vi, 460-1. Marriott's speech is reported in very much greater (and unnecessary) length in *The Political Magazine*, iii (1782), 354-60. In view of the circumstances, it may be doubted whether he took very seriously his argument about American representation through the manor of Greenwich: the context suggests that he felt himself in danger of drying up and so of failing to spin out the debate.

[4] Not 246 to 250 votes, because five or six government supporters who had voted on the 8th were unavoidably absent on the 15th for non-political reasons. [5] P. 350 above.

motion on 27 February, and Alexander Garden and Sir Samuel B. Fludyer, who had abstained from that division.[1] Only in one of these cases — that of Garden — had Robinson anticipated a vote adverse to the government: Child and Fludyer he had regarded as hopeful.[2] 'Opposition depend on *our* rats', he wrote next day to Sandwich.[3] Once more it was the deserters who wrecked his calculations and disappointed his hopes. Without these nine votes the opposition would have secured only 217 votes in the division, and the government's majority would have been somewhere between 20 and 30, figures which would possibly have turned the tide of the political battle.[4] A further factor contributing to the opposition's success was the failure in all but one instance, of Robinson's attempts to secure the absence of at least five county members who were expected to vote adversely — John Rolle, J. P. Hungerford, Lucy Knightley, Charles Penruddock, and Noel Hill: only in the case of Hill was he successful.[5]

The course of the division was determined particularly by the decisions of the nineteen men whose voting so upset Robinson's calculations, former friends of the government who now either abstained or voted against it.[6] To some extent the members of this group appeared, in point of age and classification, a random sample of the House: they included two civil servants, two army officers and one naval officer, but there were no less than five business men (three of them bankers), a number far in excess of the proportion of merchants in the

[1] It is possible that Nesbitt, like Melbourne, may have been influenced by the Prince of Wales, into whose circle of friends he was moving about this time (A. and C. Nesbitt, *History of the Family of Nisbet or Nesbitt in Scotland and Ireland* (1898), 46-8).

[2] '15 March 1782, Remarks', Abergavenny MSS.; Fortescue, v, p. 390. [3] [16 Mar. 1782], Sandwich MSS.

[4] 'We reckon today upon a majority of from twenty to thirty. . . .' If near thirty, 'the old Ministry and their friends will hold up their head.' Selwyn to Carlisle, 15 [Mar. 1782], H.M.C., *Carlisle MSS.*, 593.

[5] '15 March 1782, Remarks', Abergavenny MSS.; Fortescue, v, 390, entries in the third and fifth columns. Hungerford and Knightley were approached by Lord Wentworth at the instance of Lord Sandwich — Wentworth to Sandwich, no date, Abergavenny MS. 448A.

[6] Dawes, Douglas, D'Oyley, Jackson, Lord Lincoln, Lord Melbourne, Neville, Sinclair, Lord Trentham, Sir J. B. Warren, Child, Dimsdale, Sir Gilbert Elliot, Farrer, Sir S. B. Fludyer, Garden, Nesbitt, Whitbread, Sir John Wrottesley.

House. Four members of the group belonged to the circle of court and administration, and six to parties or factions connected with the government. Nine were independents, and among these last were four Scotsmen, two of whom, Elliot and Sinclair, were later to have distinguished public careers, and all of whom were of considerable standing in their native country; of the other two, Archibald Douglas, grandson and heir-at-law of the last Duke of Douglas, had various connections with the Scottish aristocracy, and himself received a British peerage in 1790; and Alexander Garden, member for the county of Aberdeen, though the most obscure of the four, was nevertheless the possessor, according to one newspaper account, of 'a very large fortune, and many of the first connections in the shire . . . very moderate in his political conduct . . . in general subjects a friend to Government but . . . uniformly opposed them in the particular and important question of the American war'.[1] One marked feature of the group (not unexpected) was that less than half of its members had sat in parliament since before the commencement of the American War. Ten entered the House in or after 1776, eight of these at or after the general election of 1780: a high proportion of the group thus consisted of men who had had no part in American politics between the passage of the Stamp Act and the skirmish at Lexington, and whose views had not been formed amidst the heated controversy over the events which had led up to the war; with no long-established habit of support for the North ministry, they were perhaps the more easily able to turn against it.

Few of the nineteen men made much mark in parliamentary life — most of them, if they ever made speeches, did not do so in the great debates and were rarely or never reported — so there is little direct evidence available regarding their opinions in March 1782 or the reasons for the course of action they then adopted. Sir John Warren's letter of the following day to Lord Sandwich reflects a general discontent with the North ministry in his private circle, with which he evidently had sufficient sympathy to risk jeopardizing his client-patron rela-

[1] *Parliamentary Characters, 1779–1781*, 25.

tionship with Sandwich (which, in fact, now came to an end).[1]
John Sinclair, by his own account, had become convinced that
Sandwich was not fit to be at the head of the Admiralty; [2] it
may be surmised that this disapproval was now extending to
the whole ministry. In recent years Sir John Wrottesley had
expressed very critical views about the abilities of ministers.[3]
He would certainly appear to be one of those, described by
Sir Gilbert Elliot, who were extremely anxious that the
American colonies should not be lost, and who long supported
the North government because a Rockingham ministry — the
only alternative — would have abandoned the war. 'However
much they . . . [might] be dissatisfied with the abilities of
the ministers, or disgusted with their mismanagements and
misfortunes, yet [they] had no choice left them', Elliot wrote.
'This I take to have been the true bond between Parliament
and the late Ministry, and the true key to its otherwise un-
accountable longevity.' [4] Elliot, then, shared this view with
Wrottesley. But it would be rash to apply his generalization
to other members of the group, or to any other men who, at
an earlier date, had abandoned the cause of the North ministry;
it certainly did not apply completely to two at least of the
nineteen — Alexander Garden and Richard Jackson: though
in general supporters of administration, they had from the
beginning disapproved of the American War.

The nineteen did not represent the whole extent of the loss
of support which the government had suffered since the early
days of the new parliament. To picture that loss in full,
account must also be taken of the defection on 8 March of
J. P. Hungerford, and of about a dozen other desertions which
had already occurred by 20 February, four weeks before.[5]

A comparison of the 'state' of the House prepared by

[1] 16 Mar. 1782, Sandwich MSS.
[2] Sinclair, *Correspondence*, i, 77.
[3] Almon, *The Parliamentary Register*, xvi (1780), 102-4; Debrett, v, 148.
[4] Countess of Minto, *Life and Letters of Sir Gilbert Elliot* (3 vols., 1874), i, 76.
[5] Adeane, Barrington, Clarges, D. P. Coke, A. Eyre, Drake, senior, Sir Henry Gough, Holdsworth, Sir Herbert Mackworth, Richard Myddleton, John Pennington, John Vaughan.

Robinson in February 1781 with the division list of 15 March and his observations upon it shows that twenty-seven members who, in the earlier part of 1781 could be counted as supporters or as at least friendly, had by 15 March given up supporting the North ministry. There were fourteen men whom Robinson in 1781 had classed as 'pro': Adeane, Barrington, Dawes, Sir Gilbert Elliot, Anthony Eyre, Farrer, Holdsworth, Jackson, Melbourne, Nesbitt, Sinclair, Lord Trentham, John Vaughan of Carmarthen, and Sir John Wrottesley. There were six more whom he had classed as 'hopeful': Hungerford, Sir Thomas Clarges, Child, D'Oyly, Garden, and Richard Myddleton. There were five whom he had over-cautiously put down as 'doubtful': W. Drake, senior, of Amersham, described about that time in a newspaper report as 'Tory in principle and a great admirer of Lord North, votes with the ministry in general, but sometimes with the minority';[1] Sir J. B. Warren, who until 15 March 1782 voted regularly as his patron, Sandwich, requested; Sir Herbert Mackworth, described in Robinson's lists for February 1782 as 'pro absent'; Sir Henry Gough, described in the same lists as 'hopeful'; R. A. Neville, noted in the list of 27 February as 'friendly'. And lastly, there were two men put down by Robinson in February 1781 as 'con.' but later proved friendly, Samuel Whitbread — he voted with the ministry on 12 December, 22 and 27 February, and 8 March — and D. P. Coke, who also voted with the government on 12 December and was classed 'hopeful' by Robinson on 22 February. Altogether these men included four members of the court and administration group, six members of ministerial factions, and seventeen independents: fourteen of these twenty-seven, eleven of them independents, voted on 15 March against the government; the remaining thirteen abstained (three, Eyre, D'Oyly, and Mackworth avoided voting altogether during the crisis between 20 February and 15 March, and three more, Neville, Gough, and Myddleton, appeared only once in a division, giving their votes for Conway's second motion). The undermining of the government's majority was mainly due to the actions of independents (though desertions by members of

[1] *Parliamentary Characters, 1779–1781*, 15.

parties and of the court were not negligible). A comparatively small number only of desertions was necessary to bring down the government. The North ministry had not had an assured majority: its safety had lain in the indifference of a marginal portion of its actual and potential critics, and once that indifference had been replaced by active condemnation, its position quickly became impossible.

With a majority reduced to nine, the last hopes in ministerial circles began to die. Dundas, who had pledged himself to give support to the last, thought the situation irretrievable: Rigby agreed; and North was clear that the time had come for him to resign. Even Robinson was losing heart, felt there was nothing more he could do, and looked to his friends to work a political miracle. To Jenkinson he wrote: 'Can't the Chancellor and you *devise* some change that might give a *temporary philip* (*sic*) and we should I think then still do'.[1] 'Opposition', he told Sandwich, 'say they will run us until they beat us, if they can but decrease our majority one at a time, and indeed if we cannot increase it, the number will not keep up'; but Sandwich doubted if anything more could be done.[2] The opposition, with victory almost in their grasp, prepared to challenge the ministry once again on Wednesday, 20 March, putting down a direct motion for their removal.

For a day or two the King still held out stubbornly. For the first time in these weeks he began to think of abdication. On the 15th he wrote to Thurlow: 'the changing from one party to another can answer no real good; besides I must then give up my principles and my honour, which I value above my crown': and on the morning of the 17th he wrote acknowledging North's report of the last division: 'I am resolved not to throw myself into the hands of Opposition, at all events, and shall certainly, if things go as they seem to lead, know what my conscience as well as honour dictates as the only way left for me'.[3] It seemed to him insufferable that parliament should foist upon him a ministry composed of men

[1] 16 Mar. 1782, Add. MSS. 38567, f. 92.
[2] [16 Mar. 1782], Sandwich MSS.; H.M.C., *Abergavenny MSS.*, 52, no. 455.   [3] Fortescue, v, nos. 3563, 3561.

who were publicly pledged to yield outright to the demands of the Americans : it would appear to be about this time that he drew up a draft message announcing his abdication, in which he wrote : 'His Majesty is convinced that the sudden change of sentiments of one Branch of the Legislature has totally incapacitated him from either conducting the war with effect or from obtaining any peace, but on conditions which would prove destructive to the commerce as well as essential rights of the British Nation'.[1] On the morning of the 18th North still found him unyielding. But by then it was becoming clear that the adverse effect of the division upon the House of Commons had been decisive : even well-wishers were coming to the view, that the ministry could not go on, and that it must be sacrificed at once in order to deliver the country from the dangers of a political deadlock. That same night North informed the King of the resolution of Thomas Grosvenor and some other country gentlemen : [2]

> '*That, being now convinced that the present Administration cannot continue any longer, they are of opinion that vain and ineffectual struggles tend only to public mischief and confusion, and that they shall think it their duty henceforward to desist from opposing what appears to be clearly the sense of the House of Commons.*' If these gentlemen persist in this resolution, Your Majesty will perceive that we shall infallibly be in a Minority even on Wednesday next, when the House will be moved, in direct terms, to resolve '*That it is their opinion that the management of public affairs ought not to be continued in the hands of the present Ministers.*'

Intent upon averting a constitutional crisis and upon saving the King from the consequences of too stubborn and foolish a stand about his honour, North repeated as firmly as he could his conviction that the House of Commons was tired of the government and that it was the King's duty to accept its verdict : [3]

The votes of the Minorities on Friday sevennight, and on Friday last contained, I believe, the genuine sense of the

---

[1] Fortescue, v, no. 3601.   [2] *Ibid.* no. 3566.   [3] *Ibid.*

House of Commons, and I really think, of the Nation at large; Not that I suppose the minds of men in general exasperated against the individuals who compose the Administration, but they are tired of the Administration collectively taken, and wish at all events to see it alter'd. The torrent is too strong to be resisted; Your Majesty is well apprized that, in this country, the Prince on the Throne, cannot, with prudence, oppose the deliberate resolution of the House of Commons : Your Royal Predecessors (particularly King William the Third and his late Majesty) were obliged to yield to it much against their wish in more instances than one : They consented to changes in their Ministry which they disapproved because they found it necessary to sacrifice their private wishes, and even their opinions to the preservation of public order, and the prevention of those terrible mischiefs, which are the natural consequence of the clashing of two branches of the Sovereign Power in the State. The concessions they made were never deemed dishonourable, but were considered as marks of their wisdom, and of their parental affection for their people. Your Majesty has graciously and steadily supported the servants you approve, as long as they could be supported : Your Majesty has firmly and resolutely maintained what appeared to You essential to the welfare and dignity of this Country, as long as this Country itself thought proper to maintain it. The Parliament have altered their sentiments, and as their sentiments whether just or erroneous must ultimately prevail, Your Majesty having persevered, as long as possible, in what You thought right, can lose no honour if you yield at length, as some of the most renowned and most glorious of your Predecessors have done, to the opinion and wishes of the House of Commons.

Since a ministry on a 'broad bottom' was unattainable, and since there were 'no persons capable and willing to form a new administration' except Rockingham and Shelburne, it was imperative that they be approached directly. A refusal to send for them would, in the event of North's defeat in the Commons on the 20th, leave the country without a ministry, and this situation with its obvious dangers ought at all costs to be avoided.

On the 18th George III set on foot a new approach through the Chancellor to Shelburne.[1] But he was still determined not to have either wing of the opposition storm the closet, and he wrote next morning to North :[2]

> After having yesterday in the most solemn manner assured you that my sentiments of honour will not permit me to send for any of the Leaders of Opposition and personally treat with them, I could not but be hurt at your letter of last night. Every man must be the sole Judge of his feelings, therefore whatever you or any man can say on that subject has no avail with me.
>
> Till I have heard what the Chancellor has done from his own mouth, I shall not take any step, and if You resign before I have decided what I will do, You will certainly for ever forfeit my regard.

But during the next twenty-four hours his resistance was overborne. On the 19th North urged once again that the administration's situation was hopeless :[3]

> I hear from every quarter that we shall certainly be beat to-morrow : Those who staid away last Friday will vote against us and many of those who voted for us will be absent; in short, Sir, there is no chance of keeping the present Ministry in place any longer, and if there should be anybody who informs Your Majesty that there is the least hope left of doing so, he deceives you, being himself probably misinformed. The fate of the present Ministry being certain, Your Majesty should act accordingly, and do what is wisest, and best upon that supposition, without expecting any turn in favour of your present servants, which will not happen. I hear that Lord Shelburne has told the Chancellor to-day that he will speak to no person but Your Majesty : as an honest man I think myself bound to advise Your Majesty to see him immediately, and to try what arrangement can be made.

Similar reports from Robinson were passed on to the King by Jenkinson. Writing to Jenkinson at 6.30 on Wednesday morning, Robinson commented on the widespread despondency

---

[1] Fortescue, v, 3566.   [2] *Ibid.* no. 3567.   [3] *Ibid.* no. 3568.

among government supporters and the damaging effect of Grosvenor's defection : 'Many gentlemen think that we should not fight the battle today ; that everything may be lost by it, and nothing can be gained, for that with small majorities if we even have them, altho' many think we shall not, but that we shall be beat, it is impossible to carry thro' the taxes and public business. Mr. Grosvenor on the part of some of the country gentlemen says so, others of them hold the same language, and indeed I am very sorry today that this language is held so openly by too many, that it must add to our weakness, and I fear create more rats.' His canvassing of members gave little encouragement. Five friends had 'gone out of town' ; and 'what more may desert us, God only yet knows'. Three friends whose attendance he hoped for represented little real accession of strength, for two of them had been pairing in previous divisions ; so far as he knew only three opponents had left Westminster (in only one of these cases was his information correct).[1]

Evidence from the opposition side shows that the forebodings of North and Robinson were only too well founded. A list published by Stockdale gives the names of 241 members who attended the House on 20 March to support the opposition motion for the removal of the ministers.[2] All but two of those who had voted with the minority on the 15th were again in the House and fourteen others who had not then voted were now present ; so that the opposition (allowing for two tellers) might, if there were no pairing in the interim, divide 239 against the government. Three of its recruits were men who on the 15th had stayed away or gone out of the House before the division — in one case certainly, and in the others probably, after urgent requests from the ministers.[3] Robinson's minutes of the early morning of the 20th provisionally indicated a reduction of two votes on the government side, so that, if there were

[1] *Ibid.* no. 3571 encl.
[2] *Monumentum Aere Perennius, that the public and the world may know to whom this country and its posterity will for ever stand indebted for their* DELIVERANCE FROM POLITICAL DEATH, *endangered by a system of* DESPOTISM, INFAMY *and* CORRUPTION, . . . Polhill MSS., Sevenoaks Public Library.
[3] R. A. Neville, Richard Myddleton, Noel Hill.

no pairing, the ministry might divide 243 : but there was no certainty about his figures ; only three or four defections were required to put the ministers in a minority ; in any case victory by three or four votes would be no better than an outright defeat.

It may be presumed that Robinson's reports, forwarded independently, may have helped North to prevail in the closet on the 20th. No account is known of the last stages of his argument with George III ; but by the time he left St. James's for the House of Commons, the King's protests had been overborne, his threats of abdication had been abandoned, and the ministry was authorized to resign.

At about half-past four that afternoon the last of the formal business was disposed of in a House crowded and tense with expectation. Lord Surrey stood up to propose the motion for the removal of the ministers, which stood in his name as the first order of the day. At the same time North rose to make the announcement which he hoped would bring about an adjournment of the House. The Speaker, turning a blind eye to the opposition side of the House, pointed to North ; but the opposition instantly set up a cry of 'Lord Surrey', until all in the Chamber were deafened by the uproar. After the clamour had ceased and one opposition member declared that North was out of order, especially as Surrey was already on his feet, the Speaker denied that Surrey was up before North, and declared that North had the floor. North began to speak ; but on his saying that he had it in his power to make a declaration which might convince the House he was justified in moving for an adjournment, his voice was drowned by renewed opposition shouts of 'Lord Surrey' and 'no adjournment'. Further clamour and confusion followed, till Fox restored order by putting before the House the motion, that the Earl of Surrey should speak first. Another hour or more was consumed in debate on this question, before Surrey at last agreed to withdraw his motion. North assured the House : 'those persons who had for some time conducted the public affairs, were no longer his Majesty's ministers. They were no longer to be considered as men holding the reins of government and transacting measures of state, but merely remaining to do their official duty, till other ministers were appointed to take their places.' Though the chief spokesmen of opposition showed little charity to North in the hour of their triumph, testimonies of personal regard came from more independent members of the House. John Courtenay, a ministerial supporter but a close friend of Fox, declared that, 'his amiable and engaging disposition had procured him many friends; his unrivalled wit had created him many admirers; his unassuming manners (although twelve years at the head of the Treasury) had prevented him having any enemies; his mild and forbearing temper . . . was seldom provoked': though his ministry had been unsuccessful, there could be none more devoted to the interests of the country than it had been.[1]

At about six o'clock the House adjourned for five days, to give time for the formation of a new administration. North had at least saved himself from the painful experience of having a vote for his removal recorded in the Journals. Nor at the last did his wit and good humour forsake him. As he went out of the House, members who had anticipated a long sitting and whose carriages had to be summoned from a distance, hung around the entrance, watching the snow drift down on the darkening courtyard. But North's coachman had been forewarned, and the fallen minister still had spirit to turn the situation to a jest. 'Goodnight, gentlemen,' he said as he turned to his coach; 'you see what it is to be in the secret.'[2]

[1] *The Morning Chronicle and London Advertiser*, 21 Mar. 1782; Debrett, vi, 491-510.   [2] Wraxall, ii, 247.

EPILOGUE

THE parliamentary events of February and March 1782 swept out of office the little group of ministers and their associates in whose hands the conduct of public affairs had rested throughout the greater part of the American crisis. North had entered the cabinet as Chancellor of the Exchequer in 1768, and, as First Lord of the Treasury, he had been since 1770 the minister chiefly in the King's confidence. Sandwich had been in charge of the Admiralty since January 1771. Bathurst, as Lord Chancellor and then as Lord President, had been a member of the cabinet since 1771; Dartmouth, as American Secretary, then as Lord Privy Seal, since 1772. Hillsborough, another member of this political connection, had only recently re-entered it, in 1779; but he had been a member as American Secretary between 1768 and 1772. Dartmouth excepted, these men had come to the fore during the fateful period of political fumbling and intrigue which followed the formation of Chatham's administration — disastrous years when the Rockinghams, who by compromise might have stemmed the drift towards war, had sacrificed any possible chance of exercising a moderating influence on American policy by their insistence on having all power or none at all. Of the other leading ministers, Stormont, a professional diplomat, recruited to the cabinet in 1779, had not previously had close political connections with the North-Sandwich group. But, having accepted place from North, he enrolled himself under his banner and was involved in his downfall. Germain, a former follower of Grenville, had stood apart from this group until he took the American department in 1775, and indeed he was never closely identified with it. But having been as clearly committed as any of the ministers to the policy of asserting imperial authority over America, his political career also came to an end in 1782. Discredited by failure and defeat, this group of ministers was swept into political limbo. The extent to which their reputations had been destroyed was not fully apparent for another two years. If their brief, triumphant return to office (but not to power) as members of the Coalition Government of 1783 encouraged a belief that their careers were not yet ended, disillusionment came swiftly when they were deprived of place again for good by the East India crisis at the end of that year. Stormont alone was to enjoy a further short period of office after 1794 as an associate of Portland in Pitt's war coalition. Of the members of North's cabinet in 1782 only Thurlow, the Lord Chancellor, stood sufficiently aloof from his colleagues not to be involved in their overthrow.

The political extinction of the ministers was the due desert for the incompetence with which they had schemed and acted during the American War. Till at least 1778 they never clearly defined their objectives, and, throughout, their decisions were based upon a complete and profound misunderstanding of the forces at work in America. Were the Americans to be conciliated or subdued ? On the whole they took the former view, believing that loyalist sentiment was far stronger than in fact it was. Consequently they frittered away forces in attempts to support loyalist risings, and failed to concentrate adequate armies against the main centres of disaffection. Swift and effective concentration might have enabled the rebellion to be crushed before foreign intervention made this impossible. But in 1778 the entry into the war of France, and still more that of Spain in 1779, tipped the balance of forces decisively against Great Britain. Had the Bourbon Powers used their naval and military strength in America in 1779 and in 1780, with a proper appreciation of strategic principles, instead of indulging in a grab for West Indian islands, Clinton's and Cornwallis's successful campaign in the southern colonies would have been impossible, and the high hopes which carried the government through the general election of 1780 and buoyed up its majority for a further year could never have been kindled. In a sense the North ministry owed the last two years of its existence to the faulty strategy of France.

Apart from the ministers' fatal errors of policy, they showed no capacity to turn the clumsy machinery of central government into an effective instrument for the waging of war. The main brunt of organizing the war in America fell upon the American Secretary. But co-ordinated action by other departments was essential. If whole-hearted agreement was reached in the cabinet, this might be forthcoming. But if not, independent action within departments created friction, and plans and preparations were thrown out of gear. A cabinet of equal and independent ministers, recognizing no superior over their departments except the King, could not provide a unified and energetic direction of the war. Nor was the necessary ministerial calibre available : not one of the members of the cabinet had the energy or abilities to take the lead, to command his colleagues, to drive the departments as part of one machine. The task required the daemonic energy of Chatham in his prime. But the ministers were a collection of second-rate men. Able as some of them were within their departments, none of them possessed a spark of Chatham's genius. Perhaps one, and one only, of the men in the House of Commons, Charles James Fox, might in office have displayed talents of that order ; but his impetuosity and instability of temperament had relegated him to fruitless opposition.

By 1782 the ministers had palpably failed, and the House of Commons asserted its right to oust a government which could no longer serve the interests of the country. The mere threat of a vote of censure was sufficient. The fall of North opened a new political scene. The crisis raised anew the conflict of principle within the system of 'mixed government', between the King's right to choose his ministers and parliament's right to veto his choice. The main theme of domestic politics for the next two years was to be the search once again for a stable administration which would command the confidence both of the House of Commons and of the King.

THE POLITICAL AFFILIATIONS OF MEMBERS OF PARLIAMENT

THE following sources of information concerning the political conduct of members deserve particular mention.

First, there are the manuscript collections of various leading politicians. The papers of Portland, Rockingham, and to some extent also of Burke, provide a good deal of information about the personnel of the Rockingham party and about the individuals who, without being in a real sense party men, were to some extent connected with it. The papers of the fourth Earl of Sandwich and his letters to John Robinson in the Abergavenny MSS. give a fairly complete picture of the nature, and the eventual collapse, of his political connection. Further scattered information about other members is to be found here and there in Robinson's papers and in those of his friend and confidant, Charles Jenkinson.

Next, there are the parliamentary division lists. These hardly ever contain any annotations about members' political connections, but they provide much information about the consistency or otherwise of their voting habits. Even division lists falling outside the span of this parliament are of service, since only about a hundred and fifty new members entered the House at each of the general elections of 1780 and 1784. Voting during the last years of North's ministry can be followed at fairly short intervals through the list of the minority of 4 December 1778, the division list of 3 March 1779, a consolidated list of the five divisions of 21 February, 8 and 13 March, and 6 and 24 April 1780, the division of 12 December 1781, and the four divisions of 20 and 27 February and 8 and 15 March 1782. Later, voting substantially on party lines is again on record in the list of the division of 18 February 1783, on the peace preliminaries, of 27 November 1783, on the East India Bill, of the minority on Pitt's Irish propositions on 13 May 1785, of the division on Richmond's fortification proposals on 27 February

373

1786 and on the various resolutions concerning the Regency in the winter of 1788-9.[1]

Thirdly, there are various parliamentary lists and states drawn up by politicians who were trying to gauge the reactions of members of the House during the confused period 1782-4, and again when a group of independents planned to hold the balance between Pitt and Fox in the spring of 1788. The first attempt to chart the parliamentary confusion which followed the collapse of North's ministry was made by John Robinson on behalf of Shelburne.[2] A completed list, drawn up probably after his initial draft had been subjected to considerable re-scrutiny, was preserved by Shelburne in a notebook, in which the members were listed alphabetically under the four headings, 'pro', 'hopeful', 'doubtful', 'con'.[3] The last section only of this parliamentary list is helpful towards an understanding of party groupings, as it names forty members who were known to be the core of the irreconcilable opposition clustered round Charles Fox and the friends of the late Lord Rockingham. Then two lists of some value exist for the early months of 1783. The division list of 18 February 1783, printed in the *Morning Post* of 27 February, was annotated by someone reasonably well-informed about North's political following, who identified eighty-eight members as '*old* friends of the *good* Lord North and his *new ally*'. Seventy-two of these are identifiable as supporters of North at this period, the other sixteen being known connections of Fox and his friends. A week or two later in date is the state of the parliament drawn up by Robinson after the defeat of Shelburne in aid of the attempt to construct a new ministry which would exclude Charles Fox.[4] This list distinguishes four large blocks of members, who were classed respectively as 'connections of Lord Shelburne's Government' (101), 'Mr Fox's connections' (89), 'Lord North's connections' (50), and 'Lord North's friends doubtful' (56): but not all the men here listed were party followers — all the groups included some members more correctly to be described as 'independents', and those attached to Shelburne and to North also included members of the court and administration group, only a few members of which were placed in a separate category in this document. More reliable are the

[1] Almon, *The Parliamentary Register*, xi, 119-21, xii, 52-6 ; Add. MSS. 27837, between ff. 7 and 8 ; Debrett, *The Parliamentary Register*, v, 149-58 ; pp. 390-405 below ; *Morning Post*, 27 Feb. 1783 ; Debrett, xiii, 308-15, xviii, 310-14, xix, 228-30, xxv, 90-5, 289-96, 465-71.
[2] Laprade, 42-8.   [3] Lansdowne MSS.
[4] National Library of Scotland MS. 63A (Melville MSS.).

identification of the members of eleven of the minor factions in parliament and the connection of one or two members with Dundas. The list of 104 country gentlemen and independents which it contains is also helpful, though not exhaustive. Nine months later Robinson prepared a further analysis of the House as a preliminary to the second, and this time successful, attempt to establish a government headed by William Pitt; and the draft which survives in his papers is of value chiefly for the information which it gives about the connections and attitudes of many individual members.[1] Finally, the North papers include part of an analysis of the House as at 1 May 1788. This provides lists of 108 out of the 139 members identified as usually acting with Charles Fox and of seventeen members described as 'Lord North's party'.[2] None of these lists is in itself a conclusive guide to party groupings. But, taken together and used in conjunction with the other sources of information mentioned above, they provide a firm basis for an analysis of the political structure of the House of Commons.

[1] Laprade, 65-105.   [2] Guilford MSS., Kent R.O.

THE DIVISION LISTS OF FEBRUARY
AND MARCH 1782

RECORDS of the five critical divisions of 20, 22, and 27 February, and 8 and 15 March, were kept by parliamentary organizers on both the government and opposition sides of the House. On the government side this work devolved upon John Robinson. As ministerial 'muster-master' under North, he busied himself constantly with the maintenance of records designed to enable a ready and — as he hoped — fairly accurate forecast of the government's majority to be produced immediately upon demand. The records worked progressively, each successive division list providing the basis of the next forecast. Unfortunately those for the earlier part of the session are missing. On the resumption of the session in January, Robinson prepared a list based upon the attendance at the call of the House, but only the abstract which he made from it survives.[1] It must be supposed that he drew up another on the division of 7 February, but no such list now remains among his papers. However, his lists survive for the five last important divisions of February and March.[2] The similar activities on the opposition side remain much more obscure. No manuscript lists have been found, and our knowledge of the records kept is confined to such published lists as were printed from them. Evidence about the publication of these lists has not been found. But it would appear that some parliamentary organizer — perhaps George Byng, who acted as chief opposition 'whip' — kept records similar to those of Robinson and supplied lists to the printers.[3] Publication was part of the political battle against the ministry: the

---

[1] 'Lists and Calculations on the Call, 21st Jany. 1782', and another copy of the same figures headed simply '24th' — the 24th was the day on which Fox moved for the naval enquiry, and Robinson was ready for a division in case Fox's motions were of such a kind that the government could not accept them. Abergavenny MSS. (B.M. facsimiles 340(4), f. 165).

[2] Abergavenny MSS. (B.M. facsimiles 340(4), ff. 98-104, 141-7, 82-97, 340(5), ff. 48-66 and 29-36).

[3] Philip Yorke wrote to Hardwicke about the division of 18 Feb. 1783 on the peace preliminaries: 'I doubt if the triumphant party will print

disclosure of members' votes was intended to cause pressure to be brought by constituents upon independent members to vote against the government.[1] Both Debrett and Stockdale published division lists in broadsheet form, as well as in the political literature which they produced, and they provide lists for three of these five divisions. For that of 20 February, there exists Stockdale's list given as an appendix to an analytical account of the charges pressed by Fox against Sandwich.[2] For that of 27 February there are two lists from opposition sources. One is a broadsheet printed by Stockdale.[3] The other was incorporated by Debrett in *The Parliamentary Register*.[4] Debrett also printed lists of the division of 15 March, first in the form of a broadsheet,[5] and then in *The Parliamentary Register*.[6]

What degree of reliance is to be placed on these various lists? The compilers were partisans. Moreover, each was likely to know more about the voting of men on his side of the House. In the one case where two different printed lists are known to exist — for the division of 27 February — the versions of Debrett and Stockdale agree exactly for the votes cast in opposition, but there are discrepancies between their lists of government supporters involving nineteen names. This suggests that the list handed out to them was incomplete for the government side and that both printers — independently — tried to complete it from other channels of information. Debrett's lists are more reliable for the government side than Stockdale's. This is apparent both in the avoidance of occasional absurdities — the inclusion, for instance, of a regular party man on the wrong side — and in the much greater degree of

a list of the division' (Add. MSS. 35381, f. 34). Lord Surrey furnished the Yorkshire Committee of Association with a list he had compiled of the members who voted on 7 May 1783 for Pitt's motion for parliamentary reform, and wrote to Wyvill : 'I fear there are one or two names inserted who ought not to be there ; this circumstance you will attend to, in case it is proper to be published' (C. Wyvill, *Political Papers*, ii, 255-7, iv, 295-6).

[1] 'Every artifice of party was used by the Opposition to encourage their friends, and to terrify or hold out to popular odium the adherents of administration. Lists were published and disseminated throughout the kingdom, containing the names of the members who voted on each question' (Wraxall, ii, 237).

[2] 'Substance of the Charge of Mismanagement in His Majesty's Naval Affairs in the year 1781 compared with authentic papers laid before the House on Mr. Fox's motion in the month of February 1782. To which is added a complete list of the division.' A copy of this pamphlet is preserved in a bound volume of tracts in the Wilkes papers, part of which was used to mount newspaper cuttings (Add. MSS. 30895, ff. 112-39).

[3] B.M. ref. 1881. c. 7. [4] VI, 330-41.
[5] B.M. ref. 746. f. 12(8). [6] VI, 475-86.

correspondence with Robinson's lists. I conclude that, where there are discrepancies and no outside evidence to dispel them, as a rough rule Robinson should be followed in dealing with the government side in a division, Debrett and Stockdale, with a preference for Debrett, when dealing with the opposition side. A further circumstance to be taken into account is that not all the lists preserved in Robinson's papers represent the same degree of completeness. Those for 22 and 27 February are annotated 'Minute (or State) of division', but that for the 20th is described only as a 'rough state', and for 15 March there is only an initial nominal roll of the House on which members were ticked as voting for or against the government.

Robinson was accustomed to analyse the House in terms of eight categories. Two of these were the 'pros. present' and the 'cons. present', and the lists of names under these headings represented his lists of a division. The absentees he listed under six heads : 'pros. absent', 'pros. abroad', 'hopefuls absent', 'doubtfuls absent', 'cons. absent', 'cons. abroad'. In the absence of other evidence, the position of a member's name among the columns of absentees may sometimes be considered to give some indication of his behaviour in a previous division : for instance, a man described as 'doubtful' or 'hopeful' had probably been absent from previous divisions, otherwise Robinson would have been able to class him as 'pro' or 'con'.

The following pages explain my attempt to correct or reconstruct the disputed parts of the five division lists of February and March 1782. Often independent direct evidence about a member's conduct is lacking, and I have, therefore, resorted to circumstantial evidence in the attempt to secure completeness. In particular I have regarded as circumstantial evidence the normal voting habits of a member ; and where one list, in conflict with another, records a vote in flagrant contradiction to voting habit, I have assumed that its compiler was in error.

(i)

THE DIVISION OF 20 FEBRUARY 1782

The official figures for the division of 20 February 1782 are — government 236, opposition 217. Robinson's and Stockdale's lists agree upon 217 of the names in the majority and upon 210 of those in the minority. There remain 19 'pros.' and 7 'cons.' to be identified from among the 46 members about whose voting the two lists are in disagreement.

APPENDIX II

Four of the 46 can be very easily eliminated. Sir James Tylney Long, William Pulteney, Charles Ross, and John Shaw Stewart are listed by Robinson as voting against, and by Stockdale as voting with, the government. As both the friends of government and of opposition attribute the votes of these four to the other side, most probably they were absent from the division.

Next, there are eight members who are described as absent in Robinson's list but as voting with the opposition in the other:

John Pennington	Sir P. J. Clerke	Benj. Lethieullier
Pinckney Wilkinson	George Forester	Robert Ladbroke
John Vaughan	R. P. Knight	

The absence of two of these men, Pennington and Lethieullier, is suggested by entries in Robinson's next list for the division of the 22nd. Both men are there set down as 'doubtful, absent'. Against Pennington's name in the list for the 20th is the note 'went away', and in a later list, for the 27th, he is described — although voting against government — as 'rather friendly'. Lethieullier voted later for motions to end the American war, but otherwise he was friendly towards the ministry, voting with them on 8 and 15 March. All this evidence is circumstantial, but it is supported by the fact that all the other six members in this category were strong partisans of the opposition; by their inclusion all but one of the minority are accounted for.

Thirteen men noted as absent by Robinson are stated in Stockdale's list to have voted with the ministry:

Nath. Wraxall	John Pringle	Lord George Sutton
John Campbell	John Courtenay	John Nesbitt
Sir John Henderson	Robert Child	William Graves
Sir John Eden	Lord Charles Spencer	
Sir Charles Frederick	William Woodley	

Only in one instance does Robinson's list appear to be in error. According to Wraxall's own statement, he was present and voted in the division.[1] Of the other men in this group, the absence of one or two is a certainty. Stockdale's inclusion of Woodley is an absurdity. Woodley's sympathies were with the opposition: he would certainly not have voted with the government on this occasion, and Lord Sandwich had tried, and failed, to get some assurance from him.[2] In fact, wishing always to vote against the ministry,

[1] *Historical and Posthumous Memoirs*, ii (1884), 183.
[2] Sandwich to Robinson, 16 Feb. 1782, Abergavenny MS. 431.

379

he never voted at all, because he owed his seat to a ministerial supporter.[1] The inclusion of Lord George Sutton is another of Stockdale's absurdities, for he was a member of the Rutland faction in opposition. Circumstantial evidence supports Robinson's list in other cases. Sir John Eden had obtained leave of absence from the House,[2] and he was in fact absent throughout the whole duration of the parliamentary crisis. Courtenay is described in Robinson's list as ill, and against Spencer and Child appears the note 'went away': Child's absence was in character, and it seems to be confirmed by Robinson's inclusion of him as a 'hopeful absent', not as a 'pro.' in his next list (for the 22nd). In the lack of other evidence about the remaining men in this group, I follow Robinson and class them as absent from the division.

On the other hand, I count as voting with government 15 members omitted as absent by Stockdale but included in Robinson's list:

John Craufurd	A. R. Bowes	Martin Fonnereau
Earl Nugent	J. P. Hungerford	Lord Galway
Giles Hudson	Andrew Bayntun	Henry Pelham
Sir Walter Rawlinson	Hew Dalrymple	Robert Waller
Lord Lincoln	James Murray	John Yorke

Direct evidence of Craufurd's appearance in this division is recorded among the pleasantries of Lord Carlisle's friends who were observing his vacillations with sardonic disapproval. Selwyn wrote to Carlisle the day before the division:[3]

> I hope that Government will send two Yeomen of the Guard to carry the Fish down in his blankets, for he pretends to have the gout. He should be deposited *sur son maniveau*, and be fairly asked his opinion, and forced to give it one way or the other, *en pleine assemblée*, for at present it is only we who can tell *s'il est clair ou poisson*.

'Though he assured Lord Ossory in the morning that he would not vote at all', Anthony Storer informed Carlisle a few days later, 'he came down, pretending to be sick, and divided with Government. His own party, for so I call the Opposition, despise his conduct as much as we do.'[4] Robinson's inclusion of Nugent is supported by the fact that Nugent spoke for the government during the debate, rising to oppose Fox's motion.[5] Rawlinson was a

---

[1] See pp. 64-5 above.   [2] *Commons Journals*, xxxviii, 683.
[3] H.M.C., *Carlisle MSS.*, 580.
[4] Storer to Carlisle, 24 Feb. 1782, *ibid.* 582.   [5] Debrett, vi, 248.

particular friend of Lord Sandwich and certainly would not have been absent on a question which concerned Sandwich personally. The inclusion of Lord Lincoln, Bowes, and Hungerford is upheld by the fact that Sandwich had received reassurances of their support,[1] and Andrew Bayntun belonged to the Gower group, from which support was also expected by Sandwich.[2] Hew Dalrymple and James Murray were connected with the Lord Advocate, who had agreed to support the government in their defence of the Admiralty. The remaining six members were regular supporters of the government, and on them Robinson is to be followed in preference to Stockdale.

Lastly there are five members described by Robinson as voting 'pro' and by Stockdale as voting 'con':

J. H. Blair	Sir S. B. Fludyer
Baron Dimsdale	S. Smith
John Darker	

J. H. Blair is counted as voting for the government on this question, for in his list of 'cons present' for the 27th, Robinson made an annotation against his name, indicating that he was generally friendly, though *contra* on the American question. Dimsdale I set down as voting with the opposition. His voting habits make it unlikely that he supported the government, and as the minority is incomplete without him, Stockdale's entry is probably in this case correct. Darker, I conclude, was absent — this was likely in the light of his voting habits, and especially from the fact that observers rarely seemed to be sure how he was voting; it is also suggested by his initial appearance in Robinson's list of 22 February as 'doubtful absent'. Fludyer and Smith I consider voted 'pro'. Fludyer had various connections with the government,[3] and Sandwich had just received reassurances of his support.[4] Smith was a regular supporter of the ministry, and in his case I place trust in Robinson's list rather than in Stockdale's.

As a result of these various readjustments, the minority of 20 February 1782 is to be made up by the addition of Pinckney Wilkinson, John Vaughan, Clerke, Forester, Knight, Ladbroke

[1] Sandwich to George III, 20 (should be 19) Feb. 1782, Fortescue, v, no. 3521, and accompanying list, Fortescue, iv, no. 2580.
[2] Sandwich to Robinson, 16 Feb. 1782, Abergavenny MS. 430.
[3] Through his mother he was related to the Brudenells, and he occupied a borough seat controlled by the Duke of Newcastle.
[4] Sandwich to George III, 19 Feb. 1782, Fortescue, v, no. 3521, and accompanying list, Fortescue, iv, no. 2580.

and Dimsdale to the 210 names agreed between the two lists, and the following 19 members complete the majority:

Nath. Wraxall	J. P. Hungerford	Robert Waller
John Craufurd	Andrew Bayntun	John Yorke
Earl Nugent	Hew Dalrymple	J. H. Blair
Giles Hudson	James Murray	Sir S. B. Fludyer
Sir W. Rawlinson	Martin Fonnereau	Samuel Smith
Lord Lincoln	Lord Galway	
A. R. Bowes	Henry Pelham	

(ii)

THE DIVISION OF 22 FEBRUARY 1782

The figures for the division of 22 February 1782 were: government 194, opposition 193. No list is available from the opposition side, and all that is possible is to make certain corrections in the list compiled by Robinson, which contains 216 names of government supporters and 211 names of members of opposition shown as present at the division.

Although Robinson's list of the majority is thus too large, two more members must be added to it. By an oversight Robinson omitted Henry Dundas, who was present and spoke during the debate: he must have voted, for his absence at that time would not have been compatible with the political part he was then acting — and it would have been a subject of lively comment by observers. Also, according to Robinson's list of the division of 27 February, Lord Fife voted with the government on the 22nd, although he is omitted from the list. These additions raise the number of 'pros present' to 218, 22 in excess of the division.

Fortunately it is possible to eliminate 22 names from this list. In the first place, crosses appear against 18 names. Robinson's papers referring to the later division of 8 March show that he used this notation to indicate members who were absent from a past division but whom he hoped to get up for the next. It seems reasonable to assume that this notation bore the same meaning on this occasion also (with reference to the impending division of 27 February), though, in one case, Robinson was undoubtedly mistaken; the name of John Purling is so marked, but in fact he voted for the government in this division.[1] With Purling counted as present, the deduction of the other 17 names marked with a cross

[1] J. Purling to Sandwich, 13 Mar. 1782, Abergavenny MS. 448c.

reduces the number of 'pros present' to 201. Further evidence permits the elimination of another five — George Pitt, John Craufurd, Lord Trentham, Sir James Marriott, and Abel Moysey. Pitt's name was added to Robinson's list of the 'pros absent', but was left standing in error in the list of 'pros present'. John Craufurd's absence was noted by Anthony Storer, and that of Lord Trentham reported to Carlisle by Selwyn.[1] The presence of Sir James Marriott was queried by Robinson, and subsequent investigation by Lord Sandwich established his absence from the division.[2] Abel Moysey was noted next day by Loughborough, in a letter to William Eden, as having voted against the government.[3] These deductions reduce Robinson's list of the majority to 196, and as this figure includes the two tellers, it corresponds with that given in the *Commons Journals*; but as the list is unconfirmed from other sources except in one or two instances, it probably contains some errors and must be treated with caution.

It is not possible, however, to apply a similar process of elimination to the 211 members noted in Robinson's list as 'con present'. Eleven names in this list are marked with a cross, but here this sign probably indicates only that Robinson sent out to them urgent requests for support at the next division, and annotated them as possible supporters when it took place:[4] it does not controvert, rather it makes more probable, the conclusion that they probably voted against the ministry on the 22nd — one, Sir Gilbert Elliot, certainly did so;[5] another, John Peachey, would appear to have done so, for in the next list, after the division on the 27th, Robinson noted against his name, 'generally with, but has been against us in the American question lately'; a third, Sir John Wrottesley, may have done so, though the evidence about him from George Selwyn is conflicting — Selwyn at first reported him as voting but later stated that he was thought to have abstained.[6] In default of any evidence indicating the absence of any of these 211 men, I have given their names as they appear in Robinson's list, but it must be remembered that 16 of them were not present at the division.

[1] A. Storer to Carlisle, 24 Feb. 1782, G. Selwyn to Carlisle, 25 Feb. 1782, H.M.C., *Carlisle MSS.*, 582, 584.
[2] Sandwich to Robinson, 25 Feb. 1782, Abergavenny MSS. 436, 437.
[3] Add. MS. 34418, f. 331.
[4] Two or three of the eleven normally supported Administration, and none of the others were confirmed opponents of the North Ministry.
[5] The Countess of Minto: *Life and Letters of Sir Gilbert Elliot*, 3 vols. (1874), i, 75; Loughborough to W. Eden, 23 Feb. 1782, Add. MS. 34418, f. 331.
[6] G. Selwyn to Carlisle, 25 Feb. 1782, H.M.C., *Carlisle MSS.*, 584.

(iii)

THE DIVISION OF 27 FEBRUARY 1782

The official figures for the division of 27 February 1782 were: government 215, opposition 234. For a list of the division three sources are available — one from the government side, Robinson's parliamentary state, and two from that of the opposition, Stockdale's broadsheet and the list printed by Debrett in *The Parliamentary Register*.

Although Debrett's and Stockdale's lists were undoubtedly completed independently,[1] they both tally exactly in their enumeration of the majority, and give 234 names, the correct number for the division. These names must be presumed to have come from an informed opposition source.[2] I therefore regard their agreed list as correct. Accordingly, Robinson was in error in recording Peregrine Bertie, J. C. Jervoise and Philip Yorke as absent, and John Darker, Thomas Farrer, Lloyd Kenyon and John Wilmot as members of the opposition majority; his being mistaken is confirmed in two instances: Philip Yorke's correspondence makes it clear that he voted against the government,[3] and Lloyd Kenyon's diary records that he did not vote.[4]

All three lists contain errors in their accounts of the minority. They are in agreement upon 193 names only; but there are another 16 instances in which Robinson's and Debrett's lists are in agreement though differing from Stockdale's, and this brings the established roll of the minority up to 209, leaving six names only to be identified in order to complete it. These six are readily revealed by a comparison of the lists; there are 14 members about whom Robinson's and Debrett's lists are in disagreement, with Stockdale's list supporting sometimes one, sometimes the (other see p. 385). Seven men — Burton, Dundas, Howard, Owen, Crespigny, Edmonstone, Darker — appear in two lists as having voted in the division. The inclusion of the first three is not contradicted by Robinson: by an oversight he omitted their names altogether when compiling his list. Sir George Howard was a faithful courtier.[5] The presence

---

[1] This is clear from the discrepancies between the lists of members voting with the government in these two sources.

[2] Pp. 376-7 above.

[3] P. Yorke to Hardwicke, 1 Mar. 1782, Hardwicke to P. Yorke, 2 Mar. 1782, Add. MS. 35380, ff. 194, 190.

[4] Kenyon MSS. I am indebted for this information to Mr. C. Shone.

[5] Wraxall, ii, 406.

of Dundas at the debate is established by Debrett's report of his speech;[1] moreover, his absence from the division would have been entirely incompatible with the political line he was following at this period. Burton had recently voted against the government, but his

	Conduct in the division according to:		
	Robinson	Debrett	Stockdale
Francis Burton	omitted	pro	pro
Henry Dundas	omitted	pro	pro
Sir George Howard	omitted	pro	pro
Sir John Coghill	pro	omitted	absent
John Halliday	pro	omitted	absent
Lord Melbourne	pro	omitted	absent
Hugh Owen	pro	omitted	pro
John Purling	pro: query	omitted	absent
John Strutt	pro	paired	absent
P. C. Crespigny	pro	omitted	pro
Sir A. Edmonstone	pro	omitted	pro
John Frederick	absent 'went away'	pro	absent
P. C. Methuen	absent	pro	absent
John Darker	con: query	pro	pro

classification of 'pro absent' in Robinson's next list for 8 March suggests he supported the ministry on the 27th. The presence of Owen, Crespigny, and Edmonstone is attested by evidence from observers of both sides. Darker, however, is in a different category. Each side put him down as adhering to the other, and the obvious conclusion is that he was not present at the division. This conclusion is in line with his known performance in other divisions and also with the frequent confusion about him which is apparent in Robinson's lists.

As regards the remaining seven members listed above: the absence of John Frederick and of Methuen is attested by evidence from observers on both sides; that of Methuen tallies with his behaviour on other occasions, and with the regular description of him in Robinson's lists as 'doubtful absent'. Purling's absence is confirmed by a report of his conduct which he made to his patron, Sandwich; the division of 22 February was the last he attended, and from then on he was too ill with gout to come to the House.[2] Strutt is stated by Debrett to have paired off with John Bullock, a statement for which, it must be presumed, Debrett had some

[1] *The Parliamentary Register*, vi, 327.
[2] J. Purling to Sandwich, 13 Mar. 1782, Abergavenny MS. 448c.

evidence; it is a partial confirmation, that Robinson noted Bullock as paired, though apparently not knowing with whom he had arranged to be absent. Both opposition sources concur in placing Coghill, Halliday, and Melbourne as absent from the division: there is, moreover, no room for them in the list of the minority. I conclude, therefore, that Robinson erred in omitting to delete them from his list of 'pros present'.

The names to be added to complete the list of members voting with the government are, therefore, Burton, Dundas, Sir George Howard, H. Owen, P. C. Crespigny, and Sir Archibald Edmonstone.

(iv)

THE DIVISION OF 8 MARCH 1782

In the division of 8 March 1782, 226 members voted with the government, 216 with the opposition. For this division, as for that of 22 February, I have not found any list from an opposition source, and the only one available is the parliamentary state prepared by Robinson. Excluding tellers, this lists 228 members in the majority and in the minority 217. The adjustment of these lists of names to correspond with the figures for the division is not difficult; but the results stand uncorroborated, and it would be rash to consider them as unquestionably correct — the degree of error seems to be suspiciously small.

In Robinson's state Thomas Farrer appears among the 'cons present'; but this was an error, for in an analysis which Robinson made after the next division, that of 15 March, he classed Farrer with Baron Dimsdale and Sir Gilbert Elliot as one who in the last division had voted with the government but had now turned against them.[1] The deletion of Farrer brings Robinson's list of the minority to the correct total of 216.

The consequent addition of Farrer to Robinson's list of the majority increases it to 229, three in excess of the figure for the division. However, two names in this list — William Graves and John Nesbitt — are queried, indicating that Robinson was doubtful whether they had actually voted. A further piece of circumstantial evidence for the absence of Nesbitt is that a week later, on

[1] One copy of this document is reproduced, with several minor errors of transcription, in Fortescue (v, 390), and another, also with minor inaccuracies, in Laprade (40-41). There is yet another copy in the Sandwich MSS., in the body of the letter to Sandwich from Robinson, not dated but written on 16 Mar. 1782.

substantially the same question, he voted against the government. There is also evidence suggesting that, by an oversight, Robinson failed to strike out of the list the name of John Darker: a few days later he made use of his state of 8 March to compile lists of absentees on both sides who might be brought up for the division of the 15th, and on this occasion, he placed Darker's name under the heading of 'doubtful absent'.[1] This classification is in accordance with what is known about Darker's conduct: moreover, there is some circumstantial support for it in the fact that less than a week later Darker sent word to Sandwich that he was 'very ill and confined to his bed'.[2] The deletion of Darker, Graves and Nesbitt from the list of the majority reduces it to the correct total of 226.

(v)

THE DIVISION OF 15 MARCH 1782

236 members voted with the ministry in the division of 15 March 1782, and 227 with the opposition. For this division two sources are available, one from either side. One list is provided by Debrett — copies of it exist both as a broadsheet and in the pages of *The Parliamentary Register*. A second version exists among Robinson's papers: but it is the least trustworthy of his records of this series of divisions. Whereas his other lists are, as explained above, analyses of the House, the preparation of which involved some checking and correction, this document is simply an alphabetical roll of the House, upon which names are ticked, the column in which the tick appears indicating whether the member voted for or against the government. It would seem to represent the first stage in the evolution of Robinson's parliamentary states. There are no explanatory notes or headings; indeed, the list is only identified as appertaining to the division of 15 March by the fact that the name of P. C. Wyndham, who took his seat on that day, is added to it in pencil.[3] One or two other pencil corrections appear upon it, but errors remain. Four out of the 18 cases in

[1] Abergavenny MSS., B.M. facsimiles 340 (5), f. 47, 'Pros sent to and expected', etc. Darker's is the only name out of 52 in this list, grouped under various headings, which does not appear in one of the columns of absentees in the State of 8 Mar.: his and that of Trentham are the only two in it not marked in that State with a pencilled cross, star, or query.

[2] Sandwich to Robinson, 13 Mar. 1782, Abergavenny MS. 449.

[3] Wyndham was returned on 11 Mar. at a by-election for Chichester on the interest of the Duke of Richmond. He took his seat in the House on the 15th on purpose to vote against the Government (Fortescue, v, 390).

which this list differs from Debrett's can be submitted to the test of outside evidence, and in all four it proves to be incorrect. Accordingly my reconstruction of the division list follows Debrett in all but one or two cases.

Robinson's and Debrett's lists are in agreement upon 233 out of 236 members in the majority and upon 219 out of 227 in the minority. Accepting Debrett's account of the pairing of six more members — three on each side — who are recorded as present by Robinson, there remain 18 men about whose voting the two lists are in disagreement. One of these can be immediately set aside. Philip Rashleigh is allotted to the other party by the observers on each side, Robinson showing him as voting against, Debrett as voting with the government, and I conclude that he was absent from the division.

Robinson's list allots to the majority six out of the remaining 17 men whose votes are disputed — Samuel Whitbread, John Clevland, Henry Rawlinson, Lord Melbourne, Philip Yorke, and Sir John Borlase Warren. The attendance of a seventh, Lord Galway, is confusingly both confirmed by a tick and queried by the annotation 'went away'. Debrett's list assigns Galway to the majority, and also John Buller, who is not ticked in Robinson's list, and it shows Whitbread as voting against the government.

In three of these instances the unreliability of Robinson's list is demonstrated by other evidence. Three of the men set down as present were definitely absent from the division. Warren wrote the next day to make excuses to Sandwich for his absence, provoking from his patron a stiff letter of dismissal and the tart comment to Robinson: 'I believe you will join with me in opinion that the writer of the enclosed is not only a rat but an idiot.' [1] Melbourne, to the disgust of George Selwyn who had brought him into parliament as a court follower, allowed himself to be persuaded by the Prince of Wales not to vote.[2] Yorke was *hors de combat* with an injured ankle, and informed his uncle, Lord Hardwicke, two days before the division, that he would certainly not be able to go to the House; and he seems to have been still incapacitated on the 20th.[3] I am led to conclude by these errors in Robinson's list that

[1] Warren to Sandwich, 16 Mar. 1782, Sandwich to Warren, 19 Mar. 1782, Sandwich MSS.; Sandwich to Robinson, 18 Mar. 1782, Abergavenny MS. 456.
[2] G. Selwyn to Carlisle, 18 Mar. 1782, H.M.C., *Carlisle MSS.*, 597; *The Last Journals of Horace Walpole*, edited by A. F. Steuart, ii, 420.
[3] P. Yorke to Hardwicke, 13 Mar. 1782, Hardwicke to P. Yorke, 20 Mar. 1782, Add. MS. 35380, ff. 210, 219.

no special credence can be given to the other entries in it concerning Galway, Whitbread, Clevland, Henry Rawlinson, and
Buller. On Galway there is 'semi-agreement', since Debrett supports one of the two conflicting entries on Robinson's list: he can
therefore be reasonably counted among the majority. Whitbread
is placed by Debrett in the minority, and I accept this, following
the principle that Debrett is a good authority for the opposition
side in divisions. Two more members are required to complete
the majority. Of the remaining three who are here considered,
the two most likely to have voted were Buller and Clevland: both
belonged to the government circle, the first having some connection
with North and the second with Sandwich. Rawlinson, as an independent, is the likeliest of the three to have been absent. But as
between these three selection is a matter of conjecture, and I have
noted this in the corrected division list.

The inclusion of Whitbread in the minority leaves seven other
members of it to be identified. Here I follow Debrett as the better
source and include John Hanbury, Lord George Sutton, Admiral
Keppel, Pinckney Wilkinson, John Nesbitt, Isaac Barré, and Sir
William Lemon, all of whom are omitted by Robinson: and I
conclude that Robinson was in error in noting as present John
Bullock and the younger Drake. In one of these cases further
evidence supports Debrett's list: Nesbitt's vote is confirmed by
Robinson himself in the analysis which he drew up on the morning
after the division.[1]

The complete corrected division lists are given below. It
would be rash to claim that they are entirely accurate, but at least
they come closer to accuracy than any of the lists from which they
are derived.

THE DIVISION LISTS

A. 20 Feb. 1782. Fox's motion of censure against Sandwich.
B. 22 Feb. 1782. Conway's first motion for abandoning the attempt
  to reduce the colonies by force.[2]
C. 27 Feb. 1782. Conway's second motion, of similar effect, which
  was carried.
D. 8 Mar. 1782. Cavendish's motion preparatory to a request to the
  King to remove the ministers.
E. 15 Mar. 1782. Rous's motion of no confidence in the ministers.

[1] Fortescue, v, 390.
[2] Robinson's list of opponents present at this division, which stands
uncorrected by any other list, is sixteen in excess of the number who actually
voted.

Notes:

The letters P (*pro*) and C (*con*) are used to indicate votes cast for or against the government.

Votes which are not agreed in Robinson's and Stockdale's lists for 20 February, nor in Robinson's and Debrett's lists for 27 February and 15 March, are indicated by italics. Where examination of a conflict between lists leads to the conclusion that a member was absent, this is indicated by the entry '*ab*'.

A star indicates that the member paired.

A member acting as a teller is indicated by the entry '*tel*'.

Notes that members were ill, abroad, or at sea, are based on the information in Robinson's lists.

		A	B	C	D	E
		20 Feb. 1782	22 Feb. 1782	27 Feb. 1782	8 Mar. 1782	15 Mar. 1782
	Bedfordshire					
County	Lord Upper Ossory	C	C	C	C	C
	St. A. St. John	C	C	C	C	C
Bedford	Sir William Wake, Bt.			C	*	C
	Samuel Whitbread	C	P	P	P	*C*
	Berkshire					
County	John Elwes	C	C	C	C	C
	W. H. Hartley	C	C	C	C	
Abingdon	John Mayor	P	P	P	P	P
Reading	Francis Annesley		C	C	C	C
	R. A. Neville, *el*. 21 *Feb.*	*vac.*		C		
Wallingford	John Aubrey	C	C	C	C	C
	Chal. Arcedeckne	C	C	C	C	C
Windsor	John Montagu			C	C	
	P. P. Powney	P	P	P	P	P
	Buckinghamshire					
County	Earl Verney	C	C	C	C	C
	Thomas Grenville	C	C	C	C	C
Amersham	William Drake, senior	C	C	C	C	C
	William Drake, junior	C	C	C	C	*a b.*
Aylesbury	Anthony Bacon	P	P	P	P	P
	Thomas Orde	P	P	P	P	P
Buckingham	James Grenville	C	C	C	C	C
	Wm. Grenville, *el.* 19 *Feb.*	C	C	C	C	C
Chipping Wycombe	Lord Mahon	C	C	C	C	
	Robert Waller	*P*	P	P	P	P
Gt. Marlow	William Clayton	P			P	P
	Sir J. B. Warren	P	P	P	P	*a b.*
Wendover	Richard Smith	C	C	C	C	C
	John M. Smith	C	C	C	C	C

APPENDIX II

Constituency	Member	A	B	C	D	E
		20 Feb. 1782	22 Feb. 1782	27 Feb. 1782	8 Mar. 1782	15 Mar. 1782
	Cambridgeshire					
County	Ld. Robert Manners, *at sea*					
University	Philip Yorke [1]		C	C	P	a b.
	John Townshend		C	C	C	C
	James Mansfield	P		P	P	P
Cambridge	Benjamin Keene		C	C	C	C
	Jas. Whorwood Adeane		C	C	C	C
	Cheshire					
County	Sir R. S. Cotton			C	C	C
	John Crewe			C	C	C
Chester	Thomas Grosvenor	C	P	P	P	*
	R. W. Bootle	C		C	C	*
	Cornwall					
County	Sir William Lemon, Bt.		C	C	C	C
	Edward Eliot		C	C	C	C
Bodmin	George Hunt		C	C	C	C
	William Masterman [2]	P	P	P		P
Bossiney	Charles Stuart, *abroad*				P	P
	Henry Lawes Luttrell, *abroad*					
Callington	George Stratton	P	P	P	P	P
	John Morshead	P	P	P	P	P
Camelford	John Pardoe	P		P	P	P
	James Macpherson	P	P	P	P	P
Fowey	Philip Rashleigh		C	C		a b.
	Lord Shuldham	P	P	P	P	P
Grampound	Sir John Ramsden, Bt.		C	C	C	C
	Thomas Lucas		C	C	C	C
Helston	Richard Barwell [3]			P	P	P
	Lord Hyde			P	P	P
Launceston	Chas. Geo. Perceval	P	P	P	P	P
	Thomas Bowlby	P	P	P	P	
Liskeard	Wilbraham Tollemache		C	C	C	C
	Samuel Salt		C	C	C	C
East Looe	John Buller, senior	P	P	P	P	P[4]
	William Graves	a b.	P	P		P
West Looe	John Buller, *out c. 5 Mar.*	P			va c.	va c.
	Sir William James, Bt.	P	P	P	P	P
Lostwithiel	George Johnstone, *at sea*				P	P
	Lord Malden	P	P	P	P	P
Newport	Lord Maitland		C	C	tel.	tel.
	Sir John Coghill	P		a b.	P	P

[1] Absence on 15 Mar. due to illness.   [2] Absence on 8 Mar. due to illness.
[3] Absence on 20 Feb. due to illness.   [4] See Henry Rawlinson (Liverpool).

		A	B	C	D	E
		20 Feb. 1782	22 Feb. 1782	27 Feb. 1782	8 Mar. 1782	15 Mar. 1782
Cornwall (contd.)						
Penryn	Sir Francis Basset, Bt.	P		P	P	P
	John Rogers	P	P	P	P	P
St. Germans	Edward J. Eliot		C	C	C	C
	Dudley Long		C	C	C	C
St. Ives	William Praed	P	P	P	P	P
	Abel Smith	P	P	P	P	P
St. Mawes	Earl Nugent	*P*	*	*	*	*
	Hugh Boscawen					P
St. Michael	William Hanger	P	P	*	P	P
	Francis Hale	P	P	P	P	P
Saltash	Sir Grey Cooper, Bt.	P	P	P	P	P
	Charles Jenkinson	P	P	P	P	P
Tregony	John Stephenson	P	P	P	P	P
	John Dawes			P	P	
Truro	Bamber Gascoyne, senior[1]	P		P	*	P
	Henry Rosewarne	P	P	P	P	P
Cumberland						
County	Sir Jas. Lowther, Bt.					
	Henry Fletcher		C	C	C	C
Carlisle	Lord Surrey		C	C	C	C
	William Lowther		C	C	C	C
Cockermouth	John Lowther		C	C	C	C
	John Baines Garforth		C	C	C	C
Derbyshire						
County	Ld. George Cavendish		C	C	C	C
	Nathaniel Curzon	P	P	P	P	P
Derby	Ld. G. A. H. Cavendish		C	C	*	C
	Edward Coke		C	C	C	C
Devon						
County	John Parker		C	C	C	C
	John Rolle		C	P	C	C
Ashburton	Robert Palk			C	C	C
	Charles Boone	P	P	P	P	P
Barnstaple	John Clevland	P	P	P	P	P[2]
	Francis Basset	P	P	P	P	P
Beeralston	Lord Fielding	P	P	P	P	P
	Lawrence Cox	P	P	P	P	
Dartmouth	Lord Howe		C		C	C
	Arthur Holdsworth		C	C	C	C
Exeter	Sir C. W. Bampfylde, Bt.		C	C	C	C
	John Baring			C	C	C

[1] Absence on 22 Feb. due to illness.   [2] See Henry Rawlinson (Liverpool).

392

		A	B	C	D	E
		20 Feb. 1782	22 Feb. 1782	27 Feb. 1782	8 Mar. 1782	15 Mar. 1782
Devon (contd.)						
Honiton	Sir Geo. Yonge, Bt.		C	C	C	C
	Jacob Wilkinson		C	C	C	C
Okehampton	Richard Vernon	*		*	*	
	Humphrey Minchin		C	*	C	C
Plymouth	Sir F. L. Rogers, Bt.	P	P	C	P	P
	George Darby	P	P	P	P	P
Plympton	Sir Ralph Payne, K.B.	P	P	P	P	P
	James Stuart	P	P	P	P	P
Tavistock	Richard Rigby	P	P	P	P	P
	Richard Fitzpatrick		C	C	C	C
Tiverton	Sir John Duntze, Bt.[1]					P
	John Wilmot			C	a b.	
Totnes	Sir P. J. Clerke, Bt.		*C*	*	*	*
	Lancelot Brown	P	P	P	P	P
Dorset						
County	Humphrey Sturt		C	*C*	C	C
	George Pitt				P	P
Bridport	Thomas Scott		C	C	C	C
	Richard Beckford		C	C	C	C
Corfe Castle	Henry Bankes		C	C	C	C
	John Bond	P		P	P	P
Dorchester	George Damer, *abroad*					
	William Ewer	P		P	P	P
Lyme Regis	Henry Fane	P		P	P	P
	David R. Michell	P		P	P	P
Poole	Joseph Gulston	P		P	P	P
	Wm. Morton Pitt		C	C	C	C
Shaftesbury	Hans Winthrop Mortimer			*C*	C	C
	Sir Francis Sykes, Bt.	P	P	P	P	P
Wareham	John Boyd	P		P	P	P
	Thomas Farrer		C	C	a b.	C
Weymouth & Melcombe Regis	Welbore Ellis	P	P	P	P	P
	John Purling[2]	P	P		a b.	*
	Gabriel Steward			P	P	P
	Wm. R. Rumbold	P	P	P	P	P
Durham						
County	Sir Thomas Clavering, Bt.	P	P	P	*	P
	Sir John Eden, Bt.	a b.		*	*	*
Durham	John Lambton		C	C	C	C
	John Tempest		C	C	C	C

[1] Absence on 8 Mar. due to illness.
[2] Absence after 22 Feb. due to illness.

		A	B	C	D	E
		20 Feb. 1782	22 Feb. 1782	27 Feb. 1782	8 Mar. 1782	15 Mar. 1782
Essex						
County	John Luther	C	C	C		C
	T. B. Bramston	P	P	P	P	P
Colchester	Sir Robert Smyth, Bt.	C	C	C	C	C
	Christopher Potter, *uns.*			*C*		
	4 *Mar.* Edm. Affleck, *abroad*					
Harwich	Geo. Augustus North	P	P	P	P	P
	John Robinson	*tel.*	*tel.*	*tel.*	*tel.*	*tel.*
Maldon	John Strutt	P	P	*	P	P
	Eliab Harvey, *at sea*	P				P
Gloucestershire						
County	Sir William Guise, Bt.		C	C	C	C
	James Dutton				P	P
Bristol	Matthew Brickdale	P	P	P	P	P
	George Daubeny	P		P	P	P
Cirencester	James Whitshed	P	P	P	P	P
	Samuel Blackwell	P	P	P	P	
Gloucester	Charles Barrow		C	C	C	C
	John Webb		C	C	C	C
Tewkesbury	Sir Wm. Codrington, Bt.		C	C	C	C
	James Martin		C	C	C	C
Herefordshire						
County	Thomas Harley	P	P	P		P
	Sir Geo. Cornewall, Bt.	C	C	*C*	C	C
Hereford	John Scudamore	C	C	C	C	
	Sir Richard Symons, Bt.	P	P	P	P	P
Leominster	Lord Bateman	P	P	P	P	P
	Richard Payne Knight	*C*		C	C	C
Weobley	John St. Leger Douglas	P	P	P		P
	Andrew Bayntun	*P*	P		P	P
Hertfordshire						
County	William Plumer	C	C	C		C
	Thomas Halsey	C	C	*		C
Hertford	Baron Dimsdale	*C*	C	C	P	
	William Baker	C	C	C		C
St. Albans	John Radcliffe	C	C	C	C	C
	Wm. Charles Sloper	C	C	C	C	C
Huntingdonshire						
County	Earl Ludlow	C		C	C	C
	Lord Hinchingbrooke	P	P	P	P	P
Huntingdon	Lord Mulgrave	*tel.*	P	P	P	P
	Sir Hugh Palliser, Bt.	P	P	P	P	P

APPENDIX II

		A	B	C	D	E
		20 Feb. 1782	22 Feb. 1782	27 Feb. 1782	8 Mar. 1782	15 Mar. 1782
Kent						
County	Charles Marsham	C	C	C	C	C
	Filmer Honywood	C	C	C	C	C
Canterbury	George Gipps	C	C	C		C
	Charles Robinson	C	C	C	C	C
Maidstone	Sir Horatio Mann	C	C	C	C	C
	Clement Taylor	C	C	C	C	
Queenboro'	Sir Chas. Frederick, K.B.	a b.			P	P
	Sir Walter Rawlinson	P		P	P	P
Rochester	George Finch Hatton	P	P	P	P	P
	Robert Gregory		C	C	C	C
Lancashire						
County	Sir Thomas Egerton, Bt.	P	P	P	P	P
	Thomas Stanley		C	C	C	C
Clitheroe	Thomas Lister	C		C	C	C
	John Parker	C	C	C	C	
Lancaster	Wilson Braddyll	C	C	C	C	
	Abraham Rawlinson	C		P	C	C
Liverpool	Bamber Gascoyne, junior	P	P	P	P	
	Henry Rawlinson	C		P	P	P[1]
Newton	Thos. Peter Legh					
	Thomas Davenport	P	P	P		
Preston	Sir Henry Hoghton, Bt.	P	P	P	P	P
	John Burgoyne		C	C	C	C
Wigan	H. S. Bridgeman, *abroad*					
	Horatio Walpole		C	C	C	C
Leicestershire						
County	John Peach Hungerford	P	P	P	C	C
	William Pochin		C	C	C	C
Leicester	Booth Grey		C	C	C	C
	John Darker	a b.		C	a b.	a b.
Lincolnshire						
County	Sir John Thorold, Bt.		C	C	C	C
	Charles Anderson Pelham		C	*C*	C	C
Boston	Lord Robert Bertie, *d. 10 Mar.*				va c.	
	Humphrey Sibthorpe	P	P	P	P	P
Grantham	Francis C. Cust	P	P	P	P	P
	George Sutton		C	C	C	C

[1] Of the three members, John Buller (E. Looe), John Clevland (Barnstaple), and Henry Rawlinson (Liverpool), two only were present at this division, but which I have not been able to discover.

		A	B	C	D	E
		20 Feb. 1782	22 Feb. 1782	27 Feb. 1782	8 Mar. 1782	15 Mar. 1782
Lincolnshire (contd.)						
Great Grimsby	John Harrison	C	C	C	C	C
	Francis Eyre	P	P	P	P	P
Lincoln	Robert Vyner	P	P	P	P	P
	Sir Thomas Clarges, Bt.	C	C	C	C	C
Stamford	Sir George Howard, K.B.	P		*P*	P	P
	Henry Cecil	P		P		P
Middlesex						
County	John Wilkes		C	C	C	C
	George Byng	*tel.*	*tel.*	*tel.*	*tel.*	*tel.*
London	Sir Watkin Lewes		C	C	C	C
	John Sawbridge		C	C	C	C
	Frederick Bull		C	C	C	C
	Nathaniel Newnham		C	*	C	C
Westminster	Sir George Rodney, Bt., *at sea*					
	Charles James Fox		C	C	C	C
Monmouthshire						
County	John Hanbury		C	C	C	C
	John Morgan	P		C	P	P
Monmouth	Sir John Stepney, Bt.	P	P	P	P	P
Norfolk						
County	Sir Edward Astley, Bt.		C	C	C	C
	Thomas William Coke		C	C	C	C
Castle Rising	John Chetwynd Talbot	P	P	P	*	P
	Robert Mackreth	P	P	P	P	
King's Lynn	Thomas Walpole, *abroad*					
	Crisp Molineux			C	C	C
Norwich	Sir Harbord Harbord, Bt.		C	C	C	C
	Edward Bacon [1]					
Thetford	Charles Fitzroy Scudamore, *ill*					
	Richard Hopkins		C	C	C	C
Great Yarmouth	Charles Townshend	P	P	P	P	P
	Richard Walpole		C	C	C	C
Northamptonshire						
County	Lucy Knightley		C	C	C	C
	Thomas Powys		C	C	C	C
Brackley	Timothy Caswall	P	P	P	P	P
	John Wm. Egerton	P	P	P	P	*
Higham Ferrers	Frederick Montagu		C	C	C	C

[1] Absence on 20 Feb. due to illness.

		A	B	C	D	E
		20 Feb. 1782	22 Feb. 1782	27 Feb. 1782	8 Mar. 1782	15 Mar. 1782
Northamptonshire (contd.)						
Northampton	Lord Althorp	C	C	C	C	C
	George Rodney	P	P	P	P	P
Peterboro'	Richard Benyon		C	*C*	C	C
	James Phipps		C	C	C	C
Northumberland						
County	Lord Algernon Percy, *abroad*					
	Sir William Middleton, Bt.		C	C	C	C
Berwick	John Vaughan	P	P	P	P	P
	Sir J. H. Delaval, Bt.	P	P	P	P	P
Morpeth	Peter Delmé	P		P	P	P
	Anthony Storer	P	P	P	P	P
Newcastle	Sir Matt. White Ridley, Bt.		C	C	*	C
	Andrew Robinson Bowes	*P*			P	P
Nottinghamshire						
County	Ld. Edw. C. C. Bentinck				C	C
	Charles Medows		C	C	C	C
Newark	Sir Henry Clinton, K.B., *abroad*					
	Lord George Sutton	ab.			C	*C*
Nottingham	Robert Smith		C	C	C	C
	Daniel Parker Coke		C	P		
E. Retford	Lord Lincoln	*P*	*P*			
	Wharton Amcotts	P	P	P	P	P
Oxfordshire						
County	Lord Wenman, *ill*					
	Lord Charles Spencer	ab.	P	P	P	P
Banbury	Lord North	P	P	P	P	P
University	Sir William Dolben, Bt.	P	P	C	P	P
	Francis Page	P	P	P	P	
Oxford	Lord Robert Spencer		C	C	C	C
	Peregrine Bertie		C	*	*C*	C
Woodstock	Lord Parker	P	P	P	P	P
	William Eden, *in Ireland*					
Rutland						
County	Thomas Noel					
	G. B. Brudenell	P	P	P	P	P

		A	B	C	D	E
		20 Feb. 1782	22 Feb. 1782	27 Feb. 1782	8 Mar. 1782	15 Mar. 1782
Shropshire						
County	Noel Hill	C	C	C		C
	Richard Hill	C	C	C	C	C
Bishop's Castle	William Clive	P	P	P	P	P
	Henry Strachey	P	P	P		
Bridgnorth	Thomas Whitmore		C	C	C	C
	Hugh Pigot		C	C	C	C
Ludlow	Lord Clive	P	P	P	P	P
	Frederick Cornwall	P	P	P	P	P
Shrewsbury	Sir Charlton Leighton, Bt.		C	C	C	C
	William Pulteney	*ab.*	P	P	C	C
Wenlock	Sir Henry Bridgeman, Bt., *abroad*					
	George Forester	*C*	C	*	*	*
Somerset						
County	Sir John Trevelyan, Bt.		C	C	C	C
	R. Hippesley Coxe					
Bath	Abel Moysey	C	C	P	P	P
	John Jeffreys Pratt	C	C	C	C	C
Bridgwater	Anne Poulett	P	P	P	P	P
	John Acland					
Ilchester	Peregrine Cust	P			P	P
	Samuel Smith	*P*	P	P	P	P
Milborne Port	John Pennington	*ab.*		C	C	C
	John Townson	P	P	P	P	P
Minehead	John Fownes Luttrell					
	Francis Fownes Luttrell	P		C	P	P
Taunton	*one seat vacant*					
	John Halliday	P	P	*ab.*		P
Wells	Clement Tudway		C	C	C	C
	Robert Child	*ab.*		C		C
Hampshire						
County	J. C. Jervoise	C	C	C	C	C
	Rob. Thistlethwayte	C	C	C	C	C
Andover	Sir J. G. Griffin, K.B.	C	C	C	C	
	Benjamin Lethieullier	*ab*		C	P	P
Christchurch	Sir James Harris, K.B., *abroad*					
	John Frederick	P	P	*ab.*	P	P
Lymington	Harry Burrard, *abroad*					
	Edward Gibbon	P	P	P	P	P
Newport	Sir Richard Worsley, Bt.[1]	P		P	P	P
	John St. John	P	P	P	P	P

[1] His absence on 22 Feb. was due to the hearing of a charge of adultery against his wife, Horace Walpole to Sir Horace Mann, 25 Feb. 1782.

APPENDIX II

		A	B	C	D	E
		20 Feb. 1782	22 Feb. 1782	27 Feb. 1782	8 Mar. 1782	15 Mar. 1782
Hampshire (contd.)						
Newton	Edward Meux Worsley	P	P	P	P	P
	John Barrington					C
Petersfield	William Jolliffe	P	P	P		P
	Thomas Samuel Jolliffe	P	P	P	P	P
Portsmouth	Robert Monckton, *ill*					
	Sir William Gordon, K.B.[1]	P	P	P		
Southampton	John Fuller	P	P	C	P	P
	Hans Sloane	P	P	P	P	
Stockbridge	John Luttrell	P	P	P	P	
	James Luttrell					
Whitchurch	Thomas Townshend		C	C	C	C
	Lord Midleton		C	C	C	C
Winchester	Henry Penton	P	P	P	P	P
	Lovell Stanhope	P	P	P	P	P
Yarmouth	Edward Morant		C	C	C	C
	Sir Thos. Rumbold, Bt.	P	P	P	P	P
Staffordshire						
County	Lord Lewisham	P	P	P	P	P
	Sir John Wrottesley, Bt.		C	C	C	C
Lichfield	George Anson		C	C	C	C
	Thomas Gilbert	P		C	C	P
Newcastle-u-Lyme	Lord Trentham	P				
	Arch. Macdonald	P	P	P	P	P
Stafford	Edward Monckton		C	C	C	C
	R. B. Sheridan		C	C	C	
Tamworth	John Courtenay[2]	ab.	P	P	P	P
	John Calvert	P	P	P	P	P
Suffolk						
County	Sir T. C. Bunbury, Bt.		C	C	C	C
	Sir John Rous, Bt.		C	C	C	C
Aldeburgh	Martin Fonnereau	*P*	P	P	P	P
	P. C. Crespigny	P	P	*P*	P	P
Bury-St.-Edmunds	Sir Chas. Davers, Bt.		C	C	C	C
	H. Seymour Conway, senior		C	C	C	C
Dunwich	Sir G. W. Vanneck, Bt.		C	C	C	C
	Barne Barne	P	P	P	P	P
Eye	R. B. Philipson	P	P	P	P	P
	A. J. Skelton	P	P	P	P	P
Ipswich	Thomas Staunton		C	C	C	C
	Wm. Wollaston, *abroad*					

[1] Absence on 8 Mar. due to illness.   [2] Absence on 20 Feb. due to illness.

		A	B	C	D	E
		20 Feb. 1782	22 Feb. 1782	27 Feb. 1782	8 Mar. 1782	15 Mar. 1782
Suffolk (contd.)						
Orford	Lord Beauchamp	P	P	P	P	P
	Rob. Seymour Conway	P	P	P	P	P
Sudbury	Sir Patrick Blake, Bt.		C	C		
	Sir James Marriott	P		P	P	P
Surrey						
County	Sir Joseph Mawbey, Bt.		C	C	C	C
	Augustus Keppel		C	C	C	*C*
Bletchingley	John Kenrick	P	P	P	P	P
	Sir Robert Clayton, Bt.		C	C	C	C
Gatton	Lord Newhaven	P		P	P	P
	Robert Mayne	P	P	P	P	P
Guildford	Sir Fletcher Norton		C		C	C
	George Onslow	P	*	P	P	P
Haslemere	Edward Norton		C	C	C	C
	Walter Spencer Stanhope		C	C	C	C
Reigate	John Yorke	*P*		P		P
	Sir Charles Cocks, Bt., *abroad*					
Southwark	Nathaniel Polhill		C	C	C	C
	Sir Richard Hotham		C	C	C	C
Sussex						
County	Lord George Lennox		C	C	C	C
	Thomas Pelham		C	C	P	P
Arundel	Thomas Fitzherbert	P	*	P	P	P
	Peter Wm. Baker		C	C	C	*
Bramber	Sir Henry Gough, Bt.			C		
	H. Fitzroy Stanhope		C	C	C	C
Chichester	William Keppel, *ill, d.* 1 Mar.				*va c.*	
	P. C. Wyndham, *el.* 11 Mar.					C
	Thomas Steele		C	C	C	C
E. Grinstead	H. A. Herbert	P	P	P	P	P
	Sir John Irwin, K.B.	P	P	P	P	P
Horsham	James Wallace	P	P	P	P	P
	Sir George Osborn, Bt.	P	P	P	P	
Lewes	Henry Pelham	*P*	P		P	
	Thomas Kemp		C	C	C	C
Midhurst	Henry Drummond	P	P	P	P	P
	Sir Sampson Gideon, Bt.	P	P	P	P	P
New Shore-ham	Sir Cecil Bisshopp, Bt.	P	P	P	P	P
	John Peachey	P		C	C	P
Steyning	Sir T. G. Skipwith, Bt.		C	C	C	C
	John Bullock		C	C	*	*a b.*

APPENDIX II

		A	B	C	D	E
		20 Feb. 1782	22 Feb. 1782	27 Feb. 1782	8 Mar. 1782	15 Mar. 1782
Warwickshire						
County	Sir Robert Lawley, Bt.	C	C	C	C	C
	Sir G. A. W. Shuckburgh, Bt.	C	C	C	C	C
Coventry	Edward Roe Yeo	P	P	P	P	P
	Lord Sheffield	P	P	P	P	P
Warwick	Robert Ladbroke		C	C	C	C
	Chas. Francis Greville	P	P	P		P
Westmorland						
County	Sir M. Le Fleming, Bt.				C	C
	James Lowther	C		C	C	C
Appleby	Philip Honywood	C	*	C	*	C
	William Pitt	tel.	C	C	tel.	C
Wiltshire						
County	Charles Penruddock	C	C	C	C	C
	Ambrose Goddard	*	*	*	*	C
Gt. Bedwin	Sir Merrick Burrell, Bt.					
	P. C. Methuen			a b.		P
Calne	Isaac Barré	C	C	C	C	C
	John Dunning	C	C	C	C	C
Chippenham	Henry Dawkins	C	C	C	C	C
	Giles Hudson [1]	P				P
Cricklade	Paul Benfield, *abroad*					
	one seat vacant					
Devizes	Henry Jones	P		P	P	P
	Sir J. T. Long, Bt.	a b.	P	P	P	P
Downton	Robert Shaftoe	P	P	P	P	P
	H. Seymour Conway, *junior*	P	P	P	P	P
Heytesbury	Francis Burton		C	C	P	
	Wm. P. Ashe A'Court		C	C	C	C
Hindon	Lloyd Kenyon		C	C	a b.	C
	Nathaniel Wraxall	P	P	P	P	P
Ludgershall	Geo. Augustus Selwyn	P	P	P	P	P
	Lord Melbourne	P	P	a b.	P	a b.
Malmesbury	Lord Fairford	P	P	P	P	P
	John Calvert, *junior*	P	P	P	P	P
Marlborough	Earl of Courtown	P	*	P	P	P
	William Woodley	a b.				
Old Sarum	Thomas Pitt		C	C	C	C
	Pinckney Wilkinson		C		C	C
Salisbury	Wm. Henry Bouverie			C	C	C
	William Hussey		C	tel.	C	C

[1] Absence on 8 Mar. due to illness.

		A	B	C	D	E
		20 Feb. 1782	22 Feb. 1782	27 Feb. 1782	8 Mar. 1782	15 Mar. 1782
Wiltshire (contd.)						
Westbury	Samuel Estwick		C	C	C	C
	John Whalley Gardiner		C	C	C	C
Wilton	Lord Herbert		C	C	C	C
	Wm. Gerard Hamilton		C	*	C	*
Wootton	Henry St. John	P	P	P	P	P
Bassett	William Strahan	P	P	P	P	P
Worcestershire						
County	Edward Foley		C	C	C	C
	William Lygon			C	C	*
Bewdley	Lord Westcote	P	P	P	P	P
Droitwich	Andrew Foley		C	C	C	C
	Edward Winnington		C	C	C	C
Evesham	Sir John Rushout, Bt.		C	C	C	C
	C. Wm. Boughton-Rouse		C	C	C	C
Worcester	Thomas Bates Rous		C	C	C	C
	William Ward	P	P	P		P
Yorkshire						
County	Sir George Savile, Bt.[1]			C		C
	Henry Duncombe		C	C	C	C
Aldborough	Charles Mellish	P	P	P	P	P
	Sir S. B. Fludyer, Bt.	*P*	P			C
Beverley	Sir James Pennyman, Bt.		C	C	C	C
	Evelyn Anderson		C	C	C	C
Boroughbridge	Anthony Eyre					
	Charles Ambler					
Hedon	Christopher Atkinson	P		P	P	P
	William Chaytor	P	P	P	P	*
Hull	William Wilberforce		C	C	C	C
	Lord Robert Manners, senior					
Knaresboro'	Lord Duncannon		C	C	C	C
	James Hare		C	C	C	C
Malton	Edmund Burke		C	C	C	C
	William Weddell		C	C	C	C
Northallerton	Edwin Lascelles	P	P	P		P
	Henry Peirse		C	C	C	C
Pontefract	Lord Galway	*P*	P		P	*P*
	William Nedham		C	C	C	C
Richmond	Lord Graham	P	C	C	P	P
	George Fitzwilliam		C	C	C	C
Ripon	Frederick Robinson	P	P	P	P	P
	William Lawrence		C	C	C	C

[1] Absence on 8 Mar. due to illness.

		A	B	C	D	E
		20 Feb. 1782	22 Feb. 1782	27 Feb. 1782	8 Mar. 1782	15 Mar. 1782
Yorkshire (contd.)						
Scarboro'	Earl of Tyrconnel	C	C	C	C	C
	Charles Phipps	P	P	P	P	P
Thirsk	Sir Thomas Gascoigne, Bt.	C	C	C	C	C
	Beilby Thompson	C	C	C	*	*
York	Lord John Cavendish	C	C	C	C	C
	Charles Turner	C	C	C	C	C
Cinque Ports						
Dover	John Henniker	P	P	P	P	P
	John Trevanion	C	C	C	C	C
Hastings	Lord Palmerston	P	P	P	P	P
	John Ord	P	P	P	P	P
Hythe	Sir Charles Farnaby, Bt.	P	P	P	P	P
	William Evelyn	P	*	*	*	*
New Romney	Sir Edward Dering, Bt.	P		P	P	P
	Richard Jackson	P			P	
Rye	Thomas Onslow	P	P	P	P	P
	William Dickinson	P	P	P	P	P
Sandwich	Philip Stephens	P	P	P	P	P
	Sir Richard Sutton, Bt.	P	P	P	P	
Seaford	John Durand	P	P	P		P
	Christopher D'Oyly					
Winchelsea	Charles Wolfran Cornwall, *Speaker*					
	John Nesbitt	ab.		C		C
WALES						
Anglesey	Lord Bulkeley		C	C	C	C
Beaumaris	Sir George Warren, K.B.		C	C	C	C
Brecknock	Charles Morgan	P		C	P	P
Brecon	Sir Charles Gould	P	P	P	P	P
Cardiganshire	Earl of Lisburne	P	P	*	P	P
Cardigan	John Campbell	ab.		P	P	P
Carmarthenshire	John Vaughan		C	C	C	C
Carmarthen	George Philipps				P	P
Carnarvonshire	John Parry		C	C	C	C
Carnarvon	Glynn Wynn	P	P	P	P	P
Denbighshire	Sir W. W. Wynn, Bt.		C	C	C	C
Denbigh	Richard Myddleton			C		
Flintshire	Sir Roger Mostyn, Bt.		C	C	C	C
Flint	Watkin Williams	C	C	C	C	C
Glamorgan	Charles Edwin	C	C	C		
Cardiff	Sir Herbert Mackworth, Bt.					
Merioneth	Evan Lloyd Vaughan		C	C	C	C

		A	B	C	D	E
		20 Feb. 1782	22 Feb. 1782	27 Feb. 1782	8 Mar. 1782	15 Mar. 1782
WALES (contd.)						
Montgomery-shire	Wm. Mostyn Owen	C		*C*	C	C
Montgomery	Whitshed Keene	P	P	P	P	P
Pembrokeshire	Sir Hugh Owen, Bt.[1]					
Haverford-west	Lord Kensington	P		P	P	P
Pembroke	Hugh Owen	P	P	*P*	P	P
Radnor	Thomas Johnes	P	P	P	*	*
New Radnor	Edward Lewis	P	P	P	P	P
SCOTLAND						
County members						
Aberdeen	Alexander Garden	P		C		C
Argyll	Ld. Fred. Campbell	P	P	P	P	P
Ayr	Sir Adam Fergusson, Bt.	P		P	P	P
Banff	Earl of Fife	C	P		C	C	C
Berwick	Hugh Scott	P	P	P	P	P
Caithness	John Sinclair	P	P		P	
Cromarty	George Ross	P		*		P
Dunbarton	Geo. Keith Elphinstone, *at sea*					
Dumfries	Sir Robert Laurie, Bt.	P	P	P	P	P
Edinburgh	Henry Dundas	P	P	*P*	P	P
Elgin	Ld. William Gordon	P		P		*va*c.
Fife	Robert Skene	P	P	P	P	P
Forfar	Arch. Douglas					
Haddington	Hew Dalrymple	*P*	P	P	P	P
Inverness	*vacant*					
Kincardine	Ld. Adam Gordon	P		P		P
Kirkcudbright	Peter Johnston	P	P	P	P	P
Kinross	George Graham	P		P	P	P
Lanark	Andrew Stuart	P	P	P	P	P
Linlithgow	Sir W. A. Cunynghame, Bt.	P	P	P	P	P
Orkney and Shetland	Charles Dundas			*	*	*
Peebles	Alexander Murray[1]					P
Perth	James Murray	*P*	P	P	P	P
Renfrew	John Shaw Stewart	*a*b.		C	C	C
Ross	Lord Macleod, *abroad*					
Roxburgh	Sir Gilbert Elliot, Bt.	P		C	P	C
Selkirk	John Pringle[1]	*a*b.			P	P
Stirling	Sir Thomas Dundas	P		C	C	C
Sutherland	James Wemyss	P	P	P	P	P
Wigtown	Keith Stewart	P	P	P	P	P

[1] Absence on 20 Feb. due to illness.

		A	B	C	D	E
		20 Feb. 1782	22 Feb. 1782	27 Feb. 1782	8 Mar. 1782	15 Mar. 1782
SCOTLAND (contd.)						
Borough members						
Dunbar, etc.	Francis Charteris	P		P	P	P
Dumfries, etc.	Sir Robert Herries	P	P	P	P	P
Inverness, etc.	Sir Hector Munro, *abroad*					
Selkirk, etc.	Sir James Cockburn, Bt.	P	P	P	P	P
Wigtown, etc.	William Adam	P	*tel.*	*tel.*	*tel.*	*tel.*
Stirling, etc.	James Campbell	P	P	P	P	P
Dundee, etc.	George Dempster					
Dysart, etc.	Sir John Henderson, Bt.	*ab.*			P	P
Crail, etc.	Sir John Anstruther, Bt.	P	P	P		P
Aberdeen, etc.	Adam Drummond	P	P	P	P	P
Dornoch, etc.	Charles Ross	*ab.*		C	C	C
Elgin, etc.	Staats Long Morris	P		P	P	P
Glasgow, etc.	John Craufurd	*P*			P	P
Ayr, etc.	Sir Arch. Edmonstone, Bt.	P	P	*P*	P	P
Edinburgh City	James Hunter Blair	*P*		C	C	P

INDEX

407

INDEX

THE END OF NORTH'S MINISTRY, 1780–82

Harrison, John (1738–1811), 211 n. 4, 212 n. 1, 218, 396
Harrowby, Lord. *See under* Ryder
Hartley, David (c. 1732–1813), 133, 218
Hartley, Winchcombe Henry (1740–1794), 211 n. 2, 212 n. 1, 218, 263, 390
Harvey, Eliab (1758–1830), 394
Harwich, 65, 89, 102, 107, 168 n. 3, 394
Haslemere, 37, 56, 102, 119-20, 168 n. 3, 169 n. 1, 225, 400
Hastings, 65, 89, 403
Hatton, George Finch (1747–1823), 395
Hayley, George (d. 1781), 136-7, 227
Heathcote, Sir Thomas (1721–87), 76, 77
Hedon, 80, 85-6, 153, 402
Helston, 59, 153, 169, 391
Henderson, Sir John (1752–1817), 316, 329, 348 n. 2, 379, 405
Henniker, John (1724–1803), 173 n. 3, 182 n. 3, 203 n. 1, 403
Henniker, John (later Henniker-Major) (1752–1821), 153
Herbert, George, 2nd Earl of Powis (1755–1801), 55, 66
Herbert, George Augustus, Lord Herbert (1759–1827), 192-3, 402
Herbert, Henry, 10th Earl of Pembroke (1734–94), 55, 62, 231, 239-240
Herbert, Henry (1st Lord Porchester) (1741–1811), 76
Hereford, 51 n. 1, 109, 394
Herefordshire, 48, 394
Heron, Sir Richard (1726-1805), 12
Herries, Sir Robert (1730–1815), 179, 182, 405
Hertford, Earl of. *See under* Seymour Conway
Hertford, 51 n. 2, 152, 394
Hertfordshire, 48, 394
Hervey, Frederick Augustus, 4th Earl of Bristol, D.D., Bishop of Derry (1730–1803), 54, 217-18
Heytesbury, 55, 56, 168 n. 3, 169 n. 1, 401
Higham Ferrers, 26, 55, 108, 115, 214, 396
Hill, Arthur, Lord Fairford (1753–1801), 202, 401
Hill, Noel (1745–89), 318, 359, 367 n. 3, 398

Hill, Richard (1733–1808), 318, 354, 398
Hill, Wills, 1st Earl of Hillsborough (1718–93), on North, 5 ; character, 6 ; 15, 27, 34, 39, 41, 89, 256-257, 274, 370-2
Hinchingbrooke, Lord. *See under* Montagu
Hindon, 401
Hobart, John, 2nd Earl of Buckinghamshire (1723–93), Lord Lieutenant of Ireland, 4-5, 6, 11-12, 39-41, 241
Hoghton, Sir Henry (1728–95), 153, 336-7, 347, 395
Holdsworth, Arthur (1757–87), 56, 65, 318, 361 n. 5, 362, 392
Holmes, Rev. Leonard Troughear (c. 1732–1804), 57, 96-7
Holroyd, John Baker, 1st Lord Sheffield (1735–1821), 133, 203, 401
Honiton, 80, 85-6, 153, 168 n. 2, 393
Honywood, Filmer (c. 1745–1809), 125, 168 n. 3, 194, 395
Honywood, Sir John (c. 1710–81), 56
Honywood, Philip (c. 1709–85), 212 n. 1, 216, 237-8, 401
Hooper, Edward (c. 1701–95), 56
Hopkins, Richard (1728–99), 330 n. 1, 396
Horsham, 55, 90, 96, 100-2, 168 n. 3, 169 n. 1, 400
Hotham, Sir Richard (1723–99), 78, 125, 132, 212 n. 1, 218, 282 n. 5, 400
Howard, Charles, Earl of Surrey (1746–1815), 53, 128, 162, 330 n. 1, 368, 376 n. 3, 392
Howard, Frances, 56
Howard, Frederick, 5th Earl of Carlisle (1748–1825), 53, 54, 207, 241-2
Howard, Sir George (1718–96), 124, 203 n. 1, 384-6, 396
Howard, Thomas, 14th Earl of Suffolk (1721–83), 78
Howe, Richard, 4th Viscount Howe (1726–99), 145-6, 153, 177, 330 n. 2
Howe, Sir William (1729–1814), 145-146, 153, 158
Hudson, Giles (d. 1783), 181, 329, 380-2, 401
Hull, 51 n. 1, 133, 402
Hume, Sir Abraham (1749–1838), 109-10, 158

416

INDEX

THE END OF NORTH'S MINISTRY, 1780-82

Palmer, Sir John (1735–1817), 22, 126
Palmerston, Viscount. *See under* Temple
Panmure, Earl. *See under* Maule
Pardoe, John (1711–98), 92, 99
Pardoe, John (1757–96), 92, 99, 204, 206, 391
Parker, George, Lord Parker (1755–1842), 397
Parker, John (1735–88), 392
Parker, John (1755–97), 218, 395
Parry, John (1724–97), 175, 227, 403
Parsons, John, 155-6
Payne, Sir Ralph (1739–1807), 100, 101 *n.* 3, 393
Peach, Samuel, 142
Peachey, John (1749–1816), 331, 348 *n.* 1, 383, 400
Peeblesshire, 404
Peirse, Henry (1754–1824), 57, 402
Pelham, C. A. *See under* Anderson Pelham
Pelham, Henry (1759–97), 255, 329, 332 *n.* 4, 348 *n.* 2, 380-2, 400
Pelham, Thomas, 2nd Lord Pelham (1728–1805), 55
Pelham, Thomas (1756–1826), 255, 315, 331 and *n.* 1, 332, 334, 348 *n.* 1, 400
Pelham Clinton, Henry, 2nd Duke of Newcastle (1720–94), 55, 74, 81, 89, 90-1, 146, 209, 313, 316, 329, 357
Pelham Clinton, Lord John (1755–1781), 209
Pelham Clinton, Thomas, Earl of Lincoln (1752–95), 81-2, 132, 135, 313, 329, 357, 359 *n.* 6, 380-2, 397
Pelham Holles, Thomas, 1st Duke of Newcastle (1693–1768), 187
Pembroke, 404
Pembroke, Earl of. *See under* Herbert
Pembrokeshire, 66, 404
Pennant, Richard (1737–1808), 84, 138, 158
Pennington family, 50, 128
Pennington, John (1737–1813), 50, 128, 332 and *n.* 3, 333, 349, 361 *n.* 5, 379, 398
Pennington, Sir Joseph (1718–93), 128
Pennyman, Sir James (1736–1808), 402

Penruddock, Charles (1743–88), 359, 401
Penryn, 102, 104, 153, 392
Penton, Henry (*c.* 1738–1812), 57, 76, 202, 399
Perceval, Charles George (1756–1840), 98, 169 *n.* 1, 199-200, 202, 255, 310, 391
Percy family, 49
Percy, Lord Algernon (1750–1830), 168 *n.* 3, 209, 397
Perthshire, 404
Peterborough, 54, 127, 218, 397
Petersfield, 56, 399
Philipps, George (*c.* 1742–84), 316, 329, 348 and *n.* 2, 403
Philips family, 90
Philips, Jonathan (*c.* 1704–98), 57, 92, 107
Philipson, Richard Burton (1723–1792), 44, 399
Phipps, Charles (1753–86), 204, 403
Phipps, Constantine, 2nd Lord Mulgrave (1744–92), 8, 62, 177, 202-3, 204-5, 268, 308, 310, 394
Phipps, James Farrel (1744–86), 397
Pigot, George, 1st Lord Pigot (1719–1777), 177, 204
Pigot, Hugh (1722–92), 177, 204, 212 *n.* 2, 217, 398
Pitt, George (1751–1828), 130, 315, 329, 348 and *n.* 2, 383, 393
Pitt, John (*c.* 1706–87), 192
Pitt, Thomas (1737–93), 21, 57, 271, 401
Pitt, William, 1st Earl of Chatham (1708–78), 70, 226, 370
Pitt, William (1759–1806), 70, 81, 169 *n.* 1, 171, 172 *n.* 1, 175, 176, 220, 222, 225, 229, 320, 339, 345-6, 374, 375, 401
Pitt, William Morton (1754–1836), 192-3, 318, 393
Pleydell Bouverie, Jacob, 2nd Earl of Radnor (1750–1828), 55, 78
Plumer, William (1736–1822), 110, 211 *n.* 4, 212 *n.* 1, 215, 216, 220, 394
Plymouth, 51, 65, 102, 120 *n.*, 154, 393
Plympton, 54, 96, 99-102, 168 *n.* 3, 169 *n.* 1, 393
Pochin, William (1731–98), 126, 222, 395
Polhill, Nathaniel (1723–82), 78, 125, 400

422

and *n.* 1 ; parliamentary calculations, Mar. 1782, 351-2, 356-9,
366-8 ; 363, 373-5 ; his parliamentary lists, 374, 376-89 ; 394
Rochester, 51 *n.* 2, 66, 102, 107, 152,
395
Rockingham, Marquis and Marchioness of. *See under* Watson
Wentworth
Rockingham Party, 24-5, 26, 43, 47,
70, 74, 107, 117, 125, 129, 132,
188, 194, 210-21, 227, 229, 230,
241, 251-2, 356, 370, 373
Rodney, George (1753–1802), 397
Rodney, Sir George Brydges (1719–
1792), 30, 76, 81-2, 104, 132, 173
n. 3, 177, 302 *n.* 3, 396
Rogers, Sir Frederick Leman (1746–
1797), 328, 330, 332 *n.* 3, 348 *n.* 1,
393
Rogers, John (1751–1832), 392
Rogers, Thomas (1735–93), 133, 168
n. 2
Rolle, John (1756–1842), 190, 301,
328, 330, 332 *n.* 3, 333, 349, 359,
392
Rosewarne, Henry (*c.* 1731–83), 58,
180, 392
Ross, Charles (1729–97), 332 *n.* 5,
379, 405
Ross, George (1700–86), 404
Ross-shire, 404
Rous, George (1744–1802), 158
Rous, Sir John (1750–1827), motion
of no-confidence, Mar. 1782,
352-3 ; 399
Rous, Thomas Bates (1739–99), 147-
148, 151, 402
Rouse, Charles William Boughton
(1745–1821), 227, 402
Roxburghshire, 69, 404
Rumbold, Sir Thomas (1736–91),
168 *n.* 2, 399
Rumbold, William Richard (1760–
1786), 393
Rushout, Sir John (1738–1800), 57,
402
Russell, Francis, 5th Duke of Bed-
ford (1765–1802), 52, 54, 121
Russell, Gertrude, Dowager Duchess
of Bedford (1715–94), 82, 94, 108,
121, 127, 207
Russell, John, 4th Duke of Bedford
(1710–71), 70, 121, 172, 206-7
Rutland, Duke of. *See under*
Manners

Rutland, 397
Ryder, Nathaniel, 1st Lord Harrowby
(1735–1803), 55
Rye, 65, 96, 107, 124, 403

Sackville, Charles, 157
St. Albans, 51 *n.* 2, 394
St. Christopher, loss of, 345
St. Eustatius, 261
St. Germans, 56, 392
St. Ives, 57, 181, 392
St. John family, of Bletsoe, 121
St. John, Frederick, 2nd Viscount
Bolingbroke (1734–87), 54
St. John, Henry (1738–1818), 200-1,
402
St. John, Sir Henry Paulet (1737–
1784), 76
St. John, John (1746–93), 96, 100-1,
168 *n.* 3, 174 *n.* 2, 200-1, 211-12,
398
St. John, St. Andrew (1759–1817),
121-4, 211 *n.* 4, 217, 390
St. Mawes, 54, 57, 392
St. Michael. *See under* Mitchell
Salisbury, 51, 55, 80, 401
Salt, Samuel (*c.* 1723–92), 63, 94, 110,
175 *n.*, 212 *n.* 2, 215-16, 219, 391
Saltash, 65, 89, 98, 106, 392
Sandwich, 51 *n.* 2, 65, 89, 96, 102,
152-3, 168 *n.* 3, 403
Sandwich, Earl of. *See under*
Montagu
Saratoga, 10, 179
Savile, Sir George (1726–84), 17, 19,
25, 48, 115, 122-4, 211 and *n.* 2,
212 *n.* 1, 213, 218, 219, 260, 265,
317 *n.* 1, 330 *n.* 1, 402
Sawbridge, John (1732–95), 81, 136-
137, 211 *n.* 4, 227, 396
Scarborough, 66, 80, 222, 403
Scarsdale, Lord. *See under* Curzon
Scawen, James (1734–1801), 77, 124
Scotland, electoral system of, 66-9
Scott, Henry, 3rd Duke of Buc-
cleuch (1746–1812), 295
Scott, Hugh (1758–1841), 168 *n.* 2,
404
Scott, John (1739–98), attorney-
general in Ireland, 39-41
Scott, Robert, 94 *n.* 1, 158
Scott, Thomas (1723–1816), 78, 211
n. 4, 227, 393
Scudamore, Charles Fitzroy (1713–
1782), 170, 173 *n.* 4, 302 *n.* 11,
317 *n.* 1, 396

INDEX

Townshend, John (1757–1833), 162, 211 n. 2, 212 n. 1, 217, 391

Townshend, Thomas (1733–1800), 57, 226, 249, 399

Townson, John (1725–97), 99, 398

Tregony, 54, 392

Trentham, Lord. *See under* Leveson-Gower

Trevanion, John (*d.* 1810), 403

Trevelyan, Sir John (1735–1828), 143-4, 398

Truro, 58, 107, 153, 180, 392

Tudway, Clement (1734–1815), 57, 175 n., 398

Tufton, Sackville, 8th Earl of Thanet (1733–86), 55, 216

Turner, Charles (1726–83), 111, 113-14, 237, 403

Tyrconnel, Earl of. *See under* Carpenter

United Provinces, 12-13, 243-50

Upper Ossory, Earl of. *See under* Fitzpatrick

Vanneck, Sir Gerard William (1743–1791), 57, 212 n. 2, 216, 399

Vaughan family, of Merioneth, 66

Vaughan, Evan Lloyd (1709–91), 403

Vaughan, John (1748–95), 208, 397

Vaughan, John (1752–1804), 361 n. 5, 362, 379, 381-2, 403

Vaughan, Wilmot, 1st Earl of Lisburne (1730–1800), 173 n. 3, 202, 208, 267, 403

Vermont, 322

Verney, Ralph, 2nd Earl Verney (*c.* 1712–91), 57, 211 and n. 2, 212 n. 1, 215, 390

Vernon, Richard (1726–1800), 94 n. 2, 207, 393

Villiers, Thomas, Lord Hyde (1753–1824), 316, 356, 391

Virginia, 26, 242

Volunteer Movement, 11

Vousden, Mr., of Winchelsea, 107

Vyner, Robert (1717–99), 88, 133, 173 n. 3, 313, 396

Wake, Sir William (1742–85), 22, 152, 330 n. 2, 390

Wales, electoral system, 66

Wallace, James (1729–83), 100, 174, 202, 260, 327, 340-1, 343-4, 400

Waller, Edmund (*d.* 1788), 57

Waller, Robert, 380-2, 390

Wallingford, 88, 95, 157, 222, 390

Wallop, John, 2nd Earl of Portsmouth (1742–97), 55

Walpole, George, 3rd Earl of Orford (1730–91), 30, 55, 90-1, 204

Walpole, Horatio (1717–97), 8, 24, 296-7

Walpole, Horatio, 2nd Lord Walpole (1723–1809), 216

Walpole, Horatio (1752–1822), 60, 211 n. 2, 212 n. 1, 216, 395

Walpole, Richard (1728–98), 212 n. 1, 216, 396

Walpole, Robert, 1st Earl of Orford (1676–1745), 53, 170

Walpole, Thomas (1727–1803), 212 n. 2, 216, 302 n. 9, 396

Walsh, John (*c.* 1725–95), 83, 147, 158

Walsingham, Lord. *See under* De Grey

Walsingham, Robert Boyle (1736–1780), 168, 177

Ward family, 151

Ward, John, 2nd Viscount Dudley and Ward (1725–88), 150-1

Ward, William (1750–1823), 150-1, 402

Wareham, 51 n. 3, 56, 90, 92, 94 n. 1, 393

Warren, Sir George (1734–1801), 158, 227, 403

Warren, Sir John Borlase (1753–1822), 204, 205 n. 3, 357, 359 n. 6, 360-1, 362, 388, 390

Warwick, 51 n. 3, 55, 401

Warwick, Earl of. *See under* Greville

Warwickshire, 47, 401

Watson Wentworth, Charles, 2nd Marquis of Rockingham (1730–1782), 24, 25 ; and North's proposals for a coalition, 1780, 26-9 ; 43, 44, 48, 52, 55, 70 ; and the general election, 103-16 ; 121, 123, 124, 126-7, 158, 177 ; his party in the Commons, 210-21 ; and opening of the new parliament, 231-3 ; and the Speakership, 235-7 ; 237-9 ; view of affairs just before Yorktown, 269 ; 343 ; approached to form a 'broad-bottom' ministry — his terms, 350-1 ; 365, 373

Watson Wentworth, Mary, Marchioness of Rockingham, 81, 115

INDEX

THE END

PRINTED BY R. & R. CLARK, LTD., EDINBURGH

Jan '59   H 30   D. G. Barnes of West River.